P9-CRP-037

Memoirs of the New Mexico Congressman

Just Fly the Plane, Stupid!

STEVAN PEARCE

Just Fly the Plane, Stupid!

Copyright © 2013 by Stevan Pearce

All rights reserved. In accordance with the U.S. Copyright Act of 1976, the scanning, uploading, and electronic sharing of any part of this book without the permission of the publisher is unlawful piracy and theft of the author's intellectual property. If you would like to use material from the book (other than for review purposes), prior written permission must be obtained by contacting the publisher at www.justflytheplanestupid.com. Thank you for your support of the author's rights.

Initial edit by Whitney Pipkin.

Literary development and design: Koechel Peterson & Associates, Inc., Minneapolis, Minnesota.

Books may be ordered at www.justflytheplanestupid.com.

ISBN 978-0-9899992-0-5

Printed in the United States of America

To my wife, Cynthia,
one of three strong and independent women in my life
who brings light and laughter to my life;

. . . my mother, Charlotte Allyne Pearce,
who taught me discipline and to never give up;

. . . my daughter, Lori Bova,
whose clarity of thought and integrity in life give me joy;

. . . to my father, Melvin Pearce,
the steady, reliable force in my life,
who went to work every day
and came home to be with his family;

. . . and to Coach Dennis Shaw,
who left coaching to become a preacher,
dying suddenly at a young age.

To Michael Turner
It is An Honor
to serve with you!

NA-2
2015

ACKNOWLEDGMENTS

The idea for the book began when my friend Rebecca Allen gave me a college graduation gift—a book titled, *This Is Your Life*, by Stevan Pearce. The pages were all blank, and I was supposed to fill them in as my life unfolded. The gift was great in making me think, but it was too confining for me. My life is not lived or written in the nice organized pages of a journal but on the run, hurriedly scratched on scraps of paper as thoughts, images, and memories flash by. My desk is covered in loose papers, my computer has open documents and files, and I have boxes of notes that I was going to transpose to that gift from a friend . . . but never have. I was too busy living life to be a good chronicler, having developed the notion that there are two categories of people—those who live life and those who write about it. I chose the former, but I am going back now and trying to correct that mistake. The decades of notes, thoughts, and pictures needed much solitary time to understand what has transpired.

Tim Keithley urged me to write a memoir and was the one who finally moved me to take the first step. Rebecca Allen helped my story become more vivid.

My friend Joe Yue has been a sounding board for ideas.

Mary Haarmeyer encouraged me to start writing, and Carol and Bob Richardson have contributed greatly to the project. Maryam Sabbaghian Brown offered insight and encouragement along with Ralph Drollinger, Latayne Scott, Dennis Boesen, Marita Noon, Fred Huff, and Kimberly Reed.

Eric and Shannon Layer offered valuable suggestions.

Whitney Pipkin took my rough draft and edited it into a comprehensible product.

I am eternally thankful to all the men and women of Lea Fishing Tools, who helped forge a company that was vibrant and energetic and with whom it was a joy to work; to the men and women who have helped in my congressional office through my time in D.C., and finally to the gracious people of southern New Mexico who have entrusted me with one of the most noble responsibilities I have had in life.

CONTENTS

1

AIRSPEED

In 1998, as the beginning date neared for the second session of my first term as a New Mexico state representative, my wife, Cynthia, decided she would spend time in Springdale, Arkansas, with our daughter while I was in Santa Fe. One day after work in early January, we took off in our small plane for the quick flight over parts of Texas and Oklahoma.

The weather briefings told me that, while most of the flight would be routine, a fast-moving cold front might cause flight conditions to worsen. I might need to fly an instrument-aided approach at the Springdale airport.

With decades of experience as a professional and military pilot and more than ten thousand flying hours under my belt, I was comfortable in most weather. That was especially true when at the controls of our 1984 Mooney 231, a single-engine aircraft with good instruments and a great autopilot in which I had already logged a thousand hours flying.

As we crossed Oklahoma, the forecasted cold front pushed across our route. The inflight advisory about the storm grabbed my attention as it mentioned deteriorating weather and possible icing conditions in the portion of northwest Arkansas into which we were headed. Icing is especially dangerous for small aircraft, and pilots know they should never willingly fly into such conditions.

I immediately checked with the closest flight service station, a ground-based FAA installation that provides up-to-the-minute weather to pilots in the air and on the ground. The conditions at Springdale Municipal Airport were still suitable for landing in a small plane; ceilings and visibility were lowering but considerably above the minimum requirements, and no ice was present. We continued, but now I was in a hurry to get Cynthia on the ground and to get back out of the area as soon as possible.

Clouds, rain, low ceilings, and falling temperatures greeted us as we transitioned from eastern Oklahoma into northwest Arkansas, just minutes from our destination. A routine landing at the Springdale airport left me confident that I could get off the ground and out of the area before conditions worsened.

After dropping Cynthia at the terminal, I got a quick weather briefing for the return trip, filed my instrument flight plan, and pitched Cynthia's headset and the charts into her empty seat as I strapped back into mine. Although the threat of icing existed on the return trip, pilot reports showed it was at higher altitudes than what I planned to fly, so I was still confident about making the flight.

The little Continental engine sprang to life; the checklists were normal. Taxi, takeoff, and climb-out were all uneventful. Passing through ten thousand feet, I hooked up my cannula and started breathing oxygen. Wanting to be as high as possible without picking up ice in the winter skies, I chose my altitude by temperature and stayed in air that was five degrees above freezing.

It is my habit to hand fly the aircraft during climb-out to keep up my proficiency, and that night was no exception. Leveling out at fourteen thousand feet, I engaged the autopilot and got comfortable for the less than three-hour flight back to Hobbs, New Mexico. Everything was routine. I had been alone in the dark and in weather like this many times. I glanced at Cynthia's headset in the other seat, a connection to her that brought a smile to my face. We had sacrificed a lot together to have the plane, but it was the joy she brought to my life that caused the glow.

Because of the clouds at lower altitudes, I had opened the alternate air valve during the climb. But when I found myself between cloud layers in an expanse of clear air after leveling off, I closed it. The valve provides air to the engine if the air intake becomes obstructed with ice accumulated during the flight. Having experienced little precipitation and no icing during climb-out, I had no way of knowing I would regret that decision later in the flight.

The Red Warning Light

The flight plan would take me over Lawton, Oklahoma, just south of the restricted areas around a military base there, across the Texas Panhandle to Lubbock, then directly home to Hobbs. It was a flight I had made many times since our daughter, Lori, had gone to work in Arkansas as a buyer for Walmart.

The dark night became lonely fast, as I was the only small aircraft on the frequencies used for lower-altitude traffic. An occasional airliner passed above me as the air traffic controllers passed me from one sector to the next. After overflying Lawton, I noticed the airliners above me were deviating north or south of the airway, indicating there was some image on their radar they wanted to avoid.

Seventy miles out of Lubbock, and using a short-range radio navigation system known as the VOR, I set my course needle to the Lubbock station and wondered aloud to the controller, "Fort Worth Center, this is November 95886, with a question."

"Roger, 886. Go ahead."

"I hear the airliners deviating. Is there weather ahead that I need to be concerned about? Maybe a thunderstorm?"

"Negative. The radar is clear between your position and Lubbock. My radar is not as accurate in detecting weather as the airliners', but I'll keep an eye on it for you."

My small Mooney aircraft had no radar, but it had a Ryan Stormscope, a lightning detection device made for small aircraft. Its screen was clear of the dots that would indicate electrical discharges, confirming what the controller had said. But I continued to monitor the airliners with their radar—pilot-to-pilot communications are discouraged—to help me guess what might be in the dark ahead. The clear layer I had been flying in was squeezing shut since passing Lawton. I was back to flying in clouds, but a glance at the outside air temperature showed the temperature was still five degrees above freezing and no ice was forming on the wings.

Then something caught my attention on the far right side of the instrument panel. The red alternator warning light had quietly flashed, alerting me to a possible electrical problem. A quick check showed everything was normal with the alternator, but I brought my emergency checklist within reach, just in case.

A few minutes later, the quiet blink occurred again. This time, my investigation revealed the alternator was producing erratic voltage. As I watched the voltage pulsating back and forth, trying to make sense of it, the meter suddenly dropped to zero. The alternator had failed. Fortunately, the failure occurred while I was looking at the gauge, otherwise precious moments could have lapsed and battery power would have been depleted before I discovered it.

"Fort Worth, this is 886. I just lost my alternator," I said, trying to remain calm. "I need to get on the ground as soon as possible. Lubbock is not much farther than Childress, but I do not need to fly through a thunderstorm. Still no radar returns on a storm between my position and Lubbock?"

"Negative. It looks good," he replied. "Do you need to declare an emergency?"

"Negative on the emergency," I answered. The loss of the alternator was very serious, but I had caught it as it happened and felt confident about my ability to land somewhere. I was already thinking about how to get the problem fixed the next day.

I had never lost electrical power in flight, but the training says to be ready. So every flight, day or night, I had a habit of checking my batteries and keeping the flashlight nearby. On night flights, I flew with it on the seat between my legs so I wouldn't have to fumble for it. In thirty years, I had never needed the flashlight so quickly.

I had developed habits over the years, preparing for in-flight crises I had never experienced. That's what discipline is all about, and it had paid off several times before. For instance, I check the fuel tank for water before every flight, though I had never found more than a teaspoon upon looking. Water in the tank can be sucked up by the fuel pump and delivered to the engine, where it could wreak havoc in flight. Once, when a friend flew my aircraft back from Midland to Hobbs, delivering it to me for a hurriedly scheduled flight, I was tempted to get into the air without checking the tank, since it had just been flown.

In aircraft emergencies, there is no time to do what should have been done before. Complacency can creep in—even on the most careful pilots—and especially when in a hurry. Discipline caused me to check the fuel tank anyway. Sure enough, I found not just a few drops, but seven cups of water. It was the only time in more than three decades and thousands of hours of flying that I have found any significant amount. It would have definitely caused problems, maybe even engine shutdown, had I flown without checking.

Pilots train, prepare, and practice for emergency situations, but that's not always enough. Emergencies demand discipline and mental composure as much as knowledge. Confidence and the ability to continue flying the airplane are psychological challenges that can overwhelm a pilot as certainly as mechanical failures. Sometimes there are scenarios for which you cannot prepare, and this was one of them.

But right now, I had to decide where to land—and soon.

"886, What Are Your Intentions?"

Lubbock had better and more varied instrument approaches, a control tower, emergency equipment, and a service center that could repair the alternator the next day. Childress, the closest lighted airport with an instrument approach, was only thirty-five miles away, forty-five degrees to the right of my course, but it had no control tower and no emergency equipment. I preferred Lubbock even though it was twice as far away.

While talking to the controller, I was turning off the navigation radios, the backup communication radio, and all lights to save power, pausing before turning off the pitot heat, but with temperatures above freezing level, I turned that off as well. (The pitot tube protrudes into the airstream and has a forward-facing opening. The pressure in the tube varies with airspeed, and that pressure is piped to the pilot's airspeed indicator. The pitot heat keeps ice from blocking the tube and rendering the airspeed indicator inoperative. The alternator failure had already rendered it inoperative, but I failed to realize that.)

I left the autopilot and one communication radio on as the only drains on the battery, felt for the flashlight, and made sure that it was operating. I had a standby radio that would allow me to shut even those last components down, but it was tucked in the most rearward part of the cabin, out of reach. When Cynthia is on board, she usually crawls over the seat to reach our safety bag when we need it. But in the hurry to get off the ground, I had neglected to move it within reach.

Once I reduced electrical drains on the battery, with the autopilot controlling the aircraft, I planned to crawl to the plane's rear seats to get the radio. Having it in hand would allow me to shut down all powered equipment while maintaining communication with the controllers.

I never made it to the backseat—or to that radio.

Losing the alternator in conditions that require electrical instruments is a big problem, since small planes have only a twelve-volt battery, smaller than most car batteries, to keep the lights and vital instruments operating without an operating generator.

"886, what are your intentions?" The air traffic controller interrupted my thoughts.

We were both tiptoeing around the actual declaration of an emergency, which triggers a series of actions on his part.

"Roger, 886 is continuing to Lubbock, shutting down all nonessential electrical equipment. I will leave only this radio on for communications, but would appreciate it if you would monitor my route and let me know whether I am drifting off course. And you might keep an eye on the weather. I am still concerned about the airliners deviating."

"Roger, I'll keep an eye on the weather and on your flight track."

Just when I was thanking God for keeping me calm through the problem, factors beyond my control began to take hold of my small plane. Lightning, thunder, and turbulence all hit at once, throwing the plane around like a ping-pong ball in a bingo tumbler. Snowflakes and ice pellets suddenly flecked the dark skies, striking my windscreen before I could see them coming. The storm the controller knew nothing about was suddenly all over me. With a failed electrical system, let alone a thunderstorm, I knew my circumstances could become deadly.

I snapped off the autopilot and broke one of the cardinal rules of instrument flight, rolling into a steep sixty-degree banked turn to get out of the storm.

"Fort Worth, 886, I just got into a monster ride. Must be what I was hearing the airliners avoiding. Request permission to deviate from my course."

"Roger, my radar still does not show anything, but you are approved to deviate left or right of course as needed. Let me know when you can proceed direct to Lubbock."

"Roger."

It took all of my focus to keep myself under control as the storm tossed the aircraft around the sky. The violence nearly inverted the plane, rolling it one direction and immediately back the other way. I cringed as my head struck the roof, turbulence slamming me against my shoulder harness and seat belt just before smashing me back into the seat.

Fear coursed through my veins like the electrical discharges outside the airplane. *Would the aircraft hold together?* The fleeting question became a knot in my stomach.

Then a blue orb of St. Elmo's fire—harmless static electricity that will scare the water out of you the first time you see it—formed inside the windscreen and dissipated as it rolled over the panel and fell into the cockpit. Although it was harmless, it was enough to feed the panic pushing its way up my throat, threatening to overwhelm me.

"God, I Need Help!"

I was just fifteen seconds into the crisis, trying to maintain the steep turn that would reverse my course and get me out of the storm. The discipline that I had built up over years to keep my fear from running the show was being put on trial. Already, I could barely process what was happening, let alone deal with it. And I had barely begun the wild ride.

Just then my airspeed indicator started decreasing, slowly at first, then more rapidly. And faster than I could say "165 knots," which was my airspeed going into the storm, the indicator fell to zero. I was as near panic as I had ever been during a flight. Now I only had seconds to react and just one chance to get this right.

Airspeed generates lift from the wings; without it, an aircraft will succumb to gravitational pull and return to earth. Without airspeed, flight stops and fall begins. And my airspeed was gone—all of it!

When a pilot is in a situation like mine, with no airspeed, he is desperate—and trained—to get it back. The urge to maintain flying speed is so strongly trained into pilots that it dominates all other sensory urges. Without airspeed, disaster is certain.

All a pilot has to trade for airspeed is altitude. My training told me I needed to push the nose down, start a descent, and get my airspeed back, assuming that, in my rush to click off the autopilot and begin the steep turn, I had pulled the nose up and lost speed. Above all, I didn't want to stall the plane in the midst of severe turbulence.

I have read aircraft accident reports since my first days as a pilot, trying to learn from the mistakes of others. I concluded that pilot error is the cause of many accidents. Oftentimes, it's hard to figure out what the pilot was thinking when he did what he did.

At that moment, I realized I didn't have the composure to solve the problems before me. In a second, I uttered aloud the most desperate prayer of my life. *"God, I need help! I'm overwhelmed and don't know if I have the skills to get out of this."* My lifelong fight with gravity, with the things that held me down, had turned deadly.

Within seconds of uttering the prayer, and despite fighting fear and emotional overload, I found myself almost inexplicably contemplating some of the most perplexing aircraft accident reports in which small planes fly straight down so fast that they rip the wings off before reaching the earth. I could never understand what would cause a pilot to speed downward while seeing the airspeed build to the point that they reach the structural limit of the aircraft.

But it made even less sense that I was allowing this distraction to disrupt my concentration. I was agitated at the interruption.

Then suddenly, in that steep turn, in the violent weather, with death staring me in the face, I experienced a sudden revelation—just in time— that I later recognized as an answer to my prayer: *Pilots ripped their aircraft's wings off because they were seeing what I was seeing—zero airspeed—when, in fact, they had plenty. My airspeed was there; it was just not displaying!*

Things were happening too fast at the moment for me to process why the airspeed was not displaying, but that recognition saved my life. (I would realize later that the temperature in the storm dropped twenty degrees and suddenly froze my airspeed sensor shut, giving the illusion of "zero" airspeed.)

I struggled with all my might against a natural tendency to lower the nose and start a mad descent, which could have built up enough airspeed to break up the aircraft in flight. Instead, I gripped the controls against severe turbulence, amid the growing prospect of losing self-control, and tried to get out of the storm.

Psychological factors can lead to catastrophe just as certainly as mechanical failures. In just a few seconds, I had become completely overloaded with the onslaught of problems, having to remind myself second by second that, if I could maintain control of my emotions, the airplane could fly. Pilot error was my biggest adversary.

I was still in the midst of a 180-degree turn to exit the storm. The flight that had been so calm and predictable had become anything but. Flight— and life—can change that quickly.

"886, what are your intentions?" It was the air traffic controller trying to help.

"I'm pretty busy right now. I'll call in a second." The battery was getting weaker, so he could not hear my responses. He had an airliner come up on my frequency to relay radio transmissions to and from me. The airliner transmitted my comments. "Fort Worth, this is American 568. 886 says he will call you in a minute."

"Roger, keep me posted. I am not reading his transmissions." I could tell by the controller's voice that he was concerned. I could hear the anxiety in both their voices.

And then another problem arose as the engine began to sputter and chug. I could tell by the mushy controls that this time I was indeed losing airspeed. I jammed the mixture all the way in, dumping more fuel into the engine in the belief that the injectors might be getting plugged. It didn't help. I wanted to give up, to let go and let the airplane go, to quit trying.

"Fort Worth, 886, I have just lost my engine." My voice revealed that I was fraying at the edges. I was still physically restraining myself from chasing the airspeed, guessing that I was going fast enough to stay in the air.

The airliner relayed, "Fort Worth, American 568. 886 reports he has lost his engine."

I could hear in his voice an element of helplessness, as though he was talking for and to a dead man.

"Roger, American 568. Ask 886 if he is declaring an emergency."

It was surreal. I could hear them talking about me as if I was already beyond hope. It seemed the controller, the other pilot, and maybe even I did not believe I would survive. But I didn't have time for self-pity. I heard the request and answered the airliner before he could relay. I did not want to seem quite that hopeless.

"American 568, you can tell him I am declaring an emergency." He relayed to Fort Worth with a level of emotion in his voice that was almost too much. I fought to not let anything be the last straw.

My voice was now shaking and uncertain, struggling to complete the sentences. "American uhh . . ." I could not remember his number. "American, can you have ummm . . . Fort Worth give me a vector to Childress. . . . And my airplane is bouncing so much in the turbulence . . . and I have my cockpit lights off and having trouble aiming the flashlight. Can you . . . tell him to let me know ummm . . . when I am headed toward Childress . . . and I am declaring an emergency."

"Roger, 886. Fort Worth knows you have declared emergency. I will get the vector for you."

Declaring an emergency triggers a series of responses on the part of the air traffic controller, including notifying the airport where the troubled plane will land, clearing any other aircraft out of the route of flight, and calling the local sheriff.

Then the struggling engine shuddered to a full stop. I could quit worrying about that; it was gone!

"Just Fly the Plane, Stupid!"

"Don't give up! Just fly the plane!" I started shouting the words aloud as commands to myself. I could not tolerate the thoughts of self-pity filling my mind, thoughts that I would not get to see our grandkids grow up, not get to spend my golden years with Cynthia. I glanced over at her headset. The sight, so sweet at takeoff, was now the source of profound sorrow.

"Snap out of this. Just fly the plane, Stupid!" I grabbed the headset and threw it out of sight into the rear seat. I had to get every distraction out of my mind. Only one thing would save me, and it wasn't self-pity and abstract thoughts.

"Trust God. JUST FLY THE PLANE!"

As an aircraft commander and instructor pilot in the Air Force, I had given instructions to other pilots in training situations. Now I was instructing myself, aloud. It was the last lifeline I could find.

"American 568, tell 886 that the sheriff has been notified and has dispatched people to the area."

The airline captain relayed to me, but I was so despondent I couldn't answer. I didn't want my aircraft wreckage and body to be found by a Texas county sheriff. My mind strayed to Cory, a pilot who worked with us years before at a small aviation company. He'd gotten himself into trouble with weather beyond his capabilities. We, his fellow pilots, found him in the wreckage.

"886, did you copy?"

I clicked the microphone twice, the universal signal that I had heard his transmission.

Childress had been forty-five degrees to the right of my flight direction toward Lubbock. My steep turn to get out of the storm had been to the left. The controller told me to keep my turn going.

I did not know how much airspeed had bled off since I lost the engine. The turbulence was dying down, the lightning flashes had slowed, and the precipitation against the windscreen had stopped, but I was without power, a little more than thirteen thousand feet in the air, just starting a glide toward the earth. Landing without power and without a runway is harrowing in daytime. At night, survival is rare.

"Don't panic! Just fly the plane!"

All my thoughts had been distilled to these two simple commands. One part of me was shouting them at the other.

I was not trying to start the engine or figure out the airspeed problem. I was trying to keep from stalling the plane with no indication of airspeed. I was trying to keep the turn going until I was pointed at Childress. I was trying to keep myself from giving up.

I began to process just a little bit of information, approximating the point at which gravity would win and the aircraft would hit the ground. Gravity always wins, but an operating engine gives the pilot some control about where. Tonight, that would not be the case. The gravitational pull of the earth would determine the touchdown point, and it appeared to be about fifteen miles short of the Childress runway. I asked the airliner to relay this information.

The solemn, unspoken recognition of pending disaster persisted in their voices, but my own desperation had become a bit calmer. I told myself, "Use your altitude. Feel the aircraft and airspeed; get the most out of your glide. Do what you can with what you have."

I broke out of the clouds at fifty-one hundred feet above the ground, after almost seven thousand feet in a controlled descent. I could see the lights of Childress and the flashing red lights of the sheriff's car pulling out of town. At the lower altitude, the engine suddenly began to sputter and cough, as though it was coming back to life. The airspeed indicator began to bounce off zero. Then it hit me—ice had restricted the pitot tube and engine inlet in the storm. It was now melting, bringing my engine, and a bit of hope, back to life.

With the sputtering engine generating a little power, my rate of descent slowed. Maybe I could milk enough power out of it to stretch my glide to Childress. My trembling hands and legs had calmed enough to try to land without power. I was at least considering it. If I could just get a little consistent power, I could extend the glide to the runway.

I found myself inside the fifteen-mile range that I thought would be my point of impact, and I was still fairly high above the ground. I didn't know if the glide rate of the Mooney would carry me to the runway, but I thought I'd try.

My heart was still pounding, but my hands were steadier on the controls. The engine had partial power, and it shook the entire airframe as it fired on a few cylinders. I was getting closer to the field, but lower and lower.

Now I was battling another pilot instinct, a tendency to stretch the glide. It is a reflex action; if the runway is close, one concentrates on trying to get there, failing to notice that the attempt to keep the aircraft in the air is bleeding off airspeed. The scenario played out in my mind: Airspeed would dissipate until the plane stalled, one wing would drop and strike the ground, causing the aircraft to cartwheel side-over-side. It is better to crash-land with wings level, just before the runway, than to stretch the glide only to cartwheel.

My years of flying crop dusters were paying off. In a spray plane, the aircraft is always tickling right at the edge of a stall, and a pilot learns how to keep it at that point, a knot or two above the stall speed. Experience helps you know the feeling in the control yoke when you can do no more.

I was at that point. Either I could make it to the runway or I couldn't, but I was determined to get every foot of forward glide I could squeeze out of the Mooney's partial engine power.

The words of my first flight instructor, Greg Quinones, played in my mind: "It would be a shame, my friend, to land on this side of the concrete," he said once, in his thick Hispanic accent, when I was about to land in the boondocks short of the Las Cruces airport. I did not need to stall the airplane this close to the runway.

"Just fly the plane." I was no longer shouting but quietly coaxing a little more out of the plane—and out of myself. "Hold steady, don't want to stall. Let her touch down out here if she wants, wings level. Nice and easy. If it hits, make sure the wings are level. Don't want to cartwheel this baby."

The engine steadied and the glide continued to extend closer to the runway, past the stretch of dirt before it. And, finally, somehow, the wheels touched on the pavement.

Still rolling, I made the call to the airliner that was now barely in range, asking him to let Fort Worth Center know they could close my flight plan; I had touched down. The weak transmission of his radio signal could not hide the surprise and relief in his voice. Somehow, I had escaped a desperate emergency.

As he signed off, my weakened battery sighed its last breath, and the entire plane went dark as the radio popped and shut down. I was still rolling to a stop on the runway.

The magnetos, which provide power to the spark plugs, separate from the electrical system, kept the engine running despite the dead battery and alternator. But I was totally without lights or communication. Somehow, I made my way to the dark ramp, parked, pulled the mixture to idle, shutting down the engine, and sat in the dark.

I didn't move; I couldn't move. I was spent. Empty.

Instant Replay

Sitting there alone, the chain of events began to replay through my mind—the alternator failure, flying into the storm that hadn't shown up on radar, the loss of airspeed, or so I thought, and the near panic that resulted. Then the complete despair as the engine sputtered before failing.

Slowly, the cause of this chain of events began to dawn on me. The temperature inside the storm was much colder than it had been in the air seconds before. My five-degrees-above-freezing temperature became fifteen-degrees-below-freezing inside the storm. I had flown into severe icing conditions, but my mind was telling me that icing could not be a problem.

When the alternator failed, the heater that keeps the pitot tube from freezing shut was disabled, allowing the accumulation of ice. The tube had frozen shut, thus it was not sensing my speed, though it was far from zero. And the same icing conditions that froze my pitot tube had been forming ice in the engine inlet, partially obstructing it. With less air getting to the engine, it began to sputter and chug.

The recognition hit me like a lightning bolt—if the alternate air valve had been open, the engine failure could have been averted. I could have avoided the most harrowing part of the emergency, the part that took me to the point of almost giving up.

As in most catastrophes, it is the accumulation of problems that leads to near disaster. Together, they had overwhelmed my ability to process information.

Many aircraft accidents happen because the pilot concentrates on the problem and does not fly the aircraft. I faced the sober realization that, despite decades of training, I almost lost control by locking in a few variables: airspeed, a failed engine, and fear.

During my military years, I read a report about an Air Force aircraft whose No. 3 engine had come unbolted from the wing while flying thirty thousand feet above the ground. The engine rocketed ahead, its thrust unhindered by the weight of the plane, until it ran out of fuel. All of the pilot's training to maintain composure played out in his calm response: "There goes the No. 3 engine."

Life, like flying, has a rather mundane quality to it most of the time, with repetitive tasks making up the bulk. But harsh and sudden realities can accompany both. There are rules and laws and practices that, if broken, can lead to death. Flying dramatically brings to light consequences that, in the rest of life, may take years to surface.

While such composure is trained into pilots, it isn't easy to achieve in flight. I now knew that. Discipline, while it can feel routine and boring to implement, quickly proves its worth in an emergency.

Several minutes after landing, I saw the sheriff's flashing lights turn into the airport. My knees were shaking, but that was not what kept me sitting, unmoved in the dark. It was a deeper recognition that many had failed to survive the exact situation I had just faced. Without an answered prayer, I would have fared no better.

The deputy pulled up and parked beside me, staying in his vehicle, respectful of the gravity of the situation. Finally, he got out of his car and knocked on my window. I turned, looking absently at him for many seconds. My focus returned, and I unlatched the door.

"Evening," I said, my voice still trembling. "Pretty cold out here."

The deputy had seen fear up close before and knew what to say. "Yep, pretty cold. You need a lift?"

Preparing for Life's Emergencies

Life, like flying, has a rather mundane quality to it most of the time, with repetitive tasks making up the bulk. But harsh and sudden realities can accompany both. There are rules and laws and practices that, if broken, can lead to death. Flying dramatically brings to light consequences that, in the rest of life, may take years to surface.

We take for granted the things necessary for life until they are gone. At any moment, the ride can become harrowing. It is discipline in the boring and everyday that prepares us for the sudden and unexpected.

There is a saying among pilots that the most useless things to him are airspeed he does not have, runway behind him, and altitude above him. All are essential, but once they have been lost or used, they take precious moments to regain. Sometimes you have those precious moments, and sometimes you do not.

There are experiences, resources, and people that prove essential in each of our lives. When we lose them, getting them back takes precious time and energy. Sometimes you have time to get them back; sometimes you don't.

Pilots rehearse the mental discipline necessary in emergency situations over and over in simulators and flight training. As much as the practice helps stabilize those beating hearts and purify bad tendencies, in an emergency there are only precious seconds to make those rehearsed decisions. There is one chance, maybe two, to avert failure.

For some reason, we do not practice for many of life's emergencies. Sure, we may have a flashlight tucked away somewhere in case the power goes out, and we may have rehearsed the fire exits once upon a time, after our kids learned about it in school. But we don't practice how we will react when those same kids come home past curfew or with a boyfriend we don't like. We don't go through the motions, rehearsing for the death of a loved one or the loss of a job. We save and we plan a bit, but it pales in comparison to the preparation of a pilot before flight.

We do not study accident reports of failed marriages or careers spoiled by scandal. We act as though these things would never, could never, happen to us. These problems are no-notice exams that test our preparation, our character, our very foundations. They affect the rest of our lives and how long we live them. And our reactions to them affect how well we live the lives we have left.

INTRODUCTION

I was born the third of six children to a sharecropper in West Texas who didn't stay there long. When two successive droughts broke the family, financially and otherwise, my mother and father left the dry land farm and headed west in an old pickup truck with their three children, myself included. Three more would be born later.

When the truck broke down sixty miles west on the New Mexico-Texas border, we hitchhiked three miles to Hobbs, New Mexico, and I grew up there.

In Hobbs, my father got a job as a roustabout, on the lowest rung of the oilfield hierarchy, raising his family on $2.62 an hour. In those early days in Hobbs, my parents collected Coke bottles and redeemed them to help make ends meet. Later, after we moved to the five-acre farm at Nadine, we sold vegetables we raised to help pay for school clothes.

Despite our humble beginning, I was able to finish high school and college, become an Air Force pilot, fly in the Vietnam War, and then return to Hobbs, where I met and married Cynthia. Together, we built an oilfield service business that grew from four to fifty employees over fourteen years.

After experiencing the burdensome regulations and obstacles our government has created for all industries, I decided to act instead of just complaining, running for and being elected to the United States Congress, representing southern New Mexico for eight years between 2003 and 2012.

People tell me mine isn't a typical path to the Congress, that I have a story worth telling. But there are multiple "poor boy succeeds" stories out there, examples far better than mine. However, the changing of financial circumstances was a mere backdrop to my life, as I experienced abiding changes to the characteristics that had for so long defined me.

I don't know whether my path is typical. I only know my story, and the more interesting one behind it that drills down into my progression from a son of a sharecropper to congressman and the transformation going on behind scenes.

I didn't learn to ride a bike when other kids in the oil camp neighborhood did. I was afraid and would not be coaxed out of it. The fear of falling and the fear of failure left me on the sidelines, envying the exhilaration of others as they broke free from the guiding hands of parents to wheel by, knuckles tightly clenched to handlebars as they embraced the childhood rite of passage. It would be several years before I took the chance on two wheels.

I had trouble expressing my feelings and was easily discouraged at anything I tried.

As my seventh birthday approached, I experimented with my first attempt at assertiveness: pleading with my mother for a birthday party. I imagined myself breaking out of my shell and taking my place as the center of attention, becoming an outgoing boy like my brother Tom. My pleas, however, did not work; we could not afford a party, she told me. In a rare display of strength, I persisted in my requests, all to no avail.

As the twenty-fourth of August approached, my enthusiasm deflated and my attempts to break free of my old self withered on the vine. I dragged through the big day without interest, well into the afternoon when Mom called me in from the backyard where I was busy moping. I walked into our tiny house to find that all the kids in the oil camp had gathered for a birthday party, for me.

When everyone shouted "Surprise!" the fears won out. I bolted to the bedroom, crawled under the bed, and cried.

Mom came in first, trying to lure me out of hiding. One after another of my friends came, too, entreating me to join the fun. But I was utterly unmovable under the bed, in the dark. As I rejected appeals, my resolve hardened, and I wore the refusals like a badge of honor. Eventually, they tired of reasoning with the pair of shoes protruding from under the bed and retreated to the fun of the party without me.

Instead of being the charming, center of attention I had envisioned, I once again embarrassed myself in a display that took a decade to over-come. Mom found the disaster confounding, and she wasn't sure what to do. We never discussed the event, and I never requested or received another birthday party.

"I Am the Weakest of My Brothers"

There are many doors that prevent us from moving from where we are to where we dream of being. Sometimes dreams do not even exist; we simply know that we are not satisfied with who we are. That was the case for me. I had to be taught how to dream and see the possibilities that others seemed to understand from birth.

There were as many closed doors in my life as in any life I have seen . . . , and most of them were in my mind. I was riddled with insecurities and fears, lacked knowledge or vision, and struggled with the embarrassment of poverty, shyness, and my own introversion.

> For so long, I kept myself locked in a cell of fear, unable to move from where I was to where I wanted to be. But the doors that restrain us, I've found, are seldom locked. With a little push, they swing wide to welcome a life we never imagined.

I can see in the young lives of my grand-children ideas and ways of perceiving that simply never existed in me at an early age. I am amazed even today at the creativity, insight, and freedom of expression in others that I had to learn and develop one step at a time.

God provided; somehow he used this flawed vessel. Through prayer, practice, and persistence, I overcame the obstacles and learned not only to ride a bike but to fly supersonic jets. I learned not only how to relate to others but convinced a number of them to vote me into elected office.

This book is a compilation of the events that shaped my life. As my family evolved financially, I changed dramatically, facing childhood fears and insecurities while learning self-reliance—and a bit of gumption.

The real story is my fight to overcome these internal obstacles, a fight I found far more difficult than overcoming the ones placed in my life by external forces.

This book is my story of overcoming. In the process, I have helped a few others, some of whose stories are included.

In biblical Israel, God chose Gideon to be a judge over the squabbling, disjointed clans and tribes of Israel. Gideon's response? "I am from the weakest tribe, the weakest clan, the weakest family, and I am the weakest of my brothers. Why me?"

That is very close to the way I feel.

For so long, I kept myself locked in a cell of fear, unable to move from where I was to where I wanted to be. But the doors that restrain us, I've found, are seldom locked. With a little push, they swing wide to welcome a life we never imagined. If just one person pushes at those closed doors, then this book and this story will be worthwhile.

I know that God has blessed me, renewed me, refreshed me, and redeemed me, and he is still at work. For that, and for the blessing of living in a time of liberty, I am eternally thankful.

3

SAND-WORN CEILINGS AND PURPLE PAINT

William Goyen once said, "I don't think anyone ever recovers from the place he was born." Growing up in a small town in East Texas during the Depression, his roots influenced his work as a writer for his entire life. I know as well how deeply my roots have influenced me.

In my forties and suddenly curious about my family's history, I asked my dad to show me where he grew up and where I was born. He was reticent but finally agreed to make the trip. We set out in the pickup on a Friday morning in the fall of 1991, and I would soon learn why he hesitated.

The two of us spent two days driving through the sandy farmland towns surrounding O'Donnell, Texas, forty miles south of Lubbock, where we lived until I was just over a year old. Except for his brief stint in the Army at Bryan, Texas, Dad hadn't ventured beyond places where either his family or he and Mom had lived, places such as New Moore, Draw, Redwine, Tahoka, and Lamesa, all of which were within twenty miles of his birthplace.

In Redwine, he showed me the collapsed heap of a stucco house where Grandmother Henry (his mother's mother) lived, where he had visited every weekend in his teens. He showed me the cistern that his father and other family members dug by hand.

Dad seemed lost in another dimension as he described the time he, as the eldest grandson, was lowered into the hole to stack and cement building blocks to form the walls of the cistern. The memory seemed painful, and he didn't go into deeper detail. (Nor did he seem to like that I retrieved a section of the cistern wall to carry home with me.)

He showed me where he would walk on daylong trips into the Breaks, the rough and unbroken land to the east of his grandmother's home. He showed me where Mom was born in Draw and the high school in O'Donnell where he and Mom graduated, and the football field where he found a taste of stardom.

When we visited the little museum at O'Donnell, he paused in front of a large photograph of Bobby Dan Blocker, whom he knew well when they were in school together. Blocker headed to Hollywood and played Hoss Cartwright on the TV series *Bonanza*. Dad also showed me with pride his WWII service hat in a display case at the museum.

As we drove the highway between O'Donnell and Lamesa, he pointed out a small rock house west of the highway. "That's where we lived the year you were born," he said, almost as an aside.

I focused my eyes on the humble farmhouse, not sure whether to believe what I saw. I asked him to drive closer. From a distance, it looked tiny, and I couldn't imagine how the five of us fit in it. He looked as though he'd rather keep driving by, but I pushed, "It will just take a few minutes. I want to see it up close."

As he turned onto the farm road leading to the house, the pickup's tires bogged down in the soft sand. "Let me get out and walk," I suggested.

He stopped, shut the engine off, and replied tersely, "I'll walk with you."

Our feet sank into the soil, and we both began to get sand in our shoes. It took me back to the shoes full of sand all us kids would get when we went to the New Mexico sand hills to hunt for arrowheads. We would get out of the car and walk out through the sand dunes, looking for places where the wind had, just maybe, exposed an artifact. Never owning a pair of hiking boots, we wore our low-top school shoes, which allowed the sand to come in, under our feet, and into our socks. The small spears of grama grass poking through the sand would pierce like harpoons through our socks and into our feet and ankles, forcing us to stop and pick them out.

As Dad and I continued toward the house, he shook his head in silent disagreement with what we were doing. He did not appreciate going back this close to that period of his life, and I silently wondered if this was more painful than the scene at the cistern had been.

I started down the weed-choked driveway toward the house but he interrupted, "Not that one. My cousin Tech lived in the big house." He directed my gaze instead to a corrugated tin building that stood to the side of the main house. It was the size of a portable storage unit someone would put in his backyard.

"We lived over here."

Tech's house was pitifully small, a visible reminder of how hard life was for farmers in those days. But the house for our family of five had been nothing more than the chicken coop; they had to relocate the chickens before moving in.

Peering through the boarded-up door, I was shocked by the primitive shelter that, forty years later, still had a dirt floor, no insulation, no Sheetrock, exposed studs, and just the bare tin walls. The windows were mere cutouts in the tin wall with wire over them to keep the chickens in and the foxes out. Light shone through the wall in places where rats or foxes had crawled in. Though the chicken manure had long since been scraped out, the smell of sand soaked with animal urine was still pungent. I was embarrassed, and somewhat hurt, that I had never been curious enough to know the circumstances my parents had lived through trying to provide for us kids.

The worst part, when I surveyed the surroundings, was that the structure stood squarely in the middle of the plowed sandy fields. I asked Dad if these were the fields he plowed, and he replied with an affirmative nod. The hurt in his eyes seemed to keep him from saying more at first.

When the wind blew, he told me, Mom put cardboard in the windows to keep the sand out. But it came in anyway, covering every surface. They lived in this little house for two to three weeks at a time while Dad was plowing and cultivating the crop at this farm.

My folks alternated between living here and at a house in New Moore, a few miles away, when Dad was cultivating another field. It was not much bigger than this one and equally battered by the sandstorms.

"You Were a Sharecropper?"

I stood quietly, lost in speculation about those days before my memory, visualizing what it must have been like for the five of us, cooped up in there. I thought of a memory I did have, of driving through sandstorms when I was five, scared and overwhelmed by the grinding sand against the windshield. What was it like in this house with the sandstorms coming inside?

I pictured Mom wrapping damp cloths around our heads, covering our mouths and noses and securing the cloth at the back of our necks, making us look like little bank robbers. She had to be worried that we were breathing more sand into our lungs than they could sustain. I imagined the dust and sand covering the food as she tried to serve up meals.

What was it like for Mom, trying to make it work, living here? Dad was wild at heart. He could tolerate anything, but what about her? What was it like as the spirit drained from her and she thought about a lifetime she would have to spend in these places? I couldn't grasp the full depth of it and wearied of the attempt to imagine her hardship.

I had wondered before at how some people can snap, at how young mothers can run off and leave families in the middle of the night, looking for the city lights and long ball gowns they dreamed of while they were growing up. But now, looking at the lifestyle my parents called their own in the prime of their dreaming days, at twenty-two and twenty-three years of age, it was harder for me to comprehend how they had stayed, how they had made do.

Dad did not speak. I think, from the way he was standing back, he didn't want to be part of what was going on inside me. I broke the silence. "This is pretty tough. I know you said you worked for your cousin, but how exactly was that set up? "

"I farmed on the halves with my cousin Tech McLaurin. He was my age and inherited this farm at twenty-two when his father died. All the McLaurins died at an early age. Heart disease. Tech never worked too hard, went off down to Juarez on frequent partying trips. Had a second family down there, ended up losing the farm. He was too young to have that kind of property and responsibility."

"What does it mean that you farmed on the halves?"

"Tech owned the land, and I farmed it. When we got the crop in, we split it down the middle. We each got half the proceeds."

"You were a sharecropper?"

"No!" he snapped, suddenly defensive.

And I let it go. I had heard enough not to press.

When the Ceiling Collapsed

The other house in New Moore, where Dad also farmed, was a little larger than this one, but the constant sandstorms had already left their mark long before we arrived. When we moved in, Mom did the same thing she has done in every house her entire life, whether she owned it or not. She cleaned with a vengeance, sweeping out the sand, dust, and loose balls of black hair left from the years of occupation by bracero and migrant farm workers from Mexico. The stubborn hair proved to be her cleaning nemesis. Masses of black hair had accumulated in the screens that had been nailed on the windows. Mom cleaned those and the rest of the outside of the little house. Finally, she felt she had a home clean enough to cook and eat in, where her three boys would be safe. She piled all the trash from inside and outside the house into one stack and burned it.

After all the cleaning and disinfecting, during one of the frequent sandstorms, the ceiling lost a long struggle with gravity and caved in. The weight of sand that for years had sifted through the cracks in the roof, accumulating in the attic, came crashing down. In the piles of sand deposited unceremoniously in the kitchen, Mom found more masses of hair.

The constant blowing sand had worn down Mom's desire to be on the farm. The ceiling collapsing was a vivid reminder that all the time she thought the house to be safe, the germs, lice, and filth had been drifting silently over their food and clothes each day. It was unnerving for her, and, at twenty-two, she made the decision to get away from the blowing sand and the farm, to find a safe place to raise her children.

That was 1947, the year I was born . . . another drought year. Dad nursed his cotton through the difficult season of planting and cultivating and chopping out weeds. It survived the boll weevils and the drought, but the crop was sparse. For the year's worth of work, Mom and Dad made two hundred dollars.

One week, Mom helped Dad hoe all week long on the farm. She went to Cousin Tech to be paid, and he told her, "I am paying Melvin (Dad), and the wife always comes as part of a package deal. I am not going to pay you."

Mom responded, "I don't work that way. When I work, you pay me." So he paid her.

Dad's family was too involved in the young couple's life. His parents found an old car that had a good motor and a cab, but the rest of the body had been stripped off. They insisted that it was all my dad could afford, but Mom refused to ride in it.

Her refusal, along with her stance that she was not part of a package deal with Cousin Tech, earned Mom a reputation in the family. They began to say she imagined herself as "too good to live by their standards." They were poor folks and had accepted it.

The Pearce family had a routine for Sunday dinners in which Mom and Dad were expected to participate. One Sunday, the extended family, consisting of three sprawling related families (the Pearce, McLaurin, and Henry families), all met at the Henrys' house on my grandmother's side of the family. The next week they met at one of the Pearce homes.

With large families and multiple generations all in one area, the events ballooned to gaggles of people. These Sunday gatherings took precedent over church, causing Mom to chafe at the expectations and brood about missing church. She also didn't like expectations that she consult with Dad's parents on household matters. Mom bought a refrigerator once without asking the advice of Dad's family, and they threw a fit at "the brazen show of independence."

Yet, it was okay when Grandmother Pearce found a discarded secondhand stove and delivered it to our house. When Dad installed it and lit the burner, it was clear why it had been thrown out—the flames shot clear to the roof. Mom was furious that Dad had put the family at risk rather than speaking up and telling his family "no."

Between the blowing sand and dust, the crowding in-laws, and the economic stress, Mom was choking. She needed breathing room.

She announced one day that she would have no more of this farm life. Everyone knew the unspoken part—that she was not going to live with secondhand stoves delivered by the in-laws and forbidden refrigerator purchases. The family whispered, knowing full well she could hear, "Allyne (Mom) will have the say over everything; she will eventually run the family."

Gravitational Pull of the Family

Gravity, like family, has its proper role. It gives order, predictability, and certainty to the patterns of life. If there is too little, things come unhinged.

Without it, things on earth would fly off into the atmosphere, which itself would refuse to cling to the earth. But in life and family, when the gravitational field is too strong, things become heavy and burdensome.

Just as the planets orbit around the sun because of a gravitational pull, families naturally orbit around parents. In Dad's family, the orbits were far too close to extended relatives, causing habits that threatened to stifle family relationships and invited interfering suggestions about every aspect of life.

Dad's parents, my grandparents, were good, well-meaning people, but their love beyond a certain point proved smothering. They exerted strong gravitational pulls on all their children, wanting to keep them close and tied in to the family, even in adult years, to help them "avoid bad decisions." As poor people, they had learned from their experiences that bad decisions could sink their flimsy economic lives. They had learned to fear life.

This strong influence stifled Mom's input about her own husband and children, and she silently stewed for those five years. Slowly, she began to stew more vocally as she started to pull free from Dad's family. It's not that she wanted chaos. She wanted enough distance that the pull of the family would not disrupt the development of her husband and children into their own distinctive family unit.

Gravity must be just right in the family; we need the right proportion of it in our individual lives as well. Not unlike planets orbiting around the sun, it takes the perfect amount of gravitational pull—not too much, not too little—to maintain meaningful and healthy relationships among family members. While family units may be properly balanced, an individual family member could disrupt that balance if he or she is too fearful to "leave and cleave" or too careless to keep close contact.

Mom was feeling stagnant, as though nothing would change and that Dad would never make a decision to better their lives because of the strong influence his family exerted. It is because of these dynamics that the Bible tells the man to leave his father and mother and cleave or cling to his wife. Hard feelings and friction arise if parental bonds are not broken at the right time.

Purple Finger Paint

It was 1948 and another drought year across the entire region. Drought is hard for any farmer, but for a dry land farmer in West Texas, it is catastrophic.

At just under one, I was still crawling, but my brothers Mike and Tommy were old enough to be into everything. One day, my parents were driving around on the New Moore farm, sharing one of the few moments alone and dreaming about the future when they found their pig lying dead about an eighth of a mile from the barn. It had purple paint on its snout.

Consumed with guilt and fear, they hurried home to check on the kids and found Mike proudly displaying his purple hands and the pur-

Not unlike planets orbiting around the sun, it takes the perfect amount of gravitational pull—not too much, not too little—to maintain meaningful and healthy relationships among family members. While family units may be properly balanced, an individual family member could disrupt that balance if he or she is too fearful to "leave and cleave" or too careless to keep close contact.

ple handprints they had both painted on the outside of the barn. When Mom asked where the purple paint came from, Mike showed her the one hundred-pound sack of peas stored in the barn waiting for planting season.

The purple color was arsenic painted on the peas to keep the mice and insects from eating the seeds before they could germinate. After Mike opened it, the pig rooted it over and ate some of the deadly peas. Mom carefully shepherded Mike and Tom while she washed their hands; her nerves ever closer to the breaking point.

But there were moments when even Mom discovered the joy of farming. As the first rains came, the cotton crop germinated with the green leaves breaking through the soil. Sandstorms can cut the tender young shoots off before they get a chance to grow. But when the plants got through this phase and matured, blooms and squares set that would form the bolls; the size of the crop was no longer speculation.

Anticipation built as the young couple toured the crop week to week. Despite the drought, Dad, and even Mom, grew excited to see the crop survive from one stage to the next.

Boll weevils can decimate a crop at this stage, but miraculously his crop escaped, and the cotton began to burst out of the bolls rich and thick. Despite the drought, Dad's rows of cotton were full and long; the cotton had opened and was ready for picking. The anticipation of the summer gave way to the excitement of harvest as they drove through the fields looking at the bountiful crop.

On a Thursday, the pickers stopped by to see when Dad wanted to start harvesting, and they all agreed to begin the following Monday. By now, nothing could go wrong and the young couple set aside the caution and temperance that controls all farmers, spreading the bills from the full year of farming on the table in preparation for paying them off.

The next day, a Friday, it rained all day. On Saturday, the sand blew all day. (Such is life in West Texas. The sandy soil soaks up the rain as soon as it hits the ground, and it can easily be blowing within an hour after a rainstorm.) Sunday it rained again. After the cotton absorbed the rain on Friday, the blowing sand then stuck in the wet cotton. And the rain on Sunday caused the heavy, sand-soaked cotton to start falling out of the husk.

The excitement and hopes that were so vivid three days earlier had been dashed. The cotton they managed to pick had so much sand in it that it barely ran through the gin. It had little value. They made fifty dollars for the entire year of work, hope, and worry.

"Melvin," Mom said, "this is no way to live or to raise a family."

He did not respond. He was concerned about what he would tell his parents. He was frozen in place, immobile, afraid of what his parents would say should they choose another life.

Shortly thereafter, Mom began her own gravitational pull, telling Dad that she did not want the farm life anymore. She strongly declared that they could and should make a living somewhere else. She was ready to get out of the orbit they were in.

Mom suggested they take a vacation to get away before the dreariness of winter and more blowing sand. They loaded all five of us in the pickup truck and departed, full of excitement, on a three hundred-mile trip west toward Juarez. But the pickup broke down sixty miles later, at the New Mexico state line. We hitchhiked three miles into Hobbs, where we stayed with Mom's uncle, Jay Webb.

Mom saw one of Jay's paycheck stubs from the oilfield job and was flabbergasted to learn he made more in a week than they had made in a year.

Jay was sympathetic to the young family's circumstances and said, "Melvin, you are never going to make a living in farming. I can help you get a job in the oilfield." They had no money to fix the truck. Their choices were few.

With Jay's encouragement, Mom's insistence, and a little breakdown intervention, Dad began to believe he could get a job somewhere other than the farm. He believed that he might be capable of more, that he might be able to survive away from his family.

4

MOVING TO THE OILFIELD

With Mom and Jay's backing, Dad steeled his nerves, walked into one of the contract gang companies, and asked the manager about going to work. The manager did what all managers in the oilfield at that time did; he told Dad he would give him a job.

The oilfields in those days were boom and bust. Transients and winos always knew they could work in the oilfield, but the managers never knew who would actually show up. They told everyone they had a job. But once they all showed up, the managers took their pick of the crop of workers and doled out jobs to only a few, dismissing many who thought they would have work that day.

Filled with the lightness of having launched out and believing he had gotten a job, Dad went back home to get the furniture and move it to Hobbs. He was surviving on his own, away from the safety net, out where his parents had told him he could not. He was not only defying his parent's warnings about "the outside world," but also the gravity that had kept him rooted in place his entire life.

When Dad told his parents of his intentions, they warned him that, if he moved to Hobbs, his family would "go to the dogs." All the things we would be exposed to in that rough town, they said, would ruin us.

Dad showed up for work on Monday full of expectation. But after the crews were all filled out, the man told him there was no job for him. Confused, Dad insisted that the man had promised him a job. Dad had believed far more into the promises than the jaded offer had really contained. He made a small scene—a farm boy sheepishly asserting himself in this new dog-eat-dog world—and the man told him to get out of the office.

Dad's brief attempt at independence was a flickering flame, and he felt it dimming back toward reality. The warnings of his family crowded back into his mind, joined by his own fears that he was just not smart enough to make it on his own. As he was shown out of the office, he wondered if his folks had been right, if all that was left was to "go to the dogs." He walked with leaden steps back to the parking lot and got into the pickup, knowing that if he was to feed his family, he had to go back to the farm. Back to work for his cousin.

As he pulled out of the gate, he glanced in the rearview mirror and saw the manager running out the door, waving his arms. Dad started to ignore him; he was too depressed for another letdown. But his gentle, helping nature would not let him leave an arm-waving man, not even one who had just thrown him out of his office.

Out of breath, the manager told him that one of the crews had just shown up missing a roustabout who, drunk from the night before, refused to get out of bed. The crew needed someone immediately. Could he start right then?

That is how close things were for my family. Providence stepped in to change the outcome of our lives, but it had hinged on whether Dad hit the brake or pressed the accelerator, throwing gravel on the man who'd misled him.

To the Edge of the Earth

Dad got the job and consistent work on a contract roustabout gang in the oilfield. Mom got a job at Franklin's Dress store on Broadway, working on a commission. She did very well, and they wanted to send her to be trained as a manager. But her father advised against it, and she followed his advice. Later, she went to work at Mead's Fine Bread, a local bakery, because they offered her more money.

Dad was making more in a month than he had in a year on the farm. But even with the boosted income that off-the-farm work provided, life was hard for the five of us in early 1949. Living expenses were not that much more than they had been, but my parents still could barely put food on the table.

They didn't have money for a babysitter, so Dad took us kids with him when he went hunting one day. I was not yet two years old, and we all got pink eye. (I was so scared when the doctor came to give us each a shot that I crawled far under the bed. The doctor followed me, grabbed me by the ankle, and pulled me out for the shot, setting the frightening experience like concrete in my already fear-filled mind.)

> Providence stepped in to change the outcome of our lives, but it had hinged on whether Dad hit the brake or pressed the accelerator, throwing gravel on the man who'd misled him.

Shortly after arriving in Hobbs, a rare blizzard rolled in and froze everything. Dad only had one pair of thin, summer-weight khaki work clothes to wear through the coldest winter to hit Lea County in decades. Along with their jobs, Mom and Dad also gathered Coke bottles and redeemed them for two cents each to help put food on the table.

When I was about three, I displayed my first free-market tendency. I asked, "Mutter, if I wash the dishes, would you pay me a quarter a week?" She agreed, and I dutifully pulled a chair to the sink and washed dishes each night. Even at that age, I figured out that she was paid each Friday, and I met her at the door when she got off work to ask, "Mutter, where's my quarter?"

The move to the new normal for our family wasn't easy, but it was alive. Dad had traded, however hesitantly, familiarity of home and family for a fresh start. He was making more money than he had ever made, but it, too, came at a cost—jealousy and resentment from his family. The rest of his brothers and sisters remained in place, in the familiar surroundings, with the poor wages of dry land farming, joining his parents in describing the peril that lay out there in the oilfields: honkytonks, loose women, fast talkers, and shysters.

But over the next decade, as they saw us standing strong against the temptations around us, each of Dad's brothers and sisters began to ask quietly just how much Dad was making. They were intrigued by his experience, wondering whether they could survive on their own. Eventually, each of them overcame their fears and left the farm as well, living independent of the big family gatherings and feeding their families with off-the-farm jobs.

Each of Dad's brothers and sisters ended up working in the oilfield around Odessa, Texas. We were the only ones who ventured beyond the edge of the earth—into New Mexico. I chalk that up to Mom's independence, but it might be that this was a secondary reason; the primary reason being that Hobbs is just where the truck broke down.

From Contract Gang to Major Company

The Hobbs area was home to Shell, Texaco, Marathon, Mobil, Humble, Gulf, Getty, and all the other established oil companies at the time. The contractors were just what the name implied, hired by the major companies to fill in around the edges and to do the jobs the company employees didn't have time or desire to do.

As a contractor, Dad made less than he would on staff with the major companies and didn't receive health insurance or retirement benefits. Mom soon understood the difference between the contract gangs and the major companies and began eyeing an opportunity for Dad to break into the latter.

But openings at the major companies, she noticed, were filled before the new family in Hobbs even knew about the jobs. One day, Mom was working her job at Mead's Fine Breads when a coworker told her he had been offered a job at Humble Oil Company in Eunice but was not going to take it. "Do you think your husband would want it?"

Mom immediately saw it as an answer to prayer and was quick to respond. "Who does he need to talk to?"

"The superintendent's name is Hoot Carlson." He explained that the job was west of Eunice, about five miles out of town.

Mom was excited to discuss the news with Dad, but he received it with uncertainty. Dad was always hesitant to make changes, and they had found what he longed for in the small house on Cecil Street: a small group of friends, a set routine, and a stable home. Uprooting from the certainty of the farm and away from his family had taken a lot of adjustment, and here was Mom, suggesting yet another move.

Dad craved predictability more than the lure of increased pay. Mom was more directly involved with the finances, and she entreated Dad to seek more stability in this area as well as the others. Finally, Dad drove to Eunice, west to the Humble Arrowhead Camp, and asked for the job. And he got it.

Providence provided the open door, but Mom gave the final push through it. Dad would later be glad he took the opportunity that someone else had turned down, one that our family had been waiting for.

5

SANDSTORMS

I sat in the backseat of the 1948 Chevy Coupe, huddled between my two older brothers with my knees squished up to my chin. The only place to rest my feet was the hump of floorboard covering the driveshaft in the middle of the backseat. If I put my feet on either side of the hump, an older brother would elbow me for getting on his turf.

We were driving from our new home at the Humble Oil Camp to my favorite destination: O'Donnell, where my dad's family lived. I loved them and loved visiting them.

But Dad was having trouble enjoying this trip, and Mom was just as anxious sitting in the passenger's seat. Dad was hunched over the steering wheel, squinting into the dark afternoon skies. Blowing sand had blacked out the winter sun setting low in the southern sky. It was one of the fiercest sandstorms yet.

At five years of age, I was too short to see over the dashboard, so I sat toward the front of my seat and strained up to peer out the windshield. Even if I had been taller, I could barely see beyond the hood through the thick blowing sand. The howling wind drowned out any other sounds.

Cars coming toward us came into view briefly before they inched silently by in the other lane, headlights barely visible.

We were quiet, wondering if everything was okay, believing Dad could see farther than we could. But as he strained to see, he grew uncharacteristically serious. The radio was off, and he was not singing any of the old country songs like he did when we were having fun. When he was like this, we knew to keep mum—no distractions from the backseat. Mom was quieter than usual, worried, helping Dad peer out the front window as if there was something she could do. If a car happened to be in our lane, we would not see it until it was too close to avoid.

We drove mile after mile—through Seminole, straight east toward Lamesa. I knew from previous trips that all around us were flat fields of sand, waiting to be picked up by the raging winds and blasted against every possible surface and being.

Once the storm relented, I knew Dad would inspect the front of the car, noting each place the paint had been sandblasted off of the hood and front fenders. The clear glass lenses in the headlights would be crazed, cloudy and mildly opaque from the constant onslaught.

From the state line east, past Lubbock, O'Donnell, and Lamesa, the agricultural land was plowed in the spring, and the wind would blow it all over the state into the late fall and winter months. The tons of airborne topsoil would join the sand that was already blowing eastward from our county, blacking out the sun during intense winds.

At the wheel, Dad flinched as a tumbleweed the size of a man emerged from the dark in front of the hood. I jumped as the scraggly ball hit the front of the car and exploded into dried fragments, some of which we would later pick out of the radiator.

In spots where farmers had not intervened with their plows, the tumbleweeds rolled furiously, like whirling dervishes, following the first onslaughts of sand, smashing headlong into us or darting around and over the car. The biggest ones would roll under the car and cling to its frame, scraping along the pavement for miles. The scraping sound frightened my five-year-old mind, as though the overgrown weeds were trying to claw through the floorboard of the car.

Eventually, the asphalt would sand them down until the little Chevy choked them out behind us. Thrust into the gale, they catapulted and disappeared into the dark. As we passed into land where the farmers kept the edges of the field more carefully cultivated, the onslaught of tumbling weeds stopped.

We drove on and on through the darkness. The "Are we there yet?" mantra ran silently through our heads. I wanted to be there, to be inside my grandfather's home, the only place I knew them to live until I was in high school, except for a brief period of time they lived in Eunice when we lived a the oil camp. The house was well built against the fury of the winds. It didn't shake like our little one at the oilfield camp, nor did the dust come in around the window frames as it did at our house on Cecil Street.

As we passed through Lamesa and turned north toward O'Donnell, we drove into the epicenter of raging sandstorms. There were no mountain ranges for hundreds of miles to slow the winds, leaving an endless supply of sand to be blown from every direction. The closer we got to the destination and to the safe haven, the darker the skies grew. The sand tapped furiously against the car's exterior, accompanied by the whirling tumbleweed that bounced off every side.

If we could just hang on a little longer, it would be quiet. Dad could relax, sip coffee, and talk in quiet tones to my granddad about how rough it had been, his eyes bloodshot from the strain and the sand that had gotten into them as he loaded everything into and out of the car.

Finally, we arrived.

Grandfather's Oasis

Once I was inside my grandparents' house, I hurried through the familiar rooms and went straight to my favorite place: the hidden passage.

Their house had two closets, separated by about three feet, which opened into rooms on opposite sides of the house. Each closet had a small door, hidden behind the coats and clothes. You could go in one closet and come out the closet in the other room.

I was fascinated by that dark escape route and ran to it each time I got to their house. The clothes in the closet never changed; they smelled of mothballs and musk that I hated. But the idea of a quiet, safe retreat, and the secret passage, enticed me beyond the odors and darkness. It felt so wonderful to be safe.

In the summer, my grandfather kept a small garden in his backyard. He fought off the drought with a water hose, growing peas, beans, tomatoes, okra, and squash there inside the city limits. The sand did not blow and rake across his garden. It was a haven from the summer dust storms, an oasis that led me to connect water with life.

My grandfather had a huge apricot tree just to the right of the driveway. In the years when the fruit did not freeze, he would have us crawl high into the branches to retrieve the golden fruit too high for him to reach from the ground. I would climb slowly, clutching the branches as I moved along, afraid of gravity before I knew what it was.

In contrast, my cousins Gerald and Mark, who were closest in age to me, had absolutely no fear of falling. They would shimmy up the trunk, swing from limb to limb and jump out from halfway up the tree. They didn't need Granddad to watch and warn them about falling, and when they did fall, they got right back up, proudly displaying their cuts and bruises.

While they were unafraid of a few scratches, I convinced myself that a fall would leave me paralyzed . . . or worse. Were it not for those apricots, I might never have ventured off the ground. To eat one of the plump fruits, I would hold on with one hand and wrap the other arm around a limb before daring to pluck an apricot and quickly devour the juice running down my chin, unable to wipe it as I grabbed hold again.

"Don't fall!" Granddad would shout. *There was little chance of that*, I thought. It was more likely that the tree bark would wrap itself around my hand like it does around a barbed wire that's been wrapped around a tree trunk for too long. I would spit the seed as far as I could and shout back, "I'm okay!"

I felt like I was in a skyscraper, so far up. When I look at the pictures of the tree now, he could have grabbed my foot from where he stood.

Later, safely inside the house, "Mama," which is what we called my grandmother, would have her usual request for me, "Stevie, go out to the cellar and get me a quart of those peaches and a pint of the black-eyed peas."

"Yes, ma'am," I'd respond, though dreading what was to follow.

Most of the houses in West Texas had storm cellars. Theirs, about the size of a small bedroom, was in a corner of the backyard and had been dug by hand through the sand down into the clay, eight- to ten-feet deep. The cellar had a wooden door that lay flat against its frame over the opening of the cellar.

The tornadoes that came each year destroyed everything in their paths. Families would huddle in the musty darkness of these cellars until danger passed. But the cellars also housed homegrown and canned vegetables, peaches, and pears for my grandparents, stored in the coolness of the underground room.

I dutifully went outside and approached the door, afraid to pull it open, to walk down the steps cut into the clay and into the dark. While the dark solitude of the hidden passageway had given me comfort, I associated this underground room with all things frightening—with black widow spiders, tornadoes, and the hard clank of a door behind me.

After a few minutes of stalling, I would retreat empty-handed into the house and sidle up to Mama in the kitchen. "I couldn't remember if the quart is the big jar or the little jar. And which one is the pint?"

"Now, Stevie," she would prod me, never frustrated, "you just watch out for those spiders and go on down in there and get the jars. I have told you a dozen times which one is which. The big ones are quarts and the small ones pints. Now go on and help your ol' grandma," and she would laugh her jolly laugh, letting me know it was okay to be afraid

I grew up believing the sandstorms of my formative years were the way of life, and that the darkness and dreariness that accompanied them was inevitable. It was as though it was reflective of the dreariness inside me.

Back outside, I lingered again. Finally, I would muster the courage, grab the handle, and fling open the light and floppy door, letting it fall to the side. I used a stick to sweep away the cobwebs that made the journey into the darkness so treacherous. *One step at a time.*

The only light came from the opening, and it took a minute for my eyes to adjust. As soon as I could see, I grabbed the peaches and peas, quarts and pints, and flew up the steps and back into the house. My grandmother knew she hadn't heard the cellar close. "Stevie, you did just fine. Now run back out there and close the door so no critters get into the cellar."

"Yes, ma'am," I said, still trying to catch my breath and racing heart.

When Fear Is Cultivated

I grew up believing the sandstorms of my formative years were the way of life, and that the darkness and dreariness that accompanied them was inevitable. It was as though it was reflective of the dreariness inside me.

In the hardest storms, I could feel the small pea-sized pebbles striking my face, and I'd retreat inside. The blowing wind would hit the side of a house and the fence, changing directions constantly as it deposited its cargo of sand anywhere it pleased.

When I was in the house with my grandparents, I was comforted. I was safe from the spiders and darkness and tornadoes. But they also reinforced the dangers in life, dangers I had internalized since birth, whether it was the spiders or falling or tornadoes. Despite their good intentions, their words of caution often helped fill in the gaps of my imagination, laying the groundwork for bigger, more lifelong struggles with fear that kept me frozen in place—immobilized.

Only when I graduated from high school and saw the grass return and experienced the wind without the dreary blowing sand did I realize how severe nature had been in the place and time of my youth.

Lea County is on the eastern edge of New Mexico, and though it has mostly dark, sandy loam soil, the eastern edge of the state and the county gives way to the deep red sand that makes up that area of West Texas.

The farmers of that period didn't have the technology of deep-breaking plows that can turn the heavier clay to the top and stabilize the blowing sand. With the severe drought of those years, the eastern side of the state, along with the ranches in Texas, lost their grasslands. Without grass roots to hold the soil in place, the heavy windstorms picked up the topsoil and carried it for miles.

Decades later, I discovered rainfall charts and understood what it was we had lived through in eastern New Mexico and West Texas in the early 1950s. The charts showed long periods of drought throughout the last two thousand years in New Mexico, sometimes up to two hundred continuous years with below-average rainfall. Though there have been worse droughts in that region's history, the lack of rainfall we experienced during my childhood made that period one of the driest times in the last two hundred years.

That was how I lived my young life—in a shaken snow globe of a desert.

6

THE MAJOR OIL
COMPANY

Mom had been looking more intently than Dad for the next step up on the ladder of life. This was it—working for a major oil company.

I was five years old when we moved from our Cecil Street home to the Humble Oil and Refining Arrowhead Camp, west of Eunice. There were two Humble camps in Eunice, one just east of town and ours to the west. The oil companies began to close the camps in the 1960s and '70s. Humble gave camp property to the city of Eunice around that time. Today, the Eunice golf course sits on the land where I lived from ages five to nine.

In his previous job, Dad was making $1 an hour. Humble paid $2.62 per hour. The extra pay would be nice, but what the growing family needed as much as the pay increase was the health insurance Humble provided.

The perk that even Dad got excited about was the company-sponsored savings plan—Humble matched every dollar saved by an employee. Dad really liked that the company was helping them build a nest egg for retirement years, for long-term security. He reviewed the stock report every month and spent the rest of his life recounting the many times the stock split, doubling the number of shares he owned. Even with all the financial struggles we faced, my parents demonstrated a lifelong discipline of spending less than they made and planning for the years when they could no longer work.

Camp living was a standard practice for oil companies during that period. Shell, Gulf, El Paso Natural Gas Company, and other companies had similar camps near their fields. Our camp was one of the smallest.

The superintendent lived in the largest house at one end of the camp with the engineers close by. We lived at the other end—the wrong end, the poor end. The superintendent and engineers lived in large, well-built houses maintained by the company and provided to them at no cost.

We were the new family. Dad had no experience in the oilfield and was hired as a roustabout, the lowest rung in the industry's corporate ladder. In the social strata of the camp, we were at the bottom of the pecking order, too.

My parents paid nine hundred dollars for our house in the camp, buying it from another family that was transferring. They borrowed the money from the Humble credit union and made payments of ninety-five dollars per month.

My sister was born shortly after we moved to the camp, then my brother Philip. Seven of us lived in the 800-square-foot ramshackle structure that had been thrown together piece by piece. The last piece seemed to be a lean-to addition.

Life in the Camp

Our camp had a single paved street with six or eight houses on each side and large Chinese elms in the yards on both sides of the street. The men worked together; the women gossiped together.

There was an administrative office, a recreation hall, pipe yard,

warehouse, playground, and a locker room for the crews to change out of their oily clothes each day. A wire fence surrounded the whole compound, with snake-proof fencing running along the ground.

Occasionally, Dad would get to fill in for a pumper when one was on vacation. The pumper drove from well to well, gauging the tanks to see how much oil had been pumped and making sure that each well was working as it should. Dad recorded the level of oil in each of the tanks all day long. Then at night, he would transfer those numbers from the tally book to forms that were submitted to the accounting office to calculate the amount of oil that would be sold each month.

After starting school, I discovered I was good in math, and it became a source of pride to me that I could sit down at the dinner table and help Dad add all the rows of numbers, giving me the sense I was helping the family.

Life in the camp was routine, and yet it had its exceptional moments. One late spring afternoon, the men gathered after work to discuss the threat of a tornado projected to come through southern Lea County later that night. As families walked to their houses in the dark, one or two men were assigned to listen to the radio and alert the rest of the camp if the threat materialized.

In the middle of the night, alerted by the watchmen, all the families awakened sleeping children and, still in pajamas, hurriedly pushed them into cars. All the cars in the camp joined in a procession like an old-time wagon train: out the front gate, onto the highway, fleeing east toward safety. We drove the five miles into Eunice and continued east thirty-eight miles to Andrews, Texas. Arriving there in the early morning, we parked along the wall of the cemetery and slept in the cars. The night skies were stormy and rainy even there at our refuge.

The next morning, when the sun came up, the men huddled again. It was obvious from the clear skies that the bad weather had moved out of the area. On the way back to our camp, we were listening to the local news. As it turned out, the line of thunderstorms had missed Eunice and instead spawned a tornado that, according to the announcer, had passed right over the Andrews cemetery. It touched down half a mile south of where we all parked in our search for safety!

During the early 1950s, there was no television in southeast New Mexico. Midland, Texas, less than one hundred miles east, had a broadcast station. But we could not get the signal in our camp, so families developed their own pastimes. There were square dances in the recreation hall, but we did not attend because Mom and Dad were members of the Church of Christ and would not have anything to do with dances.

Our recreation instead entailed the entire family huddled around the radio in our living room, listening to the Louisiana Hayride and the Grand Ole Opry. Dad liked Kitty Wells, Hank Snow, and Web Pierce, but I absolutely loved Hank Williams. Something about his mournful songs spoke directly to my five-year-old soul. "Your Cheatin' Heart," "I'm So Lonesome I Could Cry," and "Honky Tonkin'" were all favorites.

My brother Tom was born a performer, appearing in plays, singing, and performing skits. I tried to follow in his footsteps by singing Hank's song, "Say Hey, Good Lookin'." My youthful pronunciations and tentativeness led to boisterous laughter at the Pearce family gatherings: "Say hey, good wookin', whacha got a cookin'? How's about cookin' sumpin' up wit me?"

I enjoyed the attention but was suspicious of the laughter, not knowing if people enjoyed the performance or were laughing at me. When my Grandfather Pearce mimicked my song one day, it convinced me that I was being laughed at. I retreated inside my shell, not to sing again until after high school. Later, I realized the family was not making fun of me, but I was easily discouraged at stepping out of my comfort zone.

Hunting Coyotes

During that period, Dad partnered with some men who made money on the side by hunting coyotes using greyhounds. With my two older brothers in school, I was the one invited to join him on the ventures. Dad would appear in the bedroom we three boys shared to wake me at 4 a.m., gently touching my shoulder. Without making a sound, I was to get up, slip on my jeans, shirt, and shoes, grab the coat I had laid out, and silently follow him, being careful not to crack my shin on the console radio in the living room.

All bundled up, we drove out the back gate of the camp, loaded the grey-hounds into the old pickup, and drove half an hour to a designated meeting spot. There, we joined three or four other pickups full of dogs ready for the hunt. While I stayed in the pickup, Dad got out and visited briefly with the other men in the early morning cold. I hated the dark cold venture.

A few minutes before daylight, the caravan eased off the highway and onto the ranch roads in the pasturelands. We bounced around the open range looking for coyotes. Because the coyotes killed the livestock, a bounty or reward was offered to those who could round them up and remove them. But the money was secondary to the thrill of the chase.

The excitement and anxiety of the dogs in the back of our pickup began to build with barks and howls. They knew the drill and leaned on the cab with their front paws, looking just as intently at the road before us. If a dog got too close to or stepped on another, I would hear a yelp as the fangs of the offended one grazed skin in a warning to the other.

When we saw a coyote, things kicked into high gear. It was then that I saw my father the most freed. I could see in his face that he was wild at heart. The weight of supporting a family would, for a moment, be lifted as he let himself be carried away by the chase. While he was transported into another realm, I, in the time before seat belts, clung to the door with both hands and wished I were at home.

As the pickups shifted into a higher gear, the howling from the back of the truck rose to a fevered pitch, and we would sail off the road and into the open range, flying after the coyote. The trucks angled to cut him off as the dogs licked their chops.

I remember the coyote's tail streaming straight out behind him, wringing in circles as he kicked in his afterburner. When we moved within range, Dad slammed the brakes.

The most aggressive dogs were over the side while we were still moving, rolling head over heels and coming onto all fours in full pursuit. The other dogs waited until we stopped and Dad ran around to lower the tailgate. I always wanted to be like the over-the-side dogs, hitting the ground running, but I was more like the ones who'd wait.

One of the best dogs we ever had was a big staghound we called Rattler. He would stand on top of the doghouse in his pen waiting eagerly for us when we went to the barns. Though the dogs were part of the family, we maintained a healthy fear, knowing what they could do on a hunt. When let loose from the pickup, Rattler was fast, agile, and could easily tackle a coyote by himself.

After catching the coyote, the dogs would stand on it and continue to hold it in their jaws, shaking their heads furiously. Dad would reach into the melee, at the risk of having his hand bitten, and grab a hind leg of the coyote to pull it out of the mass of dogs. He would pitch it in the back of the pickup to retrieve his bounty later.

Kids in the Camp

As kids, life in the camp was the best we had known. There was safety and—for kids—fun to be had in numbers. In the summertime, the kids would gather and move through the camp like a herd of gazelles. They would gather up and begin to move, first this way, then that, a fluid mass that had a central point but no leader. The older kids dominated but the younger ones, if they had an appealing activity in mind, could lead by suggestion.

"All right, we're going to swing on the swings to see who can go the highest," one of the leaders would shout, and the entire herd would raise a dust cloud heading to the swings. These were oilfield swings, made with two-inch pipe. They were much higher than the typical commercial backyard swings.

With the older kids setting the benchmark, we would all see how high we could swing. If you could not go higher than the crossbar from which the swings hung, you could not compete. When the swing got that high, it lost the centrifugal pull against the crossbar, came loose from gravity, and floated for a moment, only to drop like a rock back toward earth. The chains would catch the fall with a snap as the swing fell back inside its arc.

There were half a dozen swings on the set, so a whole team could compete at once. Built by oilfield workers, the swings were cemented in place and could easily withstand the hard activity. After all had mastered the art of going higher than the crossbar, the older kids again led the way in "parachuting" out of the swing when it was at its apex. They would free-float for just a moment before crashing back to earth, ten or twelve feet below. My fears ruled the day when I tried to parachute out at about half the height of my swing, again dissuaded by the fall to earth from the higher altitude. I never did make the jump.

Eventually, that thrill wore off though, and the boldest kids began to swing so hard and so high that the swing actually made a full circle over and above the crossbar, wrapping a loop of the chains around it. I never worked up the nerve to do that.

Suddenly, the herd would evaporate away from the swings and materialize at the slides. The slides, like the swings, were oilfield-sized but still too slow for our daring desires. So we tore strips of waxed paper from the rolls in our mothers' kitchens and set the slide on fire with a new kind of speed. We had contests to see who could fly

I always wanted to be like the over-the-side dogs, hitting the ground running, but I was more like the ones who'd wait.

the farthest off the end of the slide. To satisfy our thrill seeking, we eventually tried coming down the slide standing up, then later standing up on the waxed paper. I was never the leader in these games nor did I win the contests of distance or speed. By the time I processed how to go about it, the group had moved on to other games.

In the midst of an activity, someone in the group would shout, "War!" and the energetic mass of young humanity would fly from the playground at the front of the camp, down through the main street and all the way to the other end, screaming and shouting about cowboys and Indians, Germans and Japanese, whatever phrase seemed to fit the day. When we got down to the industrial end of the camp, down where we lived, there were all sorts of toys. We used the jaws of pipe wrenches as pistols and gathered up bolts from the oilfield that were an inch and a half across, pretending they were hand grenades.

In the camp, there were railroad ties that were used to store pipe and keep it off the ground. When not in use, they were stacked up in squares that were up to eight-feet tall. These stacked railroad ties made perfect forts. We climbed up the ties and down inside the middle of the square, the fort, lobbing hand grenades from one fort toward the other. I was about six years old when one of the bolts hit me above the eyebrow, tearing a big gash. I had to be rushed to the hospital and get stitches to close it, an experience that only increased my natural fears.

I was tentative when it came to all the roughhouse games—afraid of getting hurt, afraid of heights, afraid of flying and of flying objects. But in baseball, I could hold my own even with the older kids. We would play until the cover literally came off the ball. Then we would wrap black electrician's tape around the string of the ball to keep it from unwinding and just kept using it until someone was able to get a foul ball at the high school game and sneak away with it. The dirt and rocks in the field in our camp quickly scuffed and ragged any new ball.

When Mom was pregnant with my brother Philip, a new roustabout named "Red" Lovett moved his family into the camp right across the street from us. The typical oilfield humor began to circulate as Mom's pregnancy became more evident. The people in the camp joked that, with the new guy in the camp being a redhead, our next baby brother would be redheaded, too. It was all very standard oilfield humor. They would have said it about any of the women if they had been pregnant.

But when Philip was born, he was indeed redheaded. It was one of Mom's most embarrassing moments, though there was no truth behind the rumors. Eventually, the whispering, gossiping neighbors in the camp began to crowd in on Mom's idea of family and privacy. Just as Dad's family had intruded, the closeness of the camp neighbors began to suffocate Mom's independent spirit. Meanwhile, Dad began to yearn for a small farm where he could have a milking cow, a few chickens, and a garden.

7

VISUALIZING

We lived in the oil camp until I completed the third grade at Eunice Elementary School.

From the very first, I loved school and loved my first grade teacher, Mrs. Bartholomew. But I hated one aspect of school. I could tell it was time for "that part" when Mrs. Bartholomew had us put away our Big Chief tablets and the pencils with the extra thick lead.

"Now, class, we will have our music lessons."

I looked down at my crude drawings of airplanes, with the streak marks indicating speed and the splashing soil where my machine gun bullets were spitting up dirt. Here I was, reaching the high point of my art life, and I had to put it away.

Mrs. Bartholomew continued, "Now, children, fold your arms on the table and put your head down."

I was one of her favorites, but she knew I hated this part of school. The dread began to build in me as I placed my head on my arms and squeezed my eyes shut, dutifully complying. Soon, the sound of Mozart began to softly flood the room. It was not that I hated the music; I actually liked it. But I hated the questions. I knew that when the music stopped, the questions would start.

"Nancy, tell us what you saw when the music was playing?"

"Yes, ma'am. I saw a field of flowers, and the breeze was moving them."

"Oh, that is wonderful. Sol, what did you see?"

"Oh, it was great. I saw colored water coming over a waterfall and hitting in a pool. And it sprayed on my face."

"Oh, Sol, you are so descriptive. Stevan, what did you see?"

My face was already beet red in anticipation of the question. We had been down this track many times before. I began to stammer and stutter, searching for an answer. Mom's description of what happened to liars kept me from spitting out a contrived answer, so I did the same thing I always did. I said nothing. The girls started snickering. I wished I could disappear into the floor . . . but it never swallowed me, so I just sat there.

"Come on, Stevan. Surely you saw something."

"No, ma'am. When I close my eyes, I only see black. I have looked real close. If I look at the light right before I close my eyes, I can see a shape that looks just like the bulb, but it is all fiery and orange colored. Then it fades and goes out."

The boys in the room were snorting with amusement. I wanted to fight them, but I didn't have the nerve, and Mom threatened what would happen if we ever fought. So I just sat in humiliation.

Everyone else saw sunflowers, Roman warriors, and mountain peaks with goats on rocky crags. I saw nothing. I closed my eyes and saw black. I saw myself wondering what I was going to answer if someone called my name.

I hated the music lessons more and more. Curiously, that hatred of these lessons, and these moments, never carried over to my teacher. I loved her like my own mother, despite her persistent music questions.

Several years later, when we had moved to Nadine, my brother Mike got a stereo for Christmas and began to buy classical music. As the oldest child, he had complete control of the bedroom that we five boys shared.

When he was ready for bed, he'd stack six of the long play vinyl albums on the record changer, and they would play one after another while I drifted off to sleep.

During my late elementary and junior high years, I recognized many classical works but really liked Beethoven's Fifth and Ninth symphonies. When NBC used a few Beethoven notes for its network theme music, I recognized it right away and was sure they had committed some heresy by stealing them.

We listened to Tchaikovsky's work, including Capricco Italien, Marche Slave, the 1812 Overture—with real cannons firing in the climactic conclusion—and his Symphony No. 6 in B minor, Pathetique. I knew the lyrics and music to every word of *Porgy and Bess*, especially "Methuselah lived nine hundred years."

Everyone else saw sunflowers, Roman warriors, and mountain peaks with goats on rocky crags. I saw nothing. I closed my eyes and saw black. I saw myself wondering what I was going to answer if someone called my name.

Of course, with Mike's developing expertise and knowledge of music, he and Dad had a friendly rivalry. Dad preferred the country music of the Louisiana Hayride, the Grand Ole Opry, and the country radio stations around Hobbs. I grew up in the country, but learned to love both country and classical music.

But all of this music and the words to these lyrics were trapped in an unspeaking part of my mind. I still did not see images or feel feelings, though I was pretty sure I enjoyed it. I did not sing or play music until much later.

To this day, I cannot visualize scenes when I close my eyes to listen to music, and that's just one example. An inability to visualize songs, concepts, and how to get from point A to point B has plagued me from childhood. I simply could not visualize. There was little raw material to work with here, and I've had to learn to work around it.

"Surely You See Something"

And the torturous creative exercises didn't end with the first grade.

In the sixth grade, Mrs. Pate assigned an art project to be completed over a six-week period in time for parent night. Each of us was given an eleven-by-fourteen sheet of paper to fill with our best creation. No other instruction. My mind was blank, and I sat there for the hour of art each day for a week—not even a pen stroke. The teacher pushed, "Surely you see something in your mind that you can paint."

I didn't. Finally, I decided to draw a horse like I had seen Dad do. He could sit down and draw a perfectly dimensioned and proportioned horse in a few minutes. I had five more weeks to do it. I began to labor, huddled low over the project, one stroke at a time. I could have been filling the entire page with ink dots I was so finely crafting each line. I finished with a feeling of triumph without a day to spare before parent night.

The day of the parent-teacher conferences arrived. The centerpiece of the night was for our parents to see our art projects, hung on the cork strip above the blackboard, high on the wall. Parents were "oohing" and "aahing," but mine kept looking. Finally, Dad asked, "Stevan, where is yours?"

I was aghast. He might as well have been asking where my male member was. The other parents were bragging on their kid's art project, the sheets filled with paint. In front of the class I led them to the part of the wall where mine hung.

From my perspective hunched over the meticulously drawn horse, it seemed life-sized. Viewed from where we stood, the whole horse could have been covered by placing a silver dollar over it. The rest of that massive sheet of paper was blank. The girls in the room snickered. I had a crush on LaRell Roberts, the undertaker's daughter, and could just see her and her best friend, Elaine, laughing behind my back. I wanted to hide. I hated art. I hated that I could not see things in my mind.

Years later, when I was in pilot training, I had the chance to put my art and visualization (or lack thereof) to work one more time. Each class designs its own patch, worn on the shoulder by all the members. It sets the class apart as you walk around on base among the other uniformed soldiers, granting us some individuality and distinction.

Most class patches were ornate cartoon characters with a snappy saying, such as "Born to Fly," "From Hot Styx to Aces," "Piece O'Cake," and

"Non Perspirus," which is Latin for "No Sweat" (or close enough for us Air Force guys). The artwork is always creative and colorful, filled with gooney birds, angels, unicorns, T-38s, eagles, etc. I was among a group of airmen who lobbied for the class patch we would design together to be simple. As you can see, it has the same sort of creativity that I had on that sixth grade art project.

The patch was all black, the white numbers in the middle are our class number, 71-06, that was required on all class patches. That was it. No sayings or cartoons.

It speaks to who I am.

CAMEL CIGARETTES
AND "SI SABES"

My grandfather Pearce was a slight, delicate, tidy man, who had a confident way about him. His humor was as dry as West Texas, and I learned to keep up with him as I grew older.

He was exposed to mustard gas in World War I when he was assigned to a unit fighting in the Argonne Forest in France, and though he lived to a ripe old age, he always seemed on the verge of bad health. We often took him for solemn visits to the VA hospital in Big Springs. But through it all, he smoked a pack of Camel cigarettes a day and occasionally rolled his own cigarettes (I suspect to save money).

My grandfather loved to argue with me about my favorite baseball players: Whitey Ford, Mickey Mantle, Roger Maris, and Yogi Berra. Starting at ten years old, I was strictly a New York Yankees' fan and could not be shaken, but he always took the other side.

He was many things in life but, as was true of my dad, never lived to his potential. In his younger years, he drew the plans for an improved cotton gin but never did anything to pursue the idea, even though he continued to work seasonally at the local gin for the rest of his life.

Grandfather was a carpenter and helped my uncle GR build a house from scratch. He understood the necessity of building things to the square and how to line up a wall to be perpendicular, and that became a euphemism for how I viewed his character. He lived squared up to truth; there were no angled walls or tilting structures in his life. As an untrained carpenter, he intuitively knew things had to be square. Equally, in life, truth was never a question. Life had to be squared up with truth.

My grandmother was a large delightful woman, who loved to laugh and cook and eat, tasting each spoon as she stirred the pot and eating the last bite from the pan as she scraped them clean. She was forty-five and my grandfather was fifty when I was born.

While we lived in the oil camp, things must have gotten difficult for them, because they moved to Eunice and my grandfather went to work as a janitor for the Eunice Public Schools. They were only there a short time; they seemed out of place, both in my mind and in theirs, and moved back to O'Donnell within a year. Gravity drew them back to familiar surroundings as surely as it pulls planets into familiar orbits around the sun. Maybe they believed the warnings they sounded to Dad, that they might go to the dogs if they stayed longer in the oilfields.

Other than my grandfather's seasonal work at the gin and my grandmother's weekly Avon route, they were basically sedentary from the time of my earliest memories. When I spent time with them in the summers, one day each week, Mama, which is what I called my grandmother, would approach me with her kindly instruction, "You and I are going to deliver Avon this afternoon. Are you ready?"

"Yes, ma'am."

"Do you have on clean underwear? You never know when we might be in a car wreck, and I wouldn't want the hospital to find you with dirty underwear."

"Yes, ma'am."

As I got older, I wondered if she had ever calculated that getting in a wreck might be a bigger problem than having on dirty underwear. But I loved her too much to ever say anything.

About the most I ever said growing up was "Yes, ma'am" or "No, ma'am." The ladies at the church in Hobbs teased me, "Your brother Tommy is a fine boy; he visits with us. You never say a word. Are you sure you're his brother?" My face would get red, and I would respond, "Yes, ma'am." The more my shyness was noticed, the more I pulled into my shell.

After the quiz about my undergarments, Mama and I piled into her 1951 Ford auto and drove to visit family and friends on her Avon route. I never heard anyone order anything; rather, my grandmother would laugh and visit and fill out an order and people would sign it. They seemed too polite to say they didn't want what she sold them. We kids also knew what we were going to get at Christmas time and always thanked her profusely, but the unused bottles of Avon piled up in our bathroom.

Every time we drove the twenty miles north to Tahoka, she would point to the small lake on the left side of the road. "Now you be careful around water. You remember your Papa helped pull that neighbor boy out of the water. He was no older than you. Drowned right there at that spot," she would say, pointing as she mentioned Granddad Pearce.

"Yes, ma'am," I would say, absorbing a new fear. The swimming pool in O'Donnell was off-limits to us because of the danger.

That was my earliest memory of water; that it would drown me. By the time I was six, I was sure I was going to drown sometime soon. Since she was the one who warned me of the danger, I would ask her, "Mama, if I was asleep on my back outside and it started raining, could I drown in the rain?" It didn't rain much in New Mexico, but given the constant warnings, I began to watch for the ways in which water might catch me unaware. I knew I would never purposefully get into anything other than a bathtub.

When I was seven, the extended Pearce clan converged for a weekend camping trip on the Delaware River, south of Carlsbad, New Mexico. I again received the usual warning about drowning. Being preoccupied with not getting in the water made me vulnerable to an invisible force that seemed to pull me toward it. Sure enough, I slipped on the slick clay of the bank and slid down the ten-inch bank into the river, certain my end had arrived. The Delaware is not deep enough to drown a person at its normal state, so I could easily have stood up in the water, but my fear was self-fulfilling. They had to pull me from the water, shaken and scared, the implanted fear now becoming a more vivid possibility.

Until college, all my attempts to learn to swim were miserable failures, even with Dad's coaxing and coaching. When I decided to learn, I had to wear one of the "eggs" that were used to help problem swimmers learn. In my first attempt at swimming the backstroke without the egg, I bumped into someone coming the opposite way, lost my velocity, and sank like a rock. My instructor pulled me from the bottom of the pool. Fear can be positively paralyzing.

Fears of War and Flying

My fear of water was deep and wide, but no fear paralyzed me more in my youth than the thought of war. In the early 1950s, World War II was a fresh scar in the minds of Americans, and even more so in small towns, because everyone knows one another.

In those days before television, after dinner the large Pearce gatherings often drifted into contemplations of life and death. Predictably, they just as often drifted into quiet, reverent discussions of the casualties of the war. As a kid, I was expected to be quiet, but that did not stop me from listening. I soaked up every danger, every warning, and every risk at an early age. I knew the things that could get me. I knew even then that I did not want to die in war and be the topic of conversation.

Karl King, my grandmother's nephew, who enlisted in the Air Force and trained as a pilot, was killed when his jet crashed not long after the war. Among the risks of war that were imbedded as fears in my mind, a fear of flight took a primary position. It seemed like the easiest way to die in a war.

Growing up, these fears of dying, drowning, and flying were planted deeply in my psyche. At that same time, my mother's brother Sonny was denied entry into the military because of flat feet. Having overheard the comments about how wearing boots caused his feet to be flat, I insisted that I get boots to wear. My folks were not enthused, as they were much more expensive than the regular school shoes and were harder to pass down to younger brothers, nevertheless they relented.

Once I got them, the boots were horrible to wear. My very high insteps made them uncomfortable, and within weeks, my seven-year-old mind chose comfort over the threat of war a decade or more in the future. Off and on, I tried to wear boots and do things that might change my feet, in order to save me from the perils of war. But when I took my induction physical years later, my high insteps were still perfectly shaped, ready for service.

In all of this, I do not mean to cast shadows on my grandparents. They were only trying to warn us of the dangers in life, the things that made them cautious and fearful of life, but my psychological makeup made those warnings larger than life. My brother Tommy, who was two years older than me, did not seem to be bothered by the warnings. He was the first to slip out from my grandparents' home and go to the pool. He never cared about war or flying enough to consider the dangers.

My brother Michael is four years older, and the stories did not bother him. He loved planes and the water. He had model planes, read about them, and knew the F-100 was the first supersonic fighter and that the "B" in B-17 and B-52 meant bomber.

The oil camp where we lived was about a mile from the Eunice airport. Mike had figured out how to get into the hangar, and once inside, he crawled up into the airplane seat and pretended to fly. When I was five or six, Mike dragged me along on one of his visits to the unattended hangar, but I wouldn't

> My fear of water was deep and wide, but no fear paralyzed me more in my youth than the thought of war.

go near the planes. Later, when we moved to Nadine, he would lie down at the end of the rows of Mr. Jobe's field and watch the crop duster fly above him, pulling me along one day to watch. The experience did not thrill me.

The early childhood warnings never troubled my brothers, but I chewed on every possible threat, dreaming up ways to avoid war and airplanes and never once going to the swimming pool unescorted.

Mom's Parents

My grandfather Garnett, Papa Ed, was a whiz at math, according to the family. When other kids his age in school were given a string of two-digit numbers and asked to add them on the blackboard, the teacher would read him a series of complex numbers in the thousands and ten thousands instead. By the time he had written the last one on the board, he would write the answer down, having added them in his head.

Although he never got an education to maximize his talents, he used them in his cattle trading and could guess an eight hundred-pound calf within a pound of its actual weight. With that skill, he was always able to get the better end of a deal when he bought and sold cattle.

The first story I heard Uncle Sonny tell about his mother, my grandmother Garnett, was a time when the kids were still young. Grandmother Garnett had the entire brood that had been born up to that point in the cotton field chopping cotton alongside the braceros. Something about one of the Mexican men set her off, and she was berating him, shifting suddenly from low gear to second and into full throttle when the man interrupted, "Yo no se. No sabes ingles." ("I don't understand English.")

Without missing a beat, Grandmother lifted her hoe as high as she could raise it, and swinging it in an arc designed to split his skull in half, she bellowed, "I will sabe your ass with this hoe!"

Narrowly escaping death from the swinging hoe as it buried itself in the soil where he had been standing, he screamed in terror, "Si sabes! Si sabes!" She had that effect; she could make you understand the most complex things in life without a long educational process.

Once, when Mom was still a teenager at home, a neighbor man stopped to visit grandmother. Mom made a comment that was critical of the visit, and Grandmother, who was eight months pregnant, picked up a small table and used it to beat her, then chased her out of the house and into the pasture. Mom was wearing only a flimsy dress and panties and was without shoes. After Grandmother retreated into the house, Mom crept into the cottonseed bin, where she buried down with only her head showing until her father got home, well after dark.

There were no terms of endearment used for her—no "Nana," no "Mama"—we called her Grandmother Garnett. We "sabe."

An expected dynamic existed until I got into the Air Force. All of us were very close to the Pearce grandparents, but we seldom went to the Garnetts.

Grandmother had her own children the same age as her grandchildren—a son, Dennis, was born twelve hours before my oldest brother, Mike, and a daughter was born the same year as Tom. It was probably too far of a stretch to love them all. In fact, she would not have anything to do with us.

As Mom explains it, Grandmother Garnett never liked us six kids. I suspect that came from Mom's troubled last year of high school, when she dared to point out flaws in her mother's character. Mom was kicked out of the house that day, but she refused to leave, protesting that Grandmother had a responsibility to see that she got an education. A guarded truce ensued until the day Mom graduated from high school, whereupon Grandmother picked all her clothes up and threw them out of the house, and with that, Mom was on her own.

By the time I was five years old, I understood that we were not Grandmother Garnett's favorites. My brother Tom, in his gregarious way, ignored it and sometimes went with Mom to her family gatherings, but the rest of us fought against the notion.

One of the telling comments was made when we all were coerced into going to visit Mom's parents one Christmas. All her nine brothers and sisters were there with their many children, but Mom was up to six children, five of us being boys. While looking at the boys, Papa Ed asked Mom when she was going to "quit having all those mules." It made Mom mad, and she had Dad herd all us "mules" to the car while she "finished the conversation." It was probably the same one she was having when she got kicked out of the house fifteen years before. My uncle Sonny, a peacemaker, drove to catch up with us, flagged us over about ten miles out of town, and convinced Mom to come back.

During one visit, Grandmother sent Don, another of Mom's younger brothers, to buy soft drinks. When he returned and walked through the door with them, she kicked him in the crotch, which was her favorite place to kick. My four-year-old brother Philip confronted Grandmother and said,

"But he buyed them." Every movement in the room stopped as family members silently watched for the blowup. Such a question of Grandmother's authority never succeeded, but she did not respond. On the way home, Mom and Dad talked about my brother's bravery. From my position, I was not sure it was that at all; I have always been conscious of the thin line between bravery and stupidity.

Tom always had the ability to work through controversy and conflict, and Grandmother was no exception. He gave her a silk flower arrangement that she watered for days. Later, when he explained it, she laughed about it with him. Tom had that gift. I, however, concentrated on staying out of sight when we were at her house.

When I started pilot training in Lubbock, I visited them more frequently than any other time in my life. On one visit, Papa Ed was home alone and invited me to stay for lunch, and I gladly obliged. After rifling around in the refrigerator, he produced some Colby cheese with mold on it, and he got out the bread, which also had mold spots. We scraped the mold off the cheese, pinched the bread clean, and made a couple of oddly shaped grilled cheese sandwiches. As we finished eating, he carefully wrapped everything exactly like it had been and placed it back in the exact spot it had been in and commented, "If we hide the evidence, she won't know we've been here."

He saw my eyebrows shoot up and continued as if to answer my unasked questions, "I know your grandmother is pretty hard and people want to know why I didn't make her change. . . ." He paused, obviously thinking back through the years before continuing, "To this day, I remember meeting her, and she had this fierce independent spirit that I loved from the moment I met her. Why would I change the thing I loved the most?" It was the only significant comment he ever shared with me about his relationship and is a testament to his kind and giving spirit.

For me, I can't get over the most dominant memory of my grandmother's interaction with Papa Ed. He pulled up in front of their house at Christmas in his pickup with the sideboards and cow manure splattered over the side. (He was a cattle trader his whole life.) Grandmother Garnett waited until he got into the house and all his daughters were fussing over him, and she bellowed, "Get that slut wagon out from in front of my house!"

Such stories might make it seem that Grandmother Garnett was plain mean, but all of her ten children grew up to be wonderful people, so she did something right. After rearing ten children, at age forty-nine, she enrolled in a nursing program at Texas Tech, completed it, and served people as a nurse well past her retirement years. I doubt too many patients got away with giving her grief.

9

MOVING UP IN
THE WORLD

After my parents decided they wanted to leave camp life, they started looking for a small farm in a price range they could afford. Satisfied with my dad's pay and the job at Humble Oil, they decided to stay in Lea County. Dad saw that small farms in the northern end of the county had irrigation, so he and Mom set their sights there. They looked for one with good soil, free of the rocks that filled some farms in the area, and, most importantly, one that came with water rights. Water can be pumped to irrigate the farm only when you own the rights to pump it.

With the right soil and hard work, they could expand my grandfather's backyard oasis concept into an idea that would feed the family with the fruit of our labor. But they understood that none of that could occur without water. In the arid Southwest, water is more than a convenience, more than something to wash your car or bathe in—water is life.

In 1957, my folks found a five-acre farm with irrigation for fifteen thousand dollars. To buy it, they had to overcome the thing they feared most, which was to borrow money from the bank. The courage to make this decision would transform our family in ways no one could have imagined, and especially my life.

They also bought an old rambling ranch house near Eunice for fifteen hundred dollars, which they intended to move twenty miles to our newly acquired land, a common practice of the day. According to old timers, the house was built in the late 1800s; if that was true, it was one of the oldest houses in Lea County.

After paying cash for the house, Mom began to negotiate with house movers. Everyone she talked to questioned whether the house would survive the move, because it lacked interior wall strength. The house was built "box style," which meant it had no studs in the walls. Several movers turned the job down. Some of the movers said if they could cut the house in half, they would move it. Finally, Mom found one man, Ray Campbell, an uncle to the famed country western singer Glen Campbell, who said he and his brother could move it intact.

But on the day of the move, Ray and his brother didn't show up. Ray lived in an old motel on the south end of Hobbs, so Mom went there to find him. He hadn't been able to afford to eat in a while, and he didn't know where to find his brother. Mom picked up Ray, found the brother, and cooked them a large meal with cobbler and ice cream. Then she took them to the house to start work. She had paid her money for the house and would not be denied moving it.

> From watching my dad I learned one principle that always applies to improving your life circumstances: Start where you are and use what you have.

Dad and some of his oilfield buddies braced the inner walls with discarded, greasy oilfield boards. They placed three-by-twelves under the house on the truck to keep the unwieldy structure from breaking into pieces during the twenty-mile move.

Mom and Dad followed the house in our pickup, but she was so afraid it would break into pieces that she hid her head in a pillow and didn't watch. The most treacherous part of the journey was the last few feet as the truck hit the decline off the highway onto our five acres. The highway is built higher than the land around it, and the drop is sudden and steep for a house that was at risk of splitting. Ray didn't hesitate, aiming the truck at the opening to our piece of ground and bouncing across it. He made the turn without a hitch.

The workers took a day to place concrete blocks under the house and set it, and we moved in the day they put it on the ground—with no plumbing or electricity. It was several weeks before the septic system was complete and we could use the indoor bathroom.

From the time we got the farm, Dad basically worked two jobs. Every morning he got up at 4:30 a.m. and went out to the barn to feed the livestock, milk the cow, and do other chores. Each of us kids had to help, but we rarely made it out of bed when he did. He left for work at 6:30, was back home by 4 p.m., and went back to work, farming and tending to the animals.

Start Where You Are and Use What You Have

All Dad ever wanted in life was that small farm and enough water to irrigate it. He was content with his life of working in the oilfield, planting crops, tilling the soil, building a championship pig herd, and helping his kids and the others in the 4-H club. Those were his rewards in life and, for him, they gave it meaning.

From watching my dad I learned one principle that always applies to improving your life circumstances: Start where you are and use what you have. The five-acre farm, as humble as it was, improved our potential tremendously, and eventually helped pay the way for all of us kids to go to college as well as my mother. We could now grow crops, raise livestock, experience responsibility, and move toward self-sufficiency. None of that had been possible living in the camp.

Even when we were struggling, my folks never considered taking government assistance. They saw how it ruined the spirit of many people. They just wanted the freedom to raise and provide for their family. This farm became a part of that.

10

NADINE

Over the years, and for a variety of reasons, I've often been asked, "How did you end up the way you did?" The following conversation is a summation of the many conversations I've had in trying to explain how I became who I am.

"Nadine is how I ended up this way."

"Nadine? Is that your mother?"

"No, no. Nadine is the place where I grew up. I liked it; it's what made me who I am."

"Why was it so special? Did it have a mall or park?"

"No. There was nothing. It was mostly an intersection."

"What? How could you like an intersection with nothing there?"

"I don't know. We visited Albuquerque every year at the state fair. It just seemed like it was too big and too many people. I was lost all the time. I didn't know who I was there. I was nobody when I was there, in the big city."

"How many people lived there?"

"There was nobody in Nadine. Well, a few families just like ours, but there was no one special. But I knew where I belonged there. After awhile, I could see who I was. I didn't know that before we moved to Nadine. But in the big places, I could never find out who I was. That's why I am the way I am."

"Oh, I never cared about all that, so I was happy when we moved to California—L.A., the Dodgers, the Rams, Disneyland, freeways, Knott's Berry Farm."

"Knott's Berry Farm? Do they grow berries there? Strawberries? Blueberries?"

"That's stupid. Why would they grow berries there? They have roller coasters and a big Ferris wheel. You can see all of L.A. from the top of the Ferris wheel. They don't grow anything there."

"Jeez, don't be angry. It was just a question. It made sense to me."

"Made sense to you? You don't know anything. Who are you? You're from Nadine."

"When I am in Nadine, I know who I am."

"Is your Nadine intersection on a freeway?"

"No, it's just a country highway. A guy from Eunice rolled his car once, right in front of our house. I was the first one there. The blood was running everywhere. I could see his shinbone sticking out. He couldn't get out."

"What did you do?"

"It's not what I did, but what he did."

"What was that?"

"Well, I was just squatting there looking at him in his crushed up Pontiac. I thought he was dead. Suddenly he reached out and grabbed my hand and said, 'Son, I need your help.' Imagine that, a grown man needed help from me. Eleven years old, and he needed my help."

"That's a dumb story. We have ambulances and fire trucks and policemen in L.A. We never even have to slow down when something like that happens."

Suddenly we were both quiet.

Nadine, New Mexico

I lived my formative years in Nadine. I tell people that we were moving from Eunice to Hobbs, twenty miles north, but ran out of money five miles short and ended up there. It's only a partial stretch of the truth.

Nadine, named for the daughter of a forgotten rancher in the area, is five miles south of Hobbs. It did not have a school, a post office, or a church when I was growing up. It was more of an intersection than a town, situated where the main highway heading north and south crosses with a county road that leads to Texas, just three miles away. The New Mexico portion of that road running west was not paved but was made of caliche, a white powdery rock native to the area, and it dead-ended within a mile. The community was no more than a few families scattered along two miles of the main highway when we moved there, surrounded by the open-range ranches of the West.

Riley Meyers ran the only business in Nadine, a little service station a mile from us. We'd walk there to buy sodas and candy, as a form of recreation mostly. Riley kept his candy bars in the refrigerator to keep them from melting in the summer heat, but the chocolates always had a white film from being refrigerated. He also ran a commercial chicken house behind the station until Tyson's used muscle and political influence to run all the small egg producers out of business.

West Texas is home to the Permian Basin Oil Field, which extends a few miles under New Mexico's Lea County. For decades, Lea County was the only part of the state that enjoyed the oil field's prosperity, having jobs and filling its tax coffers to the resentment of the rest of New Mexico. But none of the oil wells in Lea County were close to Nadine, and the prosperity that came with them missed Nadine as well. Today, with oil at around one hundred dollars per barrel, even Nadine has prosperity. Ranchers, faced with drought and debt, have sold off highway frontage, and heavy industrial businesses are locating there to service the growing oil economy.

Nadine also sits above the very western edge of the Ogallala Aquifer, which is part of what drew Dad there in the first place. He found five acres of land that had twelve-acre-feet of genuine water rights, proved up and signed off by the New Mexico State Engineer. In the arid state of New Mexico, irrigation is essential if you plan to farm.

But just because the land had water rights did not mean that it had water. Dad had to baby the well; pump it too hard, and it began to yield red sand that filled our water tank and the irrigation ditch. The underground water played out a couple of miles south of Nadine, so Eunice has to pump water for the town from wells twenty miles north.

Lea County is bordered to the east and south by West Texas, where they speak a dialect that is similar to English but uses a few more syllables to say everything. Kids routinely have two first names, such as Bobby Dan or Lou Ann. In northern New Mexico, Lea County is referred to as "little Texas," which is not a term of endearment. We picked up the West Texas dialect and shared the Texas oil; people in northern New Mexico hated the sound of the county with good jobs and prosperity. One of the persistent rumors of my years at Nadine was that Texas and New Mexico were going to swap two counties. Texas was going to get Lea County, and New Mexico would take El Paso. It hasn't happened yet.

When our 4-H group needed somewhere to meet, Mom talked a local rancher into donating a vacant lot behind Riley's chicken house to locate a 4-H building. She and another mother supervised the moving of an abandoned building from the carbon black plant north of Eunice to the vacant lot, where it became the home of all the town's community activities for several decades. Teen groups from Hobbs even came to use the big building.

The kids from Hobbs, though, were yearning for Cushman motor scooters at the time, while none of the Pearce kids in Nadine even had bikes. Being five miles from town ensured that we did not live the same hurried, hectic lives as those in town. In the absence of activities, we came to know ourselves and our surroundings better.

The community of Nadine was populated with people like us, just ordinary folks who could not afford or did not want to live in town, desiring simplicity and space as my mother did. Most of them lived below the radar of the rest of the world, but not all.

Brigitte

We called the stretch of blacktop going to Texas the Nadine Road. Dinah Avary, a year older than me, lived a mile down that road. As was true of everyone who lived at Nadine, her family had drifted in, looking for a cheaper place to raise a family. Her home was a dilapidated, 1940s travel trailer, made long before travel trailers were cool. The rumor was that she bathed across the Nadine Road in the dirt tank that lay on the edge of Will Terry's ranch. I don't know; I never saw.

When Dinah got to high school, she joined the drama department, started trying out for the school plays, and adopted the name of Brigitte. She had aspirations, and the name change indicated where she hoped they would take her. In the late '50s, the French actress Brigitte Bardot was about as risqué a figure as there was in the world, other than Marilyn Monroe. But Marilyn did not create the sense of allure or outrage that Brigitte, the French version, did. Her name was too common to evoke hot sweat in the middle of the Nadine nights.

Before digital photography, you took pictures with your camera, delivered your rolls of film to local camera centers, and they sent them by mail to larger towns where the film was developed and printed. It could take up to two weeks to get your pictures developed and back in your hands. Rumor was that there were censors at these centers who would delete photos that were too explicit.

Polaroid cameras had been around for decades, but changes to the camera in 1963 made them commonplace in households by 1964. The Polaroid cameras gave artistic freedom—and the opportunity for uncensored photos—to amateur photographers.

The Polaroid played a big role in the scandal that rocked Hobbs High School in 1964. Brigitte, the Nadine version, wrote a letter that appeared in *Playboy* magazine. In the letter, she complained that they never gave small town girls a chance to be in the magazine. She enclosed one of the new Polaroid photos of herself in a bra and panties. And, lo, her letter and the picture appeared in the magazine!

The news swept through the high school like wildfire. When students found out Brigitte rode my school bus, they came running to find out more. It was the peak of my high school popularity. I withheld information, yielding only the morsel about her bathing in the stock tank. Of course, I never admitted that I had not seen the evocative sight.

Brigitte graduated that year and evaporated from the town as quickly as the summer irrigation. Over the summer, the thrill died down, and Nadine slipped back into obscurity. My brothers and I resumed putting the catfish in the tank. (We had suspended that, just in case she was bathing there.)

I began my senior year in the fall of 1964, forgotten, now that Brigitte had moved on. But the schoolyard scandal flared back to life the next year when *Playboy* flew Brigitte to New York for a photo shoot and made her the centerfold in December of that year. By that time, she had gotten married and moved to Odessa. The girl that sat at the back of my school bus, unnoticed, had suddenly become much more noticed. All of her.

It was in Nadine that I gained full understanding of what the biblical character Gideon knew—that I, like him, was among the "least of these." I would later learn, however, that these are just the type of people God chooses to use sometimes—whether small in stature as was the shepherd/psalmist David, or just from a small town as I was.

Having studied her for the years she had been on the bus, I was curious enough to borrow a copy of the magazine (those, along with dancing, were not allowed at the Pearce house) to see what she looked like when the shades were pulled up in her dressing room. The layout editors did their best, stretching her upward and backward in a pose designed to hide the fact she was somewhat short of curves.

Her celebrity status was a big deal in Hobbs, which held a main street parade with Brigitte as the grand marshal, presenting her with the keys to the city at a ceremony. (Nadine didn't have keys to give her; it stayed unlocked all the time.) Brigitte was the first and last centerfold from Nadine—1964 to 2013—as long as the dry spell since the Cubs last won the big one.

I used to lie awake at night and dream of the Texas girls whom I saw at the baseball games and at the fairs. Our family often visited to O'Donnell, where my grandparents lived. When I was a sophomore in high school, I met Jo Ella, the prettiest of the girls who raised and showed 4-H pigs with us. She was from O'Donnell, where my dad had graduated from high school and where my cousin Terry Phillips went to school. O'Donnell, like Nadine, had no water and no oil, but agriculture was big and respected there, unlike in Lea County. As the daughter of a landowning farmer, Jo Ella was in a tier of society that farm boys from Nadine could never reach.

I eventually married one of those Texas girls, and it was everything I dreamed it would be, but she was not a farm girl. Cynthia's father, as did my father, made his living in the oilfield. At 135 pounds, he worked in one of the toughest jobs in the oilfield as a roughneck. He carried sacks of drilling mud that weighed almost as much as he did, swung the dangerous drilling chains, and died at 78 without ever having owned his own home. You didn't have to be from Nadine to know poverty.

It was in Nadine that I gained full understanding of what the biblical character Gideon knew—that I, like him, was among the "least of these." I would later learn, however, that these are just the type of people God chooses to use sometimes—whether small in stature as was the shepherd/ psalmist David, or just from a small town as I was. It all comes down to trusting Him.

11

COMMITMENTS AND PLEDGES

In the forgotten and barren intersection known as Nadine, despite the drought of the late 1940s and '50s, I began to sprout, grow, and blossom. It may seem strange to some, but my personal growth began with commitments and pledges when I was nine years old. These commitments revolved around three main focal points: the Pledge of Allegiance, 4-H, and church.

The Pledge of Allegiance

School kids in the '50s and '60s stood every morning in every classroom in the nation and recited the Pledge of Allegiance, starting in the first grade.

At first, I did not understand it, but about age ten, I began to think about its words and what it meant. In its small way, this pledge was a dot that connected. For me, with my trouble visualizing, it gave me a constant, something to focus on. The familiarity of the solemn oath was a tie that bound me to the kids standing next to me. It was a routine that eventually allowed me to start every day on a familiar theme. That was a big deal to my ten-year-old perspective.

The progressives today say we cannot pledge allegiance to the flag because to do so would require us to pledge to all flags. I don't see it that way. What they have done is remove a constant, at least one thing on which we could all agree—the commitment every growing child makes to this country and the commitment that student makes to the one standing next to him or her.

We are more divided than ever before in our history, because, as a people, we have no common belief or commitments. We make no pledges.

4-H

When Mom signed us up for 4-H, we said the 4-H motto and pledge before every meeting. These, too, became part of my consciousness, a part of my internal gravity that tugged at me every time I compromised them. The pledge went like this:

> *I pledge my head to clearer thinking,*
> *My heart to greater loyalty,*
> *My hands to larger service*
> *and my health to better living*
> *for my club, my community, and my country.*

(In our generation, we were content to save the country. The additional burden, "and my world," was added to the pledge by a later generation.)

I could get my head around the idea of clear thinking, being loyal, and helping the people in our club and community. Nadine was so small that you knew everyone; when you helped the club, you helped the community.

In big cities, it seems people grow up isolated, not believing it's within their reach to help the community. The calling to serve others seems too large, and it overpowers the individual. The idea of using my hands to serve was an example constantly being shown by my parents and the people in our small community. These were the footholds that helped me climb out of the pit in which my young and selfish mind and body were trapped.

The greatest acceleration of learning and moving outside myself began at fourteen, when all 4-H'ers are challenged as senior members to participate in a project called Junior Leadership. Older members coach and mentor younger members in their livestock projects, public speaking, citizenship, and a host of other activities. The saying is true: If you want to learn, teach.

While teaching others, it was soon apparent that many kids, whose families were just like ours, without wealth or standing but who shared our values, were also afflicted with frailties and limitations, much like my own. They might not be as pronounced, but everyone, at least in Nadine, seemed to have fears that I understood. For kids younger than myself, I could help them through, and I began to see myself as a potential leader.

The 4-H motto is "*To make the best better.*" Starting at the age of nine, I pledged myself to a lifelong belief that, even when I gave it all I had, I could do better next time.

Commitment to Faith

The same year we started in 4-H, I walked alone down the aisle at church to be baptized, joining my parents and older brothers in committing to the lifestyle of a Christian. I began then to think about what that meant. Bible stories had always been a part of our discussions at home, but I began to view them from the perspective of having made a commitment to God. It was those stories that led me to believe I could be more, and it was through my involvement in 4-H that I found the realization to this truth. It gave me the courage and then the experience to take leadership positions outside of 4-H and continue to grow and find myself.

Discipline at Home

Mom, as a child, the second of ten, was placed in positions of responsibility for her siblings. She had to get them all up and out the door to church and school. When her oldest sister, Venita, started first grade, she was afraid to go alone, so Mom, as the second oldest, went to school with her. Mom learned the lessons along with her sister and was promoted and stayed a grade ahead of her age group in school.

Her status as the disciplinarian growing up barely paused between raising her siblings and then her own children. She married immediately after high school, and my oldest brother was born a year later.

Having seen the effect of drinking, carousing, slothfulness, and similar sins in others during her youth, she did not tolerate any of these in her own children. Moral lessons were a constant as we grew up. The rules gave me a much-needed structure in which to live my life.

Gravity

Without knowing or fully understanding these commitments to our country, to my faith, and to the club and community around me, I was establishing an internal gravitational field that helped me make sense of life and the world around me. This certainty of knowing what my community was—and that I had pledged to help it—was an understanding that began to grow and thrive in my ten-year-old mind. That understanding was rooted into our lives, built around the traditional concepts of church, patriotism, the family, and community spirit where we joined in potluck dinners, church socials, and a shared belief in the moral, spiritual, and fair-dealing values—the basic values of rural America.

Life for most in the small community of Nadine revolved around the 4-H meetings and the county fair, where the idea of pitching in to help those you were competing against was second nature. All dirtied their hands to help unload a competitor's animals, get them to the pens, and even help wash and groom a rival's animals if it was needed.

In helping the younger kids and seeing the other families up close, I began to construct my own individual identity. That identity has stayed connected in my mind all my life, avoiding the tendency in some my age as they began to try to establish any number of identities until one decouples from the knowledge of their own self.

One such example came to light when I attended a funeral for a long-time pastor of a black church in Hobbs. The all-black choir was rejoicing in our common faith and, at certain points, for emphasis, their hands and arms would fly up toward heaven. Each time that happened, I noticed a flash from the corner of my eye. At first I thought it was the flash from the sun reflecting off a mirror as a car drove by, but it happened multiple times, so I concentrated on the choir.

Finally, I saw it. One of the choir members had white arms that flashed when the arms went up and gravity pulled the arms of the robe down. I studied the person to see who it was and, with a start, recognized a man who graduated from high school the same year I did. He had his face, hands, and arms painted black!

There were Anglo kids who took on characteristics of the American Indian, Hispanics, and other races. For me, the days in the fields with the braceros and the early childhood with different races in the Nadine 4-H club left me with the impression that I did not need to change my identity to help someone of a different race. To do so requires one to give up the gravity of their own life. The most powerful thing I can do is to treat them the same as everyone else.

Without knowing or fully understanding these commitments to our country, to my faith, and to the club and community around me, I was establishing an internal gravitational field that helped me make sense of life and the world around me.

As a kid who feared gravity from the moment of birth, I was beginning to discover its positive effects: The calm of having an internal system of order, of responsibilities and commitment, and the external support network of other adults and friends who believed the same tenets.

When my friends in high school asked me to go drinking with them, my internal gravity helped me reply, "We don't drink at our house, and besides, I have to exercise our pigs at 4:30 in the morning. If I stay up 'til midnight, I can't get out of bed." Not exercising the pigs had grave consequences, such as a less chance to make the sale at the county fair and the increased possibility that we could not pay the bank loan—a note that I had signed and pledged to pay back. My commitments began to give structure to my thinking and responses.

Meanwhile, friends who did not have these commitments wrestled with answers to the same questions and, with no real reason not to go drinking, wound up going along toward wasted days, wasted years, and not a few wasted lives.

Without understanding it, my fledgling beliefs and gravity gave me courage, responsibility, stability, and certainty.

I am afraid as America transitions more to big cities and away from the rural communities such as Nadine that there is a loss of connection and a loss of a belief that, as a single kid on the streets of New York City, you can do anything to help your community or your country.

12

LEARNING TO WORK

We moved from the oil camp to the farm in 1957, and at nine years old, I learned how to work. The farm-taught habits stuck, and as an adult, I find myself working long hours just as my father and mother did.

Our first spring on the farm, Dad prepared to plant onions as soon as the ground was warm enough. He bought bundles of onion shoots and soaked the ground the night before. At 4:30 in the morning, Mom, Dad, and we three oldest kids headed out into the cold darkness to work the muddy rows.

Dad had sharpened short round sticks so we could punch holes in the ground, but the sticky mud soon rendered them ineffective. So we used a finger to make the holes, then pushed an onion in each hole and filled it with soil. We planted a quarter of an acre before Dad left for work at 6:30, then changed clothes and were on the school bus shortly after 7 a.m.

In the afternoon, Dad transplanted the tomato plants from small containers he bought the day before. We lugged a five-gallon pail of water and carefully soaked each plant to give it a good chance of survival—replacing a dead plant represented a loss of several days in the growing season, so each of us learned to take care of the fragile new garden.

Dad had a knack for growing things. We had rows of onions, tomatoes, squash, corn, jalapenos, green chilies, and watermelon—nearly three acres of crops that first year. All of us kids experienced the fun and boredom of plowing with the tiny Farmall Cub and, later, the 8-N Ford tractor.

When the crops began to ripen in mid summer, the whole family harvested them. As soon as Dad got home in the afternoon, he took the day's yield into town and sold them to Tootie's Supermarket. As kids, we sometimes worked a stand Dad set up on the side of the road, selling eggs, vegetables, cantaloupe, and watermelon. The money went into the family cookie jar to help make ends meet. It was at the farm stand that I learned to make change and negotiate with customers.

Mom canned the crops that were not sold, but that project also involved the entire family. Dad and all of us kids picked the vegetables while Mom readied the canning operation, boiling the glass jars and setting up the pressure cooker. Then we all shelled the peas or beans and helped blanch the vegetables before placing them in the cooker that would boil out any bacteria and sealing them into jars. It took an hour to pressure cook the jars of vegetables, and our responsibility as kids was to have the next batch ready to put into the sterilized jars. It was an all-day operation.

It often became my job to milk our Jersey cow as well. On winter mornings, carrying a bucket of hot water to the barns to wash the cow's udder before milking, I began to hate cold and snowy weather. I had to break the ice in the trough so the animals could get a drink, and the cow would need special cleaning after lying in the mud and muck of the snow.

With only one pair of shoes, I wore the same ones to do the chores that I wore to school; they would inevitably pick up mud and manure from the barnyard. Later, in the heat of the school classroom, the muck would thaw and permeate the classroom. I was so shy that I didn't need the extra embarrassment of the teacher asking who had the smelly shoes.

We did not have a concept of "rich" or "poor," but most people would have called us poor. Each of us kids worked from as early in our youth as we could effectively swing a hoe, milk a cow, or gather the crops. Each summer morning, we got up and worked in the garden. I was ten when for the first time I was tasked by Mom to hoe an entire row, which seemed to extend beyond the horizon. It felt insurmountable, but step-by-step, I hoed. After hours of work, I got the entire row done.

Although the farm tasks never got easier, it was on the small farm at Nadine that I first conceived of doing things that require time and discipline. It was there, planting, tilling, and caring for the crops, that my work ethic was developed and I learned that big projects take time. But one step at a time, one row at a time, and one day at a time, they can get done.

Holidays at Nadine

In my family, holidays were often like bonus workdays—not a day off. Companies in the oilfields that have workers on duty 24/7 have to pay them double time on holidays. If Dad happened to be going into overtime, holidays were triple pay. With so many hungry mouths to feed, Dad would announce he had to work on Thanksgiving or Christmas with a sense of anticipation. Everyone knew the next paycheck would be a little larger. If the company didn't need his services, he was available to work with us around the farm, and we would tackle big projects.

One Christmas, Dad bought a load of feed shocks—the stalks of milo that are cut and bundled after the grain is harvested. To get them home, we loaded up as much as we could into the single-axle stock trailer, taking four or five trips to get it all stacked inside our barns and ready for winter feed.

To keep costs of feeding our livestock lower, we started to mill our own feed. In the summertime, we could just put the milo on the ground and cover it with a tarp. It rarely rained, so there was little risk of losing the investment. The winter was different; the possibility of rain or snow kept constant pressure on us to mill the grain before it was ruined. All of us played sports or had activities after school, and the shorter days meant there were fewer opportunities to get the work done.

Christmas and Thanksgiving were days when there were no sports, no concerts, or any other complications. We could pick up a load of milo, haul it, and grind it all in one day. Dad would carry a couple of kids to help shovel the grain into the trailer. Two of us would hook up the long belt between the mill and the tractor; one of us would feed the grain into the mill and another would hold a sack under the outlet to catch the ground feed.

By the end of the day, we were covered with milo dust from head to toe. It was a horrible, itchy job, about as miserable as any I have ever done, but we did it willingly because it meant more money at the end of the project. I valued the profit and the eventual chance to go to college more than I valued comfort.

As I grew older, I sought out the oilfield jobs and also worked on the holidays. During college, the day after we got home for Christmas break, I would often show up at the well service offices at 5:30 a.m. I worked every day possible to pay college tuition and expenses. I especially tried to work on Christmas day, for the same reasons as my father.

The big lesson I was learning is that people can and will adapt to any circumstance to make their lives better. They just need the opportunity to work harder to earn their own success.

My First Paid Job

Mom got us all Social Security cards at early ages, and I was nine when I got my first paid job outside the home. (Child labor laws restricting this experience came years later.)

Dudley Thorpe was a local farmer who needed help moving aluminum irrigation pipe every morning and every evening. He saw all of us kids in front of the house that had just been moved into Nadine, so he stopped and asked if one of us wanted to help him. Somehow, I got selected.

I got up at 4:30 in the morning with my dad. Mr. Thorpe came by the house and picked me up shortly afterward. For the next two hours, before school, we moved pipe—my four-and-a-half-foot frame on one end and a grown-up on the other. He had been irrigating all night, so the field and crop were wet, and in the early morning and even in the summer, it was always cold.

Every two weeks, Mr. Thorpe stopped by the house to pay me. Using his pickup truck as an office and the hood as a desk, we'd settle up. I'd add up my hours and then Dudley figured the total pay, deducting Social Security and taxes. Knowing what I was getting paid by the hour, I could easily figure out how much the check should be. It was always less. At a very early age, I realized that my pay was being diminished by payments to a government I didn't know much about.

Getting paid was something new to me. I liked it, but I never spent much; I was a saver from the beginning. My brother Tom, on the other hand, was a consumer. It was a pattern that showed up early and never changed for our entire lives. When we worked together, Tom spent all his money by the end of the same day, purchasing Cokes, candy, peanuts, and toys at Wacker's 5-and-10 Store. He never saved.

When I did splurge on an occasional RC Cola or candy bar, we had to walk to Riley Meyers' store, which was a mile away at the Nadine intersection. To get there, we had to pass the Flowers' farm. They had three big scary dogs—a collie and two German shepherds. To avoid the dogs, we'd cross the four-lane highway in front of their house and move about one hundred yards into the pasture. Sometimes the dogs still came after us. Bobo, our big chow-mix, was no match for the three of them, and we would hightail it past their farm, three or four kids and our big yellow dog.

Early one morning, a wild racket outside the house woke us up. The three neighbor dogs had gotten too close, and Bobo took them on by himself. They were on his turf, and he battled the three of them with a ferocity we had never seen in him. He drove them off, and we never had another problem with those dogs chasing us. Why he hadn't done that earlier was beyond me.

When we took the vegetables to Tootie's Supermarket, I saw they had a kid who gathered up the shopping carts and brought them back into the store. It struck me that the work looked easier and the pay was better than Mr. Thorpe's, and I wouldn't be cold and wet all the time, and I could work more hours at the supermarket. I knew I could do the job, but asking for it was the hard part.

Mom agreed to take me to the store to meet with Tootie Schnaubert, but I had to ask for the job on my own. When I stood face-to-face with Mr. Schnaubert, I stumbled and stammered, but Mom was coaxing me out of my shell. I was hired and, at the age of ten, started my first summer job in town.

I knew that if I worked hard, I could get paid. When I got paid, I felt like I was able to help out my family and have some perks too! I didn't realize at the time that the greatest "perk" from these jobs would be learning to communicate, a skill I'd need my entire life.

The Rascons

Behind our farm, Mr. Jobe had a cotton field managed by Mr. Rascon, whose family lived in a little concrete-block house about a mile from ours. The Rascon family seemed to be a host for workers in the bracero program, which allowed Mexican nationals to take temporary agricultural work in the United States. Each summer, I saw the workforce around the Jobe farm swell as the cotton fields needed chopping, or in the fall as the bolls opened to be picked.

While my dad was working in the oilfield and we were out of school, Mom took us oldest kids to join the Rascon family and work alongside the braceros in the fields. The work crew assembled in the dark of the morning around Mr. Rascon's pickup to start at daylight. We stretched across the field like a Civil War battle line, fifteen or twenty people abreast, each working a row. If I thought the rows were long in our five-acre field, these seemed to stretch to infinity.

The braceros worked so fast that often my brothers and I would be paired on a row, leapfrogging each other to try to keep up with the more efficient pros. We picked the cotton into heavy-duty canvas sacks that were six-feet long and slung over one shoulder with a strap or pulled along the ground behind the picker. They paid the workers for each pound of cotton picked, and stuffing the sacks full of rocks, unripe bolls, and leaves was not acceptable. It was hard work that left our hands bleeding.

I watched with envy as the braceros hung their one hundred-pound sacks on the scales and, using a small pad and a pencil, marked the weight of each sack on a page in the book. As we worked or waited in the heat, we all drank water from a communal metal cup that we dipped into a barrel, with no concern for germs or sanitation. And when the field was hoed or the cotton was fully harvested, the workforce would quietly vanish to the next farm.

To this day, the cotton scales, the smell of the cotton field, and the early morning dew on the cotton—which was chest high to my ten-year-old frame—take me right back to those fields. The biting corrections of a kindly Mr. Rascon, who was trying to get a good day's work for a day's pay from us kids, showed me that most corrections are not personal attacks but just the way it is. I am still comfortable with a straightforwardness that would make most squirm.

Mr. Jobe would never have gotten the field picked without the help of the braceros. They were efficient and effective. The workers showed up season after season and fed their families in Mexico for a full year on the seasonal farm work. That bracero program was eventually terminated in 1964 amid charges of exploitation and due to efforts to unionize the farm workers in this country. As recently as 2010, millions of pounds of crops were left in America's fields because there were not enough workers to harvest them.

In 2011, I took an early morning cab ride to the Lubbock airport. The driver was about my age and had grown up in and around Lubbock. His father had been a bracero, and he was one of fifteen kids. Their family would follow the crop cycle each year, pruning in the winter, chopping cotton in the spring and summer, picking fruit in the late summer, picking cotton in late fall and early winter, using as many of the family members as were able to work.

The driver said that his dad bought and paid for a house in one year with the wages from the family. I asked if the transiency hurt his education. He replied that he and each of his siblings had had good lives, because their parents taught them to work and to make their own way.

If I have the ability to work across racial and cultural boundaries, it is rooted in the many experiences I had growing up. In a cotton field, any concern about differences melts away amid the hard work of twelve-hour days.

Mom also showed us what it looked like to transcend those boundaries. Mrs. Rascon lost a child one year and desperately needed someone to sit and listen. We were their only real neighbors, as the rest of the people in the Rascons' lives were transient. Mom did the neighborly thing and stayed with her for two full days, letting her talk. Of course, the talk was conducted throughout the day as they fed and cared for her large family. Mom came home having learned how to make tortillas, sopapillas, and authentic Mexican dishes. Out of appreciation, Mrs. Rascon gave Mom a molcajete to grind our peppers and spices.

Years later, Mom also helped Grace Rascon, who was my brother Mike's age, get a scholarship to New Mexico Junior College. Mom saw her every day, carrying her little sack of books, head held high, as the door to education was opened for her.

The jobs I had growing up were stepping-stones. Each helped me get experience and move up to other more complex positions.

Some people in this nation have driven hard agendas to get higher and higher minimum wage laws passed, but in the process they have gotten rid of all the stepping-stone jobs. Kids that used to get experience in jobs that do not justify more pay cannot get that experience now. Those jobs did not pay more just because legislation was passed that said the company had to pay more. The companies instead went out of business, stopped hiring, or moved overseas. If we want people to prosper, to graduate up and out of the lower class, we should bring back those entry-level jobs.

When people in the society are lifting themselves up, the country will become stronger. Strength does not happen because laws are passed; it happens one family at a time. Parents who are teaching their kids by example are the bedrock of a strong society, and families making their way out of poverty are the building blocks of a vibrant economy.

Self-reliant families produce strong individuals, and strong individuals make for a strong country. I was blessed to grow up in such a family, but many of the poor families today are waiting at home to have their lives changed.

Nadine 4-H Club

Who I was changed dramatically between the ages of ten and twenty. I tired of being afraid, shy, and separated from the other kids and faced at least some of my fears to change that.

The first major development began when Mom started a 4-H club soon after we moved to Nadine. She drove around in her 1954 Mercury and visited the families in the area, so they all knew about the opportunities 4-H offered. Mom believed that 4-H had lessons for every kid in the county and soon expanded her recruiting beyond Nadine and toward the southern edge of Hobbs.

The Armitage children who joined the group were black, but that did not seem to be anything different to Mom. Despite the racial tension that rocked the country in the late 1950s, the Nadine 4-H club had white kids, Hispanic kids, and black kids all working together. Looking back, I'm sure there were more problems than Mom and Dad let on, but the idea of excluding any kid from the club never came up. We were all just kids in need of the training Mom saw we could get from 4-H.

Once, when we went to El Paso, people were shocked when they saw there was a black kid from our club showing pigs. Eventually, more black kids joined and later formed the Gold Star 4-H club in Hobbs. Mom led both clubs for several years.

Maria Quiroz was a shy Hispanic girl who was my age. Mom had helped her sew her own dress and said it was one of the best she had ever seen. She was hopeful for Maria's chances as we approached the county contests, but Maria's dress did not win.

Mom demanded to see the judges' scorecards. She could only whisper what she saw on them; the affront was too great. The judges marked Maria down because her dark skin color could be seen through the dress's delicate yellow fabric. It was like a collective slap in the face to all of us who were pulling for the fellow club member.

I don't remember discussions around the dinner table about racial discrimination. My parents lived the sermon instead of preaching it, demonstrating with their lives a better way.

4-H Work

Every morning, we had to exercise our 4-H animals to get them fit and ready to show at the fairs. "Exercise" meant getting twenty or so pigs and about the same number of lambs out of the pens and herding them along Mr. Jobe's fence for about a mile each morning and each afternoon. This resulted in animals that were toned, just like athletes. And the animals were easier to handle and show than those that were not worked during the year.

> When people in the society are lifting themselves up, the country will become stronger. Strength does not happen because laws are passed; it happens one family at a time. Parents who are teaching their kids by example are the bedrock of a strong society, and families making their way out of poverty are the building blocks of a vibrant economy.

We raised pigs and often had twenty to thirty of them at a time. We took them to the fairs—originally in a single-axle trailer that Dad pulled behind his pickup truck. It only held six or eight pigs, so he had to make numerous trips to get all the pigs to the fair.

The 4-H club had many adult leaders, and we were like extended family. Mom was just as proud of every project from the club as she was of our own family. Lou Jean Denton had a toothbrushing demonstration that Mom was sure would win the district contests.

Dad helped all the families in our club find pigs that he knew could beat ours at the fair. If one of the other kids' animals won over ours, we were excited for them, even if it was an animal my parents had bought for them. We learned that, if we lost, we could try again next year. We could do better. We could get a better animal or feed it better. We learned to compete.

The idea of service to others was never preached by my parents either; it, too, was a lifelong demonstration. My parents helped the other kids and sometimes even worked to find money for a kid who couldn't afford an animal. Dad often helped the kids in the club get animals to the fair, then he helped shear and groom the animals until late in the night during fair week.

4-H wasn't just about the animals. Even though most of the families at Nadine were desperately short of cash, Mom wanted our club to give back to our community. Every year she organized projects that involved us knocking on doors and selling candy, candles, and even brooms to collect money for worthy causes. The March of Dimes was a big fundraising event for the Nadine 4-H club each year. No matter how poor, we were taught we could work to make a contri-

bution. Taking advantage of the freedom of this country meant giving something back also.

When I ran for political office, the confidence I developed knocking on doors in those days with the Nadine 4-H club helped me in my campaigns. When I started my first political campaign, I articulated my values as faith, family, freedom, and service. The service part was learned through the years of giving back to our community.

4-H Accounting

Part of the 4-H experience was calculating the costs to raise and show the animals. As a child, I started making "T" charts. On one side of the vertical line were the expenses for the animal and the income on the other.

We'd track each animal individually and understood what each pig cost to buy, the medicine costs, how much feed it ate, and what it sold for. Each T was tallied to show a profit or loss for that animal. At the end of the year, we'd add up all the Ts to know if we made or lost money and which animals caused the profit and which caused the loss. It was simplistic but effective.

For me, math came easily. With my 4-H projects, I began to quickly grasp how costs, revenues, and profits came to be. I quickly learned that investing in better stock would reap the benefits of higher revenue if we made the sale at the county fair, rather than having a pig sold at the lower packer price. Some animals did well; others did not. We stopped buying and raising the pigs that didn't make money and bought pigs that did.

Even now, with a degree in economics and an MBA, I still do T charts in my head to figure out the big picture of where budgets lose money. This simple skill has been a valuable lesson from my 4-H years.

Learning Banking

Many people cannot imagine sending a fourteen-year-old to talk to the bank president about getting a loan, but in rural New Mexico in 1961, that is exactly what Mom had me do. My folks could not afford all the costs associated with our 4-H activities, especially buying and feeding the growing livestock herd. The pigs were our business, and we took on the responsibility of financing them.

I was a middle child with two older brothers, two younger brothers, and a younger sister. My oldest brother, Mike, had the job of signing the loan papers. But when he went to college, it just worked out that I would be the next one to go to the bank and meet with the president. I had to convince him that we would work hard enough to repay the two thousand dollar loan, which was a lot of money back then.

From my earliest years, I knew what it was to balance my checkbook and reconcile the bank account. I knew what it was to lay awake at night calculating in my head the value of each pig and knowing how the pigs had to place to pay the loan back. I learned to handicap the pigs that I thought were good enough to make the sale at the fairs and bring more revenue. I learned to tally up the ones that were just going to bring market price. It was scary, but I learned.

Even after we had a reputation with the bank that we paid our bills, the president still made me come in and meet with him. I put my signature on the loan and knew what it meant to give my word. Looking back, I can see that the bank president and my mother were training me.

Years later, Mom confided to me that when they first moved to New Mexico from the farm near O'Donnell, Texas, Dad would not go into the bank. He was too shy to talk to the bankers, too embarrassed to ask for a loan. My mother went to the bank and asked for the loan to buy our first little house on Cecil Street. She didn't want me to be as shy as my father was, and she constantly pushed me out of my comfort zone.

The 4-H projects helped feed us and paid for each of us to go to college. Mom was hungry for the chance to get ahead. The 4-H projects also paid for her college when she was in her forties. Once she got more education, she got a teaching job, and our family's economic condition improved dramatically.

Many people might have looked down on our little enterprise, but for us it was the stepping-stone, it was our only way out of poverty and the only way out of Nadine. It was our opportunity to use what little we had: five acres of space for barns and crops, an irrigation well, and one small tractor. We raised chickens to have eggs, a cow for milk, pigs and sheep for meat, and grew our own vegetables.

Decades later, those childhood experiences were the foundation for knowing what the bank needed to see and verify before they would process our application and lend us the money to buy our first company.

Truth—Growing Up Poor in Nadine

James Hearst wrote a poem called "Truth," in which he said, "How the devil do I know if there are rocks in your field, plow it and find out. . . . the *connection* with a thing is the only truth that I know of, so plow it."

Growing up poor was hard, but it was handy in some ways. It made us figure out truth and connections to things more quickly than if we had money. If a particular sow did not have many pigs or her offspring did not win at the fairs, we either got rid of her or we'd go broke. It was that simple. If we ignored the truth, we could experience the emotional thrill of keeping our favorite sow, but we would not pay the bills.

We knew that Mom and Dad did not have the money to bail us out if the revenue at the fairs didn't produce enough to pay the bank, so we gained every advantage we could by exercising and feeding our stock right and buying the right stock in the first place. If we didn't pay the bank, we wouldn't get a loan for the next set of fairs.

Many people might have looked down on our little enterprise, but for us it was the stepping-stone, it was our only way out of poverty and the only way out of Nadine.

Similarly, if we didn't save, we would never go to college, because the truth was that my parents could not afford to send us. By working out these truths in our own minds, then planning accordingly, each of us kids had the opportunity to go to college. Many other families just like ours never saw one of their kids graduate from college, because they never dared to confront the harsh truth.

Years later, these same simple truths, disciplines, and processes allowed me to evaluate complex business decisions about expansions of our company's business lines. Formal accounting is valuable, but all the information in the world is not helpful if you can't figure out what makes for a profit and what results in a loss.

13

TOOLS OF IGNORANCE

Once we were settled in Nadine, Mom enrolled us at the school in Hobbs. I attended the fourth grade at Will Rogers Elementary, under the supervision of Mr. Murphy, the dark-skinned and austere principal.

One day he called the entire school into assembly to inform us that a bank robbery had occurred at the New Mexico Bank and Trust on Broadway Street, about ten blocks away. His son was working inside the teller's cage and was the one the masked man confronted as he waved a gun and demanded all the cash. Mr. Murphy told our assembly how frightened his son had been. It seemed he called an assembly just to tell us that. None of us questioned why our principal needed to do so, to voice his emotions about his son's experience. The crime was never solved, and continued discussions about the event only gave me more reason to fear life.

All of my early life, I felt as though I was trapped in a cell, looking to be set free. Those three years at Will Rogers were no exception. I was trying hard to make friends, but life on the farm provided little opportunity for companionship. During that first year at the school in Hobbs, Mom enrolled us in vacation Bible school at Taylor Street Church of Christ, where

I met a kid my age named Aaron. We struck up an immediate friendship. On the last day of the program, we were playing during the recreation period, and his hand accidentally struck me in the face. Though it didn't hurt me, my teeth left a blood blister on his finger. We studied it intently and wondered aloud how long it would take to disappear.

The next day, his family went on an outing to a lake in our area. When Aaron dove into the water, his head struck a rock and he drowned. At his funeral, I could not get past my memory of looking at the blood blister just a few days earlier, wrapping my mind around how recently we had been getting to know each other. The event only magnified my fear of drowning.

I was looking to get past the fears and take hold of life, but it kept slipping away. The cell door kept slamming shut just as I tried to venture out.

At nine years old, I thought I had broken free of my shell when I talked Mom and Dad into signing me up for Little League baseball. Being new to Hobbs, no one knew me or wanted me on their baseball team, so I had to make it through tryouts. I convinced my parents I could walk the mile and a half from my elementary school to the baseball field for practice and games.

About halfway to the park, I stepped inside an old neighborhood grocery store to get out of the weather. I rarely had money for a soft drink, so I just loitered around. The owner's son, who looked to be in his forties, was mentally impaired and confined to a wheelchair. He used one foot to drag himself along, his arms hanging limp at his side. His baggy brown sweater, worn year-round, had drool on the front from misshapen lips that could not hold themselves together. Those lips muttered indistinguishable syllables that scared me, driving me out of the store. Some days he was out of sight, and I would dart in out of the wind. But it seemed as though he had a transponder on me and could tell when I arrived, because he would pull himself out of a back room and come up and try to talk. I was confused and, trying to find my own voice, could not help him with his need to be understood. When I began to cross the street and pass on the opposite side of the street, he pulled himself to the door and would shout garbled sounds across the street. I began to run past the store.

One foot at a time, I made my way down the streets, paralyzed with the fear of not making the team, fear of the distance, fear of the grocery store, and a fear of being.

Saying Yes to Opportunity

After the tryouts, a sympathetic coach picked me up to play for Parkway Cleaners' minor league team. He used me as a catcher on that team for nine year olds, only because I was slow to react. When the coach told us to find our positions in the outfield or infield, I was the last to move, finding someone in every position before I arrived. I ended up wandering around the infield like a kid at the prom with no date.

The coach called me in and told me I would be the catcher, because no one else wanted the spot. Although I didn't want it either, I dutifully complied. It was that unwanted assignment, taken without complaint and saying yes to the opportunity, that put me in position eight years later to receive some of the most important coaching of my life. And it remains a valuable life lesson for me: God can use the most innocuous events to direct our lives, if we are willing vessels, saying yes to the unexpected (or being too quiet to say no).

I had to walk to baseball practice every day along the same path from school, past the store, to our field, where I waited for over an hour for everyone else to arrive. Richard Johnson, who also arrived early, was a black kid who was two years my senior and threw a notorious fastball; he was also just plain mean. Richard could tell I was afraid of him and chose an unusual method to break the ice, shouting curses and throwing dirt clods at me. I cowered behind the sandpile beside the fence and rolled myself into a defensive ball; the harder he chunked, the tighter I curled.

Between the grocery store crossing and facing Richard, I was fully traumatized by the time the coach and the rest of the team arrived. I felt as though every day was filled with horrors that would strike fear into the heart of Ulysses, let alone me. But a dogged determination kept me going despite the fear.

My brother Tommy, who was two years older, was in complete contrast to me. From his earliest days, he sang in talent contests and dressed up in costumes for roles in school plays, proudly wearing what Mom made for him. I was embarrassed to be seen in public; the thought that I might have to wear a handmade costume petrified me. But Tom was not good in sports, so I found myself, with all of my insecurities, trying to encourage him. He was left-handed, had an awkward throw, and was erratic with a bat. Something was out of place in his sports endeavors, but for reasons I never understood, I desperately wanted him to succeed.

I talked my coach into letting him be on our team. He went along to placate me, but Tom's heart was never in it. He was eleven and on a minor league team with nine year olds, but he didn't seem to mind. Our games were played on a grass field with no mound and no base paths. He could throw hard compared to us younger kids, so, as the catcher, I convinced the coach to let him pitch. Then I had to try to get him to throw it over the plate. The occasional times he did, we were a great team. When he got ready to hit, I was his biggest cheerleader, telling him exactly what he needed to do.

One day, late in the season, he hit the ball what seemed like a mile away, and I knew we had arrived. I knew that now that he had the taste of connecting the sweet spot of the bat with the ball, things would be okay. I knew all he had needed was the sense of success that came from one good at bat. But I was wrong. We wrapped up that season, and he never went out for another ball team for the rest of his life.

Like a Prisoner in a Cell

The next year, a major league team picked me up to play. The manager, Weldon Irving, a local plumber and devout Christian, asked for a volunteer to be the catcher. Although I had dutifully complied by being catcher the previous year, I still envisioned myself playing in the outfield like Mickey Mantle. I tried to move back in the pack to avoid being seen.

In the same way a teacher knows who wants to be chosen the least and is driven to choose him or her, Mr. Irving asked me to step forward. Everyone snickered and laughed as he explained how to use the protective equipment (shin guards, chest protector, and a catcher's mask) that he called the "tools of ignorance," implying that you had to be pretty ignorant to play the position at all.

With my two years of baseball experience at that point spent behind the plate, I became a catcher in perpetuity, in my mind and in the mind of Hobbs' youth baseball coaches. I caught for the rest of my baseball career.

While in little league, I sat quietly behind the plate, catching Jimmie Denton's fastball and Marvin Horace's cannonball. Marvin was a tall lanky black kid who had a snake-like windup. When he released the ball, it was heavy and hard, like a shot from a cannon. Jimmie, on the other hand, was small and slight. While his fastball had as much velocity as Marvin's, it popped the mitt like a hard wasp sting instead of hitting heavy.

Between the two of them, we had an excellent pitching staff. Each threw no-hitters, each reached nearly eighteen strikeouts in the six-inning games. We played at Paul White Park, which had dugouts, a pitcher's mound, and chalk lines on the base paths. I believed I was getting out of my cell when I made the All-Stars my final year in the league.

Mr. Baker, an aging hulk of a man I knew from church who used crutches to get around, was our sixth grade Phys. Ed teacher at Will Rogers. I was excited when the tryouts for the all-city sports competition rolled around, believing I was among the best in our school.

In the softball throw event, I stood at the far northwest corner of the schoolyard with the rest of the kids. We were supposed to throw the ball toward the basketball courts, where a fence would stop the roll of the ball so Mr. Baker could hobble over to throw it back for the next competitor, carefully marking the spot where the ball had landed. When my turn came, I threw the ball over the twelve-foot fence and into the basketball courts. Besides Mr. Baker, who had to retrieve the ball, everyone celebrated the throw, and I glowed warmly in their praise.

The next event was the fifty-yard dash. Ronnie Jett and I were well matched in speed, much faster than any of the other kids. Mr. Baker watched our warm-up sprints and offered me some friendly advice: I was

> I was like a prisoner who, up for parole, stumbled beyond an imaginary line and was sentenced again for an innocent mistake. I was back inside the box that only introverts and shy people know.

losing speed with my flailing arms and needed to hold them close to my body. Mr. Baker, on crutches, could not demonstrate what he meant. I tried to visualize in my mind what that would look like.

On the next run, I held my arms tightly against my body without moving them. Of course, Mr. Baker had been advising me to pump them like pistons, close to my sides, but I could no more visualize what he was telling me to do than I could see visions while listening to Mrs. Bartholomew's music. Without the ability to process and visualize the information or clarify through questions, I just went with my perception.

He saw my running, which probably looked quite comical, and exploded. I realized years later that he thought I was mimicking his disability. Instead, it was simply that I did not understand. I was trying to get out of my jail cell and was willing to accept any coaching to do so.

Mr. Baker railed and shouted, disqualifying me from all events. The sting of his words was even sharper, having just experienced—and only tasted—the triumph and praise of my over-the-fence softball throw.

I was like a prisoner who, up for parole, stumbled beyond an imaginary line and was sentenced again for an innocent mistake. I was back inside the box that only introverts and shy people know. My running career was over before it started. I never again believed I could run.

14

MY FATHER

The pictures of my dad in high school and during his military service show a lanky, six-foot-one young man, confident in his own abilities. You could tell by the way he cocked his military hat that he was left-handed.

He was good in all sports, especially football, basketball, baseball, and tennis. The Pearce family regaled us with stories about the year he made it to the Texas state finals in singles tennis. That was outstanding for a kid from the little farm town of O'Donnell. His brother GR also made it to the finals in doubles tennis.

Dad sometimes talked about the town's adult baseball team that included all of the much younger Pearce boys.

They could only afford T-shirts with homemade logos as uniforms, but they regularly beat the teams from the larger towns, the ones with professional-looking uniforms and all the latest gear. Dad got a kick out of how surprised the men from the big towns were when these country yokels sent them packing.

But outside of organized sports, Dad had a sort of wild streak.

After graduating from high school, he paid Ed Garnett, his father-in-law, sixteen dollars for a mare that was pregnant with a "true blooded horse." I was never sure what that meant, but it was significant to him. It was also significant that he took a chance on a yet unborn colt. Dad was not a big risk taker, and the price was astronomical in those days. When the colt was born, he named him Tony, and when the horse was old enough, he broke and trained him.

That horse must have been a good one, because he talked about it up until my teenage years. He and Tony would go out hunting in "the breaks" south and east of Tahoka, a rough, inhospitable area that saw little human activity. Dad was a crack shot, which was one of the few things he ever bragged about: "When I was out hunting as a kid, I would shoot at the rabbit's eye to keep from messing up the meat, and I'd hit it." He, Tony, and his dogs would go hunting every day when he was not in high school.

While other kids his age dreamed of driving forty miles north into Lubbock, not once did I hear him dream about going to town, about big city attractions, or job opportunities. He was wild and untamed, made for the open country. Dad longed for freedom, longed to let the wild loose within him.

When we lived in the little house on Cecil Street, he brought home a couple of coyote pups one day, wrung from a den with a long piece of barbed wire. Dad's attempts to tame them were about as successful as Mom's attempts to tame him. It sort of worked in both cases, but if you reached too far into the little wire pen, the pups would still bite you.

He had a fascination with birds and always watched for nests to bring home the young birds. He once pulled two baby crows from a nest and placed them in the pickup to bring them home. They promptly displayed their only apparent defense mechanism, throwing up all over the inside of the truck. He put them back.

On another occasion, Dad spotted a roost of pigeons at one of the tank batteries and wanted to bring some home to raise, extolling the virtues of eating baby squabs and dumplings. One night I went with him and watched as he fashioned a long wire, bent a loop in it, and snagged a dozen of the roosting pigeons to carry them back to our farm at Nadine. We ate squabs the first year and never again after that. They were dirty, leaving their droppings in the pig troughs as they stole the food, and we never got rid of the pests until Dad sold the farm decades later.

He was more successful at taming the two hawks he brought home when we lived in the Eunice oil camp. One was a magnificent creature, launching away from our little yard up and around the camp. We would watch him fly, hunt, and experience the thrill of breaking the surly bonds of earth. He would come back and land, looking imperial from the effort, snapping the chunks of meat from our hand with his formidable beak.

We called the other hawk High Pockets. He had an injured wing from birth and could never soar but managed to hop-fly from one branch to the other. He was more tentative when fed, lacking the bearing and confidence of the other hawk.

I yearned to soar, to be free, just like my father. I was more inclined to hop-fly through life, never too far from the ground. Fear kept both of us rooted in place longer than most.

As the years went by, Dad's love for wild things continued, but I was not one of them.

The Natural

Early on, Dad seemed to really want one of his three oldest kids to be good at sports. Mike, the oldest, was the most talented but chose music and the French horn instead. Tom liked singing, drama, and plays. I loved sports, but I was a mediocre talent.

I think it perplexed Dad that he could not help me with sports, since it just came naturally to him. To me, it had to be explained, drawn out in detail, and hammered in. We were too far apart on the natural skills spectrum, and he eventually gave up trying to help me with baseball or any other of the things I tried to learn from him.

I would ask, "Dad, why am I not hitting the ball with power? How did you hit the ball so far?"

"I don't know how to tell you—just swing the bat, and it goes a long way. You're not bad."

> I yearned to soar, to be free, just like my father. I was more inclined to hop-fly through life, never too far from the ground. Fear kept both of us rooted in place longer than most.

I think that he never understood how he did what he did. It was just there when he picked up a bat. Years later, I found a coach who watched closely enough to analyze what I was doing wrong. Dad did not have the gift of coaching, just the gift of doing.

He was a natural artist and could draw anything with just-right proportion and perspective. As a youth, he carved model airplanes out of vegetable crates, working on the raw wood with no pattern or template. The models were precise and accurate, based on the images he had in his mind. He didn't take art classes or go to an art institute; he was just able to do it.

I wanted to be an artist, to be able to draw as he did. "Dad, can you teach me how to draw like you do?"

"Sure, you just put the pencil against the paper and let it flow. The picture will draw itself."

I put the pencil against the paper, but it didn't flow. I tried to draw horses, airplanes, pigs—anything. The picture never drew itself. I think he didn't know how to answer all the questions from me, and they put him off. But I couldn't quench my desire to learn.

"Dad, teach me how to set the carburetor."

"Stevan, you just feel the engine, hear it. It will tell you when it's set correctly."

I didn't feel it or hear it. Eventually I quit asking and trying.

Listen to Me, Mr. College-Educated Guy

Dad did what a lot of poor kids do who get into the military and suddenly have free food to eat. He put on about 40 pounds that he never was able to shed, alternating between 220 and 240 pounds the rest of his life. But one never got the idea that he was fat and sloppy—far from it.

When I was home from college one summer, working in the oilfield, we were sent on a job in the Chaveroo Field, west of Tatum. Dad said he was going to be on the same well with the Humble roustabout gang. Like every young man who has grown up and gotten too full of himself, I had developed a cockiness that was determined to surface that day.

Out on location, Dad's crew needed to unscrew a quarter of a mile of flowline (pipe that conveys oil from the well to the tanks) and lay it along a different path. They were having a hard time getting it to break loose, and I hollered, "Hey, old man, do you want me to show you how it's done out here?"

Dad was not really working on that task; he was back and forth from the heater treater to the flowline. But every time he got close, I was loading up the jabs. It was all good-natured oilfield fun, but his crew finally had enough of it. When he was out of hearing range, one of the men in his crew said, "Mister, we know you are all college-educated and everything, but you do not have a clue how strong Melvin is." They explained that the two of them together used a thirty-six-inch pipe wrench with a six-foot "cheater" attached to it for a longer lever arm, but my dad could do the same job by himself with a twenty-four-inch pipe wrench—and no cheater.

"If he can do it, I can do it," I boasted. "Where is the twenty-four?" I had lifted weights in high school and developed good arm and leg strength, I reasoned.

"Son, why don't you just do it with the thirty-six and the cheater the two of us have been using?" They were not mad, but they had heard enough. They knew Dad had a gentle nature that never responded in anger on his own behalf, and they wanted to teach me a lesson.

I jumped over to where they were, got the thirty-six by itself, and began to try breaking the connection on the pipe. It didn't budge. Confidently, I picked up the cheater, slid it over the wrench handle, and tried to break the connection loose. Then I stood up on the cheater, using my full weight to try to break the threaded pipe. Still nothing. They quietly watched. No heckles; no humor. This was too important to allow any levity.

Dad was coming over from the other side of the location, oblivious to what was going on. His fellow gang members had too much respect for him to repeat the conversation they were having with his third son. Dad laughed his good-natured laugh at the sight of me trying to break the pipe loose. He had noticed that the two guys on the cheater had not broken it either and was coming over to help.

"Let me use your shoulder to balance so I can jump on the handle," I said, only slightly less confident. It was a technique we had used when Dad had us lay fifteen hundred feet of two-inch line from the house down to the hog pens. He came over and stood respectfully to let me put my hand on his shoulder. I jumped with all my might, but the pipe did not budge.

The gang pusher came over and said, "Melvin, break that connection. This circus is holding up getting the well online."

Without hesitation, Dad picked up the twenty-four-inch Rigid pipe wrench from the back of the gang truck. He got down on one knee beside the pipe and, like John Henry, laid his mighty strength into the steel. His great biceps bulged inside the short shirtsleeves. He had barely strained when I saw the pipe move grudgingly a sixteenth of an inch. When it moves, ever so slightly, you have broken the rust and crust that holds them tight. Little by little, with that twenty-four, he unscrewed the offending connection.

I was as proud at that moment as I had been disrespectful a few minutes before. I was proud of his strength, but also of the way his crew took up for him. It was obvious they knew his strength, perhaps better than me.

A Gentle Strength

Despite his physical strength, he was a gentle, kind, and shy man.

He was talented in so many ways. When we were raising our pigs, we didn't have the money to pay a veterinarian to treat them when they were sick. Dad bought a professional hypodermic needle with a glass tube inside a big chrome body and administered medications to the sick ones. He operated on cysts and sewed up the cuts. We even held the pigs while he castrated them.

In farming, he would baby the plants, surrounding new squash or tomatoes with pieces of wood shingles to protect them from the howling sand storms and the unrelenting New Mexico sun until they had taken root. When we went fishing, he always found the best fishing holes and caught the most fish while the rest of us slogged along with an occasional nibble.

I very seldom saw him angry enough that anyone outside the family would notice. The one time that stands out was when my younger brother Philip rode his bicycle five miles from Nadine to Hobbs for baseball practice . . . and he was five minutes late. The coach told Philip to start running laps. Dad had arrived at the practice at the same time as Philip, and he was having none of that kind of punishment. He told Philip to load his bicycle in the back of the pickup. They were leaving.

As Philip put his bike into the back of the pickup, the coach ran over and started yelling at him to get back to running. When he approached Dad as though he was going to straighten him out, Dad picked up a baseball bat.

Dad had developed a reputation among his kids from the time he chucked a bat at a skunk that was about twenty-five yards away from him. The bat hit the skunk in the temple with the heavy end and killed him on the spot. To us it was as impressive as David hitting Goliath with a rock from a sling. (In our minds, Dad could do the impossible stuff, though he never saw it that way.)

Philip said it was obvious from the rhythmic way the bat was swinging in Dad's hand that he had gotten into a zone we had only seen that day with the skunk. It was obvious to Philip that he meant business. The coach saw it too and walked away.

Dad was peaceful and nonconfrontational; none of us had ever seen a response from him to any affront. I don't recall seeing him react that way again, but nothing stirred him as much as one of his kids being treated wrongly.

The Dungeon

Rather than preaching at us, Dad taught by example. He worked hard and sweated a lot. He always wore ball caps, and all of them were stained with sweat.

Other than his aim with a rifle, I never heard him boast, and I never heard him curse. He never touched a drop of alcohol and only smoked an occasional cigar in his earlier years. The regional manager of Exxon sent him a letter when he retired, congratulating him on *never* missing a day of work or being late. He was nothing if not consistent.

When I was in my teens, dreaming of playing pro baseball, I learned that my father had received an offer to play pro baseball right out of high school. "How come you didn't play pro ball?" I asked.

My question put him on the defensive. "It was different then. You rode these old beat-up buses from town to town, and they didn't make as much as they make today."

"Make that much? How much did you make farming or here in the oil-field?" I was quickly venturing beyond my boundaries, caught up in what I perceived as his lost opportunity. "What about the excitement, the roar of the crowd when you scoop the ball and make a play on the runner? What about those long home runs when you hit the ball on the sweet part of the bat? Did you get that on the farm?"

I could see my comments were hurting him, but I was already going, giving wind to my questions. "Dad, you were good. I saw you hit back in the oilfield league in Eunice. You would have made it big. I would give anything to play in the pros, but I'm not as good as you were. Why didn't you do it?"

Mom had been listening, absentmindedly reading a book in the same room. Without looking up, she interjected, "He didn't take a chance because he was afraid. The Pearces told him not to try. Fear was all your father knew. They told him he would not make the team if he took the offer to play ball. So he never tried."

Dad sagged at her comments. They had cut much deeper even than my own. I suspected my folks had visited this place many times before. His loyalty to his family would not let him question the way it had turned out.

I was filled with an immediate shame, because she said it, because I knew it to be true, and because I had opened an old wound. I was filled with shame because I was, at that moment, judging my grandparents, the ones I loved so much, for filling Dad and me with fear. I could not process then that my love for them was the more accurate of my feelings. I did not need to change that because of their shortcomings, for teaching us about the things they thought could kill us or harm us.

After I began to escape from my own dungeon, I used to encourage Dad to carve more. At other times, I prodded him to draw and paint again. I had begun to deal with my fears and felt such a release. I wanted to help him get free. He would always say, "Later," which meant he had given up. I asked him less and less and finally quit asking. It was just too hard on both of us; my wanting to see him escape and him believing that time had passed him by.

Moments of True Discovery

My particular personality had made me vulnerable to fears that were different from Dad's but just as confining. I never again brought up his decision not to try playing pro ball. I just made up my mind to get out of my own prison of fear. It was a long journey for me, and I'm not sure my father ever made it to freedom.

Well, that's not exactly true.

When Dad first started with Humble, he was an entry-level employee, a roustabout. After he had been with Humble for several years, just after we moved to Nadine, the bosses in Midland offered him a promotion to gang pusher. They wanted to transfer us to Frankel City, about forty miles east of Eunice. But Dad declined, saying he had just moved to the farm and didn't want to uproot his family.

It was the baseball offer playing out all over again. The superiors in Midland never forgot that refusal, passing him over for the next twenty-five years. He watched in silence while lesser men were promoted to pumper, gang pusher, or technician. They left him to stew in his own decision. I never heard him complain once. When you have six hungry kids, you don't have the luxury of being too prideful.

One weekend in 1985, I was riding shotgun, with Dad driving the pickup to check on his pigs. I had graduated from college, gone off to war, and come back to live and work in Hobbs. He quietly, even reverentially, shared, "They are going to promote me to field technician later this year."

I could hear the pride and triumph in his voice, as though he had renewed a lost faith or rediscovered an old truth. He displayed no outside reaction; showing emotion wasn't like him. I could hear the relief that comes from finally pushing at a locked cell door and finding that it swings open easily. Having made the careful transition from father-son to a kind of friendship, prodding him to pursue this over the years, I felt my heart bursting with pride. I looked at him and said, "That's great, Dad. I'm proud of you."

But other emotions were crowding quickly into my mind. I hurried to find chores to do at the barns farther from the house. When I had gotten some distance away, I began to weep bitter tears, for the time I had embarrassed him and for the years of life lost for him.

Over the next three years until his retirement, he shared his successes with me. On such occasions, he expressed a fulfillment and lightness of being that comes only from being able to solve problems that have defeated other men. I think these proofs that he was as smart as anyone else surprised even him. These were moments of true discovery for him and a joy for me to witness.

He called on the phone one day, which he rarely did. "Stevan, do you remember the chemical pumps that sat at the base of the pump jacks?"

"Those little square-bodied metal things, about a foot high? Sure, I remember them. What about 'em?"

"Well, we've been sending those out to be repaired by pump shops my whole career. No one ever tried to rebuild them. Today, I bought a $5.50

kit and fixed one of the pumps that we've paid over a hundred dollars each time we sent them out for all these years."

He knew that I was really good at cost controls He was sharing a profound achievement in my area of interest.

When we were kids or when I visited home, I relished the chance to ride with him in his company pickup while he made runs to oilfields. He would proudly carry any of his kids with him on his daily routine, which entailed checking dozens of wells per day. When he was in a pickup and had the freedom to do so, he would take me by the yard and tell his supervisor, "Robbie, Stevan is going to ride with me today, if that's okay."

"Sure, Melvin. I wish my kids were interested enough to come with me."

One day, when I was thirty-nine, we were driving around together checking oil wells when he asked, "How are you doing on time?"

"I have as long as you do." These moments had become extraordinarily special to me. It didn't matter what he had in mind. We drove thirty minutes to a different part of the county and pulled up on a location that looked just like every other location in the county. But I could tell from his quiet, almost respectful demeanor as we got close that something special had happened here.

Dad told me about the gas well, which they completed the previous year. But the pressure at the wellhead was too high, and his company sold into a low-pressure line. The engineers tried to adjust the choke, along with the pumpers and other technicians. No one had been able to get it set right, and the well had been having problems since it was drilled, meaning they were not getting revenue from it. A month or so before, Robbie asked Dad to shut the well in until they could get a specialist out of Houston.

"I came out here to shut it in and started looking at things. All of a sudden, I just got an idea," he told me. "I tried it and got the choke set. We didn't have to bring a specialist out of Houston. That would have cost the company one thousand dollars plus travel expenses. Not to mention, we are selling natural gas every day that would not be sold if the well had been shut in. That well pays my monthly salary in a day. Think of that, I made more for the company by getting that well on the sales line than I make in salary."

He was lost in a sense of fulfillment. Those kinds of numbers come naturally to me, and I knew before he started the explanation that his kind of experience cannot be taught. I think it was one of the proudest moments of his life. He had proved once again, to himself—and maybe to me—that he was smarter than he had believed.

"Dad, you're a natural," I told him, bursting with my own degree of pride.

The Noblest Choice of All

I recognized that Dad had a gift for visualizing, for just doing things that I do not have. I ended up more like Mom in many ways, tenacious and hard driving. When Dad slipped into his sweet spot, into his expertise, he moved effortlessly. Gravity pulls more at me. I plod toward my goals slowly, contemplatively. I have had to work hard at everything I've done.

The man or woman who chooses to go to work every day to provide a better life for his or her family is making one of the noblest choices in life. A husband and father is called to live a sacrificial life; if he does it, the country is stronger. If he does not, the wreckage of human lives begins to bog down our society and sacrifice our children.

"Remember those math classes under Rocky?" I asked him, referring to the year in high school when I worked every night until midnight or later to learn what others learned on the first pass through the textbook. He just laughed his big belly laugh that let me know he appreciated what I had said, how I was pointing out the differences between us.

When Dad let loose his moorings, he seemed to be free, to soar like the birds he constantly brought home to raise.

When he retired, he began to carve wooden airplanes again, using all the ingenuity that had been dormant for decades.

I think pushing him years before had played heavily in his decision to insist on a promotion before he retired. It still remains a profound moment in my life, when my father pushed out to freedom and shared his deepest fulfillments with me.

I never recognized his great talent until I was grown. I had been too close to recognize it before. His abilities were obscured by the lowly station

I thought he occupied in the oilfield, which was reinforced by where we lived in the camp and comments made by kids at school.

He wanted to be a ballplayer or a veterinarian. He could have done well as an artist, or a produce farmer, or raising pigs full-time, but the fear of risk, the fear of failure, and the fear of banks held him in a prison for many years. It was not until late in his life, freed from the cares of child rearing, that he began to break free.

Being afraid, being poor, getting married young, having six hungry mouths to feed, and not getting an education all robbed him of many of his dreams. Those days of talking about his triumphs in solving problems were the deepest glimpse I ever got into his sadness and losses. He was actually very smart, but had been taught that he wasn't. For all the people Mom helped escape from personal prisons, she could never help her husband escape.

But there is another side to the story. Not one of loss but of gain. One of the biblical principles that is easy to say but hard to process is when the man is encouraged to "pour himself out" for his wife and family. He is to sacrifice his life, if need be, for the security and safety of his family. I have watched many men and many families, and I have never seen a person so blessed with the skills and natural abilities of my father sacrifice all the talents and gifts to put bread on the table every day. His commitment to us was unflinching, no matter what it cost him personally.

The man or woman who chooses to go to work every day to provide a better life for his or her family is making one of the noblest choices in life. A husband and father is called to live a sacrificial life; if he does it, the country is stronger. If he does not, the wreckage of human lives begins to bog down our society and sacrifice our children.

I remember when I was seven years old, sitting with Mom as she proudly watched from the stands when my father played softball in the Oil League in Eunice, where the other players called him "Lefty." He had a left-handed swing that, in the replays in my mind, looks just like Babe Ruth's—a natural swing, using his whole body to launch a rocket over the center field fence. I could tell by the respect the teammates showed that my adoration was not just because he was my father. He was really good.

15

MY MOTHER

When we lived at the oil camp, constant reminders of our status surrounded us. The superintendents and engineers lived at one end in the well-built houses, the roustabouts at the other. Mom began to use the oil camp as her metaphor. Her kids, she'd say, were going to attend college and become engineers, so we could live at the other end of the camp. Just as she had overcome the obstacles in O'Donnell, we could defeat the pecking order of the oil camp. We could overcome gravity and move up in life.

Mom's discussions made sense to my fear-filled mind. I began to envision the way out as she had painted it. At five years of age, I asked Dad's supervisor, Ollie White, if I could have Dad's job when he died. Ollie was Dad's gang pusher, a mid-level manager, who lived about halfway between our house and the other end of the camp. I figured I didn't have to get to the other end in one move, but could start the process early. At about eight years old, I began to dream of being an engineer, moving to the other end of the camp, then building Mom a new house like the engineers had. She liked that kind of talk.

She was the one who always pushed us and encouraged us to establish a new normal, to push for greater prosperity. Dad kept to familiar tracks, seeking freedom and solitude, early on with his dogs and hunting and later trading in that hobby to grow 4-H pigs.

Mom had lived as poor in childhood as Dad; they were down-the-road neighbors. She grew up hoeing and picking cotton the same as Dad did. But she always had a belief she could and should do better, while he seemed to worry that, if he moved too high, his family would believe he thought he was better than them. Dad worked hard but was content in his circumstances, so it was Mom who kept us moving up in life, pushing against the gravitational pull of poverty and the established order. She insisted that Dad leave the farm and find a better life and that he take the job with the major oil company.

It was Mom who wanted to get us all away from the bad influences and culture of the oil camp. When they decided it was time to move from the camp, Mom was the one who traded the little house on Cecil Street as a down payment on the five acres at Nadine. It was Mom who had to look for an old house to move to the little plot of ground.

Later, when she would get us up early to hoe our garden in Nadine, she would be out there with us, flailing away with her hoe, trying to dispel the ugliness of weeds from our garden. But all the time she was also planting a different crop in us: new aspirations, beliefs, and hope.

Mom was the one who worried about paying the bills. Dad rarely concerned himself with that, believing that since he worked hard, we would have to live on whatever he made. When the possibility of a job with a major oil company came up, she is the one who calculated what the family could afford if Dad's pay were to double. It was Mom who insisted the family needed the health insurance and the company savings plan offered by the major company.

She was the one who tried to domesticate us, house break us, and make us fit for human consumption. She was the consummate teacher, wasting no moment of the day or night as a learning opportunity. Standardized lessons (i.e. school homework), lessons of the world, social graces, and maturing were all in her daily curriculum.

When I went at ten years of age to talk to Tootie Schnaubert about a job, and I could only manage to stammer, it was Mom who gently prodded me. I needed to learn how to talk to people, and she coached. She continued to work with me on this front well into my high school years.

With five boys and one girl to raise, I rarely saw Mom sad or in tears. But one day, when I was driving the car to the Pearce grandparents' for Christmas, we got a mile from their house and I hit the brakes too hard. The blueberry pie she had baked flipped off the shelf behind the rear seat and landed upside down on the fabric, spilling all about. It was supposed to be our contribution to the potluck lunch, and that was the closest I ever saw her to tears. It was like all those years, living with five boys and their heathen ways, came splattering down in that one spilled pie.

Way Ahead of Her Time

Mom took responsibility for teaching us everything we needed to know in life, and then some. Dad had an old '47 Ford pickup that we used to hunt coyotes. I was still too young for school when Mom said one day to Dad, "Melvin, don't you think it's time to take Stevan for a ride in the truck?"

It seemed to be a prearranged signal, but I didn't know what was coming. Dad never took joyrides or left with just one of the kids singled out to ride along. Something was up.

I got into the middle with Mom on one side and Dad on the other, and we bumped along out the dirt road in back of the camp, out to the low sand hills and mesquites.

Finally, Dad said, "Do you want to learn to drive?"

My interest level picked up considerably. I steered the truck around for a little while, then, out of nowhere, Mom started into an explanation of the birds and bees. "Stevan, do you remember when you asked last week about the rooster that was fighting with the hen, pecking her neck from behind?"

The fun of driving evaporated, and I realized I had been tricked. I wanted out of there.

"Well, Stevan, the rooster was not fighting or hurting the hen. They were mating. It's how animals breed. It's how babies are born."

That made about as much sense to me in my preschool years as if Mom had been lecturing on nuclear physics. But Mom never mastered the art of finesse or timing. When she saw something that needed attention, she bulldozed into it right then. She was more interested in breaking me in to the cold hard facts of life, albeit while I was learning to drive, a symmetry that stayed with me well into college.

Mom was way ahead of her time; sex education did not get talked about in general society for another twenty years or so. If she was ahead of society, she was even further ahead of me; the birds and bees and breeding were not on my radar at five years of age.

Mom's Broad Vision

Both Mom and Dad were very competitive, but in different ways. Our work in 4-H was no exception. Dad helped us win awards with our livestock, but Mom's vision was broader. She helped us win not only county and state but also national contests in events that spun off from the 4-H program.

She saw to it that members of the club completed their record books each year and that they were entered into national record book contests. She figured out the winning formula for the record books, and our little 4-H club, at the forgotten place of Nadine, New Mexico, turned out several state record book winners, two national winners, and one Presidential Tray winner as the top 4-H Achievement winner in the nation.

One of Mom's students landed in that first group of one hundred inductees into the National 4-H Hall of Fame when it was established in 2002. That class included the founder of 4-H and people who had contributed millions to the program, including J. C. Penny, the man behind one of the first clothing store chains.

Mom was also the first to speak up about right and wrong. She was both the matriarch and moral compass of our family. It's not that Dad did wrong, but he seldom expressed how and why he chose not to.

In the late '50s, the 4-H club organized a skating party. When the skating rink manager refused to let black members of the club into the rink,

Mom led everyone out the door. She was not going to tolerate discrimination. When she gathered us up and ushered us out, I was confused, not knowing what had happened. But she didn't give us explanations or a lecture on the manager's behavior; she just did the right thing. Again, she was years ahead of the national conversation that would take place in the 1960s.

She was not an activist. In fact, she had little respect for people who made public stirs. She never said much, but when issues came up, she took a stand. Dad stood beside her in that stance, but it was Mom leading the way and making the decision.

Sermons Lived

Mom had a very complex view outside the home that eventually began to make sense as well, not because I understood it theoretically, but because it made sense when I tried it. She had the capacity to completely overlook the same things in people outside the family that she would not tolerate in her own family. In things relating to us, she was all business. The rules included no alcohol, no wasted time, and similar restrictions; no unplanned sorties existed in her routine, which was driven by too many kids, too little money, and too little time.

I saw this nuanced side of her in action one spring day when the two of us were leaving Brownfield after visiting her sister. I was surprised when she took a different road. We drifted around the fields as she tried to find the right turn. I was junior-high age and had never seen her act this way. She certainly would not have tolerated such aimlessness from any of us. Finally, she saw her objective, and we proceeded in confident fashion along the dirt roads, picking our way through the freshly plowed, sandy fields to a small trailer house, not too different from the one Brigitte lived in at Nadine.

Then motioning me to get out and go to the door with her, she opened it without knocking and yelled in, "Bill? Bill, are you in there?"

When she got no response, we proceeded to enter the trailer, and in a routine that was obviously familiar, she washed the dishes, did the laundry, and cleaned the house. After that we left, never seeing Bill and with me not knowing who he was. I didn't ask and she didn't volunteer the information. She drove home in silent reflection, and neither of us brought the subject up at home among the rest of the family. She sporadically stopped at the old trailer house through the years and cleaned things up, departing without leaving a note or message of any kind. I was along on a couple of the cleaning trips but never knew who it was that Mom checked on.

I would see this same sort of unspoken intervention, in a variety of forms with a variety of recipients, for the rest of her life, especially if I watched closely.

The same year I got my driver's license, Mom solemnly approached me one day and handed me the keys to the family car and, with the seriousness of sending a child off to war, gave me instructions. "I have a friend from high school who has a drinking problem. The Stateline Bar, just east of Hobbs, called and told me he is there, passed out. I want you to take the car, go to the state line [three miles east of Hobbs], pick him up, and drive him home." It was an unspoken understanding that this was not to be one of the things we talked about, to each other or among the family.

Filled with a sense of being an insider, I went to the bar, steeled my nerves, and walked in. I had never been in a bar nor had I been around alcohol or alcoholics. All eyes turned and fixed on me. Someone motioned me toward a small man slumped over with his head on a table, dead drunk. I stood beside him, waiting. One of the patrons finally came over and roughly shook him, grabbed an arm, and jerked him up. Inside the bar, they were familiar with him. They had little patience and far more experience dealing with him. We wrestled him to his feet and more or less carried the incapacitated man to my car. We got him in the front seat before the guy helping looked at me, shook his head with sadness and a tinge of disgust, and walked back into the bar.

I drove an hour following directions that Mom had given me, which took me to the same trailer, out in the middle of the sandy farm country, where we had stopped to clean before. He was easier to rouse by the time we got to his house. I helped him inside, looked at the weeks of unfinished dishes and filth that he lived in, and turned to leave. Bill was slurring badly but began to thank me. He seemed humiliated that I was seeing him that way, but then he passed out again. Feeling my mom's compassionate tug at my heart, I stepped back in and washed the dishes while he slept before leaving without waking him.

Through the years, when Mom and I were out, she would stop by his trailer once in a while. Usually, he was not there, and the two of us would go in the unlocked front door and wash the dishes and sweep red sand out of the carpet as best we could. The cleaned dishes were the only note I ever saw her leave.

Decades later, I found out that Bill was a childhood friend who served in the army in the European theater. One night he and others were in a foxhole that was hit by an artillery shell. He got up to run, only then to realize that he had been shot as his leg collapsed beneath him. It had to be amputated just above his knee. He was a farmer at heart but felt as though he could not operate a tractor. He married a local girl, but when his drinking problem worsened, she left him.

Mom declared, "I felt like he needed help as a veteran, so that's why I went to clean his house and do other things that needed to be done." So she watched over him from a distance without ever telling anyone.

Uncle Jay's Death

One day, when I was still in high school, my uncle Jay rolled his pickup while driving on the Carlsbad highway and was killed in the accident. Uncle Jay was among my earliest memories in Hobbs. Our family stayed with him in those early days when our truck broke down and we had hitchhiked to town.

Jay and his wife, JoAnn, ran the bar at Arkansas Junction, fifteen miles west of Hobbs. She confided in us, "Jay carried all our money in a cigar box under the seat of the pickup," so Mom and I drove to the accident site. The pickup had been towed off, and the cigar box was nowhere to be found, but we combed through the broken glass and scarred ground. Sure enough, we began to find coins there in the dirt. We scraped together several dollars in change and carried it back to JoAnn. She was beside herself.

Mom and JoAnn drifted off by themselves as I stood outside the bar. I could tell by their glances in my direction that the discussion was about me, which seemed strange. Then they walked back over to fill me in. JoAnn was telling Mom that she had bills to pay, was barely scraping by, and could not afford to shut the bar down. JoAnn's problem became Mom's problem, and I had became Mom's instrument to help. It was assumed by the two women that I was their only choice. JoAnn was afraid anyone else would steal the inventory, so they hatched a plan where I would run the bar for several days until the funeral was over.

I was more than happy to help, but I was underage and did not like the idea of being in a bar or serving alcohol to people. The only time I had been in one was to pick up Bill. My folks didn't drink, and I knew nothing about which alcohol went with what and wasn't even familiar with the different brands of beer.

It seemed that the plan was in complete contrast to the moral lessons we learned three times a week at church and from both parents at home, but the years have convinced me it instead captured the essence of those lessons. Outside the home, Mom rarely spoke her sermons. She just lived them.

After the deal was set, JoAnn bolted out the door and yanked the key out as though she was jerking loose from an anchor that was pulling her to the bottom of the ocean. When she handed the keys to me, I got the impression that it was not all grief.

I began my three-day career as a bartender with no instruction other than how to manage the tricky lock on the front door.

I never had the desire to drink. I would hang around with my buddies who drank. I was the designated driver before there were designated drivers. Even in the Air Force, when I went to the Officer Club (which has some similarity to a fraternity house), I didn't drink. I didn't take my first sip of alcohol until I was twenty-eight, having seen firsthand the painful lessons it has to teach.

Breaking Free

Even as Mom was helping others, she was beginning to break out of her own cages. She started college the same year that I did, getting her bachelor's degree from Eastern New Mexico in two-and-a-half years and her masters degree in two summer sessions from Texas Tech.

The lion was unleashed in her and doing its work. As she broke free, she began to see the needs around her—everywhere. The prisoners of life needed liberating and that became her mission. Her job as a teacher and later as a counselor at New Mexico Junior College constantly put her in contact with people needing a lifeline, people with no other hope.

It was as though all the energy Mom had as a young child, seeing that her childhood family was fed and out the door each day, and later with her own six children, was too much to be contained within our walls. She had the energy to minister to the whole of Hobbs, and so she did. It was her purpose in life, being loosed with a reason and motivation to kick people in the seat of their pants, grab them by the collar to lift them up, or quietly give them encouraging words.

She had the uncanny ability to sense a need and move toward it like a soldier in battle. She could even discern which approach worked best with each person. She tolerated no weakness or self-pity among those whom she helped. Mom was not interested in creating people who would rely on her, but who could become self-sufficient. She valued counseling and would direct people who were in need to the right help.

After several years, JoAnn, Jay's widow, came to see Mom again. "I want to do something with my life. I am just dragging from bar to bar. I need to get my GED." Simple as that, Mom helped her get her GED, then enrolled her in the junior college. JoAnn finished her degree in her fifties and became a special education teacher in Alamogordo.

Mom then helped her daughter, who wanted a college education so badly she stayed in a pickup camper and washed up in the restrooms at school to finish her degree at NMSU.

A friend from Mom's class in high school was trying to get a degree to become a teacher, but she had two children. In the midst of it, she confessed to Mom, "I am going to kill myself. My husband invited a buddy from his military years to spend a few days with us, and I had an affair with him. I am not fit to live with." Mom carried her to the Guidance Center for counseling, where they helped her deal with her mistake without ending her life. She finished her degree and taught school in Lovington.

Mrs. Tripplett was working at the Lamplighter Motel as a maid when Mom told her, "You can do better." She started studying with her kids, got a GED, and got a job at a bank, where she started by making coffee but was soon promoted to teller.

The Alvarez family had six girls. Their father (whom we knew from his work at Tootie's Supermarket) was killed in a car accident and left them with nothing. Mom, aware of their situation, immediately went to work helping the women find better positions. She got one daughter, Estella, a secretary, into school. Dellia was a secretary also, and Mom told her she could be a teacher. After enrolling in school, she went on to not only become a teacher but a principal. Mom told their mother, Francis, she could go to school, too, and she became an English as a Second Language (ESL) instructor. Later reflecting on the story, Mom said, "When Francis started seeing her own potential, she shot up like she was fired out of a cannon."

Hope is in each of us; it just has to be ignited.

JoAnn brought a friend to see Mom about attending school. Faye had on a sleazy bar dress when she showed up, was overweight, and missing front teeth. But when she took her tests, she made the highest scores possible. Mom got her into the nursing program, and she became an LPN. She lost weight, got new teeth, married, was baptized, and turned her life around. Mom opened the door and let the lion do its work.

A girl came one day and asked Mom if she thought she could pass the GED. Mom thought everyone could pass. The girl tested, passed, and then ran across the campus shouting for everyone to join her in the student union, "Drinks are on me!" Students came from all over campus and celebrated with her. Later, the girl came and told Mom, "I had decided I would kill myself if you told me I could not pass, that there was no hope. But I thought, *Surely, there is someone who will believe in me.*" She came to the right place; Mom believed in everyone.

Mom went on to start a program called Women in Transition, to formalize and continue the work she had been doing with individuals. The women were transitioning after the death of a spouse, a divorce, or just trying to help their husbands pay the bills. Many people, mostly women, come up to me all the time in Hobbs and say something like, "If it wasn't for your Mom . . . ," and then they finish their particular story.

Mom knew nothing about things being too hard or too challenging. She knew nothing of defeat and believed every obstacle was just one more thing to overcome.

All the government programs in the world and all the government spending cannot do what one woman with the belief that every individual has the skills to succeed can accomplish. All the TV ads and all the articles encouraging children to stay in school do not replace the burning desire a mother can implant in her child's heart.

Outstanding Women

In 1985, the state of New Mexico initiated a program called "The Governor's Award for Outstanding New Mexico Women." At that period of the program, they chose thirty women to recognize, but they interviewed them to select just one as *The Outstanding Woman.*

In the third year of the program, I submitted an application for Mom, providing an extensive write-up about the things she had accomplished with and for women. Her lifelong passion was to keep lives, especially women's, from being wasted by helping people get out of bad circumstances, into college, and into better careers, and it deserved recognition.

Sure enough, word arrived that the judges had selected Mom as one of the thirty women being considered for the 1988 award. They invited her to Albuquerque for the interview to determine who would be the single outstanding woman of the year. She went and returned to Hobbs without saying much. She later asked if I would go with her to the awards banquet where the top woman recipient would be announced.

We drove to Albuquerque and showed up for the dinner and recognition ceremony. I sat waiting, confident that no one in the state could have done more. But instead of Mom, they chose a woman who had been state librarian for thirty-plus years. I was shocked. That woman had gone to work and done her job well for all those years, but Mom changed women's lives. She fought those early battles helping minority women get jobs, get into school, and out of bad circumstances. She had been an impact player. And the committee passed her over.

Years later, Mom told me why. She said that the interview was going well until they asked her one question: "What do you think would be the most important thing women could do for the country?" She knew the answer they wanted—a politically correct answer. She considered what she believed, weighed the consequences of that answer, then opted against winning in favor of her beliefs. It was classic Mom. No compromise.

Her answer: "The most important thing for women, if they have children, is to be home with their children, at least until the kids get into school. Women," she continued, "are making a false choice, sacrificing their children for careers. They should postpone their careers until the children are started correctly in life."

If at all possible, families should stay together and raise their children to be productive members of society. She observed that she had helped many single women and had helped others get out of destructive relationships, but that, she declared, should be the alternative rather than the first choice.

The committee, which up to that moment had been engaged and supportive, responded exactly how she thought they would, suddenly going cold. She knew they had chosen against her, just as she thought they would. She observed in the telling of the story to me, "I would do the same thing again today. If women have children, the children should be the priority."

Mom specialized in people who had lost hope. With her children, it was always a given that we would go to college, that we would have hope and compete in life. It was barely less of a mandate for nonfamily members.

Mom's tenacity, integrity, and her unflinching interaction with the problems of life dominated her decisions and fueled her desire to help others . . . and made an indelible imprint on my life.

Tanis

My only sister, Tanis, got her name from a young Hispanic girl whom Mom met when she worked at Franklin's dress shop. Mom thought the girl and the name were beautiful. There were five of us boys and one girl . . . I tell people she outnumbered the boys.

Tanis is a lot like my mom; she just sees needs around her and goes out to solve them.

In the discussion about education reform, the "educrats" usually run down the private or charter schools, stating, "They will only take the cream of the crop kids. They won't take the problem kids. If charter or private schools are allowed, the public schools will devolve into warehouses for the poor and disadvantaged."

I have always disagreed with that assertion and argued that the people who launch out away from the safety of the public schools will generally be motivated by principle. They will be trying to cure some portion of our education system.

Mom's tenacity, integrity, and her unflinching interaction with the problems of life dominated her decisions and fueled her desire to help others . . . and made an indelible imprint on my life.

Tanis is an extraordinary example of this. After teaching special ed for years, she started a charter school with the Houston Independent School District that was for kids who had been in jail. You could not get into her school *unless* you had been in jail. In Houston, she had lots of takers. That charter proved too hard, even for her, so she backed off to where you could only get into her school if you had been kicked out of every school. In other words, her school was the last resort for kids whom the school system had given up on. In her early years, she was taking seventy-eight students a year and graduating seventy-six of the seventy-eight.

I asked Tanis how she did that. She nonchalantly raised an open palm in the air and ever so slowly closed the palm into a fist. I told her I was still from New Mexico and did not speak sign language, so she would have to interpret. Repeating the motion while speaking, she explained, "You have to slow them down and stop them. Still. Quiet. After they have been still and quiet for six to twelve weeks, they can hear. Before that, they just can't focus. Sometimes I have to grip the parents and slow them down. When everyone is quiet and can listen, we make very good progress."

Not only is she graduating such a high percentage, she also makes the kids get jobs, which is teaching them responsibility and self-reliance. Of the ones who graduate, a high percentage go on to college.

But she did not begin at the point of confidence or knowing the full way forward. She said, "On my first day at the charter school, my knees were knocking. I realized we took some tough kids with extreme behavior problems . . . and gradually we sent the ones out for whom there was no way we could help."

So what motivated Tanis to do what she's doing? Struck by how fast life goes by and feeling as though time was running out, she had an urgency to step up and do more to help others. Similar to my mom, she gravitated to the need, said, "Yes, Lord, I will go," and opened the cage door. She sees the miracle waiting to happen in the ones the rest of society has declared "expendable."

Tanis looks for no recognition but says, "I felt so grateful for life and that God has enabled us to be here to experience being wives, husbands, mothers, fathers, grandparents, and teachers."

From Tanis, I see the life lessons of our family—do what you know how to do, use what you have, start where you are, and have faith in God. It's the story of life . . . her life and our lives.

Greg

My youngest brother, Greg, was a pistol from the time he was born.

When Philip was ten, he had appendix surgery and was healing slowly, walking bent over and taking it easy on the stitches. Greg, who was six at the time, came up behind him and kicked him in the backside. Philip straightened up, ripping out all the stitches.

The 4-H projects always took us to the county, state, and regional fairs. When Greg was seven, one of the 4-H adults saw him using a long piece of baling wire to burst a carnival booth's balloons. Finally, they gave him a balloon as a bribe to allow them to conduct their business. Satisfied, he marched off with the trophy in his hand.

From an early age he excelled in baseball and football. When he was nine, he won a trip to the Houston Astrodome in a punt, pass, and kick contest. Dad became a coach on Greg's youth baseball team and coached them into the regional finals. Greg went on to be the starting quarterback on the Hobbs varsity football team and a pitcher for the baseball team, winning all-district honors in football and receiving an athletic scholarship to attend college.

When I got home from Vietnam, Greg talked me into playing on their equivalent to the "semipro" team I had played on during high school. When I was taking some practice pitches from Greg, I had the old feel of the catcher in my dreams. Finally, I told him I was ready and he could throw harder. His next pitch was a heater, right down the pipe. I did not have time to move the glove, and it thunked me in the chest. I had lost a little reflex time, but mostly his pitch was that fast and hard. He was good.

It took six kids, but Dad's dream of having a star athlete in the family had been fulfilled. Similar to Dad, though, Greg was not able to use that raw talent to take him to the bright lights. The pull of gravity was too strong.

He did succeed in responding to some of the great challenges in business, being one of the first businessmen to travel to Russia as it emerged and tried to move to a free market. He was years ahead of their ability to accept entrepreneurship. He went on to engage in one of the emerging challenges for humanity . . . finding ways to clean water for reuse.

16

LIFE'S FORMATIVE
EXPERIENCES

My brother Tommy worked several summers at the local Weichmann's Nursery before he succeeded in getting me hired. It was the summer before my eighth-grade year. Tommy was good with people and worked with customers in the retail sales part of the business, delivering and planting the trees he sold. I was so quiet and shy that the manager put me out back, pulling a one hundred-foot garden hose and filling every container with water, day after day, in the summer heat of New Mexico. But I was satisfied.

That year, an infestation of webworms hit Hobbs, and Carl Weichmann sold hundreds of quarts of malathion for people to spray their trees. When the problem persisted, people worried they would lose their forty- and fifty-year-old trees. They could not spray the large trees themselves, so Mr. Weichmann bought a battered spray unit mounted on a homemade two-wheeled trailer. Then he dispatched Tommy and me in his old two-ton truck with rickety sideboards to pull the trailer up and down the alleys, spraying trees in the backyards of Hobbs. I was not old enough to have a driver's license, so Tom (in the tenth grade) drove, and I stood in the back of the truck, spraying the trees.

One afternoon I was up on the ladder spraying, when I noticed Paula Copeland in the yard next door, sunbathing in a bikini. Paula was one of the cutest seventh graders at Heizer Junior High. She was two years younger than me, but I knew who she was. When I laid eyes on her, the worms I was spraying did not die from the poison—I drowned them, with my mouth nearly hanging open. And Tom had no idea what was taking so long. Once or twice a week for the rest of the summer, I talked him into driving the old truck down that alley to douse the worms, just in case they came back. But Paula was never outside again.

The next summer, Mr. Weichmann bid to landscape the fire department substation and the yards in the new subdivision being built around Highland Junior High School, projects that promised to take up the entire summer. I still had not lost the urge to connect with Tom, to get on the same team with him, so I was happy to get the nod that the two of us would become "landscape architects." That meant I dug the holes, and Tom walked around placing the bushes. He followed me, spreading peat moss and steer manure in the holes as he planted. When I finished digging, I went back and watered the plants.

One day, we were working on the lawn of a house when the lady who lived in it came running out. "What are you kids doing here?"

Tom was the spokesman. "We are here to landscape your yard."

"You get out of my yard. I contracted with Mr. Weichmann for a landscaped yard. I expect professionals. Get on out of here. I am calling him right this minute."

I was ready to pack up and go, but not Tommy. He resolutely continued placing plants around the yard. Under his breath, he chastised me, "Keep digging those holes. That heifer is not going to run us off."

Meanwhile he was carrying on a conversation with the woman. "Ma'am, I am Mr. Weichmann's landscaper. I have worked there for three years, and Mr. Weichmann personally trained me." (All of that was sort of true—the length of service was, but Mr. Weichmann never trained

Tommy on anything. He had learned it on his own and had a natural talent for design and planning.)

I looked first at Tommy, then the woman. She kept pressuring us to leave, but Tom had engaged her about where she would like the trees placed in the yard. While she was trying to run us off, she would slip into a conversation with Tom about the placement of trees and shrubs. We didn't leave, though she didn't quit threatening us either. Tom, as usual, displayed his ability to get along with women, even getting the job done under pressure. He never told me what Mr. Weichmann said in the end.

Managing Gravity

We also got sent out to "top trees," pruning the limbs that were rubbing against a house or getting tangled in the electrical and phone wires. We used that same rattling old truck, taking a variety of long-handled handsaws to cut the highest branches in the trees. This was years before Asplundh set up its nationwide service. We were the only game in town.

I had strong arms from milking our Jersey cow, so I could get after the sawing thing. Tom liked working with me, but I was not very mindful of the physics of tree trimming at first. I dropped limbs through a couple of electrical wires and telephone cables before realizing I had to plan for gravity. Once I was clued in, my mathematical mind started calculating the geometry of the falls.

One day we got a call from the woman who lived at the house on the corner of Yucca and Fowler Streets. She wanted her tree topped, as it was getting into the wires and hanging over the fence. The house, fence, and wires were all potential targets for me to avoid hitting with falling limbs.

I had gotten pretty good at tying ropes to the branches and causing them to fall without crushing anything. This tree, however, was big and the fall lines were complex. Tom was the one in charge and always dispatched me to climb to the highest part of the tree to start cutting. He worked the larger lower branches. We had cut several limbs and the rope-tethered trajectories I laid out were working perfectly. We hadn't hit a thing. We were not defeating gravity, but managing it.

With just a few limbs remaining, I began working on a monster limb,

152 | *Just Fly the Plane, Stupid!*

nearly ten inches in diameter. It had the potential to fall on both the fence and the house, so I tied a series of ropes to it. The first one would pull it away from the fence; the next would apply pressure to keep it off the house. To reach the limb, I was standing on an even larger limb, sawing above my head. I paused to rest often, cross-checking the fall pattern each time.

Tom was working on a limb below, standing on a ladder. As I rechecked the fall line, I noticed he had taken up a position in the last radius of the planned fall path, near the tree trunk. "Tommy, I am not sure, but I think my limb is going to swing right where you are. You might move." He looked up at my contraption of ropes and at the limb I was cutting.

"You aren't halfway through. Tell me when you get closer."

I resumed sawing and stopped for yet another rest. "Tommy, you need to move."

He looked again. I still had about a third of the branch to go. A mere sliver could often hold a limb firmly in place. "You still have a long way to go." He resumed sawing on his own branch.

What neither of us was calculating was the effect of sawing from the bottom of a limb. Gravity is a constant force on the tree limbs, but it has much different outcomes when the limb is cut from the top rather than when it is cut from the bottom. I began to saw again when, suddenly, I heard a pop and a crack. The sound was crisp, not the creaking, building crack that comes when the limbs break from the top. The cellulosic fibers were giving up the struggle to hold the limb in place and pressure was building. I yelled, "Get out of the way!"

He looked up, did not see the limb sagging, and went back to work.

Just then the remaining fibers gave up simultaneously. The pop sounded like a cannon shot as the limb broke free in one swift motion. As it fell toward the fence, my first rope grabbed and changed its trajectory toward the house, then my next rope pulled taut and stopped the movement toward the house. The two acting in concert pulled the limb right toward Tommy. In a split second, the full weight of the limb slammed like a battering ram square into his back, right where I thought it would hit. He folded over the limb in front of him like a rag doll as I watched helplessly from above.

I thought he was dead. "Tommy! Tommy!" No answer. "Tommy!" I was crying, but I was too high in the tree to help him. He began to writhe around but was afraid he would fall out of the tree. Somehow, he made it half-conscious back down the ladder, knocking it down as he fell off the last step and collapsed at the base of the tree. Now I was stuck in the tree, and he was on the ground not moving, not answering.

Gradually, he came to, rolled over, and told me I had to finish the tree by myself before dark. The pay for the project only covered our labor through the end of the day. With no way to get down, I started sawing furiously. I regretted hurting him and didn't want to go over the allotted time as well. (Tommy missed a couple days of work but was okay and never mentioned the incident.)

Debt Collection

I worked the summer of my tenth-grade year at C. R. Anthony's, a regional clothing store chain in the Broadmoor Shopping Center in Hobbs. I had just gotten my driver's license. Paul Zahn, the local manager, knew Mom and hired me. He drove a new canary yellow Cadillac to work every day. One day, he took me back to his office and gave me the keys and a two-inch stack of hot checks to collect, instructing me to drive his car to the addresses on the checks to collect the delinquent cash.

I couldn't imagine doing that at all, but I didn't say a word. Instead, I took the checks and headed for the car before he changed his mind. I killed time, sorting the checks alphabetically, then by date on the check, trying to work up my courage. Finally, I organized them by areas of town. There were people in all parts of town who had written bad checks, so I decided to start in the poor side of town. I didn't feel as out of place there.

I made my first stop. To my surprise, the person who answered the door was very friendly. She knew the balance in their checking account was low but thought they had enough to cover the check. She gave me the cash, and I left. The rest of the day, taking one check at a time, I heard similar stories and got a similar reception at one house after another. Most of the people were bashful about the overdrafts and paid immediately. Some promised if I would come back later in the week, after payday, they would make good on the checks.

Late in the afternoon, I started on the houses in the rich end of town. Ironically, I had less success there. Several people were angry; doors slammed in my face. It didn't take long for me to figure out that how much you make doesn't create wealth, but how much you save. People on the rich side of town made more, but many spent more and lived payday to payday just like the rest of the people in town. They did not appreciate my being there to remind them that, with all their money and fancy houses, they were just as deeply overdrawn as the folks on the poor side of town.

By the time I got back to the store and reported to Mr. Zahn, I had collected over nine hundred dollars. He was shocked and sent me out the rest of the week. After the week of debt collections, I had gotten more than three thousand dollars from hot checks—money he thought the store would never see. We were equally surprised.

The experience was far more profitable for me than for C. R. Anthony. The store got its money back, but I learned to make cold calls on people and ask them hard questions. I also learned a lifetime of financial discipline from those door-to-door visits.

Most of my life, I have lived virtually debt free. When Cynthia and I got married, she didn't understand why I paid the credit cards off every month.

As a sophomore in high school, I learned not to spend more than I made. I developed a habit of deducting an equal amount out of the checkbook every time I made a credit card purchase. That way the money was there when the credit card bill came in, and I could pay the entire bill off immediately. I knew credit card debt is the most expensive kind to have.

Going to people's homes and seeing the shame that comes from living out of financial control forever seared the lesson into my memory. Later, I would realize Cynthia and I had failed to pass this lesson on to our daughter, who fell into a debt trap of her own after graduating from college.

JFK's Assassination

My parents were registered Democrats, but the discussions around our house were never very political, nor were either of my parents deeply involved in elections or politics. Getting through to the next paycheck, feeding and exercising the livestock, and attending the 4-H fairs consumed all of our energy. There were simply not enough hours in the day to focus on extraneous matters. But we all generally liked President John Fitzgerald Kennedy.

At 11:30 a.m., on November 22, 1963, I was sitting in Miss Wilkerson's third-hour English class when the loudspeaker in each room began to blare with a radio news program. President Kennedy had been shot. We sat in stunned silence. No one spoke. As the picture became more complete, disbelief swept through the entire school.

The tragedy brought Lyndon Johnson to the White House, and that sudden change placed into motion a series of events that greatly impacted my own life, reaching all the way to Nadine.

The $200 Boar

After raising and showing pigs for a few years, we had a family conference to discuss where to take our pig herd. Dad had used funds desperately needed in other areas and subscribed to a monthly magazine, *The Poland China World,* poring over every new issue, studying the pictures and pedigrees of the best Poland China pigs in the nation. He knew that ours did not match up and began to nurture a growing belief that we had to take a chance and invest to upgrade our stock. Dad was not much of a risk taker, but he was leading the discussion. He knew we did not have the money to make the move without risking our future projects.

The entire family gathered around the kitchen table to discuss the future of our pig enterprise. It was a good process; everyone got to express opinions. During the discussion, tempers flared, calmed, and flared again. Looking back, I can see we were not mad at one another. The volatility was a reaction to the risk of failure and the gravity of our situation. We were acutely aware that money was too scarce to sustain a bad decision. We understood that we had reached an equilibrium that could be sustained, repaying the bank loan every year and providing enough extra to fund college for the oldest brothers, but a wrong move could bring our hopes crashing down around us.

In his reading, Dad had isolated three or four farms he thought had the best stock, earmarking the pages in the magazines with his view of the best stock available. During the discussion, those magazines were flying around the table and fingers were jabbing at first one and then the other with exclamation points about their characteristics. I was never very good at picking the young pigs. Dad and my younger brother Philip had those abilities. I saw T charts and understood the business end; expenses and revenues made sense to me. Philip, who was about twelve years old, had developed the keenest eye for stock (other than Dad) and had the strongest opinions supporting the move.

By the time everyone had their say, we fully understood the risks of both acting and not acting. But deep down, we knew we had to get better or go broke. It became clear that we simply needed to make our best guess, because no clear path forward was evident; there was no security, no safety net or insurance for failure. A decision was reached and the commitment was made to push against the status quo, against the gravity of poverty, and move forward into risky territory. Those who had disagreed were on board with the need to upgrade our breeding stock.

We reached consensus to budget the unheard of (for our family) sum of $200 for a new boar.

To give the decision context, it is important to understand the economics of our pig projects. The $200 we were going to spend on our boar was about eight times the cost of our normal show animals, so we would give up eight chances for a pig to make the sale in exchange for one non-show pig that would only breed and produce pigs.

We also decided to buy a pig that was weaning age, a change from our previous purchases of mature boars obtained from other breeders. This change in strategy came with its own risks. Animals at weaning age are unsettled enough, but when they are removed from familiar surroundings and placed among new animals, they will sometimes react in confusion and panic, fighting their new companions or dashing headlong around the small pickup bed, leaping up the side boards, trying to get out. They are susceptible to sudden illness or death in the stress of a move, so there was additional tension over this decision. All these discussions and more had been brought up at that kitchen table.

The best pigs at that time were coming from Oklahoma, and the trips there were like pilgrimages for us. We kids cleaned and washed the pickup bed, covered the floor with fresh sand and clean straw, and installed Dad's homemade shelter for the young pigs. Suitcases were packed and ready before going to school on Friday. After working all day, Dad fueled the truck on his way home from work, and as soon as he got home, one or two of us would pile in beside him. He would drive all night to be in position in Oklahoma to begin looking at pigs all day Saturday and Sunday before driving back and getting home late Sunday night. Gone from the domestications of home, we would sing along with the country stations, tell tall tales, and listen to Dad play his French harp.

The return, in the middle of the night, was no less exciting than I imagine surrounded the arrival of trading ships returning from the New World. There was joyous contemplation as the hours of the evening wore on. No matter how late the arrival, on hearing the pickup pull off the highway and into our caliche driveway, Mom and the remaining kids gathered outside to see the results.

The two kids who had made the trip would go inside and go to bed, while Dad talked quietly to Mom in the dark, shining the flashlight on first one pig, then another, describing the ones left behind, and we all pondered the choices. No matter how late he got in, Dad was up at 4:30 and at work on time after working all weekend on the pig projects.

We had lamb projects and did the same thing with the lambs, but the pigs were our primary business. They were the part we all loved. My uncle Sonny Garnett was a 4-H agent, spending several years in Roosevelt County, New Mexico. He had the same zeal and the same success with lambs that Dad had with pigs.

The trip to buy the boar was similar to past trips but different. It was the same late night drive with the compressed buying of stock. It was different because of the weight of our decision and the amount of money spent on one pig.

Dad and Philip made a huge buy. For $200, they were given the pick of the entire Phipps farm, one of the Oklahoma farms in *The Poland China World*. It was a momentous day and decision for the Pearce house.

Everyone in the family made sure our new boar had the best straw and a heat lamp so he would not freeze in the winter before he was big enough to produce his own heat. He was special, and yet from the first day, something was not quite right. He was not aggressive or assertive and would stand back while all the other pigs would fight their way to the trough. Dad often fed him separately so he would get enough feed to keep growing.

The day for castration came, when all the boar pigs would be turned into show pigs. Once that operation was complete, they would have no other function in life but the market. Our new boar was not castrated, instead being separated from the others in the new pen we built especially for him.

Expectations soared as the young boar matured. The graceful lines of the new breed of pigs winning all the shows began to emerge, and our excitement built as he developed.

But this boar had a curious way of walking, as if his feet were tender and he needed shoes. Pigs are one of the smartest animals and inherently curious, but our new boar did not seem to have much interest in things around him. There was a nagging sense of something being out of place; we wanted to see him act with more authority. But after making such a big decision and big outlay of capital, our concerns were written off as just nerves.

Finally, the big time arrived—the sows were coming into heat, ready to be bred. The young stud had reached maturity and soon would be called on to perform his function in life, breeding the sows of our little herd. It was a momentous occasion. The tempers of the decision night were long since gone, replaced by great expectations. The prospects of success were materializing before our eyes.

It was an unwritten rule that breeding days were something Dad attended to alone. If we showed up, nothing was said and you were not run off, but the next time you did not go. I still am not sure about the dynamics of that.

This breeding day was different in that several of us gathered around. Mom may have even been there. It felt as though everything was at stake. Dad separated the sow in heat from the others, and all of us helped herd the boar over to her pen. The Phipps boar was not fully grown, but he still weighed over 300 pounds.

Usually, all that was needed was to get them close. When the male picked up the scent, nature took over, and he would charge down the lane and into the pen with the sow. But this was different; we had to drive him all the way into the pen. Finally, he got the notion and charged over and began amorous play. But when it came time to go to work, he just could not get it right. He tried to jump up from the side, then from the front. There was nervous laughter from all of us. Half an hour passed and nothing transpired, then he lost interest. Each of us had chores to do, so we left Dad alone with the procreation work while we tended to the more mundane tasks.

Dad came to the house late in the afternoon as the sun was setting. There had not been a successful coupling. He and Mom were having quiet discussions. All of us knew without asking that it had not been a successful outing. We wrote it off to that particular sow . . . until each sow in our herd had been in the pen alone with him. He did not perform. Dad bought hormones for our champion, then sunk more money into the failing investment by having the veterinarian look at him. This high-priced attempt to upgrade our herd was getting more expensive. The diagnosis was that he did not seem to have interest, which all of us kids had already concluded without a professional opinion.

We had never heard of such a thing as this. Nature was nature . . . these things were supposed to occur naturally, but they were not. We never knew what happened. Our boar never had interest in breeding—not that season or the next or the next. We always approached each season with the expectation that his huge bloodlines and his winning characteristics would be passed on to offspring.

I can identify with a coach when I see NFL teams bet their future on a star quarterback, who subsequently fails to make the starting lineup. Our

$200 boar, an astronomical investment for the Pearce family, did not make the starting lineup.

However, despite our concerns, the failure of our boar did not sink our economic ship. It pulled us down, but our enterprise did not crash. We just worked harder and did without. Eventually, we had a series of boars that did in fact upgrade our herd into champions. We defied gravity, paid the bills, and kept afloat.

This experience tempered our worries and fears and freed me from believing that every decision or every day was the decision or day that could ruin an enterprise. It freed me from the fear of taking a chance, of taking a calculated risk. The problems that seem to risk everything can be solved with discipline in spending, fortitude, and hard work. It is not risk that keeps us trapped; it is the desire to remain in our comfort zone that keeps us trapped. We can take calculated risks and survive if they go bad. We can become stronger from the failure. Avoiding the risk of failure is the surest way to stay rooted in the same circumstances, held in the same position by a force stronger than gravity—comfort.

Years later, when I was managing our business and beginning to fear that any particular transaction would sink our company, I remembered the $200 boar that failed and yet we succeeded. I also learned from the powerful lesson that Jesus taught through the Parable of the Talents, where he notes that risk-taking is the essential component of investing and creating wealth. Risk-taking also happens to be the key ingredient of capitalism. In that parable, Jesus congratulates the people blessed with different levels of talent or gifts for starting where they were and using what they had to invest and increase what the master had entrusted to them. The one who took no risk, who buried what he had and dug it up to return it was criticized.

Our little pig enterprise was this lesson in action. Every year we took all our profits and put it into more and better pigs, increasing our economic potential one year at a time.

But an additional lesson was being manifested. The biblical lessons instruct that mankind is forced to labor by the sweat of his brow to convert the natural resources of the world into products of value. Year in and year out, we kids, starting at a very early age, worked hard alongside Mom and Dad to grow those resources (baby pigs) into value that added meat on the store shelf. We learned capitalism from the ground up.

These lessons manifested themselves years later when Cynthia and I took uncomfortable risks and invested all we had and all we made for several years into our business. It was no different from the pig project . . . it just had a few more zeros.

The Israelites were instructed to give the very best of their herds as a sacrifice to help them remember their sufficiency was in God, not their possessions. It suddenly occurred to me one day, decades later, that our entire discussion on the $200 boar was the problem that the Israelites were warned about. When we were pointing out to one another the bloodlines that would be the salvation of the Pearce herd and the Pearce house, we were pointing at the wrong book. We were placing our trust in our own abilities versus placing our ultimate trust in God to meet our needs.

Our lack of resources at the time was a cause for anxiety that led to focusing on our personal abilities to meet our needs. We had forgotten one of the biblical promises God has given: "I will supply all your needs according to my riches." It seems we had fallen into the trap the ancient texts had warned about.

> This experience tempered our worries and fears and freed me from believing that every decision or every day was the decision or day that could ruin an enterprise. It freed me from the fear of taking a chance, of taking a calculated risk. The problems that seem to risk everything can be solved with discipline in spending, fortitude, and hard work. It is not risk that keeps us trapped; it is the desire to remain in our comfort zone that keeps us trapped.

Every person and every family can find a multitude of reasons to not trust God. We had plenty of excuses. We were barely surviving. It was easy to believe that we had been forgotten by God and that maybe he needed a jump-start for our blessing to accrue. We must, instead, exercise faith in order to unleash the blessing of God in response to man's faithfulness to his principles.

Baseball dreams as a twelve-year-old.
That's me in the middle row, the second from the left.

17

COACH SHAW

From age ten and through my high school years, I played, read about, and dreamed of baseball. As a catcher, I knew all the pitchers, and Sandy Koufax was my hero. I'd lie awake at night with a small Japanese transistor radio tucked against my ear, under the blankets so Mom wouldn't know I was listening to the late West Coast games. During the Los Angeles Dodgers games, I strained to hear about every pitch Sandy and Don Drysdale threw.

I imagined myself there in the big league stadium, in front of thousands, decked out in my tools of ignorance, catching Sandy Koufax pitches. I was in Nadine sweating every pitch when Koufax got his third no-hitter in May 1963, defeating the great Juan Marichal and carrying a perfect game into the eighth inning. When he got his fourth no-hitter, I thought no one would ever break his record. No one did until Nolan Ryan, the big Texan, another of my favorites, pitched seven of them.

That year, as a high school sophomore, I tried out for the varsity baseball team. I was still small at 130 pounds, but I made the team as the second-string catcher. I caught the second game of the doubleheaders after the senior catcher, Randy Davis, caught the first.

Against Kermit, one of the tough Texas schools, I made a play at home on a player who looked more like a fullback than a shortstop. The tank-of-a-boy bowled me over as though he was running through a leaf pile. I had to come out of the game, and Randy took my place. He was a starter on the Hobbs football team and weighed one hundred pounds more than me.

Randy's next at bat, he got on first and took aim at the shortstop. Randy was thrown out at second on an infield grounder, but he kept running around second base and hit the shortstop somewhere outside the base path, flattening him. I felt more a part of the team than ever before, thanks to Randy's payback on my behalf.

During my junior year, things really began to gel for me. Coach Jim Witherspoon was the head coach, but the assistant, Coach Dennis Shaw, and I had a connection. He was my hero, having been my eighth-grade English teacher and football coach. I liked him from my first day in his English class. He was young, just out of college, and had moved from Oklahoma to Hobbs to take the job at Heizer Junior High. He was brash, confident, and talked baseball all the time. He was a pitcher during his high school and college years and had pitched in the American Legion World Series. One of his front teeth overlapped the other, but he never seemed self-conscious about it. It made me more comfortable about the gap in my own front teeth.

Coaches in Hobbs didn't talk much about baseball; it was all about basketball. I idolized Coach Shaw. Even when he banged me around the eighth-grade football field, because I was so clumsy, small, and basically a bad player, he could not get rid of me. I had never had a hero up to that point, and I was not going to be shaken off that easily.

A Hero for a Coach

I was still small and clumsy when I entered high school, so I could only imagine what lay in store for me when he was picked as the assistant baseball coach. But I knew one thing: my hero was going to coach me in the sport he and I loved. He started teaching me the science of pitching and catching, the first real instruction I had received, and I sponged up everything he said.

He began by trying to make me think, which was no small challenge. I was as clumsy mentally as I was physically, but he stuck it out. "Pearce," he would shout, "look at the batter's feet." It was my clue that if the batter was off the plate in the batter's box, I should call for a pitch on the outside corner. Or if he was close to the plate, we should jam him with an inside pitch.

"Pearce, if the hitter is digging in on you, getting his feet set, call for the next pitch at him. Not at his head, because he can just swing his head and get out of the way. Throw at his belt. If it is at his body, he has to move his feet. Loosen his feet up.

"How many times do I have to tell you to get inside their head? Know what they're thinking, what they're confident about, and what they don't think they can hit. Pearce, you have to think to be catcher."

The truth is, you have to think to do anything, and I was not good at making those connections. I could do math and grammar with ease, but understanding how everything translated and what it boiled down to was not within my skill set. By contrast, my father seemed natural in everything, making me acutely aware that I was not.

All through the preseason, Coach Shaw pushed and cajoled. But I didn't care how much he jumped on me—he was paying attention to me. And when your hero pays attention, that's all you need.

One day he was jumping on me with particular exuberance, "Pearce, excuse the French, but get your head out of your ass!"

It was the first time I had heard him cuss or had ever heard the expression "excuse the French." We lived a very quiet life in Nadine. I was overexcited about both firsts, feeling included in his world, and yelled back, "Coach, my brother Greg is six years old. He said he wants to be just like you when he grows up!"

He didn't miss a beat. "Maybe you better try knocking some sense into him. Now get back behind the plate." His wry smile told me that he liked the compliment. I had never made such a forward comment to anyone, much less an adult, and was elated at the apparent success.

He tried to help me put the power into my hitting, something my dad did but couldn't seem to explain to me. "Pearce, when you bat, you wait until the ball is over the plate to start your swing. Visualize hitting the ball in front of the plate. Visualize, Pearce."

This was my weakest area. I thought back to elementary school, when my music teacher asked us to describe what we saw as the symphonies played. I saw nothing. This is what Coach Shaw had to work with. Here I was, being told to visualize hitting a ball before it got to the plate, and he could see that I could not "see." The last thing I was capable of was visualizing.

"Pearce, come here." He stood real close. "Hit me in the chest with your fist."

I didn't.

"Hit me."

I gave him my blank stare. I was not a hitter.

"Pearce, I am trying to help you visualize." He took my catcher's mitt. "Hit this, hard."

I rammed my fist into the mitt, but it had no pop to the punch. He then backed up so I could extend my arm.

"Now hit it."

I swung again and hit it. I could feel the power difference immediately. He could see the recognition.

"You get power as you extend your arms. When you are at bat and let the baseball get to the plate before you start your swing, you can't extend. Visualize getting the bat around and hitting the ball in front of the plate and you will get power."

I began to visualize, ever so slightly, while at bat and catching. I began to think about where the batter was in the box.

"Pearce, you never talk to the batters. You sit back there mute. You've got to talk to them, get them out of their game, break up their concentration."

"I don't know them, Coach. What will I talk to them about?" I had not made stray comments to a stranger my whole life, and here was the coach telling me to talk to everyone who comes up to the plate . . . for seven innings. The thought had never occurred to me, but I began to try.

"You guys having a good year?"

"So-so, what about y'all?" was their answer back.

"No, not too good."

It was easier than I expected. If their season or the weather didn't work, girls always would get them talking.

"There's a good looking girl behind your dugout. She with y'all?" They would perk right up and tell me how well they knew her. Sometimes it was a little graphic for my Nadine upbringing, but it got them off their game.

Taking Control

Most of the kids hadn't thought about their mental game any more than I had, but the Eunice team was different. They were well coached. Less than a third of our population and several classes down in the New Mexico divisions, they whipped us soundly every time we played them. I tried to get them to talk, but when I asked them a question, they wouldn't bother responding. They were disciplined and tough.

They had a left-handed pitcher, Otis Langley, whom I remembered from the first grade when I attended the Eunice schools. The pro scouts were watching him during his high school years. He was superb, throwing a good fastball and a couple different curves. He kept the opposing batters off balance and won consistently. Don Diamond was their catcher, and he could hit the ball a mile.

I was trying desperately to break out of my shell. All this input from Coach Shaw was invaluable as I tried to understand the obstacles and break free. I began to see and connect. Baseball was just the first venue, spurring me to begin breaking out in other arenas.

Gradually, I began to see a difference. The pitchers and I began making the strikeouts that had eluded us before. C. W. DeWitt, my best friend, was a big rawboned Missouri kid who threw hard but could never get his powerful body and legs into the action. Jim Weaver, our best pitcher, threw a live fastball that danced its way to the plate. Norman Hallmark, a tall quiet kid from church, threw a cannon of a fastball like Marvin Horace from Little League. Dickie Paul threw a good knuckleball, and Ricky Dusek threw mostly junk, all breaking pitches, but he was such a competitor that he had good success.

Coach Shaw began to ride me about taking control of the pitchers. And he harnessed the strong arm I had exhibited for Mr. Baker back in the sixth grade. "Every throw, Pearce, hit right beside the pitcher's ear on his glove side. I don't want the pitcher to use one ounce of energy jumping up or moving right or left to get the balls you throw back. And I want you to throw the baseball back to him harder than he threw to you. You don't say you are in charge; you demonstrate it."

"Yes, sir." By now the lessons were taking shape in my mind and in my game. I began to follow orders out of respect and gratitude.

"Pearce, if the pitcher shakes off a sign, you give it again. You call the game; you make him throw the pitch you want. I don't want my pitchers thinking. I want you to think for them. They have the hard job; you just wear the tools of ignorance. Sit back there and think for my pitchers."

"Yes, sir . . . and sir?"

"What!"

"My little brother still wants to be just like you when he grows up." Greg had mentioned again that he wanted to be like him.

"Pearce, you better get that little brother in control before he actually does something rash."

I grinned; it was the closest I could come to telling Coach I wanted to be just like him when I grew up.

One game, Coach Shaw noticed that Jim was shaking off my signs a lot. He called a time-out, walked out to me, and said, "Next time he shakes you off, I want you to fire the ball back even harder than usual and put it between his eyes. I want to see him flinch. He needs to know you are in charge. The pitcher has enough to do without thinking about the pitches each batter can hit and how he is standing. He has to know you mean business or he will not trust you to run the game."

"Yes, sir."

As he walked off, he turned and said, "One more thing. When your pitcher is too stressed, go out and tell him a joke to loosen him up."

"Coach, I don't know any jokes." We didn't joke around at our house.

"Well, make one up," he shouted as he walked back to the dugout, shaking his head in amazement at the challenge he had taken on with me as his project.

A couple of innings later, Jim shook off the sign. I gave the same sign again. He shook it off. A third time I gave it. We were in uncharted territory. None of the pitchers had seen an assertive action by me before. He went ahead and threw his pitch, not the one I was calling. My return throw was like a bullet, right at his eyes. He flinched and caught it just before it dropped him. He looked at me in complete shock. I took a step in front of the plate and held up the sign for the pitch I had called. He glared at me, and for the first time in my life, I held my ground.

I feared and respected Coach more than I worried about what Jim would say. I held the glare. He looked away, and I knew I had just won the battle of wills.

I was giddy with my newfound confidence and felt as though a large weight had been lifted off me as I began to understand. We got to the dugout, and I took my characteristic spot at the end of the bench by myself. I didn't want to celebrate publicly a victory that came naturally to others. Coach gave a slight nod of approval. Jim walked up and stood in front of me. "You threw the ball back hard and at my head. What was that all about?"

"I am calling the pitches, and you didn't throw my pitch. I will take your head off with the next one." It was a moment of triumph for me that no one else knew about except for Coach Shaw. The slight nod of the head was all he ever gave, and all I needed.

Freedom Tasted

Baseball became, for me, as important in my development as my religious training. In those hot spring and summer days, I sensed that I was learning more than baseball, that in focusing on the small parts of the game I was learning life lessons. The discipline to continue while friends chose to quit baseball and "hang out" became one of my signatures and one of the reasons I succeed.

The enjoyment of calling the perfect pitch for the situation, or picking a runner off first base after catching the pitch, or of repositioning a fielder perfectly by knowing the hitter and the pitch I was about to call were more than baseball lessons. They were life lessons that I was able to use in multiple ways for the rest of my life.

I began to improve in other areas. Vision and visualization come hard to me, but because of one brief season and a coach who took a few extra minutes with me each day, I could do it.

A couple of months later we were at the nicely sculpted field in Eunice. The confidence had been surging in me. The game of baseball and my appointed role in it were all coming together in my head.

Otis Langley was pitching against us and Don Diamond was catching. Jim was pitching for us. Coach Shaw had figured out that Don could not hit a curve, so every game we played against them, every pitch, Coach had me throw him curves. Every pitch. This game was no different, and this otherwise great hitter struck out every time, seeing nothing but curves.

During the middle innings when we were up to bat, I was concentrating on hitting the ball in front of the plate. Otis went into the wind up and fired a blazing fastball. I saw the ball come off the bat, a couple of inches out in front of the plate. It cleared the top of the light pole in center field, twenty feet above the concrete block centerfield wall. I did it! Coach just said, "That's what I'm talking about."

As we went back to the field, Don Diamond was up to bat.

"Don," I said, "you gave me such an easy pitch that I am going to give you a fastball. But just this first one." When I called the fastball, Jim looked in question. I stood up, moved out in front of the plate and stared. I took my position again and called the fastball. He threw it. Don was so surprised he didn't swing.

"Don, what's up, guy?" He didn't answer. He was in his zone, concentrating and focused. But I could sense that I was inside his head. "Don, I tell you what, I am going to give you a second chance, another fastball, but this is the last one." I called another fastball, but Jim shook it off. This time I just stood up and he nodded. Don was trying to outguess me now, thinking I was saying one thing and doing another. Another heater, right down the pipe, and Don watched it go by for a second strike.

I was jubilant. Everything was clicking. I was chatting it up, making the opponent think. Thinking is bad when you are doing; doing has to be instantaneous, spontaneous.

"Well, Don, I don't know what to do. You've asked every time you've been at bat all year for a straight ball, and we've had two pretty ones that you just watched." The conversation was one-sided and just loud enough for the batter to hear. It was right in my style, a hidden, quiet communication that no one knew was going on except for the batter.

"Don, I tell you what, I think we are going to give you another straight ball." He knew I was lying this time. I could tell it. We had him out before we even threw the pitch. I called the third consecutive fastball. Jim hesitated, then moved into his windup. Don was guessing curve and was completely unprepared for the blazing fastball. He took the pitch without swinging for the third strike. He just looked at me and shook his head.

Those moments of discovery are as fresh in my mind today as a rare summer rainstorm in New Mexico. I was on my way. I was emerging from the jail cell, walking free from the heaviness of wanting to change, and beginning to understand what had eluded me for so long.

The next year, I spent the winter months in the second floor of the gym, getting in shape. Coach Shaw had left Hobbs after school politics forced him out, but I was ready to meet the challenges. I was free and understood what I needed to do.

Pitchers were up there with me throwing pitches every day. I wrote letters to Sul Ross and New Mexico Highlands universities, the small-school baseball powers in our region, asking them to look at me in my senior year for a possible scholarship.

The season officially opened in the blustery spring winds. The new assistant baseball coach, the one who

Coach Shaw

replaced Coach Shaw, pulled me aside on the field the first day and declared, "Pearce, I don't think you're as good as everyone is saying. You're gonna have to prove yourself to me."

"Yes, sir." But there was something out of order. Something was different from the way Coach Shaw chewed me out. These critiques became personal; they were not seeking improvement. They were looking to prove me wrong, and they did their job. The assistant coach proved that I was not good, that I was not a starter, and I spent my senior year in the dugout on the bench—humiliated and back in my familiar jail cell, looking for an escape route.

I never did get back the swagger and insight, the sheer love of learning the game that I had that one magical season, when I hit an Otis Langley pitch over the center field fence and struck out Don Diamond with three straight fastballs by getting into his mind. The lessons were not lost; they were just out of sight.

But at the moment when I lost sight of them, all I could see was the inner walls of that cell, closing in again. The freedom I had tasted seemed out of reach again.

Rocky's Math Analysis

With a late August birthday, I started school with kids almost a year older than me. If my birthday had been eight days later, I would have had to wait another year for school. A year is a long time at that age. Stir in the fact that I was shy and introverted, and I did not mix well with the older crowd.

Nothing has come easily to me. I have had to work twice as hard to get the same outcomes as most other people. The same was true with my schoolwork. From my earliest years, I studied every night at home to get good grades, mostly A's.

Math was one of the few things I easily understood. I would even help my brother Tom, two years my senior, with the subject that was a struggle for him. When I was in the eighth grade at Heizer Junior High, I was selected along with a few others in my grade to move into the ninth-grade math class and start algebra a year earlier.

Looking back, I understand that I was almost two years younger than many of the freshmen in that algebra class. I had to admit that it was hard for me to compete. It began to distract me that I couldn't keep up with them, and I lost confidence in the one thing that had given me security. All my grades began to slip along with the math scores.

It was no one's fault. It was just that the combination of my personality, shyness, insecurities, and being placed with kids quite a bit older than me, even in my strongest subject, was too much to overcome. I floundered. My grades fell from near straight A's to mostly B's and a few A's.

The pinnacle of math at Hobbs High in those years was with a teacher we all called Rocky. Martin Rockwell's Math Analysis class came after Algebra II and probed the differential equations that many would not see until college. Mr. Rockwell was all about the process. He wanted the steps to be methodical and precise. I joined all the whiz kids my senior year in Rocky's class. He had "skid row" for the kids with the lowest scores in the class. Then you were seated by score on over to the opposite side of the room where the top students were. I always sat somewhere below the halfway spot, far below what my early potential suggested about my capabilities. I didn't get down to skid row much, but I never made the top tier either.

> Those moments of discovery are as fresh in my mind today as a rare summer rainstorm in New Mexico. I was on my way. I was emerging from the jail cell, walking free from the heaviness of wanting to change, and beginning to understand what had eluded me for so long.

To achieve the scores I did get required more work than I had ever put into anything before. Every night I studied until midnight or later. Sometimes I was up until 2 a.m. My parents worried. Dad suggested that if it was that hard, I should not be taking it. Failure was a last step I would not allow myself to take, so I just continued to work late, all year long.

The lessons that I was learning on the baseball field and the discipline to continue and to pay attention to the small things were keys to my decision to continue in that math class, which up to that point was one of the hardest things I had ever done. Only a dogged determination kept me moving forward, one day at a time. It was not pretty, but I did finish Rocky's Math Analysis class. I graduated from high school with a 3.2 GPA.

In college, every year was the same as that year with Rocky. I studied almost every night until midnight, often much later. I graduated with a 3.19. Though it was only a fraction more difficult than high school, I worked twice as hard.

4-H Takes Me off the Farm

My years in 4-H began to bear fruit during my high school and college years. With my record book, which Mom had recognized as being so important for all participants, I was selected to go to two National 4-H Congresses in Chicago, where my brother Mike had been the first national winner with his swine record book just a couple of years before.

I also was selected to attend the National 4-H Conference in Washington, D.C., where I heard Dorothy Emerson, a mainstay in the national 4-H scene for years. Her presentation entitled "KISS" (Keep It Simple Stupid) appealed to my basic and uncomplicated view of life. These trips continued to kindle the growing belief that I could excel.

18

COLLEGE YEARS

L ife gives us all challenges that will affect the outcome of our lives, depending on the choices we make.

I call the most sudden of these, the ones that you must deal with in the twinkling of an eye, *No-Notice Exams*, where, in the time it takes to answer yes or no, the flow of life is determined. How you have lived and the thoughts you have thought will determine your spontaneous actions once the exam starts. For instance, my dad's decision to turn down the company promotion affected the rest of his life in that he lost that opportunity for many years, but the same decision allowed him to choose family and stability over corporate advancement.

Sometimes the impact of these choices is financial and obvious, but other times the impact is hidden in the marrow of life, showing up in our fulfillment, anger, bitterness, frustration, or joy, and often in our relationships with others.

In my college years, I encountered several of these sudden, answer-now exams. The gravity of some decisions was obvious, while the impact of others was subtle, almost unnoticeable.

But first I had to make the decision of whether to attend college, and where. Neither was the no-notice variety of decision, since going to college was a reality I inherited from my mother, even before I knew what college was.

Neither of my parents had college educations, but my siblings and I knew that we'd go to college because Mom told us so—all the time. She planted it in our heads constantly, to the point that it became one of my earliest memories. I knew when we lived in the oil camp, before I started school, that someday I would go to college, become an engineer, and live at the other end of the camp. Mom convinced me I could.

The confidence she had was a direct result of her faith. She believed and taught us that when we did not have answers to life's questions, God would provide. I never heard my parents discuss the question of how they could afford to send six kids to college on a roustabout's salary; they walked by faith, not by sight. And it was effective. It removed the questions and stress from trying to decide whether or not we would go. There is no stress when a thing is already determined.

Based on their demonstrations of faith, I have been able to live my life with that same confidence that God's way works. Being freed from having to know every answer in life allowed miracles to work throughout our lives. We learned both that believing is work and that God works on our behalf (with work involved on our part as well.)

College was not such a sure thing for my peers. Many kids whom I grew up around spent summers and holidays working in the oilfields, just as we did. The jobs were hard but provided good pay for honest hard work. Many of those friends, without a parent to plant the dream and without a faith to overcome the lack of money, started working in the oilfield as soon as they graduated from high school and never stopped. Income opened the door to a wife, then children, and the obligations took them on paths that diverged from college.

When I was in high school, I began to consider the budget of our family and investigated Dad's pay and our expenses. Some of his payroll checks, after the deductions for taxes and gas (Exxon deducted the credit card charges for gasoline out of the paycheck) were as little as ninety dollars for two weeks. I did the math and knew that my family could not pay my way to college.

My two older brothers enrolled in college as soon as they graduated from high school. The pig projects were supplying money that was going into a savings account for all of us, but it was easy to see that I, as the third in line, would not have much left in that account to pay for my education. I began to work more hours in the summer and save more to compensate. I had made the decision to go to college, but how to pay for it was an ever-present question.

I began to research scholarships, and my 4-H experience helped me choose which college to attend. 4-H is operated by the Extension Service, which was part of New Mexico State University, and, quite naturally, the statewide 4-H competitions were held there. As a result, I'd been on the campus multiple times before high school graduation and was comfortable with the institution, so I enrolled there in the fall of 1965, the year I graduated from high school.

The same year I started at NMSU, Mom started to fulfill her lifelong desire for a college education and enrolled at Eastern New Mexico University in Portales, 109 miles from Hobbs. With six kids, and three of us in college, Mom found a way to follow her own advice, too.

I never heard one complaint from Dad about the drain on his paycheck or about having to shoulder more of the burden. About all he ever said was, "I'll sure be glad when I get all of you smart enough to live with me."

Mom took Philip and Greg, the two youngest kids, to Portales and got an apartment where they stayed during the week. My sister stayed at home with Dad and attended school there. Mom drove home each weekend to catch up with everything there.

College for six kids and my mom was accomplished without any of us or my parents taking on much debt. How they were able to manage that kind of financial burden, before Pell Grants, the Student Loan Program, and Lottery Scholarships, still amazes me.

For me, I worked and saved money every summer, plus I received two scholarships out of the several for which I applied. The main one, pretty much a full ride, was an API (American Petroleum Institute) scholarship to major in engineering. The die was cast. I was going to college to become an engineer, and I would—just as predicted long before—move to the other end of the camp.

But I hated the engineering classes from the first day and performed poorly in my core classes. After a year of struggling, I began to consider changing majors. The contemplations were painful, as a change meant giving up that API scholarship that was set to pay for most of my college expenses, about three thousand dollars per year. It meant moving back to uncertain finances and, even worse, moving away from the expectations Mom had for each of us to become engineers.

The decision, though technically not a no-notice variety, was nonetheless a crucial life choice, putting me on a drastically different path. I knew that I would have to work harder and longer in the summers and holidays to get the money to go to school. But I decided that following my heart in a field I liked rather than pursuing one determined by external expectations was key to my future.

During this period of my life, I had acquaintances who were spending their weekends at keg parties, experimenting with drugs, and following the new fads of the day. I, on the other hand, was studying, trying to justify the trust my parents had placed in me by investing in my education and foregoing their own needs that I might be freed of the constraints they had faced. Theirs was a deep sacrifice, and I felt a noble obligation. These choices formed the foundation of my life and developed in me the guiding principles by which I have lived.

Meanwhile, each semester, Mom was taking more than twenty hours and graduated with an education degree in just two-and-a-half years, an achievement indicative of her personal drive. She spent the rest of her career convincing middle-aged housewives with no hope that they, too, could go to college, get an education, and move to the other end of the camp. I had, on the other hand, slipped into a category of uncertainty.

I did not get the engineering degree my mom might have liked, but, in the end, I did get a Bachelor of Business Administration degree in economics, which merged my natural ability with numbers and love of business.

The Texas White House—1966

Taking office after the JFK assassination in 1963, President Lyndon Johnson was one of the most active presidents on conservation issues since Theodore Roosevelt, and often credited his wife, Lady Bird, with being the push behind his initiatives. I saw that firsthand.

A White House Conference on Natural Beauty convened in May 1966 and resulted in the President's Council on Recreation and Natural Beauty, chaired by Hubert Humphrey. To help give the focus a push, President Johnson also held a youth conference with a similar focus in June 1966, bringing five hundred young people who represented the twenty million youngsters involved in eleven different youth organizations to Washington for a weeklong event. A steering committee of young people organizing the event chose Jacqueline Sharp (Girl Scouts of America) and George Fox (Future Farmers of America) to be the national cochairs of that summer conference.

Mom's efforts with the 4-H club, to spearhead cleanup efforts in Hobbs—bringing groups of kids together on Saturday mornings for projects ranging from the cleaning trash off highways to cutting weeds at a local cemetery—caught the eye of the White House organizers. I was invited to attend that inaugural conference. Mom's leadership—and my participation in the projects—were beginning to pay dividends.

But since I had changed majors and sacrificed the API scholarship, I first had to decide whether to attend the conference and give up my ability to make and save money for that period of the summer. It meant losing a week's pay. Mom was the one who reassured me that we could make up the lost pay, that I needed the experience. So, at eighteen, I packed my bags and flew to Washington, D.C., a destination I assumed I would never see again.

At the conference, I sang "Cumbahyah" for the first time and attended the breakout sessions and discussions all week long. Many had planted trees as projects across the country, but I was one of the few participants with any practical experience in trash cleaning projects, granting me a fair amount of visibility during those discussions.

On June 27, we gathered on the South Lawn of the White House to meet Lady Bird and her two daughters, Lynda Bird and Luci Baines. I could not help but wonder how long the path from Nadine to the Texas ranch of the Johnsons was, and if I'd ever find out. We mingled with the first family for an hour or so until the president appeared and addressed us. He emphasized the importance of young people and our projects as he and the first lady fought to preserve the natural beauty of America. It was a message that resonated with me, given my background working for the nursery in high school and cleaning trash from our town.

At the end of the event, the youth attendees elected fifty-five of their peers to be on the steering committee for the next year. I was included in that group, because my experience with trash projects had given me a unique perspective. The conference wrapped up, and we became instant ambassadors for the Beautify America project. We were sent home to our local communities and charged to help preserve the nation's natural beauty.

As a follow-up to the original summer conference, hundreds of projects were started nationwide. I planted the tree we were sent home with in the Hobbs City Park and led another cleanup project or two—but those were due more to Mom's hatred of trash than the White House urging.

I admired the first lady for actively engaging the nation on an issue she was passionate about. She was visible throughout the country as she urged citizens to "plant a tree, bush, or shrub" to beautify the country and to clean the trash off of the highways and byways of America. Everyone in the nation knew of Lady Bird's Beautify America projects, and though many made fun of her, it resonated. People began to carry trash bags in their cars. I routinely saw litter barrels in the corners of streets in New Mexico that were full of trash, indicators that people bought into the concept of cleaning up our country. The nation began to clean up rivers and chemical dumps. It fostered a new generation of awareness.

Diana MacArthur, a relative of Lady Bird, was the head honcho on the national youth project. I continued to see her name prominently displayed for the duration of the Johnson years in the White House and maintained a special regard for her, because she included me in this unique program. In the winter of that year, I received a call from her telling me that my efforts to beautify the nation following the conference had not gone unnoticed by President Johnson or Lady Bird, and that I, along with twelve others from the conference, were being invited to the LBJ ranch outside Austin.

I told Ms. MacArthur that I had gotten a job during the Christmas vacation and going on the trip meant quitting the job and losing the income. Once again, I had a no-notice test and struggled with the decision. I asked if I could call her back. She gave me two hours but would fill the slot with someone else if I could not attend or didn't call.

Mom was aghast that I thought I might not attend. "We can work more and sacrifice; we can make up the lost pay. When can you go to a president's house again?" I thought of all my friends who never attended college because of finances. Mom's advice won out, and I called to accept the invitation.

On December 28, 1966, the thirteen of us flew from different parts of the nation and gathered in Austin to drive to the LBJ ranch, the first Texas White House. Once in the compound, we went straight to the ranch house and into the original part of the house, built in the late 1800s. The living room was typical of the ranch houses from that period; it was cramped. We sat around as you would in any rancher's front room in the country, some sitting in chairs pulled from the kitchen, some on settees and footstools, and the rest crowded on the couch. Mrs. Johnson came in and graciously visited with us for an hour or so, offering us tea and coffee.

Finally, some signal was given that the next part of the afternoon was to take place, and we went outside into the blustery wind. President Johnson joined us, and we climbed into two black Lincolns. Half the group rode with the president and the others with the first lady. I ended up in her vehicle, and she continued the down-home country chat we had been having at the house. Then the president interrupted, calling our vehicle with the latest technology of the day—the Citizen's Band Radio, better known as the CB. In his long Texas drawl he said, "Breaker, Bird, I'm going over here by the jet runway to see if we can find those deer. I want to get out and see how they're doing."

His wife answered on her matching CB, much the way any ranch wife would, admonishing her husband that it was too cold to get the kids out for long. "And Lyndon, don't you be feeding tobacco to the deer." It seemed to be an ongoing conversation.

They continued to chat back and forth while we were driving until the president did, in fact, pull to a stop next to a high fence where a few deer were congregated. We all got out and went up to the fence where he promptly pulled out some cigarettes and began to feed tobacco to the deer through the fence. I guessed they had already been addicted to the stuff, because they walked right up to the fence and began to eat from the president's hand.

Diana MacArthur changed the groups around, so I ended up in the president's vehicle for the ride back to the house. He was a gregarious, talkative, and personable man. Being from Nadine, I never figured I would meet a president face-to-face, much less be riding around in the vehicle he was driving. Of course, I never expected to ride a school bus with a Playboy Playmate either, but my life had been full of strange twists.

We got back to the ranch house and gathered under the four hundred-year-old oak tree in the front yard, where the president surprised us by issuing a proclamation that 1967 would be "Youth Natural Beauty and

Conservation Year." The moment culminated with a quick photo op with the president in the cold Texas wind. And just like that, the magic was over.

We said our good-byes and started through the carport to board the vans. As usual, I lingered toward the back when I saw an adult chaperone, a parent from our group, sidle away and behind the group. She picked up a large clay armadillo in the carport and slammed it on the concrete, breaking it into pieces, and stuffed the animal head into her coat pocket as an illicit souvenir. I suppose it was the only piece that would fit, or she might have stolen the whole thing. She never knew that I saw the transaction, but it taught me a lesson that one small action can determine the amount of respect one has for a person. Up to that moment, she had been my favorite of the adults on the trip. But her actions spoke louder than what I had liked about her before.

On to the White House

Most of the dozen or so students on the trip in Texas were also part of the steering committee, and we continued from there to Washington for a meeting to plan the following summer conference. At that December meeting, the fifty-five of us gathered to determine our plan of action, with the fresh knowledge that 1967 was to be *the* youth year.

The first order of business was selecting two new cochairs. Cheryl Sheathelm, a farm girl from Michigan, and an FFA president from the South were elected. I was second in the balloting for the male position, so when the winner declined the position—since he'd be too busy as the state FFA president—the position fell to me.

Another no-notice exam. Thinking about summer work, paying for college, and wondering how I would manage it all crowded into my mind as the facilitator asked me if I was prepared to take the position. In one of the most sudden decisions of my life to that point, when I thought I was about to decline, I said yes. Although I could not see how I was ever going to pay for my school by missing so much work, my faith declared that I would trust the future to God and simply say, *"Yes, I will go."*

So Cheryl and I replaced George and Jackie as cochairs, and within minutes of arriving in Washington, my pathway in life once again changed dramatically. Instead of just being a participant, I would now be leading out front.

It was determined that we would have a small group go to the White House to deliver a report of our actions and describe the projects that emerged from the previous summer's conference. Our other flagship event for the year would be presenting a film to the president and first lady that summarized the work. We presented the report, a booklet called

"Youth Power," during a summer White House ceremony in the Rose Garden, with me as the Master of Ceremonies.

The second event, on September 14 of that year, again included a small group of the most active participants assembled at the White House to present the film, "We Are on Our Way," to the first lady. I was designated to carry the film. Excitement crackled through the four of us as we talked on long distance phone calls about the upcoming event.

Even with all the hoopla, my circumstances had not changed. I was in the second semester of my sophomore year at NMSU and still struggling to pay for it. I had no money to speak of and left on the trip with the only ten dollars I had to my name.

I had long before mastered the art of having no money, and these trips were no exception. Airline tickets were always mailed to us, the hotel rooms were paid for by the conference sponsors, and a bus conveyed us to and from the airport. Most meals were at banquets or paid for by the chaperones. Almost every trip had some excursion to shop, but that was no problem; I just didn't buy anything. By never advertising that I had no money, and keeping myself out of circumstances that would require borrowing any, I had managed to keep myself out of awkward situations. This trip proceeded along the same lines.

But on the morning of the White House event, with only the four of us participating and all of us in college, the organizers saw no reason to have us accompanied by chaperones. The small group did not justify a bus, so we were to take a cab and file for reimbursement. I solved that by asking the group if we should all go together and just file one receipt. That seemed fine, so I asked who wanted to volunteer to do the paperwork and said I surely did not. One of the others did—no hassle, no problem.

As our cab pulled into the drive of the 4-H Center, everyone decided to make one last bathroom break so there would be no need to look for facilities at the White House. I had the film in my hands but set it on the dresser to make a pit stop. Hearing the taxi honking outside caused a slight panic, and I hurried to finish. In my haste, I left the film on the dresser, ran out, and jumped in the cab with the others.

We got to the White House, were swept along by the guards at the gate, ceremoniously escorted to the 17th Street door, and ushered inside. I was overwhelmed by the pictures along the wall at the entrance, never once thinking about the film I was supposed to present. Finally, the staffer in charge of the event came to fetch me, looking for the film, that we might secure it at the podium. Realizing too late that my hands were empty (the staffer had already realized that), I sheepishly began to make excuses.

"That's okay," she said. "Where are you staying?"

"The National 4-H Center."

"Oh, that's pretty far. This time of afternoon, I think you can make it. Did you come by car or cab?"

"Cab." My knees began to buckle. My money problem, so artfully avoided moments before, was fully back in front of me.

She responded quickly, "I will get you over to the exit, then you can just walk out the gate. I'll let the guard know you'll be back. You'll miss the reception, but no one will notice. Let's hurry."

I had seen how much the cab ride cost. My ten dollars would not cover it one way, much less the round trip. I did not have the heart to tell her I was flat broke. She had been too kind in helping me out of the first mess to burden her with another one. She got me to the exit hallway, handed me off with instructions to the guard to make sure I could get back in, and, with a wink about our secret, pushed me off.

As the guard and I walked down the long hallway, I walked slower and slower, as if the pull of the earth was getting stronger and stronger. The guard was puzzled and kept urging me on. I was thinking of just going out the gate and disappearing on the sidewalk. I could tell everyone that I had gotten lost and couldn't get back. I'll admit that it wasn't much of a plan. Finally the guard asked me, "What's the matter, son?"

I blurted out my problem, "I am supposed to be taking a cab, and I don't have enough money."

"Can you borrow some from your chaperone?"

"We don't have one this time."

As a guard in the White House, he saw thousands of kids coming in each year. He quickly evaluated that he would never get his money back if he loaned it to me. I was burning with embarrassment, and we both felt the awkwardness.

"What's so important at your hotel that you're leaving the White House?"

"Well, the National Youth Conference made this film of projects all across the country, and I was supposed to present it to Lady Bird Johnson. And I forgot it."

"Well, that's not the end of the world."

I was not convinced.

"Son, when are you leaving town?"

"Sooner than I planned when I don't get this film back in time for the presentation."

"Son, my point is this: if you are not leaving until tomorrow, we can go down to the film library, get you a film—they all look the same, and no one will ever read the label on the film can. You can present the film from downstairs, then bring your real film over here to me before you leave town. I will be talking to Bird's secretary to let her know what's up. What do you think?"

It was not so much a question as a directive. I was not convinced, but I also didn't have cab fare, so I went along with it. "Yes, sir. If you think it will work, I am willing to do that. It will get me out of a big bind."

So he led me through the bowels of the White House, through places that tours never went. I was too nervous and distracted to notice or appreciate the things I could have been seeing that few tourists ever see. I cannot remember one detail of that walk. I do remember him opening a door and ushering me into a small theater, complete with a projection room just like the theaters, soundproofing, theater style seats, a big screen, and all the trappings.

He and the film room guy had a brief discussion, and he called me over. "What diameter was the film canister?"

"I am not too good on diameters, but if you show me a couple, I can get it pretty close."

They began to pull feature films off the shelf, which were far too large. Finally, they got to the smaller documentaries. I handled a couple to see how they fit into my hand, and we chose one. The guard signed a form, and we started making our way back to the reception.

The guard said, "Son, you were supposed to go to the 4-H Center and back. Not enough time has elapsed for that to have happened, so why don't we go into the office and wait just a bit."

I'm sure he was evaluating that I was still far too nervous to pull the whole thing off, so we went into a small room and sat down. He chatted about anything to get my mind off the problem. Somehow he succeeded in making me comfortable enough to leave his presence and stand in front of people for my presentation. In the process, he gave me his contact information, so we could get the other film to him and he could make the switch.

Finally, when he determined that our arrival would not raise questions, he found the coordinator for the event and delivered me, carrying the film can tightly in my arms and obscuring the title from all eyes. The coordinator hurried me into the reception, which was just finishing. The smaller group was escorted into the East Wing. I sat down beside the first lady and the program began.

I somehow remembered my lines, and Cheryl and I presented the film. Sure enough, neither Lady Bird nor any of the other dignitaries paid a bit of attention to the title on the canister. The entire thing went off without a hitch.

We sat back down, the film safely in Mrs. Johnson's lap, the label obscure by the book on top of it.

Back at the 4-H Center, I approached a member of the young staff with whom I had become friends on previous trips to the center. She was from England and had that entirely desirable British accent. I wondered if a kid from Nadine could ever find Britain. She had told me about coming to this country with no money, and I felt safe confiding in her about the film. I asked if she could help, and she happily volunteered to go on this adventure to the White House.

When I got to the White House, I felt as though the entire world knew about the misadventure with the film. I was trying to keep it out of sight, as though I was on some sort of CIA mission, finally managing to give the name of the guard I was supposed to meet. They paged him, and he came to the gate. He casually took the film, reviewed it, looking inside to make sure it was really a film, shrugged, and wandered back toward the White House. His casual indifference convinced me that such things were somewhat routine, that behind the scenes this occurred more frequently than the higher-ups knew.

I grew up reading and believing the biblical stories of how God reached down and chose ordinary people, singling them out to do extraordinary things. David was herding sheep when God sent Samuel to anoint him as king. We raised pigs, which I figured was not much different. Though David's role was to be far greater than any I could imagine, being randomly selected from among the millions of kids to represent America's youth to the president of the United States was more than I could have imagined for my world. Being chosen to go to the White House, meet the president and first lady, even ride in their car, changed my perception of myself and ultimately changed my life.

It seemed strange that Mom's lifelong hatred of trash and her ability to move her emotions to actions would be the tool that God used to lift me up. I began to find security in the belief that, if I were true to myself and where I'd come from, I could succeed. Oftentimes, all I had to do was say yes.

The power of the circumstance was not based on who I was—our family had no political or economic status—but on what I did. This concept of how hard you work rather than who you know is the cornerstone of the country our founding fathers wanted to establish. They had grown tired of the kings and courts of Europe who determined everyone's future.

The turning point was not the recognition, the visits to the White House, or meeting the president. It was the understanding that I could succeed and lead from our five-acre farm in Nadine. It was the knowledge that God will use the most innocuous activities, such as cleaning trash along highways, to lift us up.

A couple of years ago, I heard that Diana MacArthur lived in Santa Fe and would be attending a large function I, too, was scheduled to attend. We had a great visit; she was just as gracious as I remembered from thirty years before. But, at the heart of it, I believed she wondered how I went so wrong after all that training and special attention from the Democrats of the Johnson White House, becoming a Republican. Some things are probably better not delved into, so I ignored the question, if there was one, and enjoyed the visit with someone who helped change my life.

The Lady at the Draft Board

When I was at New Mexico State University, every male student was required to take two years of ROTC (Reserve Officer Training Corps). It was one of the last public universities in the country to have the mandatory program. In my two years, I did pretty well, enjoying the discipline and, oddly enough, appreciating being forced out of my comfort zone.

At the end of my sophomore year, the ROTC staff encouraged me to enter the Advanced ROTC program. This meant that, upon graduation, I would become a commissioned officer, a second lieutenant in the U.S. Air Force. Despite their prodding, I decided that military service and the war did not fit into my future. I thought I was finished with any thoughts of serving.

The Vietnam War was in full swing, with the heaviest losses occurring between '66 and '68. The losses became personal to me when Hobbs' kids whom I knew and grew up with began to die there. Ronnie Noseff was the first, dying on September 25, 1966. In the next twelve months, Jimmie Plato and Howard Rice likewise perished. I realized my deep fear of dying weighed heavily in my decision not to enroll in the Advanced ROTC program.

In the fall of 1967, my junior year, I began to contemplate what I would do with an economics degree—maybe get a master's degree or go to law school. One night, as I went to my dorm room, I saw a group of kids sitting around the dorm lounge, deeply and emotionally engaged in conversation. There was grumbling, anger, and worry among them. They were discussing the draft. I didn't really pay any attention, as it didn't seem to apply to me. But within twenty-four hours I found out it did apply to me. I was about to experience several no-notice exams and confront two of the greatest fears of my young life: flying and dying.

The next day I got my phone call, the same one that had the other students so worked up the night before. The woman announced herself as the head of the Lea County Selective Service Board, or draft board. Every graduating high school student in Lea County knew who she was; she struck fear into our hearts with the power she wielded over our lives.

She told me that the Selective Service Board had met the night before and my birthday was No. 23 on their list. She projected they would call me up within the month and instructed me to *report to El Paso that afternoon for an induction physical!* I was stammering, but somehow got out that I was enrolled in college, and that I was going places, thinking of a law degree or a job in economics, essentially stating that her path for my life was not exactly consistent with mine.

She replied, "You are going places. . . . You are going to Vietnam." It was not a suggestion.

I exerted about as much pushback as I was capable of at that point in my life. "Isn't there a deferment because I'm in college? I'm thinking of going to graduate school."

"None," she said. College deferments were still technically in effect, but each draft board was semiautonomous. I didn't get the impression that I could argue a technicality of the law with her.

"What about joining the National Guard or Reserves?" Friends of mine had done that to avoid being drafted.

"The law changed at the beginning of 1966. If you were signed up before you got this call, it would keep you out of the draft. But since you are asking, I suspect you are not signed up."

"Marriage?" I had no prospects, but I was desperate.

"No, those deferments were ended two years ago." It was a simple and final answer.

"What if I get into ROTC?" I was grasping, afraid of going to war—determined that my path would be anything but saying yes to this "opportunity."

"That would be a possibility," she replied, but I could tell by the tone of her voice she had heard these same things before. It was also obvious that the judgment day had come, and I was confronted with a no-nonsense judge. Schemes to avoid her pronouncement on lives did not have a high success rate. I sensed that, without extraordinary luck, I would end up in her clutches.

"I will give you twenty-four hours to get into ROTC, if you think that's what you want to do." She was used to dealing with nineteen-year-old kids and was all business

"I believe that is what I will do. I want to finish college."

"I will call you at noon tomorrow to find out if you got signed up."

When I arrived at the ROTC office, they were surprised to see me, as I had rejected their recruiting efforts just six months before. I explained my new draft status and asked if they had any openings. The major in charge replied, "All we have available are pilot slots. If I remember correctly, you don't want to fly."

"No, sir. I lost an uncle in a jet crash and don't really want to fly." I thought that sounded so much better than saying I was scared to death of airplanes.

"You know, we had all the other specialties available last semester if you had chosen to sign up then, but right now the Air Force has unlimited flying positions and not much else." He was needling me.

"Sir, why do you need so many pilots?"

"The air war over Vietnam is a big part of the mission, and we are losing lots of planes and pilots." He could see my distress and popped me again. "Like I said, you could have chosen from other career fields if you had signed up last May."

The two greatest fears in my life were simultaneously rushing at me in no-notice-exam fashion, obscuring an otherwise clear and calm fall morning in Las Cruces, New Mexico. I could not get over my lifelong fear of flying, so I replied, "I need to think about it. . . ." and left without signing up for ROTC. We both knew I would not be back.

The next day, right at the stroke of noon, as promised, the woman called and got straight to the point, where the conversation had ended the day before. "Did you get signed up for ROTC?" she asked.

I started in mid sentence blurting out, "Ma'am, all they need are pilots because they are killing so many, and I do not want to fly."

She was very experienced at hearing excuses from kids. "I understand that," she responded. "They are killing soldiers on the ground, too. Now you get down to El Paso and get that induction physical this afternoon. Do you understand?"

"Yes, ma'am."

"There are no excuses—not class, not weather, nothing. You get that physical today."

I suddenly overcame my inability to visualize. The images of kids I grew up with, tromping around the vegetation of the jungles in Vietnam, were crowding into my head. Both flying and dying were back on a course headed directly toward me, but the flying part could be put off two years, while the jungle and dying part would move immeasurably closer that very moment.

I had avoided thinking about flying and those flying slots through the rest of the afternoon the day before, through the night, and up until that exact moment. With very little thought and with a sudden change of mind that I did not anticipate, I suddenly blurted, "Ma'am, can I have one more chance to get into ROTC?" In the space of half a minute, I had changed the answer on my no-notice exam. It is these decisive moments of life, which we all experience at some time, that prove up who we are in life. All the lessons our parents have taught us, all the character building we have done, and all of the courage we have summoned plays out in these exams.

"I will give you one more chance, hot rod. I will give you until 4 p.m. today, but if you don't get signed up *today*, I will drive to Las Cruces and deliver you to El Paso myself. *Do you understand?*"

"Yes, ma'am."

It was not with jubilation that I made my way to the ROTC office. In fact, as I walked from the Alumni dorm to the ROTC building, I was struck by how other people were casually coming and going, that life for them had not changed. The gravity of the decision, walking toward my two largest fears in life, weighed heavily on me. The suddenness of the change in direction made my steps drag, one after the other. The loneliness of the moment was heavy, weighed down by all the expectations and dreams that could, like that, come crashing to the floor. I had not called home to discuss the choice; I had talked to no one. My decision was made out of sheer avoidance.

One more time, I entered the ROTC office and sheepishly said, "I'll take one of those flying slots." The last thing before they closed, I signed the paperwork, hoping the war would be over before I ever had to actually go to pilot training or to the war.

Coup d'oeil is a French term used by the military and refers to the ability to discern at one glance the tactical advantages of the terrain. It literally means "stroke of the eye." Chevalier Folard declared coup d'oeil to be "a gift from God that cannot be acquired," while Napoleon simply said it is inborn in great generals. That was the case in the fall of 1967, when at twenty years of age, facing the most difficult decision of my life, I had a flash of insight that I could and would become a pilot and that I would face my fear of flying. For all my mental clumsiness and timidity, I actually have a knack for these flashes of insight.

In a little over twenty-four hours, the direction of my life was radically altered, directed by events beyond my control. There was no preparation time, no calling my trusted mentors or parents. It was the classic no-notice exam. I changed the direction of my life in that flash of insight and made it work; in fact, I embraced it as the reality sunk in.

I continue to hone this ability to analyze things at a glimpse, recognizing in a flash of insight the tactical high ground in situations of business, policy, and personal matters.

Before I deployed to Vietnam, six more Hobbs' kids would die in the conflict. I was working in the oilfield on a workover unit with Erwin Cruce's father the summer he found out his son was killed. Jerry Roberts, Stanley McPherson, who was my oldest brother's age, Charles Gass, Jaimie Pacheco, and Dan Foley all lost their lives. I personally knew all but the last three.

At the same time that I was getting my induction notice, hundreds of thousands of kids across the country were being caught in the same predicament. There were many different responses. Mass demonstrations on college campuses protesting the draft; young men were publicly burning their draft cards, going to Canada to dodge the draft, and going to prison if the offense was prosecuted.

Years later, I saw where William Jefferson Clinton, a future president, had signed up for Advanced ROTC in 1969, but resigned his position with the following statement in his letter:

Because of my opposition to the draft and the war, I am in great sympathy with those who are not willing to fight, kill, and maybe die for their country, that is, the particular policy of a particular government, right or wrong. Two of my friends at Oxford are conscientious objectors. I wrote a letter of recommendation for one of them to his Mississippi draft board, a letter which I am more proud of than anything else I wrote at Oxford last year. One of my roommates is a draft resister who is possibly under indictment and may never be able to go home again. He is one of the bravest, best men I know. His country needs men like him more than they know. That he is considered a criminal is an obscenity.

ROTC was the one way left in which I could possibly, but not positively, avoid both Vietnam and resistance. . . .

. . . I stayed up all night writing a letter to the chairman of my draft board, saying basically what is in the preceding paragraph, thanking him for trying

> In a little over twenty-four hours, the direction of my life was radically altered, directed by events beyond my control. There was no preparation time, no calling my trusted mentors or parents. It was the classic no-notice exam. I changed the direction of my life in that flash of insight and made it work; in fact, I embraced it as the reality sunk in.

to help me in a case where he really couldn't, and stating that <u>I couldn't do the</u>
<u>ROTC after all and would he please draft me as soon as possible.</u>

. . . I am writing too in the hope that my telling this one story will help
you to understand more clearly how so many fine people have come to find
themselves still loving their country but loathing the military, to which you
and other good men have devoted years, lifetimes, of the best service you
could give. To many of us, it is no longer clear what is service and what is
disservice, or if it is clear, the conclusion is likely to be illegal.

Sincerely,

Bill Clinton

The letter, as provided by the Associated Press, was written December 3, 1969. Two days earlier, the draft lottery was held, and Bill Clinton's lottery number was 311. There was no chance he would be drafted, so his attack of conscience and request to be "drafted as soon as possible" conveniently occurred two days after he was made safe by his luck in the lottery. My luck put me on the other end of the draft spectrum.

In my ROTC class, there was a very bright prospect who, like me, had recently signed up for ROTC in order to finish college. Both of us were surprised at where life had taken us, but we were adapting pretty well. When we left for the summer break that year, we promised to see each other in the fall. He never came back to school, deciding instead he neither wanted to be in ROTC nor go to Vietnam. He moved to Canada to avoid the draft, a decision shared by thousands of young men.

I was no less afraid than these men, if fear is what drove them to make excuses or to make a run for it. My enrollment in ROTC was an act of avoidance more than a yes to the opportunity of war or flying. But, eventually, I embraced the path I was on, accepting that "I will go" to war, to wherever it takes me. Thirty-four years later, this haphazard decision would pave the way for my election to public service and would inform dozens of decisions I'd make in office.

Hogar de Niños

My uncle Ed "Sonny" Garnett and his wife, Flo, started attending NMSU during my sophomore year—with the help of our family friends

Roy and Polly McLean. While there, Sonny sold me their old car for fifty dollars—a 1956 Oldsmobile that had logged 150,000 miles and had a worn steering gear that rotated through three-quarters of a turn before the front wheels actually began to follow. I perfected the art of anticipating curves while driving through the Sacramento Mountains at Cloudcroft, through Mayhill, Hope, Artesia, and on into Hobbs.

During my senior year, I worked with an orphanage deep on the southern side of Juarez. At Christmas time that year, I went through El Paso into Juarez and to the Hogar de Niños, a little Christian ministry for children, with Christmas presents for the kids. It was about dusk when I finished with the gifts and headed back to the border.

While still on the Mexico side, the generator on my car failed. Having to use my lights in the darkness ran the battery down quickly, and the car died there on a main street in Juarez. I didn't speak Spanish and was in the dark in an unfamiliar place. Soon, the gracious people on the street began to stop to see if they could help, using hand gestures and broken English to direct me to a small mechanic shop in a dark alley. Businesses that struggle to get by are open for business much later hours and a dim light bulb showed the mechanic was still working. He looked at the generator, broke it apart, and replaced the brushes. I paid him the last fifteen dollars in my pocket and got to the border about 8 p.m.

Everything was fine for 150 miles, until I passed through Carlsbad, when the generator quit again. The battery power, using the lights, would last only a few minutes, so with a bright full moon and little traffic, I turned off the lights and continued in the dark. When traffic approached, I turned on the lights until they passed, then backed off. Even with that limited use, the lights were beginning to dim. The firing power of the engine would be gone when the battery was dead. Mobile phones were decades away, and I was forty miles from my home in Hobbs and had twenty-eight miles behind me to Carlsbad. It was 11 p.m., and I had told my folks about going to the orphanage but had not been able to update them since. I was hours behind schedule.

To preserve what little battery power remained, I left the lights off as the occasional cars passed. They flashed their lights and honked angrily at the sudden surprise traffic on the dark highway. As I turned off the Carlsbad highway toward Monument, still ten miles from home, a cloud cover blocked the moon and light snow began to fall. Without the light of the moon, driving on the narrow two-lane road was even more hazardous. I was praying for battery life and no traffic. Just as I made the turn at Monument to go to Nadine, I felt a hiccup in the engine. The battery was on its last leg and quit before I got to the McNeil ranch. With fire for the spark plugs gone, the engine died and I coasted to a stop, four miles from the house.

It was past midnight, and the snow was getting heavier. I locked the car and started walking, alone, cold, depressed, and worried. The venture to help others was not feeling so good. It took about an hour to get home. Both parents were waiting up, worried. Mom was thankful; Dad blamed my troubles on the foray into Mexico to visit the orphanage.

A Sow for the Poor

The next summer, when I hatched up the idea that we should give a pregnant sow to the Hogar de Niños, Dad was still mad about the mess from Christmas. Mom was sort of on my side, but modestly so. She had seen her kids' harebrained schemes go awry before.

I pushed my vision of the orphanage having the sow whose litter of pigs was scheduled to arrive in a few weeks as putting them on the road to self-sufficiency. Just as the pig projects were paying for us to go to college, the growing pig herd could propel the little ministry into solvency.

I finally got them to agree, and we loaded the sow in our red-and-white Ford pickup on a Saturday morning and headed to Mexico. The trip was uneventful until we got to the border. The American side just looked at us with curiosity, but things got very sticky on the Mexico side. We were not your everyday tourists they were used to processing, and there were many questions, all in Spanish. None of us were fluent enough to deal with an agitated, suspicious border guard wondering what in the world we were doing with our cargo.

I kept using the only Spanish phrase I knew that I could use in front of Mom, "Hogar de Niños," then explained in English our noble intentions.

The guard neither understood nor cared about our intentions and kept demanding *"papel por la puerca"* and was equally insistent about needing a *"stampilla"* on the papers. Finally, I asked Mom what *papel* meant. She told me it meant a paper, and it needed a stamp on it. His rules called for papers to document that the animal was disease free.

Traffic had backed up and drivers were honking angrily, wanting to get on to their Saturday partying in Juarez. They didn't like being held back by some yokels at the front of the line with a big pregnant sow in a pickup truck. All the honking made the sow nervous, and she began to squeal and try to leap over the sideboards of the pickup.

For fifteen minutes the officer insisted on the papers. Dad was ready to turn back. Mom was embarrassed for holding up the traffic. My good intentions had drifted far off course. Finally, I started rummaging around in the glove compartment, got a random piece of paper out and carried that *papel* to him. *"Stampilla, necessita una stampilla."* Mom explained again that it needed a stamp. People were walking up the line and angrily shouting at us.

I went back to the glove compartment and found the registration for the pickup. It had the raised stamp of a notary on it, which I took to him. He could not read English but fingered the raised stamp at the bottom of the page as though he had found a lost treasure. With a big smile, he carried the paper into the little hut there at the border, rifled through the desk to find the right stamp, opened the ink pad, and with great ceremony stamped my original random piece of paper and slid it across the dusty desk to me. Then he stamped Dad's truck registration and carefully placed it into his desk as documentation that he had done his duty, insuring that the animal had been inspected.

I contemplated trying to convince him to return the registration but decided against it.

Dad was sullen, sitting behind the wheel. Mom was quiet, scooted into the middle. I piled in, trying to downplay the whole thing.

"Where is my registration?" Dad asked. That was about the most Dad would say when he had been pushed beyond his comfort zone. He was way past that.

"Dad, let's just go." The horns were honking.

He put the truck into gear, and I directed him through the traffic, down into the residential section on the southern edge of Juarez. Each step of the way, my father's misgivings were leading to a deeper divide in that small cab.

Finally, we arrived at the orphanage. The kids knew me by now and came rushing out to meet us. Lucita Holguin, one of the older girls, always translated when the missionaries were not there. She was surprised to see us and asked the purpose of the *puerca* in the back of our pickup.

The husband and wife who ran the place showed up and were completely unprepared for such a gift. Finally, they got the kids off the basketball court, and we unloaded the sow there. Dad pitched down the two sacks of feed we had brought to keep the sow fed until she had her babies.

Everything was very awkward, with my dad still stewing over what happened at the border. We made sure the pig had water and food before we left. Then the three of us got back in our pickup and headed back to the border in complete silence. I learned at that moment that good intentions do not always result in reverence from everyone involved.

Lucita went on to attend college in the U.S. and married a man from El Paso. She lived a good and productive life because of the efforts of the selfless missionaries. Years later, she also revealed that they ate the sow before she had her pigs.

Learning to Fly; Dealing with My Fear

At each ROTC installation, the Air Force had a program for screening potential candidates called FIP (Flight Instruction Program). In my senior year at NMSU, I reported early one morning to the University Airport that used to be south of the married student housing on the campus. (The airport was closed a year or two later and buildings replaced the runway.)

My instructor, Greg Quinones, lived in Juarez and came north to Las Cruces to fly with us. After the shock of having to fly had worn off, I tried to make the best of the situation. Looking back, I know I was too tense and too preoccupied to excel, but Greg stuck with me and taught me to fly.

My first solo was in a Piper Cherokee. It was a lot faster than the old 8N tractor on which I had logged so many hours in the fields at Nadine. On the first solo touch and go, I kicked the rudder as I dropped the flaps, and the Cherokee began to weave back and forth across the narrow little strip.

Thunk. I knocked down a runway light on one side.

Overcorrecting as I gained speed, *thunk*, I knocked another light down on the other side farther down the runway.

Back to the other side. *Thunk*. I finally got the power pulled off and stopped the aircraft on the runway.

Greg, who had been standing beside the runway, nonchalantly walked to the airplane, climbed in, and, in his heavy accent, said, "You are like a rabbit, my friend, hopping across the runway." The laughter helped restore some strength to my jelly-like legs. He got me into the air, and I soloed again that day without a problem.

As with everything I have done in life, I made flying that Cherokee hard work—harder than it needed to be. I spent hours studying and concentrating so much that I could not possibly fly well.

Before my final checkride, Greg and I were landing at the Las Cruces Municipal Airport on the wide and long runway, which presents a much different picture in the windscreen than the narrow airstrip at the university. I had descended very low on a long final approach.

The unflappable instructor looked over and said, "It would be a shame, my friend." I did not know what he meant and had no time to think about it. A second time, he said, "It would be a shame, my friend." Again, I did not respond. He repeated it yet a third time.

Finally, my brain could process the question. "What would be a shame?" I shouted.

He responded nonchalantly, with his arms still folded across his chest, "It would be a shame to land out here in the boondocks when we have seven thousand feet of concrete on the other side of the runway!"

I got the point and added power to stop from landing in the boondocks.

Burning Down Hadley Hall

On January 13, 2012, David Zott said in a speech in Las Cruces, "We have removed the fairy tales from our kids' education. Kids need fairy tales, not to convince them there are dragons; they already know there are dragons. But to convince them the dragons can be defeated."

I was one of the kids who needed to be convinced the dragons could be slain and that you could overcome the monster in the dark. I desperately wanted to believe, but I had to hear it and hear stories about it. I needed to learn there were giant slayers such as David with Goliath, because I did not believe it from birth.

After hearing enough stories and examples, I began to believe not only that there were giant slayers but also that I might be able to fight and vanquish the dragons. I began to believe the impossible was possible, testing the resolve and courage planted in me by Coach Shaw.

In 1967, a group of agriculture majors at NMSU got together to elect one of their fellow agricultural students as the university student body president. Dee Welch, Dick and Linda Ritter, and Bruce Ritter convinced their friend Houston McKenzie, a ranch kid from Tucumcari, to run for student body president. He won and served with their support.

As his term ended and elections approached the following spring, no one from the ag community stepped forward to run against the campus liberal for president of the student body. Houston, Dee, Dick, Linda, and Bruce showed up at my dorm room one night just before the filing deadline and talked to me about running. I had not run for any position in the student government, was not well known, did not have much time left before the election, and was not in the ag college. With all the obstacles, I hesitated but did not exactly turn them down.

At the last minute, I filed the required paperwork, another no-notice exam.

I knew most of the ag students from my years at the fairs and the 4-H competitions. With their support, I was elected to serve as student body president for the 1968—1969 school year. It was the only office I ran for while I was at NMSU, since I was not politically connected or active. Once again, about the only thing I did was say, "Yes, I will serve."

1969 was a turbulent year on American campuses. The administration building on the Columbia University campus was taken over by protesters and eventually burned to the ground. Antiwar protests were going on all across the country. Youth rebellion was en vogue. College students across the country were burning their draft cards, smoking dope, growing long hair. I may have been the only student body president in the country in 1969 who did not have long hair, smoke dope, or protest the war.

Years later, when I first ran for Congress, the political consultant working with my campaign declared, "You may be the only student body president from the '60s and '70s who does not mind people knowing what you were all about when you were at college." I merely lived the core values I had been taught at Nadine: faith, family, freedom, and service. An underground newspaper started on campus and gave me the name "SuperConservative." I guess they were right.

A returning student named Jim Cooper showed up out of nowhere and volunteered to ghostwrite our own underground newspaper, which we called *The Delightful Middle.* We were caught in between the college administration and the campus radicals. Roger Corbett, the president of the university, like most of the administrations around the country, was unprepared for the radicalism introduced to college campuses in the late 1960s.

The SDS, or Students for a Democratic Society, was our school's brand of radicals. They preached hate against the government, against the college administrations, against parents, and against traditional values. Meanwhile, I was more interested in getting my education, could not imagine burning down buildings, and attended church regularly while at NMSU, meeting one of my lifelong friends, Joe Herman, at that church.

I didn't mind trying to improve education, but the campus radicals were trying to encourage changes such as having coed dorms. Having grown up in the coed dorm of my family's house at Nadine, I did not have much appreciation for that.

In the spring of 1969, a few of the campus radicals set fire to a small outbuilding behind the Psychology Lab, intending it to be the warm-up for more radical behavior the next day. Sure enough, there was a call for a general march that was to convene the next afternoon at the newly commissioned student union building, the Corbett Center. The plan was to stir the crowd into a mob, march to Hadley Hall, the administration building, take it over, and presumably burn it down.

As the student body president, I decided to show up to watch what was going on. They had made an effigy of President Corbett, which was dangling from a rope on a long pole. Art Santa Cruz, a returning student who was older than most of us, stood on the retaining wall beside the student union, inciting the crowd. Jim Cooper showed up and began to quietly urge me to get up on the wall and debate him.

Just that quick, I faced another of the no-notice exams in life when action will be taken or not taken, but we will live our lives with the knowledge of our decision. I was trying to decide if I would act with courage or wilt under the test of my character and courage. Would I stand alone if necessary against untruth?

I realized how far outside my comfort zone I would be, but the longer I listened to the tripe being preached from the wall, the more I realized I must make a stand, that I must speak. I climbed up on the wall and began to debate Mr. Santa Cruz. I said yes to the debate, to standing up, not knowing how the angry mob might react.

A freshman yearbook photographer, Michael Swickard, captured pieces of the demonstration on film and placed it in the 1969 NMSU yearbook.

The last thing the organizer of a mob wants is rational debate; they need anger and raw emotion. I began to question the goals of the march, ridiculing the stated objective of the coed dorm, and wondered aloud why he was not interested in improving education, getting rid of the professors who could not teach. The organizers down on the ground tried to move the protest to its next stage, feeling that the tide was beginning to turn. They lit the effigy and began to burn it with chants of "Burn Hadley Hall down!"

A group of jocks who had been watching with half interest from the new Garcia Hall suddenly decided to come to my rescue. They swung in among the group and grabbed the pole with the burning effigy from the hippie who was in charge of it. The hulking football players waded into the crowd, slinging bodies, throwing people out of the way. The guy who had taken charge of the burning effigy began to swing it around like a lariat above his head, the flaming mass bouncing off of the gathered protesters. Pieces of the effigy began to come loose. Soon, the mob decided it was not as interested in burning things as it had been a few minutes before.

I never knew the guys who saved the day but have fondly remembered their help.

That same year, I had also been selected to serve as the Air Force ROTC Wing Commander. Nationwide, campus radicals were attempting to drive ROTC completely off university campuses, and the NMSU policy requiring participation by all freshmen males for the first two years gave them a rich target and much public sympathy. As the lead student in ROTC, I was again the target of a radical movement that was rocking the country, one campus at a time.

I was not particularly gifted at being out in front, all alone, but I developed confidence by being the target of a small group of radicals who were trying to change the values of the country. I learned to stand up against them and to voice a different view—a skill I have gone on to use all my life.

Lionel "Pappy" Haight

While all that was taking place, my studies were still primary. I had put off two required accounting classes until my senior year, but was enrolled in Accounting 101 under Professor Pappy Haight, which was consuming more than half my study hours. Rigorous accounting problems filled up entire spreadsheets and had to be completed in black ink with no erasures and only one line-thru permitted on each problem. Everything had to follow precise rules of accounting and had to balance exactly. Next to the Math Analysis class under Rocky in high school, it was the most demanding class of my school years. Professor Haight did not grade on the curve, and the tests were extreme; of the 80 people in the class, I had the fifth highest grade, and that was a low B with only one A being awarded.

At the beginning of the required second semester, I scheduled an appointment with the professor and explained, "Sir, I came by to tell you, face to-face, that I am going to drop the second semester accounting class I had scheduled with you."

He sat quietly, pondering while he bit into the cigar stub pinched between his thumb and the middle knuckle of his first finger, one eye looking off in the other direction. "Is there a problem?" he finally asked.

"No, sir, just that I worked the hardest I have ever worked in any class and just barely got a B."

He silently pulled out a folder and began to thumb through the papers. "Looks like you got the fifth highest grade. I think that's pretty good."

"Sir, a low B is not pretty good, especially for the time the homework consumed."

I was not particularly gifted at being out in front, all alone, but I developed confidence by being the target of a small group of radicals who were trying to change the values of the country. I learned to stand up against them and to voice a different view—a skill I have gone on to use all my life.

He had begun chomping the stubby cigar by this point, his slightly crossed eyes looking directly at me, mouth twitching as he chomped, then in a tone somewhere between hurt, disappointment, and disdain, he remarked, "Go ahead. You're the seventy-fifth student to drop the second semester."

The remark stung me, and I shot back, "If I were majoring in accounting, I would take your second semester, but I'm not, so I'm gonna move to the other professor and take the second semester under him." It was lame, and I regretted saying it as soon as the words came out.

But he was already signing the "drop slip," and without making eye contact, he pushed the form across the desk to me, busying himself to indicate the meeting was over.

My elation about dropping the class lost its luster as the memory of the old professor's disappointment ran through my mind, over and over, and the memory of the pride of finishing Rocky's math class tugged at the edge of my thoughts. My lightheartedness over finding an easier route gave way to disappointment with myself for taking it. I became disgusted with my actions, and the day second semester classes started, I decided to change back to his class.

Sure enough, the huge room that had housed eighty students the previous semester had just six of us left for the second half of the course. Right on cue, Professor Pappy Haight, nearing the end of a long teaching career, shuffled into the room concentrating on the papers in his hand. Standing at the lectern, he finally looked up at the small group, no sign of recognition that I had changed my mind, and stated, "As you might see, there are not many of you left. Among the complaints people gave when they dropped this class is that we never had any fun in here," and he proceeded to tell a stock joke that probably had come from his high school days.

Completing his "funny story," he concluded his opening statement, "Now I don't want to hear any more about this class not being fun. Get your spreadsheets out. All homework and tests will be accomplished in ink with no erasures. You will make every entry balance; you will be the accountant for your company and your customers."

He never acknowledged our conversation. The second semester was even more rigorous than the first. I filled wastebaskets full of spreadsheets with double-entry accounting that had a mistake somewhere before I finished the problem. During late nights hunched over my desk, I cursed my decision to take the second half of Pappy Haight's accounting class, all the while walking with more confidence and certainty for having taken the harder road on this no-notice exam. When the grades for the second semester came out, I was still fifth highest and still a low B in the class, but I was filled with enough knowledge to spot accounting errors for the rest of my life.

College Graduation

My graduation was delayed a semester due to the extra hours required to complete ROTC, so the summer of 1969 became another work summer. During my senior year, the state of New Mexico started a pilot program to let a student serve as an ex-officio member of the Board of Regents. I was selected to be the first to serve because of my position as the university student body president. I was on the search committee that ultimately chose Dr. Gerald Thomas to replace Roger Corbett as the president of New Mexico State University; he became one of the best presidents the school has ever had.

Attending the board meeting provided opportunity to meet all the members of the board. Each member offered to help me along life's pathway in any way they could. Rogers Aston, from Roswell, was the most helpful. He was a friend of another Roswell man, Robert O. Anderson, who had traded his stake as an independent oil operator for the controlling interest in a large independent company, Atlantic Richfield. Mr. Aston got a commitment from his friend that if I made my way to Alaska, the company would hire me to work on the Alaska pipeline that was scheduled to start in the summer of 1969. Without the money to buy an airline ticket, I figured out how to travel standby on military flights and made my way there.

Once in Anchorage, I joined the throngs of people who had come for the same purpose. With limited resources, I got the cheapest place to stay that I could find, a flophouse with one large open room that held approximately a hundred or more bunk beds. For a couple of bucks a night I got the top bed above an older Native American man. The place would empty out during the day as all of us reported to the yard where the pipeline activity was due to begin. Long rows of pipe filled the yard, and all the machines to carry and lay the pipe were in place. It was clear that the project was imminent.

Coming with an offer from the CEO of the company, I thought I had it better than almost everyone else there, who came with only the hope of a job. But there was a minor delay, and we were told to come back the next day . . . then the next. Something was wrong, but no one knew what it was. I was getting very low on cash and joined the crowds of people searching Anchorage for any work, even a dishwashing job, but there was nothing.

After two weeks of reporting for work every day and being sent away, I got a telegram from Mr. Aston. He reported that environmental groups had filed suit to stop the pipeline, and that it could take a couple more months. He had secured a job for me in the Hobbs office of Atlantic Richfield. The night before I left, my bunkmate shook me awake and told me he was leaving immediately and that if the police asked any questions, I should tell them I had not seen him. With a brief shake of hands, this fellow traveler in life was gone and never to be seen again by me. It was time for me to go.

The Alaska pipeline was actually delayed by lawsuits for almost five more years, a testament to the way the environmental groups hurt the poor. The oil crisis of 1973 provoked legislation that removed the legal challenges to the project, because the high price of gasoline was hurting all Americans . . . the poor most of all. And instead of killing the caribou, the Alaska pipeline has been a shelter for them, and the herds have increased dramatically. Meanwhile thousands of jobs were postponed, which kept willing workers idle when they merely wanted to feed their families. Today, thousands of jobs on the Keystone pipeline are being delayed again by the same tactics at a time when many Americans desperately need work.

I worked the rest of the summer in Hobbs and reported back to NMSU for my final semester.

During my senior year, I was surrounded by girls from Roswell, two hours from Hobbs. Becky Reed majored in journalism and worked for the student newspaper, *The Roundup*; Marilyn Hendricks, like me, had grown up on a small farm, and Melinda Erickson did math in her head and played Chopin on the piano, practicing hours each week along with her studies to prepare for competitions. She, along with Mom, pinned on my Second Lieutenant bars at the ROTC commissioning ceremony in late December 1969. We all continue to be close friends today, having been friends during one of the most turbulent periods of my life.

During that year, on a pathway to Air Force pilot training and the Vietnam War, I began to receive anonymous messages in the mail. They lovingly suggested I should think more deeply on the issues, especially the war and my participation in it. Having watched my friend from ROTC bolt to Canada and become a fugitive from his own country, I contemplated the end result of those decisions and realized I could not abandon duty for safety, no more than I could quit Rocky's math class or Professor Haight's accounting class.

After graduation and commissioning, I spent a week camping with my brother Mike in the central part of New Mexico before reporting for military duty. I would pay my debt to the lady at the draft board after all.

19

AIR FORCE PILOT TRAINING

After completing my studies at NMSU in 1969, I started the New Year driving from Hobbs to Reese Air Force Base in Lubbock, Texas, where I was scheduled to start Undergraduate Pilot Training. Having learned to fly in the ROTC program in college, flying the T-41 (the Air Force version of a Cessna) was merely a refresher.

But I knew the real test would come when we started training in the jets, the T-37 and the supersonic T-38. Realizing I had few natural skills, I hit the books hard from the first day, rarely spending time with the other trainees at the Officers Club or in Lubbock. I was serious about succeeding to become the first jet pilot in our immediate family's history. It would be my first major escape from the gravitational pull of my genetic fears and hesitations. I wanted to live and fly with the lightness of discovery I had experienced briefly under Coach Shaw, many years ago.

Captain Doyle Jorgenson, my T-37 instructor, was a great fit for my personality and modest capabilities. On one of the first flights, he asked, "Pearce, can you wiggle your toes?"

It was a question I had never considered, so I began to think about it, which only proved his point.

"Pearce, you're too tense. You'll never fly when every nerve ending is tied in a knot. You need to loosen up." He went on. "Your body can't be tense if you wiggle your toes, so let me fly the airplane, and you just concentrate on wiggling those toes."

"Yes, sir."

It was the right approach with someone like me, who had to learn even the most commonsense mannerisms. But he was sympathetic and concentrated on building a foundation of ease in the cockpit that I was able to build upon. The training included stalls, spins, aerobatics, formation, instrument flight, use of oxygen, and the basics of ejection—but I was to start by wiggling my toes.

People whom I meet now often assume that I was naturally good at things I've done, from flying jets to running a business, but that couldn't be further from the truth. Pilot training quickly taught me that whatever is worth doing is worth doing *wrong*. Who gets anything right the first time? If you plan to do everything perfectly, you will never get off the ground. And so I learned, through no shortage of failures, that success comes mostly from sticking it out.

Turn Toward the Pencils

Students are issued flight suits as soon as they enter pilot training. The suit is basically a big green sack with a zipper and sleeves for arms and legs—and pockets, lots of pockets, on the calves, thighs, and chest. And they all have a purpose. On the inside of the thigh, right up under the crotch is a slot for the orange survival knife, which is tied on a long lanyard secured through a grommet in the flight suit. The knife has a specialized hook-shaped blade used to cut the risers of your parachute if they are tangled or you need to get loose from the chute once it has done its job. You hope you never need to use this knife.

On the left outside upper arm of the flight suit are two slots for your pencils or pens. They are readily accessible in flight to write clearances or notes on the kneepad that is strapped around your thigh when you fly. The flight charts are folded neatly under the clip above the writing pad for reference in flight.

Even outfitted with all the gear, most new pilots experience a similar phenomenon under the pressure of trying to learn to fly: the inability to distinguish left from right. What came easily on the ground escaped me in air. The conversation with my flight instructor went something like this:

"Lieutenant, make a thirty-degree bank turn to the left, roll out on a heading of 270 while descending a thousand feet, level off at nineteen thousand feet, and time your turn and descent to arrive at the heading and altitude at the same time."

"Yes, sir."

The turn began first, then gradually the nose would lower and the descent would begin. About halfway through the turn, the instructor would interrupt my concentration and ask me to repeat the instructions. And I would say, "Thirty degrees, left turn . . ." etc.

"Lieutenant, which wing is low?" (Generally meaning which way are you turning.)

"Sir, the right wing is low." The concentration of controlling all parameters of flight kept the obvious from hitting my consciousness.

"Your right wing is down. Does that mean anything significant?"

"Yes, sir."

"What might that be?"

"Well, sir, I am trying to figure it out, but I may be turning to the right."

"That's correct, Lieutenant. What do you think you should do about that?"

"Well, sir, should I turn the other direction?"

"Yes, dummy, I told you to make a left turn. You should turn the other direction."

Sometimes it still took another few seconds for the recognition to translate into action. The string of invectives only increased until I actually reversed the turn.

The next time, the instructions might be to make a sixty-degree bank turn to the right to a heading of 180 while climbing a thousand feet to roll out on heading and level off at altitude at the same time. Sixty-degree bank turns require much more concentration and adjustments, because so much lift is dumped when the wings bank that much. The back pressure on the control stick and power both have to be adjusted.

It may not sound like much, but there is a pretty significant cross-check to do it all at once—watch for other aircraft, constantly adjust your bank and pitch attitude, watch altitude, vertical velocity, and heading, while the 2-G (two times the weight of gravity) makes everything happen even faster than normal because of rapidly changing aerodynamic forces as you enter and leave the turn. With so much to think about, the turn could easily go the wrong direction again, and other instructors have told me that it happens often, even to veteran pilots. Chances were that I'd end up turning to the left again. This time the corrective language would be louder and more colorful.

Finally—and you could sense that it was not the first time your instructor had been through this—he would instruct you, "Lieutenant, I want a forty-five-degree bank turn, roll out heading north, descend a thousand feet to arrive at your heading and altitude simultaneously. Lieutenant, I want another left turn . . . but to save you trying to figure out which way that is, just turn toward your pencils."

The first time an instructor shared this offensively simple revelation, my face burned red with embarrassment. I called myself stupid under my breath and thought worse of the instructor. Mad enough that I refused to reply, I did, in fact, turn toward the pencils the next time. Gradually, we all got to where we could think and fly at the same time.

Ten Feet

"Lieutenant, you're lettin' the aircraft fly you . . . fly the aircraft."

Inside the face shield of my flight helmet, the sweat was pouring down my face, running around the oxygen mask and dripping off the sides down onto my flight suit. Try as I might to control the aircraft, I knew the instructor was right. I kept repeating to myself, "Just fly the aircraft, stupid." In flying, and life, sometimes all you can manage is the basics.

"Lieutenant, you are consistently ten feet low. I want you to get the aircraft up ten feet and fly precisely on the twenty-three-thousand-foot altitude we have been assigned."

"Sir, I can't make a ten-foot correction; that's too small a change."

His immediate response represented the ageless wit of generations of flight instructors who had heard the same comment from their pupils. "Then climb one hundred feet and descend back down ninety feet." The math seemed to work fine, and it removed the pressure of making small corrections. Gradually, I, like students before me, got the changes down to fifty feet, then forty feet. Eventually, I could make the aircraft climb ten feet or even two feet.

It is in this season that I began to expect perfection. I knew that if I could consistently maintain the aircraft altitude ten feet low, I could maintain it exactly on the assigned altitude. It was simply a matter of expecting the exact. I still believe that exactness is the target, an extension of the 4-H motto of making the best better.

While I admit that my natural abilities as a pilot were unexceptional, my enthusiasm was far from muted. I found in flight the same release from the earthbound prison I had experienced under the tutelage of Coach Shaw, the same lightness of being and exhilaration of discovery and freedom. It is reflected in the poem written by John Gillespie Magee Jr. that is titled "High Flight":

Oh I have slipped the surly bonds of Earth
And danced the skies on laughter-silvered wings;
Sunward I've climbed and joined the tumbling mirth
Of sun-split clouds—and done a hundred things
You have not dreamed of—wheeled and soared and swung
High in the sunlit silence. Hovr'ing there,
I've chased the shouting wind along, and flung
My eager craft through footless halls of air. . . .

By the time of my first T-37 checkride, not only was I comfortable at the controls, I was more at ease with myself, which was reflected in an unspoken assurance from Captain Jorgensen that I would score well.

The checkride with Captain Gaines went very well indeed. My cloverleaf was symmetrical, the Immelmann Turn and Split S maneuver were crisp, the stalls and spin recoveries affirmative and clean. The entire ride was perhaps my personal best . . . until we got back to the pattern.

Regulations called for a precautionary radio call when fuel reaches a specific level, and ours was right at that limit near the end of the flight. In the real world, I would have asked the check pilot's advice about making the call. But I could not override my belief that there was a protocol that would not let me ask any question of the check pilot. I interpreted that I should do everything, and the evaluator was to be an invisible participant, so I made the call required by the book without consulting him.

Studies have shown that many shy people believe there is some secret protocol that one must guess at in social situations. This inborn tendency of mine kept me from asking for a simple clarification about the radio call, which apparently was the wrong call to make. Captain Gaines immediately jerked the stick from my hand and began to scream and violently throw the stick from side to side, bouncing my flight helmet against the side canopy. Over and over, he berated me with a tirade of verbal attacks, which brought my enthusiasm crashing to earth. Mercifully, we were in the landing pattern, and I was able to land without further incident.

After the ride, a bewildered Captain Jorgensen found me slumped in the squadron study room and asked me, "How did the ride go?" I could tell he had heard something, and that his hopes for my performance would not be realized.

"Sir, to be honest, it was one of the best flights I have ever had. My altitude control was within one hundred feet, airspeeds within plus or minus two knots the whole ride. It was scoring an excellent [the highest grade available]. Then when I made a call at minimum fuel in the traffic pattern, the check pilot lost it. He grabbed the stick, banging the aircraft and me around, lots of loud language. Sir, maybe I should have asked, but the call was not incorrect."

Captain Jorgensen shook his head in puzzlement and left. Although he never said anything, I felt from his behavior later that he had to intervene to keep me from being failed for the ride. The call was not discussed in the debriefing of the ride and never came up again with Captain Jorgensen.

Because of one radio call, the best flight of my Air Force career received the lowest grade above failing, a "Fair." Because of that grade, I was out of contention for the single-seat fighter aircraft assignments that are the apple of every jet pilot's eye. Sixty days later, I took my final T-37 checkride and scored an excellent, but the damage had been done. The class transitioned into T-38s, and the incident was forgotten, but it seriously affected my position in the graduation ranking. But, to this day, I don't know that the call was a mistake.

Passenger in Life

It was during a cross-country flight in Air Force pilot training that it struck me. In life, we will either be passengers or pilots, spectators or drivers. There was deep clarity when I decided I would determine my lot in life, not passively accept what life gave me, and that mind-set has stayed with me ever since.

I want to be the pilot of my life.

The T-38 Talon, known as the "White Rocket," was the Air Force's first supersonic jet trainer. Its two jet engines are capable of climbing from sea level to nearly thirty thousand feet in less than a minute. The high-performance aircraft boasted swept-back wings and tandem seating that placed the student in front of the instructor and both sitting on rocket-powered ejection seats. The astronauts have flown it for training since the early days of space missions. Although its maximum operating altitude is fifty-five thousand feet, flight above forty-five thousand feet is prohibited.

Cross-country missions, as the name implies, train student pilots how to convert the scattered elements of flying into the process of flying across the country from one base to another, which is more complex than it might sound. Usually, several T-38s will fly to the same destination on the same weekend so that students can compare notes about the mission after it's over. Our destination was Key West, Florida. We departed from Reese AFB in Lubbock, Texas, on a Friday for the flight, which included stops for fuel at Barksdale AFB in Louisiana and Warner Robbins AFB in Georgia.

During the flight, I was in awe of the discovery afforded through this beyond bird's-eye view. From forty-five thousand feet, I could see the curvature of the earth and the shape of the Florida peninsula jutting away from the rest of the United States. I was mesmerized, perhaps more, a lot more, than I should have been.

Keep in mind that a car going sixty miles per hour is covering a mile every minute, so the driver has to think about a mile ahead of the car to anticipate turns or stops for fuel. The faster you go, the farther ahead you have to think. If you are not thinking ahead, you are a passenger, even when you are at the wheel.

Soon enough, we were crossing into Florida. It was dusk, and we were less than an hour from landing. While I was lost in awe of the view, we were blasting toward our destination at ten miles per minute, so I needed to be thinking one hundred miles ahead. Instead, even though I was piloting the aircraft, I was more like a passenger, savoring the aesthetics of having slipped the surly bonds of gravity, climbing to the lower edge of space.

Full darkness settled upon us. We were one hundred miles from Key West and still at thirty-one thousand feet. I could tell from the silence in the cockpit behind me that the instructor was trying to make a point, but I could not for the life of me determine what that might be. Lost in the reverie of the moment, my main skill, math, was not at work. Otherwise, I would have calculated that we were less than ten minutes from our destination. Descending thirty thousand feet in ten minutes would require a very high rate of descent, more than three thousand feet per minute. But in my passenger mindset, I was still not processing the variables confronting me.

From the rear seat, I heard the telling silence . . . and in my mirror I could see the tapping of fingers on the glare shield above the instruments. Descents in any aircraft require a balancing of rate of descent, maximum allowable airspeeds, distance traveled to descend, and altitude at which the descent is initiated. *What could be the problem?* I scanned the gauges, circuit breakers, warning lights—nothing out of the ordinary.

With almost one hundred miles remaining, I saw no urgency in getting the approach plates out to review the instrument procedure since the weather was clear VFR (visual flight rules), meaning we could just use the visual contact to maneuver and land. Still, that insistent tapping. *What is that all about?*

At seventy miles, I requested a lower altitude and started a normal descent of fifteen hundred feet per minute, still not doing the math that at this rate of descent it would take twenty minutes to get to sea level. Meanwhile, we were only about seven minutes from the base.

The tapping got louder.

I got the approach plates out and was patiently working my way through, reviewing the frequencies, abstractly looking at the approach procedures, when the air traffic controller, trying to help, asked if I needed a couple of turns in a holding pattern to help me descend. I asked myself why he had made the call, but changing from passenger to pilot is not an easy transition, especially when you think you have been in control all along and your flight was right on schedule.

When we crossed the station at Key West and turned outbound for a standard approach, the world was suddenly pitch black. The ocean and a high overcast joined together to make a situation that was totally without visual references; the lights of the Florida coast and the town at Key West were behind me and the stars obscured by the high clouds. And I was ten thousand feet higher than I should have been.

The realization that I was so far behind the aircraft and mentally unprepared for what should have been a standard instrument flight caused me to hyperventilate. Every hurried breath, sucking for enough oxygen to fight off the panic, was audible over the hot microphones between cockpits. I struggled for control.

To lose altitude, I had to point the nose further down, but that caused my airspeed to build to the point that I could not lower the landing gear that would have helped me slow down and descend. I deployed the speed brakes but was still thousands of feet too high. The high rate of descent caused everything in the approach to be nonstandard.

More hyperventilation. Rising panic. And still this terrible darkness. One hundred miles before, I thought I would just watch the lights and land using visual references, never anticipating the total blackness confronting me over the ocean. My passenger ride was now like a wild roller coaster. I was supposed to be in charge, but the extreme rate of descent was throwing everything off pace, the cadence necessary for a good flight was completely missing. The hyperventilation increased, and I could not get enough oxygen. I grappled for the bayonet clips that hold the oxygen mask in place and released it. I had to breathe!

My control of the aircraft became marginal. I struggled to get my breath. With the mask that houses my radio transmitter off of my face, the controller could not read my transmissions. I had placed myself in the position of a pilot-induced crash when I should have had a routine, easily managed instrument approach. Finally, the instructor said calmly, "I have the aircraft," which meant he was mercifully going to rescue me from myself. I could go back to being a passenger. I was humiliated.

In the raucous laughter and talk over dinner, I remained silent and made a commitment that never again in life, whether it involved flying an airplane, running a business, or making the decisions for our family, would I let myself be lulled into the role of a passenger. I want to be an active part of determining the fate that lies ahead of me.

Choosing an Assignment—the Pathway of My Life

Assignments following pilot training are decided through a simple process in which the class is ranked from top to bottom, based on check-ride scores, and the pilots choose from a pool of assignments that are based on the Air Force's needs at the time. On graduation day, assignments are displayed on a screen, and the top graduate chooses first. The second chooses from among the rest, and so on, until the last person gets the only assignment left.

Because of the rocky check in the T-37, I finished about a third of the way from the top of my class, while the higher grade I believed I had earned would have placed me much higher. Going into the selection process, I was nervous about my future. This was not a no-notice exam to be sure. We had all been comparing notes about what we wanted to do all year, but the dynamics of seeing your number one choice being taken by someone else brings a no-notice element into the process.

A buzz of excitement and groans ran through the room as the list of available assignments was displayed on the screen. There were only two fighter slots; the rest were helicopters, transports, and instructor pilot slots in training command. Hidden in the mix were two C-130s going to Pacific Air Forces (PACAF), meaning they would be flying in the war effort. The 130s also are turboprops, and propellers are not extremely attractive to the go-fast ego of graduating pilots.

In the raucous laughter and talk over dinner, I remained silent and made a commitment that never again in life, whether it involved flying an airplane, running a business, or making the decisions for our family, would I let myself be lulled into the role of a passenger. I want to be an active part of determining the fate that lies ahead of me.

The top two graduates snapped up the two fighter positions, and a C-5 based in California went soon after. People were jumping at the T-38s to be in a fast jet. I could tell that, when my turn came, there would still be T-38 and T-37 instructor slots, which would keep me flying jets and delay my direct exposure to the war by two to three more years. Or I could select jet transports based in a safe stateside location. These thoughts were wreaking havoc on my mind as I tried to keep up with the quickly evolving list of aircraft left on the screen.

During the year in pilot training, I began to acknowledge that Vietnam was the event of my generation, and I had been developing deep doubts about making safe choices while others my age were dying in the war. In the back of my mind, I wondered if I had the courage to face what every person has to face: could I face fear? Would I volunteer for a war assignment?

Those anonymous letters from my college days, urging me to rethink my position on the war, began to crowd into my mind, making me think about the noncombat positions. I was conflicted about taking a slow mover (transport) copilot slot while there were jets available. How would I explain the decision to my classmates and family?

And then it was my turn. The decision I had mulled over for a year was suddenly upon me. Surprising even myself, I chose a C-130 at Clark AFB, Philippine Islands, knowing only that their primary missions were staged from Cam Rahn Bay, South Vietnam.

In the flash of an eye, I chose a blue-collar flying job in the war rather than becoming a prima donna instructor nurturing the egos of aspiring jet pilots. There were reasons for choosing the C-130, and though none were very clear in my mind, I definitely wanted to continue to defeat the fears that had controlled so much of my early life. It was in the defeat of fear that I found the greatest release from the gravitational pull of a dull life.

U.S. Air Force, 1971 Survival School

As kids, Dad would take us five boys fishing on the Delaware River once or twice a year, south of Carlsbad, New Mexico. The Delaware is a small creek with a big watershed that's far off the beaten track and flows for a few miles before joining the Pecos River that runs from northern New Mexico and down through Roswell, Carlsbad, and on into Texas. When large rains came, it would easily flood. Once, on a trip after a heavy rain, we saw a dead horse in the top of a fifty-foot cottonwood tree, so the flood-waters had been at least that deep. An old dam that was built in the early 1900s washed out quickly and stands as a mute testimony to the severity of floods that can happen on that small stream.

My mom and sister, Tanis, seldom went on these pilgrimages. It was a pretty uncivilized place even without us five boys. With us, it just was not worth the risk for the faint of heart. In decades of going there to fish, we never ran into another party anywhere along the river. Five boys and their wild-at-heart father in the middle of nowhere—not a care in the world—that was my first introduction to nature and survival in it.

I graduated from pilot training and was headed to the Philippines for my first operational experience flying in Vietnam. But combat survival training, or Survival, Evasion, Resistance, and Escape (SERE), was mandatory before going into the war theater. I showed up at Fairchild AFB in Spokane, Washington, preoccupied with the upcoming exposure to war, but my attention was redirected very quickly to survival. The experience proved pivotal in developing the growing independence and confidence that was building in me.

The training started with several days in the classroom, learning basic stuff such as don't eat the yellow snow (animals pee, too). Poisonous berries will ruin your day, so crush the small berries, taste a drop or two before you eat lots; small doses will make you a little sick, but not as bad as handfuls of them.

It was all presented in a way that was riveting and a little too real to forget. I could still perform an emergency tracheotomy with a survival knife if my windpipe were collapsed in an accident (such as hitting it while ejecting from a plane). If you don't do it, you suffocate; if you do it wrong, you ruin your voice box but will get the air. If you are suffocating, you do the process no matter what, because you need the air immediately. The instructors got standing ovations for their lectures, which was the first time I had ever seen that for any instructor.

For the actual field survival and escape portion, we were divided into groups of about a dozen, and each of us received two potatoes and an onion to eat for the next five days. The hunger aspect of survival became real very quickly. We had one parachute to share among us. We used the webbing to make belts, backpacks, and the like and converted the canopy into a tent. We were placed in the wilds of Washington State for one purpose—to survive.

I was hooked. The idea of man against nature is as old as the human race, but until we immerse ourselves in it for real, it is a hypothetical mental exercise. The Delaware River was nature, but we went home at the end of the day. This was real survival, albeit with a safety net. It was the reality show decades before TV got in on the act.

The next part of the course was how to resist the enemy if captured. We were interrogated, faced sleep deprivation, and were put to the very limits of realism in the simulated POW camp. Resistance and standing up to harsh questioning were new experiences, but I internalized them just as I had Coach Shaw's lessons.

When I got to the Philippines, I was immersed in jungle survival—the same idea as the course we had just completed, but wetter. Try sleeping in a tropical rain forest during the rainy season, knowing that snakes like dry warm places also.

From that time on, I have been an avid outdoorsman and conservationist. I have backpacked in the High Sierras, in the Gila Wilderness, and in the sand hills of New Mexico. I have been out in the wild in winter, summer, and in between. I hate when people carelessly drop their trash on the trail or in the streams and often pick up stuff someone else brought in and pack it out. It's kind of my backpacking welfare, taking care of someone else's problem.

Headed to Vietnam

My orders were to fly C-130s in Southeast Asia for eighteen months, placing me in the war zone from 1971 through the end of 1972.

As the information stated in the summary given during the selection process at pilot training, the unit I was headed to actually did very little flying from Clark AFB. Instead, most of our planes were at Cam Rahn Bay in South Vietnam, and the missions covered much of the country south of the demilitarized zone. The flights were reportedly routine, with occasional hectic or dangerous incidents, usually involving small arms fire or rocket-propelled grenades (RPGs) delivered by the enemy infantry.

When I arrived at the squadron, the first briefing told how all the enemy troops, upon hearing an approaching aircraft, would point their rifles straight up and start firing blindly, making the pilot fly through a hail of small arms bullets. The RPGs and wire-guided missiles were much more deadly.

The biggest mistake I made was reading Ernest Hemingway's *The Sun Also Rises* on the flight delivering me to the war assignment. In that book, one of the characters had his business shot off in combat. I could not get the Hemingway story out of my mind, so I memorized the entire checklist used to fly the C-130, and during every mission I flew with the two-inch thick checklist tucked between my legs, just in case one of those rifle rounds penetrated the aircraft and my seat, heading toward my sensitive areas.

With that essential preparation, I was ready for the other hazards of war.

20

LETTING THE LION
DO ITS WORK

I've heard it said that everyone will worship at the altar of something. Show me where you spend your time and money, and I can tell you what your god is.

Mom and Dad raised us in church, but Mom was the more insistent about our attendance—every Sunday morning, Sunday night, and Wednesday night. As a result, I was grounded in faith and have never drifted far from the fold. The dimensions of that faith have matured and harmonized through the years.

Faith in the 1950s and '60s in Hobbs, New Mexico, was very much a question of denomination. Were you Baptist, Methodist, Church of Christ, Catholic, or Protestant? Reflections on the deeper, more difficult aspects of faith were not a staple in our oil town. The process of faith was more prescriptive . . . a matter of memorizing the rules. There were endless discussions about instrumental music and being saved by grace versus works, but it didn't go much deeper.

As I neared graduation from high school, the hippie movement was going full steam. Most kids who grew up in church as I did were unprepared to answer the increasingly vocal critics of Christianity, subsequently abandoning their faith, rejecting organized religion, and flocking to the counterculture.

Janis Joplin was the most notable of the kids who grew up in the Church of Christ as I did. After she graduated from high school, she gravitated to the hippie subculture in San Francisco, began using drugs heavily, gained fame as one of the country's best vocal talents, and died of a heroin overdose in 1970 at the age of twenty-seven. She died sixteen days after Jimi Hendrix, another leading figure in the counterculture, who also died at twenty-seven from an overdose.

I was on a completely different track. I was busy persevering through difficult math courses and taking leadership positions at the university, where the underground newspaper tagged me as "SuperConservative" and made me stick out like a short-haired student in the '60s, which I was.

Shirley Seall

In his book *White Man Walking*, Ward Brehm wrote: "Then Lodinyo asked, 'How do you defend a lion?' After seeing my questioning look, he went on to say, 'Do you hold the lion? Protect him? No, of course not. A lion protects himself. You don't need to. It's the same with the Holy Spirit. Just let Him out and He will do the job.'" That, in a nutshell, describes my faith experience during the Vietnam War.

Exploring my faith began in earnest when I got to the war. When I was at Clark AFB in the Philippines, I attended a small congregation of believers on the base. My first night there, in the buzz of people visiting before church started, I heard a woman's voice behind me say, "I am sick." I did not know the woman or the group huddled around her, but when I heard someone in the cluster offer an aspirin, I broke in and said, "It's not an aspirin that she needs."

No one noticed the voice of the outsider except the woman asking for help. She asked through the clutter of conversation, "What do I need?"

I suspected she was talking in a bit of a riddle, so I answered in kind, "Understanding."

"What do I need to understand?"

"You need to be understood. You cannot continue to carry all the ones hanging on to you."

Her eyes found me in the crowd, and I knew from her look I was right. No one else had noticed our conversation.

After church the woman introduced herself and her husband, Earl and Shirley Seall, and invited me to a fellowship event at their home. She knew I was right and wanted someone who understood the burden of feeling questions of faith, which is hardest when those around want a friend who is a rock, one on whom they can rest their own questions and doubts. I could see that the burden had become too heavy for her, and she and her husband were looking for a kindred spirit with which to share their thoughts.

That night I listened as the group fawned over the couple, but primarily over Shirley, seeing her as a spiritual leader of sorts, telling her about their problems and seeking advice. It was obvious that she was a powerful figure in their lives. Choosing my usual path, I sat outside the group, close enough to be asked questions but not close enough to be included casually. I was content to wait my turn.

As the group faded and departed, Earl and Shirley directed their attention toward me. We began a deep discussion as though we had been acquainted for years, visiting until daylight, exploring the deep questions of our shared faith. Departing, I went to my BOQ (Bachelor Officer Quarters), changed clothes, and went to work. That night, I was back at their house, and we visited all night again.

I sensed the Holy Spirit was leading these discussions, drawing us into a relationship he would use to mature us. When the lion is let out of the cage, it has its own way.

I showered and went to work, but after considering my flying duties, I declined their invitation for a third consecutive day and night without sleep.

The hunger for discussions of the deeper aspects of faith lit a fire inside me. The fire inside them was already burning, but I was definitely heaping logs onto it, both theirs and my own, producing the fulfillment and substance of questioning and testing our theology. I yearned for insight and perspective, to understand the foundations of my faith more completely.

With them, I searched, explored, and questioned without fear of judgment and found that these exercises were key to truly embracing my faith as my own. Expressing opinions and delving into interpretations gave me more energy than I had ever experienced. The all-night visits were filling a deep void in my life, filling out and informing my faith in a new way, completing the puzzle.

The work of spiritual understanding within ourselves is arduous and sometimes painful. Finding the right balance between commandments and scruples, between a God of judgment and a God of mercy, is an infinitely intricate process. To learn the fuller aspects of Christianity, I was journeying deep into my convictions, commitments, and beliefs. Gradually, I was understanding that I was more interested in the process of tapping into the power of the Holy Spirit than the explicit dos and don'ts of a rule book.

In Jewish history, Jacob is the father of twelve sons who would each become one of the twelve tribes. He was renamed *Israel* after wrestling with an angel all night at Jabbok. *Israel* translates loosely as "struggles with God." I was in the process of struggling with God. Admitting to it gave me spiritual freedom, the kind I had been missing. The reflections and deep thinking of my life developed rapidly in this phase, though I would continue to learn and grow the rest of my life.

The actual and immediate answering of prayers was a powerful discovery. Shirley had complete faith that her prayers were answered immediately. Many times, I was scheduled for flights into Vietnam in the early morning hours following our all-night discussions. The unlimited energy of discovery and understanding usually fueled me for flight the next day. But Shirley would always ask, "Are you okay?" If I was fresh and alert headed to the flight line, she would pray for safe journey to Cam Rahn Bay. If I felt the exhaustion that comes from lack of rest, she would reassure me that I would not have to fly. On those days, with amazing regularity, the flights had maintenance delays or weather delays when she prayed. I began to pay attention to her one-on-one relationship with God. I did not understand it completely, but I did not discount it.

Because of the influence of Earl and Shirley Seall, I grew beyond memorizing the rules of our organized religion and began to search for the meaning in the Bible stories. I was in the process of growing out of religion and into being a follower of Jesus.

The lion was loose.

September 6, 1971

I was assigned to the 463rd Tactical Airlift Wing, which consisted initially of four squadrons, each with about twenty aircraft. The squadrons flew the B model C-130. It was older and lighter than the E models being flown out of the companion base in Taiwan. Because it was lighter, it could land in a shorter distance than the heavier E model, so throughout most of the war it was used to support forward field operations at bases with only the short assault landing strips.

From the time of its deployment to Vietnam in late 1965, the wing participated in some of the most dangerous missions of the war, particularly the 1968 Tet offensive in Quang Tri and nearby Hue and also the A Shau Valley in the spring of 1968. It was designated to fly the Commando Vault missions that dropped the fifteen-thousand-pound bombs to "create helicopter landing zones."

In the four years prior to my arrival, the wing lost sixteen aircraft in combat, the most recent being just months before I arrived in mid-year 1971. Although far more fighter aircraft were shot down than transports, more lives were lost in C-130 crashes than any other aircraft in Vietnam. Christopher Hobson, author of *Viet Nam Air Losses*, states that this was caused by a number of factors: larger crews, and once they were hit, few got out.

Quang Tri was just south of the Demilitarized Zone (DMZ) between North and South Vietnam. It was always an area of heavy fighting. On September 5, 1971, a major operation began in Quang Tri province to disrupt the Communist supply lines south of the DMZ. For the next few weeks, B-52 air strikes were called in by local commanders to hit enemy concentrations threatening to overrun the area.

On September 6, 1971, I was copilot on a C-130 that landed at Quang Tri to deliver ammunition and supplies to the ground troops. It was to be the most intense fighting I was to experience during the three years I was in and out of the war. On that particular mission the weather was deteriorating as we approached the field and started the approach. We received heavy ground fire during our approach and landing. Air strikes were being carried out in the area around the base as we made our approach into the field.

After we landed, ground crews worked furiously to offload our cargo, then we departed through the same hail of ground fire that we experienced coming in for the landing. During the flight back to Cam Rahn Bay, the loadmaster reported multiple bullet holes in the body of the aircraft, but fortunately none hit critical components such as propellers, engines, or hydraulic lines. For the most part, it was just another day at the office, and you just learned that the hazards of war were never predictable.

First Day in Thailand

Our 463rd Tactical Air Wing was based out of Cam Rahn Air Force Base in Vietnam. The C-130 detachment was on one side of the base all by itself, and we did not mix with the go-fast guys in other units. Mixing fighter pilots and transport pilots is very rarely a good thing. The go-fast pilots referred to us as "trash haulers," which was not a term of endearment. In fact, it was intended to convey that we didn't really belong in their esteemed company. In return, we obligingly referred to them as "fighter pukes."

Few humans have more testosterone than pilots, and fighter pilots have an extra portion. As always, when there is too much testosterone and too few women, fights were a possibility. The Officers Club bars on base in the war zone were Exhibit A of this concept, with pilots, navigators, and copilots routinely gathering there every night. The volatility of egos, danger, stress, and the universal need for a sexual outlet were constant pressures, ready to spark a melee as soldiers gathered around the watering holes after missions.

On my first rotation into Thailand's Udorn Royal Thai Air Force Base, my aircraft commander—a brash, bruising, and fearless captain—kept glancing over at me during a flight in country, wondering at my quietness. Not wanting to make conversation, I did my work and minded my own business. I was far from fearless and of medium build at 5'11" and 180 pounds. I had never been in a fight in my life, was not good at football or any contact sports, and preferred the gentlemanly game of baseball. In other words, I was a polar opposite of this muscled, courageous aircraft commander.

After flying all day, my boss instructed me that I would meet him in the bar in ten minutes and we would eat dinner together. It sounded like an order, so I showed up as directed. As we stood in the doorway to the bar, he bellowed into the room crowded with F-4 pilots, "Hey!" Sideways glances in our direction tried to determine the identity of our silhouettes, backlit by the late afternoon sun at the door. At this point, I could feel that our arrival was not going to be my typical low-key entrance.

"Hey! I'm talking to you." He shouted again, not to anyone in particular.

My heart began to race. I thought of other evenings in other Officers Clubs, when fighter pilots partook in their customary fun, practicing full-bodied versions of their "carrier landings." They would run and slide on their chests across beer-soaked tables, trying to stop their landing before going off the end. Raucous laughter would ensue.

Now, the place was quiet, and every eye was turned in our direction. He shouted so loud this time that no one could miss what he said. "I am Captain Greg LaPoint, and this is my buddy and copilot, Lt. Steve Pearce. We are trash haulers and can whip any of you fighter pukes who have the balls to take us on!"

I had never been in a fight besides with my brothers, and in my calculations, if we needed the exercise, we should have gone up to two of the smaller guys and quietly invited them to a scuffle. But here he was inviting the whole bar to brawl in response to an open insult. Jeers headed our way from every part of the room. Greg just stood there with his arm around my shoulder (I am sure to keep me from running), staring them down. There were talkers, but no takers.

As we wound our way through the tables, with him in the lead, I could feel the stares as sharply as wasp stings. Similar to wasps when their nest is threatened, the pilots were all at alert, wings and stingers erect, and ready to strike. But Greg sauntered carelessly through the room without incident, the catcalls dropping to a din as he approached and passed each table.

We made our way into the dining room and sat down. He winked and said, "I hate those arrogant fighter puke bastards. You just have to let 'em know you're not afraid."

I silently nodded, wondering how many believed I was not afraid. Death by friendly forces was not my idea of finishing well.

"Thanks," he continued.

"What for?"

"For standing beside me."

I laughed out loud; he just grinned.

No one bothered us during our entire rotation, but it was the last time I entered a bar filled with fighter pilots in such a fashion.

Today, when I encounter the Vietnam-era fighter pilots, the subject always comes up. What did you fly? When I say "C-130s," they respond that "flying trash haulers must have been almost like flying in the real Air Force." Now practiced, I respond quickly, "Once a fighter puke, always a fighter puke." Just a little of the Captain L that rubbed off on me.

Barbed Wire

During one of our standard rotations at Cam Rahn Bay, late one night, our crew was dispatched on a "top secret" mission and we were to report for duty immediately. We were to fly to Korea, pick up cargo, and return it to Bien Hoa Air Base just outside Saigon. We would not know what cargo we carried nor should we look. It was all *very* serious and high level. The flight was purposely dispatched so that we would arrive and offload around 3 a.m. to avoid prying eyes that might see the contents.

We lumbered into the night skies and headed to South Korea, arriving around midnight, and were ushered away from the plane so that the cargo could be loaded on our aircraft in secrecy. When I climbed back aboard, I glanced to the rear, afraid that if I looked too long I might end up like Lot's wife and turn to salt. I saw that the load completely filled the cargo compartment, and that it was secured and wrapped in heavy tarps. A courier, the eyes and ears of the government, accompanied the load and was to insure that no prying eyes saw the cargo and that it ended up in the right hands.

After leveling off, I declared to the aircraft commander that I was going down into the cargo compartment to stretch my legs. He knew it was a pretense to give me a chance to look under the tarp and shook his head no. However, the courier was fast asleep and did not seem to mind if anyone took a peek. Remembering the lesson about the catcher-pitcher relationship in high school, I shook my head yes, and just like the pitchers, he shrugged as if to say, "You're on your own."

At the rear of the aircraft, the loadmaster, who was just as curious, met me and showed me the spot where he had already removed the retaining straps and pulled the tarp away for me to see. In fact, he showed me several spots he had already discovered where we peered at the cargo filling the body of our plane.

Our secret cargo was . . . barbed wire! And fresh vegetables!

We were, it turns out, couriers for one small planeload of deceptive accounting, in which the Pentagon covertly moved costs from the Korea theater to the Vietnam War effort. I didn't know then, but after the war I read that many times costs of the war were concealed in just this fashion. Labor costs were assigned to the place where people were stationed. We, stationed in the Philippines, rarely had missions outside Vietnam, but our costs were not charged to Vietnam but to the Philippines.

Back in the U.S., Strategic Air Command crews routinely traveled on TDY (temporary duty) missions into the war areas. B-52 tours lasted 179 days, then they were sent home for 29 days and redeployed for 179 days. The KC-135 crews generally went on 90-day rotations and were back home 29 days before being redeployed. The explanation persisted that it was to understate the cost of the war during both the Democratic and Republican administrations.

Our C-130 TDY deployments were 15 days in country, back to Clark AFB for two days, then back in country.

Incidents such as the one with the barbed wire created a healthy skepticism about the government, government accounting, government honesty, and transparency. Decades later, this understanding of how agencies might shift costs to understate or overstate certain facts provided a foundation for me as a freshman congressman to approach the budgets and spending with a healthy dose of skepticism.

December 13, 1971—Hong Kong

As Christmas of 1971 approached at Clark AFB, I was pulling a regularly scheduled rotation on Air Evacuation Alert. It was unusual, but we received a call telling us to report for an Air Evac pickup. When we walked into the briefing room, it was crowded with bodies, more stars on shoulders than I had seen in a single room. The briefing started with the intonation from the briefer that "this was a normal, everyday air evacuation mission," which meant that it was not. Briefings never started that way, and the generals never found a reason to show up in the evening for a standard air evacuation briefing.

We would fly to Hong Kong, and once there we would pick up two passengers and Air Evac them back to Clark, where they would be flown back to the U.S. on the larger jet-powered C-141. So we departed for the flight to Hong Kong, arriving in the middle of the night. If the briefing had let us know this was not a standard operation, it was about to get more so. The tower told us that we were to taxi to the departure end of the runway and stop there, but leave the engines running and lower the cargo ramp.

We did that, wondering what was going on. Then we noticed an entire line of black automobiles proceeding to circle our aircraft, and when the circle was complete, guards posted outside each vehicle with automatic weapons held at the ready. When the guards were posted in a complete circle around us, the lead car sped off back to the terminal. Through the darkness, we could see the headlights speeding back toward us. The loadmaster who was outside the aircraft but communicating through the aircraft intercom system described the approach of the vehicle and how it parked as close to the rear opening of the aircraft as possible. Then two ordinary people, not on stretchers, got out, walked under their own power into the back of the aircraft, strapped in, the rear cargo door closed, and we were given the approval to takeoff as the circled cars opened in front of us, but all remained there to make sure nothing hindered our takeoff.

Normal, regular Air Evac . . . right.

The loadmaster, in the rear, kept up a constant update on what the passengers were doing, but we had no idea what was happening. Then we got word from the command post in the Philippines by HF (High Frequency) radio that news was breaking that the Communist Chinese had released two prisoners. Headquarters suspected this was our cargo.

During the flight, the Aircraft Commander invited them up to the flight deck. The woman was talking a blue streak, nervous and distracted. The guy, about forty-five years old, was past the point of reserved. He had a thousand-mile stare, looking without recognition. He was standing at my right shoulder, and I tried to make conversation with him. He answered with simple nods of the head and very brief answers when he spoke. He never lost the stare into the distance, never focusing inside the aircraft or on any of us.

When we arrived at Clark, we saw two C-141s parked tail to tail. They both had engines running and all the lights on, indicating they were ready for takeoff. We were instructed to use our reverse thrust to back in between the two aircraft. Our passengers would off-load and climb into one of the waiting jets. The other one was a backup in case a problem arose with the first.

Incidents such as the one with the barbed wire created a healthy skepticism about the government, government accounting, government honesty, and transparency. Decades later, this understanding of how agencies might shift costs to understate or overstate certain facts provided a foundation for me as a freshman congressman to approach the budgets and spending with a healthy dose of skepticism.

Sure enough, the next day, the news hit the world wires: the Communist Chinese had released a CIA operative they had held for nineteen years and fourteen days. Richard Fecteau joined the CIA as soon as he graduated from Yale, was shot down on his first mission over mainland China less than a year later (Korean War), and had been held in captivity since then. Subjected to solitary confinement that sometimes lasted years, long interrogations—up to twenty-four-hour brainwashing sessions—verbal insults, and psychological abuse resulted in the reclusive sort of character whom I saw in the cockpit on the flight from Hong Kong to Clark AFB. The initial doctor's reports declared that "his demeanor was extremely reserved—not used to interacting with people, he spoke in a low voice only when spoken to, and preferred to have decisions made for him"—the same things we had observed.

The girl claimed to have been on a sailboat with her boyfriend when they strayed into China's protected waters and were arrested. He died in captivity, but it was never clear who she was.

An Loc—Kontum

Shortly after my arrival at Clark AFB in the Philippines, the Air Force began to deactivate our C-130B models, the oldest Hercules that was still being flown by active duty members, sending them back to be flown by the National Guard. In March 1972, the 774th Squadron, the last squadron of C-130s at Clark AFB, received word that it would be deactivated and that our planes would be returned to the U.S. by the middle of April. We would all go home and be reassigned stateside. My war was about to end, six months ahead of time. The early departure was greeted with a mixture of relief and sadness. No one likes to be exposed to the hazards of war, but the thought of being back in the states while the war and our mission was still going on left me a little empty.

For the next three weeks, people waited in anticipation of their new assignments. Some were excited and some dismayed by the results. Meanwhile, we were still flying our missions out of Cam Rahn Bay and Thailand. Suddenly, on Sunday, April 2, all members of the squadron were told to report for a briefing. I was instructed to bring all my flight gear and enough clothes for the next several weeks. These directives were unusual and indicated that something major was happening.

Once we were all assembled, our Squadron Commander, fully serious, briefed us on the details he knew: *all* orders to new assignments were cancelled, and everyone would complete their tour of duty as previously assigned. There was stunned disbelief in the briefing room; loud murmurs and grumbling ensued. The prevailing view was that this was some sort of April Fool's joke. Some men had already sent their wives back to the U.S. to begin looking for houses at their new assignments. Furniture had been packed and was on its way to the states. When it became obvious the changes were not a joke, there was anger, frustration, and a nagging concern that anything big enough to change orders for the entire squadron couldn't be good.

Squadron members lobbed questions at the commander, but he had very little information. He knew there was a sudden demand for extensive resupply efforts in South Vietnam, which was the C-130s' mission and the reason a high level decision was made to keep us in the war effort. He explained that the four crews that had been told to bring flight gear would depart immediately after the briefing for Cam Rahn where we would fly supply missions into three principle areas: Quang Tri, An Loc, and Kontum. Our C-130 had received heavy ground fire going into Quang Tri the year before, but neither of the other locations rang a bell with us.

The four crews assembled consisted mostly of us single men who didn't have sudden problems to solve with wives and families.

What was not clear—and would not be known for months—is that General Vo Nguyen Giap, commander of the North Vietnamese, was beginning a new and major offensive. But without that knowledge, we greeted the new missions with a ho-hum attitude; the full gravity of it escaped us.

I would read later in history books and on historyplace.com website about the Eastertide Offensive and just what was upon us at the time. Some two hundred thousand North Vietnamese soldiers led by General Giap were making a sudden effort to conquer South Vietnam. His strategy, undertaken because of U.S. troop withdrawals and the increasing strength of the antiwar movement in America, involved capturing Quang Tri in the northern part of South Vietnam, Kontum in the mid section, and An Loc in the southern part of the country. It was an all-out attempt to finish the war.

Of course, we were not aware we were being sent into this situation. We were merely curious about what was happening and how long we would be gone. As a bachelor, I had no complex circumstances with which to deal. I had very little to send back to the U.S. and was one of the only people who had not yet received orders. Other people were deeply affected by the sudden change.

After the briefing, those of us with flight gear reported to the flight line and flew into Cam Rahn Bay—our normal staging base. Just as suddenly as we had received notice of the new mission, we arrived in country to news that the E model C-130s, based in Taiwan, would take the An Loc/Kontum mission, and that those of us from Clark AFB would fly "klong" missions in Thailand, resupplying all the airbases in that country. Although many of the jet fighter missions over North Vietnam originated from these bases, our resupply missions in Thailand were not as dangerous or urgent as those in Vietnam.

But the change was hardly noted—one mission seemed about the same as another. That illusion was shattered just a few days later, on April 18, 1972, when the resupply mission into An Loc claimed its first C-130 casualty at Lan Khe. Then, barely a week later, another Hercules was lost trying to resupply An Loc, and a third was lost in the same area soon after. The An Loc resupply missions turned out to be one of the most dangerous callings for transport aircraft during the war, losing five of the C-130s in just over a month. As one of the initial four crews to be flying the mission, the odds of being among the five would have been fairly high.

We never were told why those deadly missions were taken from our unit and assigned to others. Just as Providence intervened to put me in the military and into the war zone, Providence intervened to keep me away from the gravest danger that I would have faced there.

Years later, I met Neal Williams, who had grown up in Jal, New Mexico, forty miles south of Hobbs. He had also flown C-130s in Southeast Asia in 1972 from CCK, the base that picked up the An Loc-Kontum missions. He confirmed that they did indeed lose many aircraft in that month of missions and shared his eyewitness account of seeing one explode as they flew wing position beside it.

Phnom Penh—April 30, 1972

In 1970, President Nixon created a stir when he authorized the bombing in Cambodia, the country neighboring Vietnam to the south. Cambodia had delicately remained neutral until this point, and it caused great turmoil.

During 1970 and '71, several terrorist bombings targeted the U.S. presence in Cambodia, damaging the embassy and destroying most of the fledgling Khmer air force. An attempt to assassinate Ambassador Swank on September 7, 1971, failed. That same month two U.S. embassy person‑nel were killed in a terrorist attack. In the U.S., people were ready to be out of the war.

By 1972, the U.S. had begun to withdraw troops from throughout the region, leaving less manpower to impact places such as Cambodia. General Giap's Eastertide offensive in late March 1972 strained the remaining troops in South Vietnam, diverting resources in the region. Instability quickly overtook the fragile but still neutral country of Cambodia.

The Communists had moved to encircle the capitol of Phnom Penh, which had become like an island, reachable only by air or river convoys moving supplies upstream from Saigon. Some reports were that the Communists actually controlled the city.

On April 30, 1972, our crew was tasked to fly multiple trips in and out of the city. On the first trip out, we carried women and children, including Cambodian Ambassador Emory Swank's wife. Brigadier General Cleveland, the second in command military officer, appeared on the flight as an apparent escort for the families. It seemed as though the ambassador felt they should get out while the getting was good.

We would make two more trips in and out of the city, taking other nonessential personnel to safety.

I realized I would probably never be in Cambodia again and had determined to see as much of the real truth as possible. I had left my childhood fears behind and was comfortable going solo, launching away from the security and protected enclaves of the military bases overseas.

On that particular day, there were two copilots assigned to the mission, so I convinced the aircraft commander to leave me on the ground on the second trip out and pick me up on the next trip in, which was scheduled for later that day. I had worn blue jeans and a khaki shirt under my flight suit, just in case he said yes. He shrugged as if to say, "It's your skin." That said, I stripped off my flight suit, crawled off the plane, and watched it disappear into the midday sky.

As the plane grew smaller on the horizon, I was struck with a sense of, "What in the world am I doing?" Conquering my fear was something I had purposely set out to do, but I was frozen with indecision, torn between going ahead with my plan to see Phnom Penh or just sitting down beside the fence on the abandoned airfield and waiting there for the C-130 to return. Finally, I flagged down a passing taxi, negotiated in dollars the ride to and from town, and went to see this storybook place, the capital city of Phnom Penh. After exploring the town, buying a stack of temple rubbings, and a small bronze statue to help me remember the day, I saw the friendly C-130 approaching miles away. I grabbed the taxi back to the airstrip and was waiting when the aircraft landed to crawl aboard, into my flight suit, and into the right seat.

Rarely in these forays did I gain anything specific, but more a belief that I could overcome fear and the understanding that I can and should verify commonly accepted "truths." Operational duties inside the war zone offered opportunities that one might have never contemplated otherwise.

I began during that period to see my potential, to develop the courage of my convictions, to have the confidence to be on my own in very different circumstances, and to find adventure and myself in the process.

That night back in the Officers Club, I watched President Nixon address the nation, saying the U.S. had no planes or troops in or around Cambodia. It was surreal, seeing as I had been in and out of the country all day and had, in fact, gone downtown. I would have understood if he said security required him not to talk about it or that we had a few planes there. But I could not believe the "no planes or troops" argument. Again, I realized that there were those in our government who, for no real reason, would mislead people, large numbers of people.

For the rest of my life, I have verified the facts the best that I can and have always approached the official government explanations with more than a grain of skepticism.

In early 1975, Phnom Penh fell to the insurgents. Over the next four years, 1.7 million people (over twenty percent of the country's population) died in the resulting genocide. The Communists executed intellectuals,

professionals, and anyone else suspected of being connected in any way
with the former government, nearly destroying the Cambodian culture.

One-Day Millionaires

During my year and a half in the Philippines, I was staged out of multiple bases in
Vietnam and Thailand, traveling off base at
every opportunity with my notepad and
Asahi Pentax single-lens reflex camera. I
witnessed all three cultures up close.

Scenes like this were familiar to me
when most Americans my age would not recognize them. The open-air stands, while more
concentrated and with roofs and sides, are the
same sort of marketing we did in our family,
selling vegetables on the side of the highway in
our front yard at Nadine.

When we first moved to the farm at Nadine,
there was never enough money in the budget to
buy materials to build pens for our 4-H projects. Dad did the same thing
that people around the world resort to when they are scraping to get by. He
picked up the things that were thrown away by others, bringing home cast-
off tin, lumber, barbed wire, hog wire, and other materials from the oilfield.
Our secondhand animal pens didn't look all that different, I thought, from
the ones I saw in Thailand.

Our pens
with my
brothers
Philip
and Greg

Thailand workshop

I met young men and women in all three Southeast Asia cultures who were not much different than my siblings and me. They were bright, articulate, and sometimes well educated, but there was one major difference: they had no future. There were no jobs, and there was no hope in their country.

I knew I had a future because, in the land of my birth, if I worked hard, saved money, and made good decisions, I could prosper. They did not have the same opportunity. In many countries, it's not what you know or how hard you work; it's which station you are born into, who you know, or how lucky you are that counts.

There are civilian jobs on all the foreign military bases that were paid by the U.S. government and came with benefits; these were highly coveted. If a local did not get these jobs, they competed for a second tier of jobs associated with the base. In the Philippines, young women could hope to be a maid or do laundry on the Air Force base for GIs. Others resorted to prostitution to feed siblings, parents, or their own children. Young men worked hard to get positions gardening, washing the servicemen's cars, or any number of other menial jobs.

Generally, these positions were based on verbal agreements between the GI and the worker. The maids would approach you when you moved into the "hooch," dorm, or Bachelor Officer Quarters (the BOQ) and offer their cleaning services for a modest fee. For car care, you approached a group of local guys on the base (that had somehow gotten permission to be on the base). They hung out all day, every day, in and around the parking lot and had a method of passing the work around so that each one had some income.

For twenty dollars a month, young men in their mid twenties would wash and guard your car, twenty-four hours a day, seven days a week. If they were really good and friendly, they might have agreements to take care of three or four cars. The group of car washers then formed a sort of fraternity that hung together, covering for one another in sickness or on days off.

When payday came, the Filipino men sang, joked, and carried on as though they had won the lottery. They had a running joke that I could not understand at first. Finally, I asked my car steward for an explanation. He said, "We are one-day millionaires." Such happiness from having an income is an emotion we rarely see anymore in this country.

In Vietnam, several of us would live in a "hooch" that came with a nanny. She was like an aging aunt, coming and going through an unspoken rule that gave her free run of the place, no matter the time. If you had a late flight and were showering midday during her time to clean the shower, she came in anyway and cleaned the shower.

Each person paid her twenty dollars a month for all the cleaning, adding up to eighty or one hundred dollars each month, including fees for shining shoes or flight boots. For an extra fee, she would carry your laundry home and have a family member do that as well. The laundry and shoes could be placed outside your room at any time, day or night, and they were ready before you got up the next morning.

The hooch nannies paid constant attention to their work, because there was nothing else available to feed their families. They did not want to risk losing the work they did have. Off base, their country had a limited economy with few jobs to offer.

We take our jobs for granted in this country. It has been a couple of generations since most Americans have experienced the hopelessness of not having steady incomes. We carelessly gave away the great manufacturing jobs this nation once had and now have an economy that is seventy percent retail, which severely limits our economic future. Only now, with college graduates finding there are few jobs, is the nation questioning the wisdom of government policies that have shut down entire industries.

Many people in the U.S. have never seen the kind of grinding poverty that other nations have. I not only have seen hard times, but I lived them as we transitioned from the farm to the oil field and onto the five acres we called "the farm."

New Assignment

After finishing my eighteen-month tour in C-130s, I was reassigned to the 97th Air Refueling Squadron at Blytheville AFB, Arkansas. Being assigned to Strategic Air Command (SAC) was depressing. I didn't want to fly the constant training missions and was not thrilled with the command's nuclear mission. Training for an event that probably would never happen—or if it did happen would make our jobs and very lives moot—was not an ideal one for me. This job was a deterrent. I preferred operational missions with a goal I could visualize, not one to avoid.

21

RETURNING TO
THE STATES

After spending a month of leave at home with my parents in Hobbs, I drove to the new assignment, east through Texas and Arkansas, then turning north along the Mississippi River, sixty-seven miles to Blytheville AFB, Arkansas. Darkness settled over me as I approached Memphis and passed through the Mississippi River communities. Shacks, built decades before, dotted the dark cotton fields along the road. Towns that had not been updated in years left me with a feeling of foreboding that I couldn't shake.

Arriving late in the evening and checking into the Bachelor Officer Quarters, I was suddenly overcome with the greatest sense of despair and emptiness I had ever felt. I was more alone than ever.

My perceptions had been heightened during my time abroad, and the sight of power and poverty in the state was overwhelming. I was feeling sorry for myself, as though God had overlooked the hard work to escape the self-made prisons and had deposited me in this place when I deserved more. I did not realize it at the time, but it was merely another phase preparing me for the greater trials and opportunities to come.

J. Paul Getty correctly observed, "Money is like manure. You have to spread it around or it smells." If manure is spread across a field, it fertilizes the crop, creating growth and productivity. Let it pile up too much in one place, and it begins to smell and ruin the neighborhood. Money has similar results. But the spreading around cannot be accomplished by government redistribution, which creates even more problems. It should be accomplished instead by individual investors.

I was an Air Force guy, but I circulated off base across the beautiful state with the same enthusiasm as when I was overseas. I had developed a genuine curiosity about people as I watched Mom unleash the potential of those who came into her field of view, so I constantly moved outside the safe and isolated base environment. From the first day I arrived at my new duty assignment in Blytheville, Arkansas—with the fresh perspective of a man who had launched out from a small farm to seeing the world—I could detect that smell, the smell of too much wealth piled into just a few hands. As a result, growth, energy, enthusiasm, and the joy of prosperity were in scarce supply.

Even though the slaves had been freed 130 years before, there still seemed to be an unwritten social order that applied if you walked into a store in that part of Arkansas. The clerks appeared to evaluate you and calculate if you qualified socially to be there. As a stranger, new to the area, it seemed that I did not pass their tests. The sense of status that seemed to pervade that region of the Mississippi River Valley overwhelmed me every time I encountered it.

There seemed to be an unspeakably heavy wet blanket thrown over the spirit of the people. Towns looked worn out with old buildings, dilapidated infrastructure, and vacant stores because of the shortage of reinvestment. Those individuals with significant means seemed satisfied or moved to big cities, creating towns with absentee owners and little appreciation for the renewal of the communities.

Meanwhile, the people of lesser means were constantly struggling to escape the gravitational pull of poverty that I, too, had experienced in Nadine, scrimping and saving just enough to try to escape. In business start-ups, they constructed buildings that, even in their newness, were not large enough or nice enough to attract clientele and were doomed to failure. Within days of being built, buildings intended to be tickets to prosperity were instead destined to become one of the ramshackle establishments that changed hands as quickly. I could imagine as I watched the revolving door businesses that a family had sat around discussing the risk, just as we had, during my youth, with our $200 boar. Undercapitalized and lacking business skills, failure was predictable.

There was a terrible heaviness of stagnation, that it was not what you knew but who you knew that dictated success and kept it among a chosen few. Very few succeeded in breaking the class chains, and the lack of mobility hung like an anchor on the collective spirit of the region. It's not that there was more hope in Nadine, but the social order in that corner of New Mexico was not as impenetrable. I was familiar with the obstacles there, and the open horizons made me feel as though I could see the path forward more clearly.

With a bad attitude driven by the assignment and the mission, I reported for the KC-135 transition training at Castle AFB in California. I learned while there that the units at Blytheville were among the last in the U.S. to not be tasked with the nuclear alert mission and, instead, were continuing the dwindling war effort. Our planes were still in Southeast Asia, flying the war missions. With the knowledge that I would spend most of my time back in the war theater, I threw myself into the transition to the tanker and graduated at the top of my class. I was beginning to look for and find excellence in myself.

Back to Vietnam

The four-and-a-half years of college, one year of pilot training, and the transition training to first the C-130 and then the KC-135 had soaked up lots of time. I was anxious to be finished with training and fly more operational missions and have a sense of purpose, to do real things. The desire came from that small farm in Nadine, where every task could be connected to an outcome and where every day, from sunup until late in the evening, we worked hard. I asked to be assigned to a crew that wanted to be deployed to the war effort as frequently as possible.

Most of my flying in SAC through the end of 1973 was on ninety-day deployments to Kadena AFB in Okinawa, Japan, Guam, and Utapao AFB in Thailand, refueling bombers and fighters in the Vietnam War. My last rotation was near the end of 1973, and the crew that replaced us was there when we pulled all the troops out of the war in one swift and chaotic motion. Hundreds of operational airplanes, along with the fuel, ammunition, and maintenance logs that went with them were abandoned and left for the Communists. We gave them an operational air force.

It was sickening to watch our nation's leaders, most of whom had never served in the military or in combat, first cut funding to the war effort to such an extent that training missions in the U.S. were greatly curtailed, and then use the savings to provide fuel for aircraft flying missions to support ground troops who were in peril. If our country places soldiers in a combat situation, they have a moral obligation to provide everything they need—fuel, ammunition, protective equipment, and weapons. The rules of engagement should allow our soldiers to fight to win; otherwise, do not risk their lives.

Then those same legislators, who, for over a decade, put young men and women into a war to fight and die, suddenly voted to abandon the effort. Embassies were hurriedly shredding and burning documents as foreign protestors stormed in. South Vietnamese citizens who had trusted the U.S. and had worked on our bases providing intelligence faced certain death when we pulled out and turned the country over to the Communists. Our government cast them aside as useless human fodder. If our leaders lacked the will to finish the war effort, they should never have allowed it to start.

It is one of the ugliest times in our history. I was ashamed of the way we got out and hate the politicians who put soldiers in harm's way without a full commitment to prosecute the war they put us in.

I have vivid mental pictures of the helicopters loading U.S. citizens at the embassy. The Vietnamese embassy employees tried to get on but were pushed back. They then grabbed hold of the rails and dangled underneath as the helicopters lifted off, hoping for salvation. They knew they faced certain death for helping the U.S. if they stayed in Vietnam. If they could hang on long enough to get to the ships, they had a chance. In a split-second decision, they grabbed at life, leaving everything behind. Gravity always has the upper hand in such cases; muscles begin to burn, vision begins to blur, and strength gives way to exhaustion. Many could not hold on long enough and dropped into the ocean. Some made it, and they were taken in by the U.S. But millions of South Vietnamese and Cambodians who helped the Americans were killed when the Communists took over.

Timetables for leaving wars only give the local populations certainty that, if they help us, they will face hostility when we leave. We should either not get involved in the first place, or we should stay until the job is done. Too many innocent lives are lost when we plea for local help, then leave them to the mercy of the enemy when we depart prematurely.

> It is one of the ugliest times in our history. I was ashamed of the way we got out and hate the politicians who put soldiers in harm's way without a full commitment to prosecute the war they put us in.

I often hear people express fear that America might fail. They talk about finding a new country in which to live and raise their family. I see that America is worth fighting for. The helicopters leaving Vietnam brought people to the U.S., the land of hope and opportunity. When the helicopters leave the U.S. and when we grab hold of the rails, there is no other place to go.

If we want freedom and liberty, we can't give up the fight here. We must fight those who would make America a socialist country, those who hate that America for generations has been a beacon of hope and opportunity for poor and oppressed people around the world.

I have seen our fighting force today. They are highly motivated, deeply principled, and full of courage, honor, and a sense of duty. These are young men and women who risk everything to see that our liberty stays intact.

However, one of the great internal threats we face is that the nation is developing an entire class of people who are fully engaged in taking the benefits of freedom but who have no intention to fight for or defend it.

They expect others to do that for them, then they disrespect the sacrifices made on their behalf. Liberty is being perverted into a license.

The movie *Top Gun* makes war seem like a video game. It is not. I have seen the real horrors firsthand. When my country called, I didn't want to go, but I did my duty. I am grateful to have come out alive and am honored to have served the country. In Washington, the majority of our congressional representatives do not know about war or the sacrifices they ask our young men and women to face.

In 1975, more than seventy percent of our elected congressmen had served in some capacity. Today, less than a quarter of them have seen combat. It is not that veterans care more about defense issues, but those who have served in the military understand to a greater degree the human impact of their vote. They understand more fully the gravity of what they are asking our soldiers to do. I can see how each of the wartime experiences has made me better equipped to the job I do today.

22

HOW WILL I LIVE?

During my time while I was stationed at Blytheville AFB, Arkansas, rather than live on base in the BOQ, I decided to live among the locals and get to know the people and the place. I drove around for days looking for a place to live, settling on a very small house in Gosnell, five miles from the base. James and Joyce Price had four kids and were my neighbors to the west. James was a farmer and a crop duster. He and Joyce became mentors and friends. Together, they had been trying to break out of the class they had been born into.

In *Cannery Row*, John Steinbeck writes about Doc, who "tips his hats to dogs as he drives by and the dogs look up and smile at him." James had that easy way about him, and people knew he could identify with whatever they were experiencing. He made dogs smile.

Many mornings, the roar of James' Piper Pawnee engine would break the predawn stillness as he pushed the throttle to take off from the runway behind his home. Standing in the front yard, watching him fly, I began to understand the difference between a pilot and an aviator. At the Air Force base, we were all trained pilots, with checklists and procedures and wings to designate our status. But James was a natural pilot—an aviator. He didn't just strap into the airplane, separate from it; he became part of the airplane. He defied gravity.

I aspired to his ease and skill in the cockpit and in life. He and his wife, Joyce, would invite me over for meals, watch my little house while I was deployed, and generally became good neighbors and friends. We studied and thought and conspired, all of us trying to break out of the same economic chains.

James brought a sense of peace and light to those who knew him. Living in the era and just up the road from where Johnny Cash, Elvis Presley, and Jerry Lee Lewis grew up, James had the same instinct for country music. There was a sadness about James that lurked in the deepest recesses of his being, never visible, never taking away from the sheer joy of living that he brought to all those who clustered around him. It was like a country western song was always playing somewhere off in the distance, too far away to hear, but you could feel the melody if you listened carefully enough.

The Bible talks about "the man of sorrows." You intuitively knew James had seen more of life than most, the kind that brings with it a sense of sorrow. Few people around James listened as carefully as he did; they were after the sense of peace they got with him, not looking to provide it for others.

Joyce had great business sense and kept James' many efforts on track. She calculated potential earnings, kept the books, and made sure they paid the bills on time. She had an insatiable curiosity, and the two of us spent hours talking into the night, with James quietly reading the latest trade magazine. The kids were very young when I moved into the house next door. Randy and Karen had James' wild streak in them, mesmerized with motorcycles, skateboards, taking things apart, and putting them together. Susan had her mother's chattiness about her. Terry had James' peacefulness and presence.

After years of slowly building his crop duster business, James borrowed sixty thousand dollars and bought a new Ag Cat, a crop duster with much more capacity than the Pawnee he had been flying. The big radial engine had magnitudes more power than the little Pawnee's engine, and the sound as it roared down the little dirt strip by his house was music to my ears. After flying it briefly, however, James decided he did not like the way it handled on landing. He and Randy pulled the tail of the airplane into the farm shed by the runway, set the rear of the airplane up on a thirty-five-gallon drum, and rebuilt the tail wheel assembly with parts built in his farm shed.

That was James. He saw problems and solved them. He didn't worry that he had no engineering degree or that, in making the change on his airplane, he had altered the design of the manufacturer, thereby voiding the warranty. He engineered solutions to his farm equipment, cars, trucks, airplanes, and any equipment on which he worked. In my book, regardless of his studies, he was an engineer.

My college math classes taught complex mathematical formulas to calculate the area in nonstandard shapes. When he flew fields that were nonstandard, James solved these same high-level math problems with intuitive thinking. He could figure in his head the surface area of an irregularly shaped field, calculate how much chemical needed to be applied, and then fly his calculations precisely.

As someone who had had to pursue knowledge, studying hours and hours, I was in awe of the way such knowledge came naturally to James. I have read about "Renaissance Men," but they are generally descriptions of people who have studied their way to knowledge in different fields. James just knew things. He was a natural.

Philip

"Captain Pearce, you have an emergency call." The announcement on Monday morning, August 29, was ominous, not only because of the word *emergency*, but also because announcements such as this rarely occurred in the Strategic Air Command Alert Facility (SAC) in Blytheville AFB, where I was an aircraft commander on a weeklong alert tour. With a racing heart, I picked up the receiver and heard Mom on the other end whisper, "Stevan, Philip has been in an accident."

I knew from her tone it was serious. It was the way Mom handled emergencies. When faced with crisis, she toned down to the whisper I had just heard. There was no hysteria, no crying, no blaming, just one more challenge in a life filled with challenges. She seemed immune to the full reaction, numbed by the fact that she'd been poor and struggled her whole life. It seems to be the way of the poor.

"What happened?"

"He fell from the derrick."

"Mom, it can't be true. I just talked to him a couple of days ago, and he was planning to go back to Hobbs this week. No, he hasn't had time to get into an accident."

"You know him. He went to work the first day back."

I thought back to my own worry about paying for college and knew I had done the same. "How serious is it?"

"He fell fifty-six feet from the derrick. When his right foot hit, it separated his foot from his ankle, so it was dangling by skin and tendons on the outside of his ankle. His back was injured badly . . . they think the impact broke his back."

The thought of my brother, lying broken there on the rig floor—the image nearly caused me to throw up. He had worked at a local well-servicing company the two previous summers and had moved up the ranks, training for the more dangerous work of standing on a platform high in the derrick to handle the top end of the pipe being pulled out of the oil well. The derrick hand was paid more than the floor hands and got more hours, which was a big deal as he was putting money away for college.

"What hospital is he in?" I was choking back the emotion that threatened to wash over me.

"They were working on an oil well up by Tatum. It took a couple of hours for the ambulance from Hobbs to get there. He is still en route back to the hospital here in Hobbs." She continued in that quiet urgent tone, "Stevan, they said he may not live."

I knew it was the nearest she would come to asking me to drop everything and rush home.

After spending almost three years off and on in Vietnam and Southeast Asia, I thought I was immune to tragedy. Mom and Dad both had multiple brothers and sisters, and there were dozens of us in my generation. But even with all those family members, death and serious accidents did not occur often. I realized, as we sat in a brief silence, that we were as vulnerable as all. Death and tragedy strike that quickly.

"Mom, I am on nuclear alert. They may not let me off, but I will be there as soon as I can."

The Squadron Commander listened with sympathy, but finding someone who would step into my rotation and spend the rest of the week in the alert facility without disrupting the future rotations took time. I waited and prayed. Finally, my replacement reported to the gate of the alert compound and was cleared into the facility. I departed Blytheville for New Mexico.

Thoughts of pity for my brother threatened to overwhelm me as I traveled. Philip, the fifth of six kids in our family, had started out life sickly. He had rhinitis and sinusitis. Then he began to break out of his cage, much like I had done. He had just taken final exams of his junior year at Texas A&M, which was a continuation of that escape as he had transferred from NMSU for a greater educational challenge at the beginning of that college year.

This picture was taken at Christmas. The next time I saw Philip, his back was broken and he was struggling for life.

How Will I Live?

When I walked into the hospital room, I once again had to fight the urge to sink into emotional morass. The brother who had fought so hard to overcome so many obstacles in his early life was once again in a hospital. This time the question was one of survival.

The doctor's report showed that he had crushed two vertebrae at the T12/L1 level, which is the small of your back. He didn't so much break his back as severely compress the spinal column; his spinal cord remained intact but had a bone chip lodged against it. The doctors here seemed to have given up on him, resolved that they may not be able to save his life, let alone his mobility.

Philip had been working at the top of the derrick and leaned out to latch a one-inch stand of pipe that is sixty-five-feet long standing on end into the elevators when he realized he had not tethered himself to the derrick. He grabbed the stand of pipe that has little rigidity, so it flexed, then recoiled, and flung him against the derrick, gashing his head and jarring his grip from the pipe. He fell feet first and landed on the steel rig floor inches from a pipe that would have impaled him to death. His right foot severed upon impact, and he was bleeding profusely from where his skin split wide apart between his butt cheek and upper thigh.

Jim Kemp, one of Philip's coworkers and a high school classmate who was on scholarship to play football at the University of Oklahoma, was the first to reach him. Jim had taken an emergency first aid class the semester before, and his application of tourniquets saved Philip's leg and his life. He also kept Philip from trying to roll over when his back hurt so terribly, which could have added to his spinal injury.

While his coworkers did what they could at the scene, the ambulance got lost on the way, and it took over three hours for medical help to arrive. When Philip's fellow oilfield workers gathered around him, they were frozen by fear and pity, seeing his pain and the severed foot. One of the men began to throw up, distracting the others. Meanwhile, Philip calmly told them to wrap the foot in a plastic bag and put it in the ice in the drinking water can that is kept on all crew trucks. That action preserved the nerve and blood vessel endings enough that the foot had been reattached to his ankle by the time I arrived.

I wanted to dwell on Philip's courage and presence of mind, on the fact that he should not have to make his way through one more obstacle; that he was in grave danger. All these emotions threatened to remove the urgency that I should stay focused, fight the despair, get organized, do what I could, and trust God

It was a replay of the T-38 cross-country flight. Would I be a passenger or would I be the pilot. The lessons from emergency situations during pilot training kept running through my mind—*just fly the plane, stupid.*

Dad and I left the intensive care room together on Friday morning. We were walking down the hall of the hospital when the stress of the question—*Who would act on his behalf?*—overtook me, and I passed out, falling to the floor in the hallway. When I came to, Dad simply said that I needed to let it go. Life was presenting me with another of the no-notice exams; this one was testing my very foundation.

And that suddenly, the question became *How will I live?* It was the same quandary I faced in Rocky's math class when Dad said if it was that hard, I should quit. Would I be the passenger or the pilot? Would I quit now?

I did not respond to his suggestion but got up, went to the phone, and began to make calls to anyone I could think of who might be able to give me counsel on what to do. Most calls were met with sympathy, which once again threatened to sidetrack me. But gradually, through the afternoon, I learned that we needed to remove the chip that pressed against the spinal cord. Otherwise, it would cut off blood flow to the lower part of the cord and deaden it from a lack of oxygen.

People would suggest a doctor, and I would call him. Each said they were not qualified to handle the case or could not take a new patient. At about 9 p.m., after hours on the phone, I had distilled the recommendations down to a relative consensus about the best spinal doctor in the Southwest—a surgeon in Dallas who had operated on many spinal injury patients. I could tell I woke him up, but he was congenial as he listened. He confirmed that he was probably the most experienced doctor on these cases in the West and that the injury must be addressed quickly. But then he dropped the bombshell—he had just retired a couple of months before and was not willing to come out of retirement.

My heart sank as I hung up the phone. Then my brother Tom, who had been listening over my shoulder, stepped up. He was a lot like Mom in his approach, whispering a question to me about how it was going. The actress Elizabeth Taylor had contracted Tom to provide floral arrangements for parties and events at her home, and Tom had become friends with Valerie Douglas, the personal secretary for both Taylor and Richard Burton. Valerie responded to his inquiry with an immediate answer: there was a highly renowned physician in Los Angeles who worked for all the movie stars and was a spinal specialist. I called the doctor in Dallas again and ran the name by him. He knew of him and said he would be our best choice. The poor family from Nadine had found another kinsman-redeemer in Valerie, who also helped set up the transportation.

It was a replay of the T-38 cross-country flight. Would I be a passenger or would I be the pilot. The lessons from emergency situations during pilot training kept running through my mind—just fly the plane, stupid.

With that, I got on the phone to the L.A. doctor, who agreed to take Philip as a patient and would dispatch an ambulance jet the next morning. But the arrangements took precious time, and after getting the transfer from the Hobbs hospital to the one in Marina Del Rey, the jet did not arrive until late Saturday afternoon. My brother Mike snapped the photo as Philip was placed on the jet. Mom and I crawled in beside Dr. Dodge and the two nurses and settled in for the flight.

Dr. Dodge and the nurses were congenial but very concerned. They immediately started pricking Philip with needles to find out where the loss of sensation was, i.e. where the paralysis was. He had feeling well into the middle part of his feet, which was good, but they worried about the length of time the lower spine had been without circulation (from Monday to Saturday).

The Learjet was fighting the gulfstream, and time dragged on. About the halfway point, the medical action began to pick up pace and seriousness. The ink Xs marking the point where Philip lost sensation had jumped to the top of his feet. The expression on the nurses' faces told me more than I wanted to know . . . that Philip was losing his battle to walk and perhaps to live.

The next line of Xs were at the mid ankle, and the ones after that at mid calf while the flight plodded along. Finally, we arrived and were escorted to the Marina Mercy Hospital, and then another delay. The medical report from the Hobbs hospital had failed to list the blood type and another precious two hours were lost getting a sufficient quantity of Philip's rare blood type. Just past midnight, the surgery began, taking several hours.

I had been up almost forty-eight hours without sleep and waited for the report. The phone in the emergency reception room jangled occasionally as family members back in New Mexico, anxious for news, called to find out what the results of the operation were. About 3 a.m., an exhausted doctor team walked in to give Mother, Tom, and me the news. Philip would survive—they had been successful in removing the bone chip. But the delays in getting oxygen to the lower part of the spine had resulted in the spine being deadened below the fracture. So, even though Philip would survive, he would be a paraplegic; everything above the fracture would work, but everything below would not.

The news was a mixed bag. Though he wouldn't walk, I knew that I had taken a no-notice exam that involved my brother's life, that I had been able to help in some way, and that he would live.

Soon after the surgery, my brother Tom and I went to visit Philip in ICU. The nurse on duty was one whom I hadn't seen previously, so I told her that Tom and I were the Pearce brothers. In a very grave tone, she told us that there was no one in the unit for us. We were stunned, thinking that Philip must have not made it after all. Seeing the dumbfounded look on our faces, she realized that we were not from the Pierce Brothers Mortuary and connected the dots to Philip, much to our relief!

Hot Peppers

My dear friend James Price had a circle of friends that extended to Leachville, Arkansas, on the other side of the game preserve four miles to the south of Gosnell. Jimmie Kennett and the boys had built up a cabin over the swampy water at the edge of the preserve. It was mostly a man cave getaway used on rainy days and during the winter, when farming was impossible; cooking, poker, beer drinking, and feasting were normal. The tastes of Arkansas had been perfected by different men who alternated cooking barbeque pork ribs, chicken, fried catfish, and frog legs. On days when there was to be a gathering, word spread quickly in the small community, men gathered, and while the cooking was going on, a poker game broke out.

One night, a poker game got underway with a handful of farmers, retirees, and factory workers around the table. I was the quiet one in the crowd. The gathering had started after dark, and fish were still frying at 10 p.m. and the frog legs had not yet arrived. A crew was still out in the ditches harvesting them. I was not a big consumer of alcohol, given my upbringing, but I enjoyed the camaraderie and wild talk.

Doc was a 6'4", 250-pound mass of careless energy. Everyone at the table talked bad about him, but the comments slid off him as though he didn't hear them at all. As a doctor, he never had to worry about the crop, the weather, or bank loans. He always had money.

Don Oates was fifteen years older than all his pals. He lived in town and survived on his Social Security checks, always closely watching his money. He rode around with the farmers all day. They drank the hot whiskey they carried in the toolbox of the pickup, chased with the hot beer that had bounced around in the pickup bed long enough to wear the paint off the cans. Don also seemed to have a reputation for helping the widows out in town if they ever needed help moving furniture.

I never knew exactly how Don made a living, but I was told he had been a commercial fisherman for as long as anyone could remember. A commercial fisherman along the Mississippi is different than what I had visualized for shrimpers on the coast. Don had a twelve-foot flat bottom boat with a small motor, and he worked the edges of the wildlife preserve that we were sitting on. There were veiled references to wild boat chases with the game warden in hot pursuit.

Don, in everything, found the lowest cost way of doing things. In his fishing, he developed a way to boil Ivory soap, rendering it, pressing it into a cake pan where it cooled into a cake like substance. He cut the soap into squares to bait his trotlines. His frugal nature was just as evident at the card table, as he played only winning hands. Everyone had the same caustic comments to make about him that they made about Doc. He, also, did not seem to care.

By contrast, no one ever said anything bad about James. He was somehow above it all. He didn't talk bad about anyone, and everyone respected his sort of moral authority in the crowd. As a pilot, each of them had approached him at one time or another, asking for a taste of freedom from gravity and a ride in his plane. He would always oblige. Sometimes he put them in the hopper of the spray plane or crowded them into the small cockpit with him. James could figure out how to grant the request.

On this particular night, the poker game was in full progress as midnight approached.

"Don, you old cheapskate, why don't you ever gamble . . . you only play sure hands," someone accused.

"Then fold when I bet. If you are that certain, just fold your hand."

Meanwhile, Louis, a round cannonball of a man with bulging and expressive eyes, was in the process of cooking a massive turtle he had caught. He was telling about a recent trip to Memphis, "The banker was downright *belligerous*, and I got mad and walked out, never did finish getting the loan."

I had picked up on the new term but did not want to be the one to inquire. Paul Kennett, Jimmie's son, did, speaking over him, "What does *belligerous* mean?"

Louis went mute, stopping in the middle of his story, his bulging eyes blinking as he thought. When he went quiet, everything stopped at the table as he struggled for an answer. "*Belligerous* means . . . well, *belligerous* is . . . " He was fishing in his mind for the definition. I assumed it was supposed to be a derivation of belligerent mixed with religious zealotry and a bit of his Cajun background rolled in, but I was waiting like everyone else for the answer.

Conversation was resuming around the table, when suddenly Louis blurted out, "*Belligerous* . . . that is Doc Rodman." He sat puffed with pride that he had finally worked out the definition. Murmurs of understanding and a few snickers passed around the table.

Doc Rodman looked surprised, then roared his huge laugh and proclaimed, "Damn, I have to agree with Louis. I am *belligerous.*"

"Deal the cards, you tightwad," someone shouted across the table to Don.

"Boys, at least I pay my bills," he responded, and the poker resumed with this new word clearly defined in all the minds there.

At midnight, the frogs arrived with a big batch they had already dressed, fresh from the ditches. The new grease was crackling as they dropped the floured legs into the pan. Though battered the same way as fried chicken, the muscular legs are harder to cook. Fried too fast, they became rubbery and untenable, but fried just right, the way Joyce Price fried them, and they were much juicier and more flavorful than any chicken.

The cold Budweiser was flowing freely in the wee hours of the morning. The talk was loud and foolhardy. The bets were getting larger, but the large pot still might have been just twenty or thirty dollars. Don had a big stash in front of his hand thanks to hours of careful play. He drank as much as the rest but never let himself get loud or careless with the cards. Seeing their money in front of him was agitating several of the guys, but he deflected all the criticism with ease.

Around 1 a.m., Wayne said loudly, "I sure would like a hot pepper with my frog legs."

Don offered up that he might just have one available for a price. The offer and possible extortion infuriated the group. "You old fool, you don't have a pepper on you."

Don calmly replied, "I might have one in my purse, but with talk like that it will cost you."

"You old stingy bastard, you don't have a pepper."

"I guess you won't find out."

The subject died down, and I had assumed the issue of the pepper was completely gone when, out of the blue, the whiskey seemed to speak through Don's challenger: "I'll give you a hundred dollars if you have a pepper on your person."

That was more money than was stacked in front of Don. The game stopped. Everyone looked. One hundred dollars among that group was real money.

Don, careful in his dress and in his personal habits, began to feel around for what he called his "purse," which in reality was just a regular billfold. He thumbed through its money pocket, through the bits of paper that all men inevitably carry around in their wallets. He was certain it was there, but seemed to have lost it. Everyone was about to score one for Wayne when, suddenly, he produced a two-inch long cayenne pepper and laid it on the poker table, throwing down the gauntlet, as it were. It was fresh, green—and expensive!

I almost fell backward at the surprise of it. Now, all eyes turned to Wayne, who worked in a local factory. The unwritten law of the Mississippi Delta was that you did not let your alligator mouth overload a humming-bird ass. He was expected to pay up.

Wayne was sullen and angry at the recognition that he had offered to pay one hundred dollars for a pepper. He looked for a friend around the table who would offer to say he didn't have to pay. One face to the next, he looked and found resolute silence. As much as they hated to see Don and his penny-pinching ways win, right is right. Wayne fumbled clumsily for the bill, slammed it on the table, and stormed out, leaving the pepper behind. Jimmie called for him to come back in. Disarmed, he turned just in time for Jimmie to hand him the pepper, "You forgot your pepper." All was quiet at the table. Farmer etiquette had nearly been breached.

Finally, play resumed and Don discreetly tucked the one hundred dollars out of sight, back into his purse.

Wayne stewed for a while before coming back in to take his place at the table. The stormy night assured all the farmers that they would not be in the field at daylight, so they were content to play cards and eat frog legs and fish all night.

Sometime between 2 and 3 a.m., the game was in high gear. Cards were flying around the table with cash, beer, and loud talk keeping pace. Without warning, Wayne blurted out, "I sure would like another pepper." His eyes made their way around the room and came to rest on Don. "You old fool, I'll bet you that you don't have another one of those peppers." The game halted, everyone looking over at Don, who seemed to be calculating the odds.

"What about it, Don, are you on?" Jimmie asked. "Are you going to take the bet? Or do you only play on safe hands?"

Everyone had watched Don rummaging for the pepper earlier in the evening. It seemed he was only calculating whether or not to give back the one hundred dollars.

"How much are you asking to bet?" Don asked quietly.

"One hundred dollars," Wayne retorted. "I want the chance to win my hundred dollars back."

Don was playing the situation up for all the drama he could milk out of it. As a retired guy, he seldom was more than a sidekick. He didn't buy seed or fertilizer from the local businessmen, didn't command the respect of people who spent money. He was not an impact player. Now he had the audience in his hand and was handling them with the skill of an experienced showman. "I don't know. I might not have one. I can't remember. But I may have another one."

Guffaws greeted him from around the table. Wayne egged him on. "You old fart, if you had the pepper, you would have taken the bet. Come on, gamble a little." Agreement was voiced from around the room. Now the tide that had favored him in the first turn was reversed. People seemed to want Don to give Wayne the chance to win back his money.

Don asked, "What if I do have another pepper in my purse? You got kinda' mad about the last one."

Wayne replied with sarcasm, "I would be delighted to give you one hundred dollars for another pepper. I can taste it now. Cold beer, hot pepper, and another frog leg."

"Get it over with. Take the bet or deal the cards!" Paul shouted.

Don could see he was about to lose the attention. "I believe I just might have another pepper, so I will take that bet."

Wayne was ready and slapped his one hundred dollars on the table. Don carefully pulled out the one hundred dollars he had taken earlier, carefully unfolded it and laid it on top of Wayne's bill, sliding them both across to Jimmie, who had become the unofficial referee. With as much care as before, Don fished out his purse and began to rummage. For a full minute he fumbled with it. Again, the catcalls and jeers.

Jimmie asked, "Do you give up?"

"Nope." Don was all business. Calls came out to deal the cards. Don pulled every paper out of the currency compartment, then he pulled out the credit cards and looked down in those slots. Then out with the pockets that were accessed from the fold of the wallet. Everything was on the table, and he sat looking mildly confounded.

"Are you in this hand, Don? If so, ante up," Paul commanded.

Don placed his ante into the pot and continued to look.

The bet was around to him, once again he was the center of attention.

Jimmie asked, "Can I give him his hundred so we can get on with the game?"

Don refused, shaking his head no. He was intent. He set the wallet on the table, completely empty of contents, and he sat trying to remember through the fog of alcohol that had been consumed. Suddenly he brightened, picked up the wallet, and started to unfold the "secret compartment" behind the currency. He opened it, turned the wallet upside down, and began to shake it. Nothing. He held it with one hand, tapping with the other one. And suddenly, a pepper dropped out!

23

PARTIAL MAN

Jim and Debbie Phillips were Air Force friends; we flew KC-135s to-gether in Arkansas. They gave me a copy of the book *Seven Arrows* by Hyemeyohsts Storm, a collection of Native American allegories and stories, shortly after it was released in 1972. The Indians use stories to help us understand our life and the world around us.

The book caused a great controversy among the Plains Indians when it was released as there were concerns about its authenticity. Despite the turmoil, the allegory of the "Four Great Powers" helped me understand the journey I had been on and continue on, describing it almost word for word. Here is an excerpt:

Among the People, a child's first teaching is of the Four Great Powers of the Medicine Wheel.

To the North . . . is found wisdom. The Color of the North is White, and its Medicine Animal is the Buffalo.

The South is represented by the Sign of the Mouse and its Medicine Color is Green . . . it is a place of Innocence and Trust, and is for perceiving closely our nature of heart.

In the West is the Sign of the Bear . . . the Looks-Within Place which speaks of the Introspective nature of man. The Color of this Place is Black.

The East is marked by the Sign of the Eagle. It is the Place of Illumination, where we can see things clearly far and wide. Its Color is the Gold of the Morning Star.

. . . At birth, each of us is given a particular Beginning Place within these Four Great Directions on the Medicine Wheel. This Starting Place gives us our first way of perceiving things, which will then be our easiest and more natural way throughout our lives.

But any person who perceives from only one of these Four Great Directions will remain just a partial man.

For example, a man who possesses only the Gift of the North will be wise. But he will be a cold man, a man without feeling.

And the man who lives only in the East will have the clear, far sighted vision of the Eagle but he will never be close to things. This man will feel separated, high above life, and will never understand or believe that he can be touched by anything.

A man or woman who perceives only from the West will go over the same thought again and again in their mind, and will always be undecided.

And if a person has only the Gift of the South, he will see too close to the ground and too near sighted to see anything except whatever is right in front of him, touching his whiskers.

. . . After each of us has learned our Beginning Gift, our First Place on the Medicine Wheel, we then must Grow by Seeking Understanding in each of the Four Great Ways. Only in this way can we become Full, capable of Balance and Decision in what we do.

Aha Moment

At twenty-five years of age, as I read the allegory of the Four Great Powers, a great aha moment occurred. I was a Partial Man. We are all partial at birth, born with our strength at one point of the wheel, and our weakness in the others. Our task in life is to seek understanding from the other viewpoints, thus becoming whole; then we are capable of balance and decisions that are filled with understanding and impact. I did not understand that.

In my preteen days, I stumbled toward the recognition that my inborn ways of perceiving the world were less than ideal, and I committed to rounding them out, to escaping the jail cell of indecision, gaining the wisdom, vision, and courage where I lacked them. Not having a map, or teacher to point the way, it took years to figure it out.

The allegory, as taught to preteen Indian kids, lays out the Vision Quest as the journey to understanding and perceiving life from all four vantage points simultaneously . . . to become a Whole Man or Woman. To help young tribal members understand the concept, stones are laid out on the ground to represent the four cardinal directions—North, South, East, and West—joined together in a circle, much like a compass. Each of the directions is assigned an animal, a color and characteristics, recognizing the strength and weakness that accompanies each perspective.

As I read, I immediately understood that my Beginning Place was the West: Introspection, the Looks-Within Place. But I had the characteristics of the Mouse, not the Bear, experiencing life close enough to touch with my whiskers, absorbing every fear and warning. And as is the Mouse perspective, I was near the ground, unable to visualize or see anything from a distance, my vision obstructed by the blades of grass surrounding me.

While the Coyote has a natural craftiness, the mouse has almost no inborn wisdom or ability to see threats. The shadows of hawks circling overhead cause panic as there is no way to know from which direction the threat is coming. Fear is common to people born with these tendencies. All these descriptions put words to my past experiences.

The innocence and trust of the mouse was deep within me, as was the ability to closely perceive the nature of people's hearts. And true to the tendencies that come with introspection, always looking within, I was frozen with indecision in my early life.

For instance, I was given a remote-controlled airplane for my twelfth birthday and always wanted to fly it. But instead it sat in the box, high on the shelf of our closet. I pulled the box down from time to time and carefully removed the plane, running my fingers over the wings and pulling the propeller through a few cycles, listening to the whisper of the small pistons. But I never flew the plane—never. I waited until I knew how, and

I never asked or learned how to fly it. The thin plastic eventually cracked and broke after years of sitting in the box. That same indecision was at play on the baseball field at nine years of age, when I couldn't decide on a position to play and was assigned the one no one wanted.

I grew up embarrassed at my inborn characteristics, thinking that being introverted and desiring solitude—experiencing life from such up-closeness that I could barely see beyond the moment—was a great sin. As I read the allegory, I lost this self-consciousness. I learned that where I was is merely my beginning point. Life would have been far less traumatic had I known that others have an equally hard time learning their way around the circle of life. Others struggled to understand what was natural to me, this deep perception of things and the ability to let life reach out and touch me.

People who are born with wisdom or the ability to see life from great distances must make their way to the places of the heart, a journey that is no less difficult than my own had been; it simply has a different starting point.

All the years of fear and shame were wasted regretting my natural tendencies. My experience could have been immeasurably easier if I had known what I was trying to accomplish. But that would have required me to see from vantage points that I did not have, and it takes more than a little effort for a mouse to begin seeing like an eagle.

Long after I had come to recognize the changes I needed in life, this book gave me the insight and helped me to visualize the rest of the journey toward becoming a whole man. The process does not happen overnight. I have found it to be lifelong, requiring seasons of silence and solitude to observe and contemplate the realities around me from as many points of view as possible, maturing and practicing the vantage points that are not natural to me. The journey also requires teachers and mentors.

It wasn't until I first flew an aircraft that I got a glimpse of the perspective opposite mine, in a very literal sense. The ability to see like an eagle, from above the world, enthralled me. My basic tendency toward short-sightedness has not changed, so I take advantage of my time in flight. I find myself looking to the horizon every time and discovering anew what it's like to see far and wide.

Similarly, Coach Shaw taught me how to think and relate to those things around me, to gain wisdom and develop courage. He helped grow me from a timid catcher to a veritable field marshal on the baseball team.

The choice to fly, to go to war, to eventually backpack across Central and South America were all directed at ridding myself of fear and seeing life from a perspective of courage.

To become whole requires us to accept who we are and accept that we alone are responsible for the outcomes of our lives, whether we choose bitterness or happiness, anger or joy. Everyone is on a version of this spiritual journey, whether gleaning their cues from self-help guides or the Bible. For me, I knew I was being led along by a God who wanted to refine me, to meet me where I was and make me whole.

I did not by any means forsake my biblical worldview for this Native American viewpoint. But I found in it a deeper understanding of who I was and how I got to be that way. This insight, for me, has helped give meaning to some of the most frustratingly difficult and fruitful changes in my life.

Introverted and Shy

The most difficult part of my journey was that, as a youngster, I could not understand why I was the way I was. My next older brother Tom was a tremendous extrovert, mixing easily with both kids and adults, while I could barely speak to the people at church or look a person in the eye. He sought out opportunities to perform in front of people, and I was petrified at the thought. He wore costumes with ease, but even in adulthood the idea of wearing a mask to the neighborhood Halloween parties caused paralyzing fear that I could not overcome.

My first 4-H speech at the age of twelve, about the Jim Crow laws, was a total catastrophe. In my mind, the performance was a stunning delivery. But just like my sixth-grade picture of a horse, the speech, when viewed from outside, left one to wonder where it was. I did not even place, the whisper of a speech was so quiet that the judges did not score it since they could not hear it.

This fear of negative judgment carried over to my relationships and often resulted in deep loneliness. I had a crush on LaRell Roberts in the sixth grade. The idea of buying a Valentine's present traumatized me. I shopped for hours, finally settling on a small heart-shaped silver jewelry box. I was so afraid that it would not be an acceptable gift that I never gave it to her. For years, it stayed among my personal possessions, a mute reminder of my shortcomings.

While shyness in girls seems acceptable, attractive even, comments from all quarters reminded me that shyness in boys was not appealing. But try as I might, I did not know how to carry on small talk or make conversation about the latest gossip. I found myself drained when I was around people too long or too close. Meanwhile, Tom, the almost perfect extrovert, was stimulated by having people around him, giving him attention.

> To become whole requires us to accept who we are and accept that we alone are responsible for the outcomes of our lives, whether we choose bitterness or happiness, anger or joy. Everyone is on a version of this spiritual journey, whether gleaning their cues from self-help guides or the Bible.

It's not that the introvert is antisocial; he just gains energy when he is alone. I can walk in the desert alone, fly an airplane for hours by myself, think in solitary situations, and read books. All these activities charge my battery, while making small talk completely drains it.

I was not just a little shy or a little introverted. I was a ten on a scale of ten. I saw things from such a close perspective that, when I talk to people, both my eyes focus on one of theirs. When I began shaving, I did not see all the way to the mirror to see my full image. I saw part of my face and imagined the rest.

In my late twenties, still living the single life, someone commented about me losing my hair. I went home to check and, sure enough, it was gone. It took their perspective for me to see all the way to the mirror, to see even the slightly "bigger picture" of my own face.

Alaska

In 1975, I was a KC-135 Aircraft Commander on a thirty-day TDY (Temporary Duty) to Eielson AFB, Alaska. On these tours, multiple crews would come in at regular intervals to fly an ongoing mission over the North Pole. The other crews are also rotated home after thirty days. Many of the crews had experienced this same type of TDY duty in the war zone, and it rarely lent itself to getting to know other crews personally. This trip was to prove different.

We arrived in late October for our month of duty and were scheduled to leave in late November. This time we just happened to hang out a lot with one other crew that came in a few days after we did. When we were not flying, both crews usually ate breakfast, lunch, and dinner together in the icy isolation of the Alaska winter, separated from family, friends,

and any interaction with lo-cals. We became close to this crew. They joked and kidded as much as we did, but were also very professional when it came time to fly. At the end of November, we parted the way all crews depart from these tours—with a wave of the hand and a promise to see the other folks around the skies.

Seven days later, their entire crew perished in a crash. The flight lasted only a couple of minutes. They experienced a relatively minor problem; the aircraft landing gear did not retract when the copilot attempted to raise them. The aircraft commander made an initial small decision that was technically correct, but not the right decision for the circumstance. Every other decision was correct, but predicated on that initially wrong choice. The result was calamity.

The KC-135 of those days had smaller engines than today, and the heavyweight departures could easily chew up ten thousand feet of runway. The airplanes, performing at their maximum capability with little or no room for error, lifted into the air with barely enough airspeed to sustain flight. The power allowed the aircraft to accelerate to a safe climbing speed.

On this particular take off, the aircraft sounded a warning horn that the landing gear had not retracted. In such a scenario, one might decide to land and have the problem fixed. But the aircraft cannot land at the heavy weight at which it took off, so you'd have to fly a bit to get rid of fuel.

The protruding landing gear have speeds that should not be exceeded. The gear themselves will withstand much greater speeds than what is published in the manual, but the gear doors may be damaged at higher speeds (a fairly minor problem in the grand scheme). The aircraft commander, in this case, elected not to exceed that book limit.

In order to comply with the technical manual, he pulled off power to keep his airspeed below the limitations. That decision, while technically justified, was the ultimate problem. Continuing his checklist, he then raised flaps, because those also have placarded limits. When he raised the flaps, he lost lift and the airplane began to mush from the sky, just barely under flying speed. Had he left his power at takeoff thrust, the decision to raise flaps would have been routine.

With four good operating engines—albeit at their reduced power setting—the aircraft settled softly back onto the terrain near the base. They were so near flying speed that the plane was basically intact after it struck the ground, but with a full load of fuel, the plane broke into flames. The pilot got his escape window open and was halfway out when the tremendous heat overcame him. He was found right there, halfway out the window. He had survived the crash and was that close to safety but perished along with the other three crewmembers. A perfectly good aircraft, a very professional crew, a small problem, and a decision that was correct as far as training by the manual had resulted in catastrophe.

Had he concentrated on flying the plane, he would have noticed his airspeed was bleeding off, would have felt the controls become mushy, and would have known he had to add power and over speed the gear while gaining precious altitude. There, he could have analyzed the problem. Instead, the problem took over.

Since losing friends in that accident, I have been more conscious of focusing on the basics when something goes wrong in an aircraft . . . and in life. Forgetting that first rule of emergencies is the cause of far too many in-air accidents. Just fly the plane.

Small decisions of life can have the same results as the choices exercised by this crew. The consequences can be decades before coming, but they are just as inevitable as losing flying speed in an aircraft.

24

A SOJOURNER

After getting my discharge from the Air Force, I was twenty-nine and flying a crop duster for a living in Arkansas. One weekend, anxious to see my family back in Nadine, I left Arkansas late in the afternoon on the seventeen-hour drive home and drove all night. The sun began to peek over the horizon behind me as I passed through Oklahoma and hit the interstate west of Amarillo. As the new light emerged, I could see the uninterrupted horizon of the Texas Panhandle all the way to New Mexico—nothing but sky and horizon and the limitlessness of unending ranch lands stretching as far as the eye could see.

The gravitational pull of family was strong, but the pull of this place was even stronger to me. I wanted to be back where the vast distance allowed me to see with clarity. My spirit and heart expanded and soared in a way that was familiar as the spreading day cast light on the landscape where I had been raised. I realized that I'd been missing it all along. I suddenly felt free from the crowding vegetation of trees and bushes that surrounded me in the Philippines and Vietnam and followed me into Arkansas. Amid the open horizon and uninterrupted skyline, I realized this was who I was and what I was about, and—with a burst of insight—I realized I yearned to be back home, in the desert, in the land of my fathers. That became a growing desire that would build over the next few years.

Wintertime for crop dusters is like being unemployed, so for the first time since I started working at age nine, I was free for several months. Back and forth to the war zone, flying a crop duster, I had certainly not been gathering moss and had little desire to begin now. Although my faith was strong, I was undisciplined, single with no family responsibilities, and full of the love of life. The pull of home tugged hard, but the desire for adventure pulled even stronger.

As the crop dusting season ended for the year, I decided I would use the time off to achieve a childhood dream and visit Machu Pichu on the eastern slopes of the Andes in Peru, probably the most amazing urban creation of the Inca Empire at its height. Spurning the idea of a quick airline trip, I opted for an adventure by bus and train, traveling among the people. I locked my front door and hit the road, driving through New Mexico, to visit my parents.

When I shared my plans for the trip, Mom was more or less supportive, but Dad was totally opposed. He rarely got into discussions like that, and the late-evening discussion as I was preparing my backpack confounded me. Finally, he sighed in exasperation and went to bed. Mom, in a very uncharacteristic fashion, offered an insight, "Your father has always felt he married too young. He's just jealous that you are getting to do something he would like to have done himself."

The next day, I voted in the presidential election, took my backpack to El Paso, made my way to the train station in Juarez, and purchased a ticket that started me south toward Peru. I had no itinerary and no plan except to see what was ahead of me. I took only my backpack, camera, passport, and writing materials. As I sat waiting for the train to depart, I was once again overcome with fear, just as I had been when I was at Phnom Penh watching the C-130 disappear. I thought that my dad was probably right, that I should just go back to Hobbs and spend the winter. But something inside me would not let me back out; no more than I could listen to Dad and drop Rocky's math class or refuse to take the second semester of Professor Haight's accounting class.

So I picked up my backpack and climbed the stairs to board the train. The idea of being completely alone, to face my fears and push myself beyond my comfort zone, became almost a spiritual experience. The trip gave me the opportunity to reflect on myself and where I was headed, not only on this trip, but in life.

Mexico

The train made its way through Chihuahua, across the Copper Canyon to Topolobampo. I continued by bus down the coast to Puerto Vallarta, across to Guadalajara, to Mexico City, Cuernavaca, Acapulco, Puerto Escondido, across the mountains to Oaxaca, and out the southern end of Mexico into Central America. Not speaking Spanish was a hindrance, but after several weeks, I was getting to know the Mexican culture and people well, and I loved both.

In Puerto Vallarta, I camped near the beach within a few feet of a crude facility that had a table and bench and a shed to protect me from the extreme sun. A couple from Washington State, about my age, was on the same adventure, camping and making their way through Mexico.

One night after a long day of walking the city, I ended up back at my tent and noticed a Mexican man at the table, so I sat down. Too late, I noticed his red bleary eyes, the bottle of half empty mescal, and the loaded .45 in his belt with the hammer pulled back. He invited me to drink, but I declined and watched his dulled eyes try to comprehend my refusal.

A light bulb hung on a double wire with the naked copper wrapped around the positive and negative screws of the socket. The bulb dangled back and forth from the vibrations of the breakers slapping the shore. At the edge of the light's reach, a mad dog jerked at a chain, slobber running out of his snarling mouth. Absently, my companion gazed at the hydrophobia-stricken animal, slowly pulled the revolver out of his belt, and aimed it at the dog. Without squeezing the trigger, he held the sights on the dog and turned his slow motion gaze toward to me. A chill ran up and down my spine.

He repeated the motion at the bottle, an invitation to join him as he drank toward the worm, eyes now mere slits as he watched my response.

"No gracias, yo estoy enfermo." I feigned illness, knowing that more danger lay toward the bottom of the bottle. I wondered how long the chain would hold the dog and realized how far from home I was.

Slowly, he looked again at the dog, sighting down the barrel, sighed deeply, and slid the gun back inside his belt. He picked up his bottle and, without saying a word, left. I was still sitting there, unmoving, one eye on the mad dog, when the Washington couple walked up. In thick glasses, she looked more like a librarian than an adventurer. After exchanging greetings, they retreated to their tent that was staked about ten feet from mine.

Slipping silently into my tent and into my sleeping bag, I fell into a troubled sleep, waking several times with visions of the mescal-induced stupor of the unnamed visitor and what I had just experienced. At midnight, a piercing scream from the tent next to mine interrupted the still night. Grabbing the fist-sized rock I kept in the tent as a weapon, I sprang from my tent wearing only my underwear to confront the drunk or the dog, not knowing which had overcome her husband and now had the woman in the nearby tent screaming for mercy.

> The idea of being completely alone, to face my fears and push myself beyond my comfort zone, became almost a spiritual experience. The trip gave me the opportunity to reflect on myself and where I was headed, not only on this trip, but in life.

More screams followed as I emerged from the tent; she was desperate. Confronting the darkness, I saw the dog was still chained by the shed. A quick survey of their tent showed no signs of a breach, and I realized that my bookish neighbor did not need help, not that I could provide. The mad dog was still snarling and jerking at the chain, slobbering blindly at the night, eager to share his disease with any of us. But the couple in the tent next to mine was far more involved than a mad dog could interrupt, even if he broke the chain.

I crawled back into my tent . . . with new visions to disturb my sleep and a deeper gnawing loneliness. The next morning, I broke down my tent and headed out before the couple arose. I saw no sign of the man from the night before.

I thought mine was a unique idea, to travel among our southern neighbors. Instead, the route was jammed with a constant flow of young people doing the same, traveling by rail and bus throughout the region. The deeper I got into Mexico, the more risks I saw awaiting the young men and women, eighteen to twenty years old, who were on the same route. We began to recognize one another and formed a mild bond that only the road can foster. I became a sort of safe haven for those I realized were ten years younger than me. Rough men with rough ways singled out the solitary females, and it was not unusual for the girls to invite themselves to sit next to me on the bus to help ward off unwanted advances. When we hit town, they would vanish into their itineraries, and I would follow mine.

As I departed Mexico City moving toward Cuernavaca, I noticed two young French girls traveling together. They melted into the streets of Cuernavaca, and I went my own way.

The next morning, awakening in the "garden city" as Cuernavaca is called, I discovered the gardens and flowers in full array. As I took in the sight and smells of the flowers, I exulted in the beauty and simplicity. It was a spiritual experience; I was coming once again close to God. These solitary trips led me to know more about myself and have caused me to seek out the truly beautiful moments of discovery of the simple beauties of life by launching out from the known . . . out beyond certainty.

In Acapulco, the two French girls appeared out of nowhere, spraying French phrases around like machine-gun fire, all the while looking over their shoulders. I did not speak French, they did not speak English, and none of us could speak Spanish, but I knew they were scared. They had seen me enough to know they could trust me. As we started walking together and conversing, the two men physically pressing in on them decided to find other prey and left.

The girls had identified me as one of the good guys. None of us understood exactly what the other was saying, but for the next week they sat close to me on the bus and pitched their tent next to mine for safety when we camped. Together, we continued through Acapulco, south along the coast to Puerto Escondito, at that time a very small fishing village. We stayed there for several days, camping on the beach. Using our makeshift communication system, we decided it was time to move on and boarded the bus to Oaxaca. Somewhere south of Oaxaca, they split off, and I never saw them again.

Central America

Lonelier than ever, I continued south into Central America, which proved even more lawless than Mexico, The number of fellow explorers, though large, dwindled considerably the farther south I ventured.

A major earthquake earlier that year, a magnitude 7.5 on the Richter scale, had left twenty-three thousand dead and hundreds of thousands homeless in the region. In Guatemala City, the water systems had been damaged and were still unrepaired months later. Bottled water was decades into the future, but I have a strong constitution and have seldom exercised caution when eating local fare. But the polluted water in Guatemala City proved to be an exception and gave me the most violent diarrhea I have ever experienced. Alone, far from anyone who cared, I struggled to get well.

In Honduras and Nicaragua, machine guns in the hands of government soldiers were common on the streets. But armed guards in the banks carrying automatic weapons proved a wake-up call—not all countries know the blessings of safety and security.

Many people think military service should be compulsory. I am not too enamored with that idea, but I would support compulsory travel for every person when they are eighteen. Spend six months outside the country, traveling in Africa, South America, Asia, or the Middle East, and you come to see our U.S. freedom, security, and social order in a different light.

Costa Rica suited me well. It was more civilized and safer. Leaving San Jose after several days, I had to choose which way to go to Panama: west toward the Pacific and a more established route or east to the less developed Caribbean side with sketchy transportation. I opted for the latter and headed toward Puerto Limon. At Puerto Limon, locals laid out the obscure path into Panama, a once-a-week bus that traveled to a banana plantation at the end of the road. The plantation sent a noon train to Panama on the same day the bus arrived.

Waiting two days for the weekly bus, I boarded in the early morning dark, gave my destination, paid the quarter for fare to the driver. I carried my pack to the backseat, my customary place on these trips. Only one other rider was on board, a middle-aged man asleep in the seat by the front door. We bounced along the dark and dusty road, making our way south following the coast, occasionally stopping at small settlements. As the sun came up, the bus became sweltering in the morning heat.

I noted that I had told the driver the name of the village about ten miles short of my destination, but with only us two passengers, I thought nothing of it. We lurched to a stop at the town where I had said I wanted to disembark, but I sat unmoving in the rear seat.

The driver spoke kindly from the front, "Senor, esta es su destinacion."

I answered without moving from my rear seat.

"Senor, por favor, yo quiero ir a la end of the line." In the best that I could do with my limited Spanish, I explained I wanted to go to the plantation at the end of the line, not to here.

He answered, fully sympathetic with my problem, "Si, pero usted compro un bilete para aqui." Yes, he understood I had a change of heart, but I had paid for a ticket to here.

"Si, por favor, si es possible, I will pay the extra fare."

Again, "Si, entiendo, pero usted pago para llegar a este sitio."

I could not understand what was happening and still had not moved. It was a simple problem, and there were plenty of seats. There had been no ticket exchanged with a stub in a front office that would require some accounting, and I was willing to pay. He continued to be nice but insisted that I had paid only to here and needed to exit the bus. I remained unmoving in the rear.

Slowly, I saw the sleeping figure in the front seat begin to stir. He fumbled around, feeling under his seat, and finally produced a dusty and tattered conductor's hat. Slapping the dust from it and pulling it into more or less the shape it was supposed to have, he tiredly placed it on his head and gave the bill a tug to put it into its official position. With a sigh, he made his way slowly down the aisle toward me. He, too, broke the news nicely enough, "Senor, esta es su destinacion, por favor, necesita salir." As he finished the short speech, he pulled open his civilian coat and revealed the .45 stuck in his belt. Memories of the man on the beach with the mescal came vividly to my mind.

"Si, senor," I replied as I shouldered my pack and made my way to the front.

They were both pleasant as I got off the bus, and with a wave they closed the door and continued on to the plantation.

I shouldered the heavy pack, cursing both my lack of attention to detail when I boarded and my failure to fill my canteens with fresh water. With the sun bearing down and a burning anger building inside, I began to walk in the direction the bus had gone. It would be a week before the next bus or the next plantation train headed to Panama. About two hours later, the bus passed going the other direction, and both men waved cheerily from the front of the empty vehicle.

Finally, about 3 p.m., I arrived at the plantation and was welcomed only by curious glances from the workers. In my poor Spanish, I asked about the train, and they told me it was scheduled each week at noon, and clucking their tongue at my luck, they mentioned that noon was long since passed.

It was obvious that there was no hotel room in this remote location, so I sat down at a small open-air stand that appeared to be a kitchen. I asked if they served meals, and the answer was yes. I was starving, having boarded the bus before any diners opened for breakfast, and ordered, "Yo quiero dos huevos (two eggs), jamon (ham), papas fritas (fried potatoes), and pan (bread)," motioning that I would like the bread toasted. That same order had worked all the way through Mexico but something about the order of bread caused a problem.

The young woman behind the counter explained that it was not possible. I pointed to the bread on the shelf and replied I would take it plain without toasting. She said in Spanish to her companion, "El no comprende."

Becoming agitated from the long trek, the missed train, and the senselessness of it all, I replied, "Si, comprendo, yo quiero pan!"

She began to take the bread out of the sack and started cooking the eggs and ham but under her breath to the other girl once again said, "El no comprende."

I lost my composure and shouted in English, "You damned right I comprendo! I just want bread, eggs, and jamon!"

The outburst earned me total silence for the duration of my meal. While eating, I noticed a small flatbed narrow-gauge train pulled up in the shade away from the tracks with a mechanic working under it. It didn't so much resemble a train as a Volkswagen with the body removed and a flat-bed that was barely waist high with regular metal train wheels. It looked as though they had axle problems. As I finished and paid out, I walked over to the mechanic and asked whether this was the train to Panama. He shook his head yes and explained that it was delayed for maintenance.

"Will it still go this afternoon?"

"Si, senor." He was friendly, leaving me to wonder why no one had mentioned this since my arrival—that I was not too late, that I would not be there all week after all.

Just before dark, the little train was ready. Two additional flatbed cars were hooked to it. The conductor (who had also been the mechanic) washed his greasy hands, took my dollar in fare, and invited me as the only fare-paying customer to sit in the front car with him. I sat on the front of the flatbed with my legs dangling over the edge while the nonpaying customers sat on the two flat cars behind us, beside the loaded bananas. We chugged out of the plantation and into the deep dark of the jungle night.

About three hours later, we crossed the *frontera* into Panama and pulled to a stop in a small border town. The locals told me the last bus of the evening would run about 9 p.m., an hour or so from when our train arrived. Alone and dejected at the day, I waited at the small bus stop. About 10 p.m., a local walked from his house to tell me that the bus sometimes did not show up but that I could catch it at 7 the next morning. Sure enough, the next morning, the bus was right on time, and I paid to go to the airport where I bought a ticket to Colombia, not taking the time to see anything of Panama or the Panama Canal.

Machu Pichu had captured my attention in the first grade, and now it was within reach. Crossing into Colombia, I spent two days in Bogota, visiting the gold museum and other sights, before boarding a bus to Peru. I was determined to go straight through Ecuador and on to Peru, impatient to see the ruins. About 2 a.m., as the bus entered Popoyan, the border town between Colombia and Ecuador, my passport, all my writing, and half my cash were stolen. Without a passport, passage into Ecuador was not permitted. I returned to Bogata and engaged in a bureaucratic tangle trying to get a new passport, which only left me frustrated and helpless. Finally, with dwindling cash and a desire to get back to the safety of the United States, I left for a onetime entry into the U.S. to try to get a new passport there.

I was within twenty-four hours of a lifelong dream but did not make it—and still have not made it.

Roy McLean

After spending Christmas with my family in New Mexico, and with no job there, I went back to Arkansas and started the 1977 crop dusting season. The year was uneventful, but changes in the local agriculture base crop, from cotton to soybeans, made it harder to pay the bills. The reve-

nue was harder to generate since there were too many crop dusters and not enough work. The economics were beginning to stress the small operation James Price had, and I could tell he was too kind to say anything to me.

In 1978, I bought a Cessna Ag Truck, which was light-years ahead of the Piper Pawnee I had been flying. It carried more weight, was more stable in flight, and had lighter controls than the Pawnee. But the jobs were fewer and the margins less. Remembering the lessons from my 4-H projects, I knew I would have to make a decision soon or be completely broke.

One night I was reading the biblical account of Jacob, who had left home after he stole his brother's birthright and inheritance. He had been away long enough to have a dozen sons and, suddenly, found himself wanting to go home to his family and his heritage, back to the land of his fathers, and back to make peace with the brother whom he had cheated.

Though I had not run away, my own longing for home came flooding back. I realized I was deeply homesick and wanted to be back in the land of my youth, where my family lived—the land of limitless horizon, where I could feel my spirit soar in the open plains. I wanted the dry lands of the West, the desert of southern New Mexico. I longed for the days at Nadine. But I had one more adventure to complete before getting there.

Biblical stories talk about a kinsman redeemer who had the privilege and responsibility to act for a relative who was in trouble or danger. The biblical book of Ruth tells the story of Boaz, a near kinsman of the destitute widow Naomi (Ruth's mother-in-law), who acted as a redeemer in accordance with Israelite law and married Ruth.

Roy McLean was the human embodiment of that idea for all of us 4-H kids in Nadine. He had started from scratch with his own business in the oilfield and had become a millionaire. He bought our animals at the county fair and provided scholarships to us. I knew the lessons of the Bible, but they were distant. Roy and his wife, Polly, put flesh on the stories, providing for us and saving us from our bondage of poverty.

Roy and Polly had reached down and touched my life at an early age. When I was twelve, they took me waterskiing along with their own kids. Roy patiently pulled me behind the boat, time after time, trying to get me up out of the water. I was still laboring under a fear of the water, fear of new people, and a general fear of being. I never made it up on the skis for more than a few yards, but the excursion was my first connection to the two people who would become my closest mentors. When it was time to choose a college major and career fields, I showed up and talked to them on a Sunday afternoon.

In the fall of 1978, I got a letter from Roy and Polly, asking if I wanted to join them on their sailboat for a trip to the Mediterranean. The prospect of joining them on a sailboat, in this lull of my life, when I was looking for myself and for a vision yet again, seemed fortuitous.

They were going through their own trials at the time. Their oldest son, Mike, had been with them on the boat before they wrote to me. He was the sailor who had talked them into the yearlong venture. One morning, he crawled out of the boat to check on their schedule before going through the locks on the French canals. He stepped into the street to cross to the port office and was struck by a car and killed. After they buried Mike, back in Eunice, Roy wrote the letter asking me to join them. He had never asked me for anything.

My crop dusting business was barely paying the bills. The thought of going back home was heavy on my mind. And now there was this request from my mentor, one of my heroes, to join him on the boat. I had been waiting for something to jump at, some new adventure or something familiar, and this opportunity seemed to have both.

I sold my crop duster, my trailer house, and all my possessions, but kept my '52 MG-TD and a '59 MGA. I had sanded both down to bare metal by hand and repainted them. I put them into storage, packed my bags, and went, not to New Mexico, but to France, to join the McLeans and their other son, Craig, in the Mediterranean.

I met up with them in Marseilles. The thirty-five-foot sailboat was named Zia after the symbol in the middle of the New Mexico state flag. We sailed along the French coast, about thirty miles each day, and finally ended up at Perpignan, just north of the Pyrenees Mountains on the Spanish border. During those carefree days, the gentle fall breezes pushed us a bit farther south.

Back in the U.S. that year, Ron Guidry won twenty-five games and pitched the Yankees to victory over the Los Angeles Dodgers in the World Series. In college football, Billy Sims from Oklahoma won the Heisman Trophy, while USC and Alabama shared the national championship.

Discussions, like discovery, can rarely be had in one sitting. They require a certain fermenting, a layering of paint on a canvas. On the trip, I had the time to sort through things in my life and had endless discussions with Roy and Polly about where I was headed. I soon realized they were once again acting as kinsmen redeemers to me, rescuing me from danger and a purposeless life. The discussions we had during the months on the boat were just what I needed. It was like the voice of God, through these good friends, calling me back home, to my roots, to my values.

Roy shared his desire to find a captain who qualified for insurance coverage to sail the boat back to the U.S., with Craig and me as the boat crew. Without planning it, I was now on a path to crossing the Atlantic in a thirty-five-foot sailboat.

When we got to the port in Perpignan, Roy declared we would be there for a couple of weeks. I thought they needed a break from me and got a Eurorail Pass to travel across Europe, into England, to Switzerland, Amsterdam, Bavaria, Italy, and finally back to join them at the boat. During my absence, Roy had found a captain who fulfilled the insurance requirements, had paid him a fifty percent deposit, and agreed that we would meet in Gibraltar the first week of December.

Roy had planned the crossing with his son, looking at one hundred years of weather history. Never in that period had there been a hurricane or bad storm in the months of December, January, or February. When I got back to the boat, Roy was impatient to get moving down the Spanish coast. We now had a plan, and the carefree days were behind us. The calm fall weather was giving way to choppier seas and harsher winds. The sense of urgency to get farther south was ever present, but still we could only make thirty miles a day. We began earlier in the morning and kept going until dusk.

Finally, we arrived at Gibraltar and waited expectantly for the captain. One week, then a second passed with no sign of the guy who would sail the boat across the ocean. Finally, it was obvious that the captain had taken the deposit and flown the coop. Disappointed, Roy put the boat in storage, and we all flew back to the U.S. just before Christmas.

I was within days of sailing the Atlantic in a small boat and lost the chance, and still have that unfulfilled dream along with having never made it to Machu Pichu.

Once again I arrived in New Mexico for Christmas. This time, I went to Marshall Aviation at the Hobbs Airport and asked for a job. They hired me that day. I began to do some of the most concentrated flying in my life. In the Air Force, a pilot will log two or three hundred hours a year. I was suddenly flying a thousand hours a year for the next several years. After a time, I became the chief pilot and the checkride pilot, giving the FAA checkrides to our charter pilots. And soon I took on two additional positions, aircraft owner and personal pilot for a local company.

Darrell Bearden was a local manager for Climax Chemical and a private pilot. He approached me with the idea of forming a partnership to buy an aircraft and lease it back to Marshall Aviation. Dick and Ann Marshall were happy to get the sale of an aircraft, so Darrell and I flew to the factory in Florida, picked up a 1979 Piper Saratoga, and flew it back to Hobbs.

Dorothy Runnels—an Introduction to Politics

When businessman Phillip Runnels called me to fly for his company and for his father, the congressman from southern New Mexico, I was excited to get a chance to fly more frequently—and in their Mitsubishi turboprop no less. Phillip had been a naval pilot, and we had a friendly competition about whether Navy pilots or Air Force pilots were better.

Our families had been acquaintances from the county fairs when we were growing up. Phillip's father, Harold "Mud" Runnels, got his name from the business he owned, a drilling mud company. He and his wife,

Dorothy, had started small and made it big. He eventually ran for the New Mexico senate and served there before being elected to the United States Congress. He was a conservative Democrat and fit Lea County and southern New Mexico well. I was conservative but was not a Democrat, though the issue of party registration never came up.

Harold passed away from cancer on August 5, 1980, while still in office. His wife had reasonable expectations that she would be selected by the state Democrat Party Central Committee to finish out his unexpired term. It had happened that way in Louisiana with her friend Lindy Boggs, who was appointed when her husband, Congressman Hale Boggs, perished in a 1973 plane crash. But the party in New Mexico was not like the party in other states. The state constitution calls for a special election to replace House members who die in office. But state law allows 120 days to have the election. The normal November election, in this instance, would occur before the 120-day deadline, so the governor of New Mexico decided to forgo the expense of a special election.

Since Congressman Runnels had been unopposed in the general election, and the primary election had already concluded, state law allowed the Party Central Committee to select the replacement candidate. In effect, the law allowed the governor to appoint the new congressman. Longtime Governor Bruce King selected his nephew and my longtime friend, David King, to be the only name on the ballot for November. David had only moved his voter registration into the district ten days after Runnels died.

Dorothy was offended and appealed quietly to the Democrat party leadership to give her a chance. They rejected her appeal. On September 3, she changed her registration and applied to get on the ballot as an Independent candidate for Congress. But Secretary of State Shirley Hooper, Dorothy's friend from Lovington, ruled that she could not be on the ballot. A week later, Dorothy took the case to court, filing suit against Shirley Hooper. The Honorable U.S. District Judge Santiago E. Campos ruled in favor of the state and kept Dorothy off the ballot. So she declared she would run as a write-in candidate. Everybody told her it was not possible.

Up to this point, I had not had much opportunity to fly with Dorothy or to get to know her, but I respected that she did not go quietly into the night. I flew her to a campaign event in Ruidoso and heard her tell Joe Skeen she was going to run as a write-in candidate. He told her it was not possible to win as a write-in. He said if she ran, he would not get into the race—the thought being that one write-in had little chance, but two was an outright impossibility. He would siphon valuable Republican protest votes from her.

It was already mid September, and with the election in November, she had an uphill climb ahead. During that period, Eddie Chiles, who owned the Western Company in Dallas, was running a series of programs protesting the growth of government. He called his program, "I'm Mad Too, Eddie." In the West, it appealed to our independent spirit and natural suspicion of the government.

Dorothy patterned her campaign after that with an "I'm Mad Too, Dorothy" message. It captured the indignation that the governor had basically been able to choose the next congressman, who happened to be his nephew. There was a provision in the law at that time to discourage write-in candidates. In order for the vote to count, the candidate's name had to be spelled correctly when it was written onto the ballot. And there were dozens of way Dorothy or Runnels could be misspelled.

Dorothy began to educate people about how to spell her name. Then she found out that not all voting machines were the same when it came to write-in votes. She fought through one obstacle after another to keep the protest going. Late in the race, in October, the polls began to show her with a real chance to upset the only guy on the ballot. It was at that point that we went back through Ruidoso for a campaign event. Joe Skeen came out to see her and told her he might get into the race after all. "Dorothy, this upset might happen," adding that he wanted to benefit from it.

Name identification was no problem for Joe Skeen. In 1970, Joe had run unsuccessfully for lieutenant governor on a ticket headed by future Senator Pete Dominici. He also ran for governor in 1974 and 1978, narrowly losing both times. Spelling his name was not a problem. So in the closing days of the election, he announced he would run as a write-in Republican candidate for U.S. Congress in New Mexico. Dorothy had educated people on how wrong it was for the next congressman to be handpicked;

she had educated people on how to do a write-in vote. The Democrat party at that time was double the size of the Republican party in New Mexico, but Dorothy was splitting those votes with the name already on the ballot, David King.

Ron Morsbach, who was heading up the Skeen effort in Cibola County, got a call at home at 11 p.m. on election night. The Skeen campaign manager was calling to get him out of bed. "Ron, get up and get down to the courthouse. We are going to win this election, and we need you to get down there to make sure that all our votes are counted and secured." In the end, the turnout had been huge, and with the slow process of writing in names, people were waiting in line to vote, even at that hour of the night.

Joe Skeen got all the Republican votes, and with Dorothy and David splitting the Democrat votes, Joe Skeen beat David King by about five thousand votes. With thirty-eight percent of the vote, he was elected as the first write-in candidate for Congress in New Mexico history. Joe went on to serve New Mexico well, eventually ending up as a Cardinal, one of the Appropriation Subcommittee Chairmen.

The tireless Dorothy walked away from the political arena and took on the task of managing the sprawling company her husband's death had left behind. We flew thousands of miles together over the next few years. I never heard her complain about the outcome of the race, the raw luck she faced in the hard-to-spell name (although, admittedly, not the hardest), or even mention Joe Skeen promising not to get into the race and then doing it anyway.

Years later, I was giving a speech and was talking about "class acts." I mentioned Dorothy's grace in never complaining about Joe's decision. She exclaimed from the audience that she didn't know anyone else had heard his promise and didn't think anyone would have believed her!

It was during those days flying with Dorothy that I became familiar with the process of running for office. It was during those hours of discussions on our flying trips that I saw that integrity and courage do matter. It was during those discussions that she planted the idea of running for office in my own mind. I told her I would never consider it, rejecting the idea completely . . . at least I thought I had.

Cory

I was chief pilot at Marshall Aviation when a young man named Cory, about twenty years old, came into the office in 1980 to apply for a position we had flying the nightly "check run." I gave him his checkride. He was competent but light on experience. Even though he had his instrument rating, I signed him off for VFR (Visual Flight Rules) flight only. He was broke, so I allowed him to move into my spare bedroom until he could get a paycheck.

It was during those days flying with Dorothy that I became familiar with the process of running for office. It was during those hours of discussions on our flying trips that I saw that integrity and courage do matter. It was during those discussions that she planted the idea of running for office in my own mind. I told her I would never consider it, rejecting the idea completely . . . at least I thought I had.

Banks contracted with us to collect checks from drop boxes all across the region and fly them to Dallas the same day they arrived. The banks began receiving interest when they were input into the system the next morning. All across the country, small charter operations were doing the same thing.

The flights departed between 8 and 10 p.m., once the Hobbs banks got their checks to the airport. Depending on the punctuality of banks, the trip to Dallas and back would be completed by about 3 a.m. The total flight time each business night came to about six hours, and it was a good way to build flight time for young pilots.

On August 11, 1980, I was on a trip but keeping an eye on the weather back in Hobbs. The day was clear, but a high overcast was developing in the afternoon. Scattered showers were possible. As the afternoon shadows lengthened, I called and said, "Cory, I will be in about 7 p.m. I want you to wait at the Hobbs airport until I land. I'll feel better if I ride along with you tonight." I was fatigued, but the possibility of low visibility and an inexperienced pilot concerned me.

"No, Steve. I've called the weather. It's VFR all the way."

"Cory, I know you can fly the route, but I just want to be there with you. These high overcast nights are dark. You can't see the scattered showers. It will be good for you to have a second set of eyes."

"Steve, I'll be okay."

"Cory, I am giving you an order. Do not take off until I get there. I'm going to ride in the right seat with you tonight."

He agreed, but I was not convinced that he would wait, so I hurried my trip along, landed, and taxied to the Marshall Aviation hangar. The aircraft we used for the check run, N47988, was not in the hangar or tied on the ramp. I ran to the drop box to see if the checks might still be there. They were gone.

I jumped back in my plane and took off for Lovington, the first stop after Hobbs. As soon as I got into the air, I began to call on the radio. Cory didn't answer. At Lovington, I hurried over to the drop box, which was empty. A light rain was beginning to fall. I told myself, "You're just overreacting. He'll be fine." The light rain still fell, but I could see the lights in Hobbs as soon as I lifted off. The ceiling was about twenty-five hundred feet above the ground. It was still good VFR, but very dark. No horizon.

All need for hurry gone; I landed at Hobbs, put my aircraft in the hangar, and drove to my house. About two hours later, I got a call from the Roswell airport. Our plane had not shown up. I got in the car and drove to Lovington, looking for signs of the aircraft in case Cory had come back with a mechanical problem. He had not. I began to drive the approximate route toward Roswell looking for any signs in the dark. There were none.

I got back to the house near daybreak, showered, went back to the airport, and got in a plane to head out. I had alerted all of our pilots, and they had gotten into the air before I did, flying the route. Then they spotted Cory's plane—upside down off the caprock between Lovington and Hobbs. They called me on the radio. Cory was dead.

The caprock is a natural escarpment in Lea County, along the eastern edge of the Llano Estacado where the terrain suddenly drops about five hundred feet. I landed on the highway nearby and walked across the pasture to the initial impact site on top of the caprock. He had been right on course for Roswell. The scars in the damp surface of the pasture told the full story. The ground elevation increases slightly as one leaves Lovington and moves toward the caprock just a few miles away. Cory had gotten into a light shower that blocked his visual contact with the Pecos Valley. He started a slight descent to get back into VFR conditions, but he didn't have as much room to descend as he thought because of the increasing elevation at that point.

The PA-28R, a Cherokee Arrow, impacted the ground in a wings-level condition and bounced back into the air. The propeller made slices through the ranch pasture at the point of initial impact. His descent was very slow or maybe had even stopped. It might have been that the terrain rose up a few feet in the last moments before impact. The propeller had sliced the dirt before the belly of the aircraft hit—that's how close he was to safety. With the damaged engine and propeller, the aircraft slowed, the automatic gear extension lowered the landing gear, and the nose gear caught on a mesquite, causing the aircraft to flip upside down.

The plane began to slide along the ground, upside down and backward, at great speed. Cory reached up to push against the roof of the cabin, which was being crushed in as the aircraft slid along the ground. His watch was pulled off just beyond the mesquite. The aircraft continued the slide about one hundred yards, then off the caprock, dropping fifty feet to its resting place. Cory was still strapped into the seat, but a fire had flashed and then gone out quickly before it burned the craft.

I sat down and wept. My exact fears had played out. The weather conditions were not terrible but just enough to make him realize he was beyond his experience level. If I had been there, I could have taken the controls, filed a flight plan, and continued the flight. The scattered showers and dark night were not a major problem but to the inexperienced pilot.

25

INDEPENDENT WOMEN

As I celebrated the start of 1980, it began to seem as though I was late to the getting-married party—thirty-three and still single. I felt as though the rest of the field was lapping me, since some of my high school friends had already worked their way through two marriages by my age.

During college, I had begun to seriously consider what a marriage relationship should look like, especially wrestling with the biblical view of marriage. Christ had brought a revolutionary view of women into the Arab world, giving them equal status in a culture that treated a woman and wives as chattel. He made them a part of his inner circle as he traveled around, teaching his lessons.

Christian teachings declare that divorce should not be the first and easy answer, so I wanted to get it right the first time, to have a relationship and marriage that worked the way it was intended. But on another level, I was confronting my old nemesis—fear. The struggle to get myself out of my shell had been a long process. While somewhat successful in my professional life, allowing anyone to get close enough to make a lifelong commitment was a bridge I had yet to cross. During those college years,

I began to have nightmares about being trapped in a bad marriage, the wrong marriage. Then the military draft came up, and the certainty of going to war provided me another excuse for avoiding a commitment. I didn't want to start a marriage relationship on the way to Vietnam as so many did.

I discovered my deepest attraction was to strong women, independent women, with whom I could discuss ideas. These women seemed to understand my introspective nature, as though they used the same microscope in their lives as I did in mine. But they seemed to hold it in check, not letting it consume them. My introspection was relentless and quickly becoming oppressive to those around me.

Mom was a good example of an independent, thinking woman, but her relationship with Dad revealed some pitfalls. She was too headstrong for his shy and gentle nature, needing a strong partner who could provide suitable tension. If I wanted a strong and independent wife, I had to develop the strength to be paired well with her.

I spent hours thinking about the husband-wife relationship as described in the Christian teachings, trying to resolve this truth with my growing attraction to independent women. Attempts to discuss this with teachers at church went nowhere. Harmonizing these contrasting views was apparently as difficult for other Christians as it was becoming for me.

I looked for good examples of strong marriages. Some marriages seemed stagnant, with each going in different directions. It seemed as if the shared space in their house was the central point of their life together. I wanted a life partner to share the joy and adventure in life, not to share what appeared to be a mutual prison sentence.

I had spent my whole life getting out of the jail cell of introversion and insecurity and did not want to be back in a cell, trapped by a bad marriage. I wanted a wife who would express independent views, who would be a tension pulling back against my tendencies, not for the sake of disagreement but for the sake of truth, to be each other's check and balance.

Appreciation is a term we all know and understand, but it also has a definition in accounting, meaning to "increase in value." In relationships, the two terms actually merge. As we appreciate another, his or her value grows. I wanted a relationship in which mutual appreciation—especially of our differences—was a central part of the equation, thereby increasing our value to each other. The human spirit is encouraged if it is valued for what it is. Likewise, our spirit can be drained away by criticisms and discouragement.

While reading flying books, I stumbled across St. Exupery's *Wind, Sand, and Stars* and came across the expression: "Love does not consist of gazing at each other, but looking outward together in the same direction." That described it very well for me. I wanted a life partner with whom I could look outward into the challenges of life.

Later, I got to know a couple who depicted this for me. James and Joyce Price, my neighbors during my years at Blytheville AFB in Arkansas, showed me what a right relationship looked like, one with a deep mutual appreciation. They worked in their business together and discussed issues. She was strong and independent in her views, but allowed James to make the final decisions. For them, it was not a faith question—they did not go to church at the time—it was a question of practicality, one of making the best decisions they could.

I was in awe of their family model, even though I was not yet ready to create my own. I was working so hard to develop myself; how could I develop a relationship at the same time?

With all these internal questions, I was settling into a life of independence, free to come and go at will; flying, traveling, becoming selfish and self-centered, and endlessly speculating on what I wanted in a wife. And just as the Indian allegory taught, as an introvert, I found myself going over the same thoughts over and over again . . . frozen by indecision.

The constant deployments to the war zones were hard on families and equally difficult for building a relationship, giving me yet another excuse to postpone a serious commitment. Between the constant deployments (for which I often volunteered), odd working hours, and my growing comfort with being alone and having things my own way, I had endless excuses to remain single

Rosie and the Girls

I thought all my attempts at relationships were in my rearview mirror, quietly fading from view. These relationships did not fail because of some insufficiency of the women; they failed because I was making excuses. But deep down, I was tiring of superficial bonds and hungry for commitment, ready to get off the merry-go-round of dating and experience greater depth in a relationship, to start building a life with purpose and a family. I was about to be forced to reconsider my outlook.

Dad had two brothers and two sisters, three of whom had at least five kids. By now, they all had moved away from O'Donnell and the farm to places such as Odessa, Midland, and Notrees—communities clustered in Texas about fifty miles east of Hobbs. As my dad had done, they moved to the oilfield and took the lower-paid, entry-level jobs and struggled to make ends meet.

Dad's younger and unmarried sister, Emma Lee, was friends with three other single women who hung out together. They played softball, went bowling, and traveled; they had fun! These girls drove the latest convertibles, and their cars were always clean, smelling of new leather and excitement. No dried-up Pepsi on the floorboards, no crumbs from the latest foodstuffs being consumed in the backseat. No worries about how to pay for the last doctor bill, no mess of cleaning the runny nose of a sick child. Never a cross word from these girls. They seemed to have unlimited patience—and endless coolness—from my childhood perspective, but we only saw them one day a year.

At Christmas, all the cousins, uncles, and aunts drew names and each of the grandkids got one gift, something usually low on the totem pole of gifts. By contrast, Aunt Emma and her three friends would swoop in at the last second on Christmas day bringing rich gifts. These girls had disposable income, and they lavished it upon us. We loved getting gifts from these exciting and mysterious women. They were independent women. As far as I know, no one ever gave them a present in return.

Looking back, there may have been more to this group than what we guessed as kids in the 1950s. Aunt Emma had moved to Midland and was working in a good oil company job, moving up in the administrative jobs. Her friends were also career women. The leader of the group seemed to be Rosie. She was the driving force. My siblings and I just called the group "Rosie and the girls."

They seemed to make themselves part of our family, always knowing who was in which grade, who had been sick, the latest promotions or failures. We didn't know as much about them, where they came from, who they were dating, who had had the flu, nor did we ever wonder if they had their own families to go to on Christmas day. We just knew that sometime during the weekend of family gatherings, "Rosie and the girls" would show up, flutter through, and then be gone, back to a life of excitement and adventure. Other than my aunt Emma Lee, I had never had a single significant conversation with any of them . . . until I was thirty-three.

I had survived the Vietnam War, was back in Hobbs and flying as a corporate pilot. At the family gatherings, I had exciting things to tell everyone, the latest adventures of a young single man flying around the country. I didn't know or care about measles, mumps, or crying children late at night.

Christmas of 1980 was the same as most. The Pearce part of the family had gathered at Garden City, Texas, where my grandparents and one of my uncles had moved to "get away" from O'Donnell. Most of our extended family, cousins, and even my own brothers and sister had all moved away from the area and did not attend these large gatherings on a regular basis any more. The gatherings were fading as a part of the family heritage, but those of us who could still assembled for Christmas.

Right on cue, Rosie and the girls blew in with all their fanfare, but they were no longer young and vibrant. They were in their fifties, gray and fading. As they ran through the rooms chatting it up, I exchanged my usual pleasantries and went about visiting with the rest of the family, answering questions about my latest adventures. Meanwhile, they finished their rounds and were heading out, right on schedule. But when they got to the front door, they paused. A brief exchange took place, and they wheeled back into the room, charting a course directly for me.

"Stevan, we want talk to you," Rosie said.

It was not a question. "Sure."

"Not here. In the other room."

They led me into the room where all the coats were piled on the bed. I was curious, almost aloof, having learned how to keep people at a distance. One of the girls closed the door, and they gathered around me as if we were choosing pickup teams on a schoolyard—except Rosie had all the players, and they all stood facing me, each looking me squarely in the eye. I reverted to my younger self and averted my eyes, unable to hold their gaze.

Rosie, a tall slender woman, pulled herself to full height and spoke for the group. "What are you doing?"

The question was direct, and I was still processing her stern tone. I stuttered for an answer, "I am flying . . . traveling—"

"You know what I mean," she said, cutting me off. This lady, who had never spoken more than a hello to me, was suddenly all business and driving right through my protective armor. She waited in silence for an answer she knew would not come. I was shaken. It had been a long time since anyone had gotten to me in this way. The silence continued to hang in the air. None of the other girls spoke, but they all knew where this was going and had obviously discussed it at length. Finally, Rosie could see that she had made her point. "Look at us. Before continuing down the path you are on, *you had better take a hard look at us.* We had good looks, good times, money, travel, leisure, and sports. We had it all. And while we were having it all, life passed us by. No sons going off to war; no daughters going to college or getting married."

Looking at me like a modern-day prophet, delivering a message of truth and conviction to the guilty, Rosie continued, *"Life has passed us by! Don't you make the mistake we have made."*

With that, like a school of fish changing directions on some predetermined signal, the group peeled away and left me standing alone. During World War II, a woman by the same name, Rosie the Riveter, had been a national symbol of the type of feminine independence and can-do attitudes these women had. But they were letting me in on a secret—that there are costs to the career-and-adventure-driven lives they had chosen.

Rosie was right. Life was revving up, accelerating in the other lane, and I was missing it.

It was one of the most powerful two minutes of my life—a gift so precious that it took years to completely understand and appreciate the sacrifice they made, loving me enough to admit their life's disappointment. It woke me up to admit that the constant looking for perfection in a mate was simply an excuse, and that the passing by of significant milestones—family, commitment, and purpose—was not reversible. I acknowledged that I didn't have the ability to see the future or to know how a prospective wife would respond to the challenges of life. I knew I needed someone with the right qualities to counter my struggles, someone with the right degree of independence, yet with a dependence on God. I began praying for God to bring me a life mate. I just needed the right person. Although I was not dating anyone seriously when they spoke to me, I was married within a year.

Looking at me like a modern-day prophet, delivering a message of truth and conviction to the guilty, Rosie continued, "Life has passed us by! Don't you make the mistake we have made."

While looking at a strong, independent women from one direction, God delivered up my life partner from the other direction.

26

CYNTHIA

The admonition from Rosie and the girls spurred me to realize that commitment was what was missing in my life, and I had to stop with the excuses. One night, while visiting with a mixed group, I got a little mouthy, and an attractive redhead named Cynthia got right back into it with me. Her spunk and intelligence caught my attention. I glanced her way, asked her out, and we were married within a year!

It was 1981. I was thirty-four, and she was thirty-two. I haven't always been the perfect match for her, but she has been the perfect match for me. We have stood side by side, looking outward together.

In flying, there is a principle that you are not in real trouble until you run out of airspeed, altitude, and ideas all at the same time. I've applied the same concept to life in the business world. The thing is, though, I never run out of ideas, which is both a blessing and a curse. Given my propensities, I could not have been blessed with a better life mate than Cynthia. She channels me and my ideas, helping to put the good ones into action. While I have the ability to endlessly suggest solutions and see possibilities, she has a wonderful knack for sorting through mounds of possibilities to simplify, categorize, and narrow down the choices.

Cynthia can also put anything I visualize into numbers on a spreadsheet. She presents these reports to me, and I can see the answers to business questions with a clarity that I had never known before working with her. Together, we find solutions that would not be there operating as individuals. I am daily amazed by and attracted to my wife. Our mutual appreciation has not only brought joy to our lives, but also multiplied what we can accomplish.

In the details of life, Cynthia has been the one to help put my dreams and ideas into action. But to give her even more credit, these dreams weren't always her ideal in the beginning—and I certainly didn't approach everything the way she would have preferred. Because of my tendency since childhood to avoid crowds and crowded places, I often chose the harder path, the one less traveled, the one without a map to show us the way. Cynthia helped keep us on course.

When we first got married, I went to Arkansas with my new wife and insisted that we go canoeing, an attempt to recapture my Air Force days when groups of us canoed the Current River. In those trips, I sat and paddled from the front, because I was the least experienced. With Cynthia on this trip, I sat in the back, because I was now the more experienced one. The only time she turned around all day, I had just pulled my oar out of the water and had my feet propped up for a short breather. She has never let me forget the incident.

Cynthia is a redhead (if I need to say more, you have never been married to a redhead!). I love her spirit and spunk. She now gets the same amount of time in the rear seat when we canoe, and I have never looked to see if she has her feet propped up on the seat in front of her.

Lori

Part of getting married was getting used to the idea of Lori, Cynthia's eleven-year-old daughter. She was a good kid and we got along, communicating well from the first day we met. In the early part of the marriage, I asked Lori, "What do you want me to call you? Daughter? Stepdaughter?" I didn't want to make her uncomfortable or try to compete with her father.

"I don't know." These were difficult discussions for an eleven-year-old, but I wanted her to be part of the decision. "What do you think?" she asked.

I have never been a halfway person—either I do something fully or I don't do it. I don't like qualifications. I don't like the idea of a "stepdaughter." In fact, I don't like step-anything—not stepchild, not step vans, not even the two-step, come to think of it. I told her she is not a "step" with me. I didn't want the relationship to feel part-time or sound as though there may be a back door.

"I'm all in with you and your mom. If it's okay with you, I would like to call you my daughter. This is not to try to take the place of your father or anything; you need to keep in touch with him. I just want you and me to be settled on what I call you."

"I guess daughter is okay," she said in her preteen way.

So that's what we did. She was my daughter; her kids are my grandkids. Almost thirty years after that conversation, she called out of the blue one day to say, "Thank you."

"What did I do this time?" I joked back, not sure where she was going with the conversation.

"Thank you for not calling my kids 'stepgrandkids,' and thank you for not calling me 'stepdaughter.' I just hate those qualifiers when I hear them."

That was one of the most cherished calls of my life.

Wash-and-Wear Family

Marriage and accepting someone into my space did not come easily to me. After growing up clinging to and needing others, I had become independent and self-sufficient.

My job, flying charter aircraft about a thousand hours each year, did not lend itself to a healthy relationship. The first seven days we were married, I saw my new wife and daughter for a total of twenty-four hours, scattered throughout the week—eight hours here, four hours there.

It may have been the only way our marriage survived, as life with me was completely different from what the two of them had known up to that point. My belongings were scattered throughout the two-bedroom townhouse. The earliest problem was compressing or getting rid of things so that the two of them had closet space and room for their stuff. My dad helped them move in, because I left on a trip the day after we got married.

In full military-discipline style, I instituted a rule that we would have only one thing out on the bathroom shelf after we were finished dressing each morning. (Lori had her own bathroom, but Cynthia and I shared.) They both dutifully complied, sweeping armloads of makeup into the top drawer each day as they finished getting ready. But, soon enough, my rule was enforced only on one small edge of territory around my lavatory as a woman-run democracy replaced the old military order. The rest of the counters were covered with items useful to their process of getting ready, exempt from any earlier dictums.

My absence in those early days allowed the two women of the house to discuss what they had gotten themselves into, commiserating with each other while trying to find the silver linings. The more I was gone, the more they could fabricate those highlights of life with me. I improved over time, but let's just say this wine took a long time sitting on the shelf to age and oxygenate properly.

Taking a page from an old college friend Jim Walton, who had come back to fly in Lea County, I announced we were going to be a "wash-and-wear" family. If you wear it, you wash it. Cynthia asked why that was an important "family rule." I told her that, after watching other young couples, I wanted to be crystal clear: "I did not marry you to get a maid and someone to wash my clothes."

Some rules work out too well; I still do my laundry today. Often, I throw Cynthia's things in with mine and just do hers while I'm at it. Although it had not been included in the original decree, I do my own ironing, too. It somehow got lumped into the ruling on laundry. Lori began to wash her own clothes at age eleven as well—and she hasn't called to thank me for that yet.

I also announced that all of us, including Lori, would cook one night a week. It could be anything—grilled cheese or hot dogs—but she needed to plan a menu and carry it out. The two who didn't cook were in charge of cleaning. Although she struggled at first, Lori got into it and began to read cookbooks to prepare complex dishes. I recall crepes one time and moo goo gai pan another. My dish-washing career had begun very early in life, and while I still had a knack for that, I also did my turn at the cook stove each week.

In order to deal with the prospect of this new style of living, I developed a habit that still works today. Since I have a natural tendency to wake up early every morning, instead of getting up and getting busy, I started to lay awake and just look at Cynthia, lying so close to me asleep. I started concentrating on the beauty in her and in her life, the joy she was bringing into my own. Sometimes, I would take in the pleasant sight of this woman for half an hour—my wife. It was during these early morning moments, with her asleep there beside me that I began to love her with a depth that only the life ahead would reveal.

As I dove into the new relationship, I could sense a physical and emotional tiredness about Cynthia that concerned me. When she got divorced from her first husband, she had nothing; she simply went on her own, taking her daughter with her—one hundred percent accountable, one hundred percent of the time, like most single moms. That one hundred-one hundred takes a toll on single parents everywhere, and though they seldom complain about their lot in life, it is a tax on their spirit.

This close to Cynthia, I could clearly see the toll it had taken. It was painful. I wanted to help her find rest, to have her spirit renewed and refreshed. I could see her spunk and drive beneath the surface. I wanted to release the anchor of responsibility that was trying to pull her down with its weight. I asked about her dreams, the things she wanted to do. Cynthia had not traveled much before we were married, and she said she wanted to see places. Travel had given me the greatest education. I knew it could revitalize and refresh the spirit, but it is a luxury that requires money or takes the place of other commitments.

Together, we began to dream of a big trip. I had Air Force friends in Europe and suggested that she might want to take Lori there, where my friends could help if she got into trouble. The suggestion found fertile ground in her mind, and she began to think and plan. I was starting a new job and didn't have the vacation time, so they would have to go without me. We also decided that this should be a significant trip. Travel for a week or two does not get to the essence of a place; it takes longer to really get out of the routine of life back home and soak in the culture of a new place.

So, in 1984, Cynthia and Lori went to Europe for the summer on a trip they had spent weeks planning. Each took a single backpack filled with a carefully selected wardrobe that, while small, could accommodate multiple uses and looks. Lori struggled with the thought of being gone, and on the day of departure she whined about the weight of the pack and missing her friends. Cynthia had to load her daughter's pack into the car. They traveled just the two of them, without a tour group, and stayed economically in pensions, youth hostels, and with friends.

One of the things I do when I travel, to really get out of the tourist mind-set, is to shop for something specific, yet routine. In Acapulco one year, I took an afternoon looking for a Laundromat and a small box of soap to do some much-needed laundry. I could easily find a large box of detergent, but the small size we take for granted here in the U.S. was a challenge. Not speaking Spanish made the process harder. In Thailand, I looked for a furniture builder in back alleys and ordered a handmade desk.

So I asked Cynthia to bring me only one thing, a bottle of Chateau Petrus wine from the Bordeaux region of France, a very specific request; nothing else would do. She tried buying it in Germany but none was to be found. She looked in Switzerland. None. Finally, thanks to the freedom that comes with extended travel, she determined that she would have to go to France to get it. So she, Lori, and our friend Shirley Seall boarded a train and went to France to get me my bottle. They arrived in Paris, and at one wine shop after another, the French shrugged and replied that they themselves never got to see that particular wine—it was all sold on the international market.

The only solution was to continue to southern France to the Bordeaux region to get the wine. When they arrived, Cynthia found that the Petrus wine was very rare and could not even gain access to the Chateaux. In a quandary, she researched the characteristics of that Chateau in order to buy a substitute. Eventually, she found a bottle of Chateau Latour, which is a vibrant, long-lived wine similar to Petrus. It turned out to be the perfect replacement.

My request accomplished its purpose, giving her a mission and new insights into the culture by solving problems during travel. People who might not otherwise interact with tourists universally identify with them when they are solving problems. They understand the foreigner who is trying to do laundry or buy a gift of fine wine. It becomes much different than the traveler looking for directions to the nearest tourist attraction. It also changes my perspective, getting me to look up from the tour book and see people for who and what they are.

I have found a universal willingness to help around the world. In Colombia, wrestling my large backpack onto a crowded city bus, I found strangers willing to have me crowd my bag beside them in the front of the bus, while I made my way to the only open seat in the rear of the bus. They would flag me when they were getting off and explain to the person waiting to take their seat to whom the pack belonged. The new caretaker, with eye contact and a nod, would let me know my pack was safe with them as well.

When Cynthia and Lori got off the plane after two months on the road in Europe, I could see the difference in each of them. Lori, at thirteen, was a girl when she left and a young woman when she returned, having matured mentally and emotionally far beyond what a summer in Hobbs would have granted her. She

Cynthia returned with a French hat look while Lori matured dramatically.

had discovered her center of gravity and was a full partner in helping with the logistics of getting from one place to the other. She picked up her own backpack and shouldered it into the house, then helped with Cynthia's. Cynthia had renewed confidence, a freshness and alertness that has lasted a lifetime. Travel will do that for you.

Life Insurance

After Cynthia and I married, one of the questions to come up was life insurance. Although she was working full-time as an account analyst for Southern Union Refinery when we met, and even though she continued to work, she would not have had the means to pay the mortgage on our home if something were to happen to me.

"What kind of life insurance do you have?" she asked over dinner one night.

"I guess I don't have any, maybe enough so Mom and Dad don't have to pay to bury me. Why?" I was never good at the obvious.

"I need to think about my daughter and myself if something happens to you. What would we do?"

These questions were not something my family had dealt with, having the only thing they could afford, the basic policies offered by the company. I had never thought much about it after getting out on my own. Over the next week, we continued the discussion until it finally struck me. I told Cynthia, "The best insurance is if you finish college. Education is your best insurance; it lasts a lifetime, and you don't have to pay premiums."

It was Mom's voice speaking through me. I had learned from her example as she pushed college for her kids, herself, and everyone else. For Cynthia, it was as if a long extinguished flame had gotten oxygen and flickered faintly back to life. Cynthia was smart and had very good grades in high school, but she had gotten married just afterward. Although she started college, the pressures of a family kept her from finishing.

She did not make much comment that day, but I could see a new light in her eyes. Our discussions evolved away from insurance to the logistics of college. How would we work it out? I told her how Mom went to Eastern (ENMU) the same year I started at State (NMSU), and she took two kids with her to school at Portales, staying there during the week and coming home on the weekends. My sister, Tanis, stayed with Dad and went to school in Hobbs.

Cynthia asked, "What if Lori doesn't want to go to Portales?"

"Then she can stay and go to school here." It seemed obvious to me, but she was unaccustomed to finding such easy answers.

"You would do that?"

"Sure, why not?"

Eventually, we did just that. Cynthia drove ninety miles to Portales each Monday morning and came home each Thursday or Friday afternoon, depending on her schedule. Lori and I managed okay. I had stopped the charter flying and was working as a corporate pilot, which meant I was home more.

Cynthia was tenaciously focused while she was in school. She took between twenty-two and twenty-three hours each semester and, having accumulated several hours by taking college classes on and off over the years, finished her degree in just two semesters. The lion was loose inside her and doing its work, revealing a hunger to expand her mind and abilities.

Two Airplanes and a Christmas Store

Before we married, when I was single with no obligations, I had invested in a retail Christmas store business with friends of mine, Bennie and Vickie Redman. The business was suffering. The year Cynthia and I got married, Bennie and Vickie ran through their savings and called it quits. As the only remaining owner, I was left to manage a company I knew nothing about and did not have the time to run as I was gone frequently on flights.

Cynthia had been watching as an outsider, since the partnership was started before we were married. Though I considered it to be my problem, not hers, she declared one day that she would quit her job, take over the business, and pay off the bills. An indication of her tenacity and willingness to work hard, she not only carried heavy loads in college, but also managed the store and worked there on weekends when she was home. With no experience or training, she studied books on making flower arrangements and decorating trees and began to manage and run the retail business. She made it work.

When the bill collectors found out Bennie and Vickie had left and that we were the sole owners of the store, they began to call us at night, which was a new experience for me. As poor as we had been growing up, Mom and Dad never bought anything they could not afford. I don't remember a single bill collector calling during my childhood. When I was out on my own, I also paid for things on time, so these calls were distressing. Finally, I pulled all the bills out of the cardboard box and spread them on the table. There were tens of thousands of dollars in unpaid business bills and expenses that I knew nothing about. Organizing them in chronological order and placing them on a spreadsheet, I sent a copy to each of the vendors, then called each one personally.

"Here is what we owe, and the order in which you will be paid. If you call me or my wife one time, you go to the bottom of the list. I will update the list every quarter, but here is the date you will get paid on our current schedule."

The calls stopped coming as we started paying. It took almost two years, but we paid every vendor, every dollar. We have not had a missed payment since then. If we can't pay for it, we don't buy it. We don't run up credit card debt or refinance our home, make balloon notes or borrow from payday loans; we live within our means.

Often, Cynthia would wonder in frustration why so-and-so down the street could live in the house they do and we live in ours, which was not nearly as nice. Or how another couple could afford a vacation home in Ruidoso and we couldn't. My answer came from the days of collecting hot checks that tenth-grade summer at C. R. Anthony's: "They are in debt up to their eyeballs, and we don't live that way."

In 1979, while I was working at Marshall Aviation, when Darrell Bearden and I established a partnership and bought a new Piper Saratoga back from the factory, we leased it to Marshall Aviation. Just about the time we bought it, President Jimmy Carter's failed policies succeeded in getting interest rates to an all time high of 21.98 percent by 1980. Over the next two years, the airplane flew eighteen hundred hours—a pace that in normal times would have paid the loan completely off and given us free-and-clear ownership of the airplane. But these were not normal times. The interest on the loan consumed everything. We still owed almost eighty thousand dollars on the airplane in 1984 when the oil bust hit and flying stopped. It is the way government policies punish the emerging middle class. The rich do not need loans.

Before the bust, I was logging lots of hours for Marshall Aviation and for Runnels Mud Company, a local oil service company that sold drilling mud and provided mud engineers for drilling rigs. Congressman Harold "Mud" Runnels' son, Philip, who managed the company, bought a new airplane and gave me the opportunity to buy the older model Baron I had been flying. I had, in turn, lined up a buyer who would purchase it the day I got it. The stage was set for me to make a nice profit. The new plane came in; I borrowed $31,000 for the Baron, signed the papers, and as soon as the ink was dry on the loan papers and the ownership transferred, I called the buyer who had been hounding me for weeks to sell him the airplane.

He was suddenly cagey. I called the next day. He was noncommittal. He was a contract welder in the oilfield with his office in town, so I drove to his business to see him.

"You have been calling for months, trying to buy the airplane. Now I can hardly get you on the phone. What's up?"

"Man, something strange happened last week."

"What was that?"

"The phone stopped ringing."

"I don't understand."

"Customers quit calling. I think it will be okay, but I don't want to take on any more debt without some jobs coming in the door."

That's how fast the bust of the oil business happened in 1984. A local welder could tell me the day the phones quit ringing. They didn't start ringing again for years.

I was stuck with two airplanes and a Christmas store that were all bleeding cash. With a new wife and daughter, I found myself in debt and struggling to keep afloat. As the recession in the oilfield deepened, the Runnels had to sell their airplane, too, and I was suddenly without work.

Cynthia had quit her job in the spring of 1982 and was trying to pay off the bills from the Christmas store, and I was trying to sell the aircraft for almost any price, yet finding no takers.

At the height of my personal financial turmoil, I got a call from Moncor, telling me they had a new policy that "highly encouraged" anyone who had a loan with them to buy stock in their bank.

The bank officer explained, "We want you to buy $15,000 worth of Moncor stock."

"I am not in position to do that."

"It is highly encouraged, from the top levels of the bank, and I am authorized to lend you the money to buy the stock at a very favorable rate. The loan is preapproved."

"You don't understand. I have two airplanes I am making payments on, a Christmas store that is underwater, and I owe tens of thousands to vendors. I am not going to borrow more to buy your stock."

> I was stuck with two airplanes and a Christmas store that were all bleeding cash. With a new wife and daughter, I found myself in debt and struggling to keep afloat. As the recession in the oilfield deepened, the Runnels had to sell their airplane, too, and I was suddenly without work.

"The stock will make you money. You can hold it a year or two and sell it for a big profit and pay off your other loans."

"Let me repeat myself. I am not going to borrow money to buy stock in your bank."

"You know, we could call your notes."

"You can call the notes. I will give you both airplanes today, but I am not going into debt to buy your stock."

The Moncor stock was issued at $10 per share in 1982. When the bank could not talk more people into going into debt to buy stock, the price began to fall, and by July 1985, the stock was trading at $1.75 per share and was removed from over-the-counter trading. The Hobbs bank failed on August 30, 1985, with the Roswell bank being declared insolvent by the Deputy U.S. Comptroller of Currency a couple of weeks later. Ultimately, five of the six Moncor banks would fail, all pulled underwater by too many bad loans. These represented the first New Mexico bank failures in over half a century.

The high-flying Moncor was bankrupt. Local people, folks I had known all my life, had lost their life savings. I was not smarter; I just remembered collecting all those hot checks for C. R. Anthony's when I was a sophomore in high school. I didn't want to be one of the people living beyond my means, writing hot checks. I was able to sell both airplanes for a small loss. Cynthia was working day and night to pay off all the vendors from the Christmas store.

One evening, the three of us in our small family discussed my lack of a job at the dinner table. Later that night, Lori and I, still getting used to each other, went to the grocery store. When I was paying out, the clerk asked so she could document on the check, "What is your place of employment?"

"Self-employed," I shot back. Lori's head snapped around and looked at me. I didn't look back. On the way out the door, without looking at her, I said, "It sounded so much better than unemployed." Out of the corner of my eye, I could see the silent laughter shaking her body. She has always understood my sense of humor, which is usually obscure, hard to understand, and, according to Cynthia, not always funny.

27

WHO'S IN CHARGE?

In 1981, when Cynthia and I entered into our marriage relationship, I had determined to lead my new family in a loving and strong role, which did not come naturally to me.

Examples abound where Christian husbands leave their wives alone to make most of the serious, life-challenging decisions, while others misuse biblical teachings to bully their wives and families. When faced with such examples, many women conclude that to give either an absent or a dominant, mean-spirited man such power over them is not only a fearful proposition, it is able to destroy their very spirit.

In contrast, my readings suggested that Jesus taught a revolutionary idea of valuing women in a world that used them as chattel. The Christian marriages, where both the husband and wife had equal rights and the husband offered the loving headship to which he was instructed, had to impact the Roman society in which they were beginning to emerge. I reasoned that surely Jesus did not in any way teach the idea of a chauvinistic male-centered marriage.

Headship is often misused by new husbands who want to simply be master or boss. But a close study of the Bible shows that authoritarian control is not given to the husband. Headship is instead something he is charged with, and he is largely responsible for the outcomes of that marriage.

If I wanted to avoid the deep bitterness of an unbalanced marriage and have the best outcome in the relationship, I realized I must delve deeply into the biblical model to understand it fully. I have stumbled and made mistakes along the way, but I have persisted in trying to build the right relationship; perhaps the struggle I went through will be helpful to other men when they try to build or recover their marriage.

As I waded through the responsibilities that I was suddenly faced with in my marriage, I often thought back to the pilot-copilot model that was crucial to landing a C-130 Hercules at Atsugi Air Base in Japan years before. I saw value in God's design and clarity about who is responsible in times of familial turbulence. Let me tell you the story, and I think you'll see how it applies.

Landing at Atsugi

The copilot and pilot, who is usually the aircraft commander (A/C), have equal training. Generally, the A/C has more experience, but that's not always the case. Nonetheless, in this relationship among equals, one acts as the ultimate decision maker. Even when the pilot in the right seat has more rank and experience, the A/C listed on the manifest for that day has full responsibility and final authority for decisions made on that mission. Discussions might take place, the crew might offer input, but responsibility ultimately resides in the left seat. That authority can neither be avoided nor reassigned.

Submission to that authority applies to passengers as well, regardless of rank. Even though a general far outranks a captain in the Air Force, the regulations are very clear that the A/C is in charge. As a copilot on missions inside Vietnam, I saw two instances in which generals, who were onboard passengers, came into the cockpit and tried to give orders to the captains who were A/Cs. These men were trying to influence decisions that were beyond their authority. Both A/Cs knew aviation regulations well and had to threaten to kick them off the airplane if they did not return to their seats. And, both times, the generals went to the back, sat down, and forgot the issue.

Final authority has to reside in one seat. As a copilot, I made better landings and flew better instrument approaches than some of my A/Cs, but they still had authority over me. They were in charge.

In 1972, I was copiloting a C-130 that flew from the Philippines to Taiwan, picked up thirty Japanese journalists, and was to deliver them thirteen hundred miles to Atsugi AFB, Japan, near Tokyo. Soon after taking off, we began to hear alarming announcements on the radio: "All bases in the Philippine Islands are below landing minimums and closed to air traffic. Consult your air traffic controllers for rerouting." *Minimums* is a flying term that describes the minimum altitude to which an aircraft can descend if the pilot cannot see the airfield. It's illegal to breach this altitude—one of the hard-and-fast rules of flying.

Though we were not headed to the Philippines, a typhoon had developed twenty-four hours sooner than expected, affecting the entire western Pacific. An hour later, another announcement came: "All air bases in Korea are below landing minimums and are closed until further notice." The alerts were being broadcast "in the blind" and not to any particular aircraft, but we could tell from the quiet radios that we were one of just a few planes in the afternoon sky.

The bases in Taiwan closed behind us. Every base within range of our onboard fuel had suddenly closed except those in Japan. The lights turned off one by one, in every country and at every base we could use as an alternate if Atsugi AFB, our destination, closed. The typhoon raged every direction except ahead of us. And then: "Yokota AFB is now below landing minimums and closed to air traffic." It was the first base in Japan to close. We were still about an hour from our destination and suddenly in a race against time!

Growing turbulence began to buffet our plane, which had been flying in cloudy but calm skies for most of the trip. Then came the driving rain, hitting in sheets against the cockpit's windscreens. The afternoon skies went black, as if a switch had been flipped. Military aircraft are not equipped with the soundproofing that is standard fare for airliners. The driving rain hitting the metal skin of the C-130 sounded like hail striking our tin pig barns during my childhood in Nadine.

The A/C sent me below to check on our passengers. Eyes wide with alarm, they were clinging to the C-130's red web seatbacks and vomiting en masse. Holding the aircraft railing to keep from being thrown off my feet, I used the PA system to announce that we were less than an hour from our destination, that things would be a little bumpy the rest of the way, but not to worry. The words were lost in the noise of the airplane as the wild ride gave them more information than my reassurances, had they been able to hear them.

As I strapped back into my seat, the A/C was obviously worried. While I was below, more bad news had come: except for Atsugi, the rest of the bases in Japan were now closed. The Philippines were closed. Australia was too far away. We did not have enough fuel to make it anywhere that had a field above minimums. I processed the information quietly and thought aloud, "If every base in Japan is closed other than Atsugi, it's below minimums also, they're just not announcing it."

My A/C confirmed the assumption. "I think Atsugi isn't closed yet because we are headed there. They know we have no other options."

Once an airport is reported below minimum landing weather conditions, it's illegal to make an attempt to land. All flights must have enough fuel to make it to alternate landing sites where the weather is better. We had plenty of fuel to make it to our alternate when we started the mission, but the fast moving storm had closed those as well. Now we were headed to a base that was obviously below minimums with no other place to go. In silence, we let the gravity of our situation sink in.

The warnings of my T-37 training instructor, Captain Jorgensen, flashed through my mind: "You do not go below that altitude if you can't see the runway visually." But he wasn't in charge today; my A/C was, and we were running out of choices. This decision—and our execution of it—had to be right.

The A/C broke in, "You fly more precise approaches," he told me. "I want you to fly the ILS." The Instrument Landing System is used when flying "blind," with no reference to the ground. It uses instruments alone to help the aircraft arrive over the end of the runway at the lowest and safest altitude. He quickly explained the game plan: he would monitor my approach, and when we were five hundred feet above the ground, he would call out my change in altitude every fifty feet. As we descended through decision height, he would call out my altitude every ten feet. A missed approach was not an option.

He would be looking at the instruments and outside simultaneously to determine if he could land the craft. I would be flying solely on the instruments, as transitioning from instruments to visual landing and back can lead to vertigo problems that are catastrophic close to the ground.

"When I see the runway, I'll take the controls and land," he told me. "You will not look outside; you stay on the instruments. If I can't successfully land the aircraft, you'll take over and execute the missed approach."

Some A/Cs would have flown the approach and landed the airplane while I would have monitored the entire thing as little more than a bystander. But mine had given me the responsibility to fly the approach. The safety of our passengers now relied on me as much as him.

Uncertainty can be a powerful distraction from duty, and my A/C had just told me we were going to break two cardinal rules: we were going to fly an approach to a field we knew was below minimums, and we were going to fly below the "decision height." I had to quickly decide whether to follow protocol or my orders. The decision was a no-notice exam, and I had to pass. If we were going to break these rules, we could not begin the process with uncertainty. Our success hinged on being fully committed to the decision and maintaining total concentration.

With most of the precision landing systems of that time, the height for deciding whether you could land was almost always two hundred feet, which is about as close to the ground as you could get with the landing aids and equipment we had. When we hit the initial point where all instrument approaches and the descent begin, the A/C clicked off the autopilot, announcing that I had control of the aircraft. A last glance out the front windscreen (windshield) showed a pitch-black sky, driving rain, and no hint of visual references. We were in the middle of the storm.

In pilot training, I had become comfortable practicing instrument approaches with "the hood," a fabric shield that covered the student's cockpit to eliminate outside visual references. It was the best simulation of instrument conditions, but turbulence was rarely a factor in those stable training scenarios. This was no training approach.

The storm thrust us up, then slammed us right back down with the instrument readings bouncing erratically. Airspeed control and vertical velocity are both critical in precise approaches, but the turbulence was disrupting both. I didn't know exactly how fast we were descending or moving.

With the briefest of instructions, the A/C told me, "Just fly the middle of the top and bottom bounces in airspeed." It's a technique that can only be learned by experience in such unstable conditions, and this was my first time. He reassured me: "You are one thousand feet above touchdown, and as much as I can tell, you're on course and on glide path."

He talked me through the approach, telling me to "crab a couple more degrees" to offset the hurricane-force winds threatening to blow us off course, talking me down to the ground. "Eight hundred feet," he said.

Sweat poured down my face. My knees trembled, and I felt the buffet of the winds through the rudder pedals as we hurtled through the black skies. I did not want to get slow and risk a stall, so I hedged toward the top end of the fluctuations of the airspeed indicator that caused us to be a little above the glide slope. The runway raced toward us at 130 knots.

Coming in even ten-feet off in height can be the difference between seeing and not seeing the runway. The updrafts began to push us higher above the glide slope. "Get it back down on the glide path," he said, becoming more insistent. "Fly the aircraft! Make it do what you want it to do!" Now it was a command.

"Calm down," I told myself. "Just fly the aircraft. Make it do what you want it to do."

"Remember, don't change a thing when we hit 200 feet, continue to fly the approach until I say to execute the missed approach. Acknowledge."

"Yes, sir, continue the approach past 200 feet."

He counted me down, "200. Easy does it. No changes…190, 180, 170…"

I was on the edge of panic, struggling to keep my concerns to myself and my emotions in check. The instruments still showed I was about one-degree right of course and was being lifted back above the glide path. I was concerned about busting minimums, but trusted the judgment of the A/C. He was in charge and was giving orders. It's the way things are supposed to work.

"140, 130, 120 . . ." We were now at barely more than half the altitude we should be at to get a visual contact, and still had nothing. We would risk hitting the ground beside the runway if he didn't get a visual contact soon. "I think I just saw a runway light but lost it," he said. "110, 100 . . . steady . . . I have the runway in sight. I have the controls," he waggled the yoke, signaling he was taking over.

I glanced outside. We were in and out of low-lying scud with dark clouds and hard-driving rain, high and to the right of the runway. We appeared to have flown over about a third of it already. He pulled the power to idle and began the dive to the runway, the speed picking up as he put the nose down.

He shouted, "Stay on the instruments! You need to be ready and focused if I give the controls back to you!"

Tensions were sky-high. Turbulence was still throwing us around the sky. The winds were gale force from our left. He was having trouble getting over to the centerline of the runway. Visibility was less than a quarter of a mile, so we had no idea how much runway remained.

"I don't know if we have enough runway but I'm committing to the landing!" he shouted again, then barking orders. "Stay on the gauges! Cinch your shoulder harness, in case we go off the end. Be ready for a go-around."

"Yes, sir."

With a bang, we hit the runway still fighting crosswinds and unsure if we had enough rudder to win. The plane was still too fast and the hard landing caused the immense craft to balloon back into the sky, almost thirty feet above the runway. He slammed the throttles forward, using power to break the fall, and jerked them back to idle to keep the airspeed from increasing.

The tower couldn't see us through the storm and called to see if we had landed.

As copilot, I was in charge of radio calls and answered, "We are still fighting it." I was afraid if I said yes they would announce the field was closed. If we bounced once more, we would be out of runway and would execute a go-around, launching back into the turbulent skies for a second attempt. The tower could not give us permission to do another approach if they called the field below minimums, which it definitely was.

Runway was disappearing underneath us at an alarming pace. Finally, we touched down again. This time the colossal plane stayed on the runway, and the A/C slammed all four engines to reverse thrust and the speed began to bleed off. He hit the left brake to keep the typhoon winds from blowing us off the strip as we slowed and the rudder lost effectiveness. He was heavy on the brakes. I could feel the rudder pedals chattering as the antiskid sensors did their work to prevent hydroplaning on the wet runway. We lurched to a stop with only a few feet of runway left. The gale force winds kept us from the full sensation of stopping as they continued to rock the Hercules from side to side, like tremors from the storm we had just faced.

No one in the crew spoke. Slowly, I felt relief trickling in. I broke the silence first. "Atsugi tower, we are on the ground."

"Roger. This is Atsugi tower transmitting on guard frequency. Atsugi Air Force Base is below landing minimums. The field is closed to air traffic."

The last field in the Pacific where it was possible for us to land had been shut down while we were still on the runway. We had made it. It wasn't pretty, but we were safely on the ground. Passengers and crewmembers would see their families. Crew coordination, crew discipline, and a clear chain of command in the decision-making sequence had saved us all.

Questions about who is in charge—or whether that person's decisions are final—can be deadly at the moment of decision. Air Force regulations make it clear that there is no questioning the A/C. He is in charge. He makes the decisions and is responsible for the consequences.

There was no room to question, because the chain of command was more powerful than all the fears and regulations. The A/C, using his best judgment, made a decision. If he bent the airplane, he was responsible. If I bent the airplane, he was responsible.

I might have argued about the legality of busting minimums. A disagreement when there is pressure only increases it, so we are trained to trust the chain of command. Because of that, we had survived.

As a copilot, I flew with A/Cs who treated the copilot as an equal, alternating landings and instrument approaches and allowing decisions to be made by the guy in the right seat. And I flew with some who had to constantly prove to the copilot who was boss. I modeled myself after those who taught, included, and led with their knowledge and experience, not depending on rank to gain respect.

Experiences like this one greatly influenced the way I perceived decision-making throughout the rest of my life. But they proved especially telling as I prepared to enter marriage. I often thought back to the crew coordination, the different-but-equally-important roles in the cockpit, and the clarity of knowing who is in charge, especially in moments of great stress.

Leadership in a Marriage

Every relationship must have a process for making decisions, especially when it comes to life's critical challenges and disagreements. Cynthia and I were no exception. We were already married—and had made the choice to live by the same Christian principles with which we were both raised—when we sat down to discuss how we would make decisions.

Cynthia had to start the conversation: "What do you think about that verse in the Bible that talks about the wife submitting to her husband?" It seemed that I could almost feel her flinch when she asked the question.

I sighed and cringed at the word. This principle is among the most controversial of all directives coming from the Bible. Critics abound, both Christian and non-Christian. Many independent women, and Cynthia definitely qualifies, take issue with the idea, and I was not sure where she stood. Many of my friends dealt with the directive by ignoring it, afraid of seeming old-fashioned and of starting disputes with their wives. Both Cynthia and I think our beliefs should stand up to everyday life, but this one was tricky.

We are all created in God's image, I reasoned, so it could not be that the man is in some way superior or the wife inferior. But God did cast the husband and wife in different roles—a design that seems very intentional.

We struggled through this conversation for many weeks, praying and studying, not wanting to reject a principle of our faith, but to make sense of it and live it. The concept of headship in the household, however, is not the only directive in the Bible aimed at marriage. I found it must be coupled with another: that the husband must love his wife. The word *love* in this context is not the same word used for affectionate love. This love is an attitude in which the man lays aside his desires and rights and takes care of his wife, making sure her needs are met. If the precondition of nurturing and cherishing is not implemented along with the submission part, it makes for a brand of male dominance that was never God's intent.

I had a responsibility to know and trust Cynthia's insights, fears, and innermost desires well enough to merge our thoughts and make decisions each of us would make, ones that would never leave her resentful or bitter. But as the husband, I would bear ultimate responsibility for those choices. The heavy weight of this accountability, of acting on behalf of us both, came crashing down on me.

I could not expect Cynthia to accept my leadership unless I committed to this and one other principle: husbands, the Bible teaches, are to love their wives "as Christ loved the church, and gave himself for it." The husband's responsibility and love for his family must, when necessary, be sacrificial.

I realized the husband is to give up his independence and must get his priorities right, setting aside his own desires to serve his spouse and family. Only when it is settled in his wife's heart that she is the most important relationship in his life (not children, golf, work, entertainment, or other friends, though these have their place) does an independent, strong-willed wife have a proclivity for tolerating an authority-submission economy in marriage.

Once we had reasoned through the concepts, Cynthia was still curious what this should look like in everyday life, so she asked. I started to explain my thoughts with an example of what it should not look like. When I was at dinner with another couple, I saw the husband kick his wife in the shin under the table when she expressed an opinion that was different from his. He didn't realize I could see it, and I thought it was an accident at first. But when she continued to disagree with him, even more passionately, he kicked her even harder, until she stopped speaking mid-sentence.

"I never want to stop you mid-sentence," I told Cynthia. "I love your independence and decisiveness. These are some of the reasons I married you."

In matters of faith, it should be enough to know that God has laid out a commandment for us in writing. But I believe if we will work to reason through God's plan and understand the nuances, we will find a richness in life and relationships that is not possible when using the commandments as a set of rules to follow by rote memory. A deeper understanding also makes it possible to explain my beliefs and life choices to non-Christian friends.

Asking Mom

It was at this point in the discussion with my wife that I brought up the subject with my mother who, with my father, raised us in a Christian family. "Did you and Dad ever discuss the biblical idea of the wife submitting to her husband?" I asked her one day as the two of us sat visiting in our home at Nadine. My dad was still alive at this time, but I wanted Mom's perspective. I couldn't have predicted her reaction to what I thought was a fairly benign question. She shot me a look that froze my blood in place.

This was not an ordinary topic for discussion in the family, and my mom seemed to see it as an intrusion. I sat quietly, watching the emotions flash across her face for a long while; her jaw was set, her lips were pursed, and she seemed to be staring into a distant past. Finally, she started to talk.

She was just seventeen when they married, eighteen when my brother Mike was born, twenty when my brother Tom came along, and they were living on the second farm my father worked at the time (the one where the ceiling fell in). "Your father always worked hard. When he was off, he would take his horse, Tony, and go riding and hunting while I stayed home and took care of the kids. I began to suspect that when it came to supporting me when my days were in shambles, your father would not be there.

"When I was twenty-two and pregnant with you, Mike got real sick. I was afraid we were going to lose him," she said, easing into a story that seemed painful to retell. "I told your father he needed to do something—that Mike was very sick, that I could not take care of Tom and a sick kid at the same time. He didn't know what to do." Again, she stopped mid-thought. But now the floodgates were open, and the thing was going to be said. It was as if no one was there with her; she was speaking from a deep well of memory.

Tying the story back to my question, she explained that my father was never one to deal with complex issues such as submission or his responsibility in the family. And on that day, as on any other, he did the only thing he knew to do in the crush of danger and fear: he saddled Tony, picked up Tom, climbed up on the horse, and rode away, without saying a word. He relieved her of one of the children, but not the sick one nor her fears. "I know it was his way of trying to help, but he left me alone, afraid our oldest son was in the process of dying."

The emotion I had been watching form finally settled on her features: pure bitterness, one I only saw from her that day and a few more times when we talked about this subject.

She continued now, determined to get the experience, like a poison, out of her system. She had never driven a car, nor did she know how to drive, but she crawled into the only available transportation to the hospital, an old manual shift car. She placed my brother on the seat beside her. There were no infant seats or seat belts, so she tried to keep him from rolling off the seat while she taught herself to drive.

"Knowing nothing about the clutch, I jammed the gears until we started moving and somehow drove that miserable fifteen miles into Lamesa. The doctor diagnosed Mike with near rheumatic fever and told me his tonsils must come out."

There was no such thing as health insurance then, and the family couldn't have afforded it anyway. The doctor told her the tonsillectomy would cost fifty dollars, which they did not have.

"Somehow, I convinced him that we could pay it off over time, and he did the surgery," she said before falling silent once again. Then with those same pursed and bitter lips, she issued a simple observation: "Melvin should have been there, but I was alone . . . dealing with the most traumatic questions I had ever faced. I would have loved for Melvin to have been strong enough for me to lean on, but I realized I would probably have to make these decisions for the rest of our lives together."

I spoke for the first time, "Mom, I didn't mean to open up such an old wound."

It was as if she couldn't hear me, and she continued with her thoughts. "Submission? I would have been glad to submit. But if your father was not there in the tough times all families live through, why would I trust him to make decisions that might limit our future. I did not submit easily when I did not agree. I know I am headstrong, but Melvin needed to be stronger."

That one moment in her marriage—one that showed her that life's major decisions were hers alone to make—resulted in a life-long bitterness.

"I had to be the strong one. Your father is not a bad man," she said, trying to soften the blow. "He is a good man and worked every day to provide for us . . . , but he should have been there."

During all of these discussions, I suddenly realized a deep character flaw in myself. It was as if blinding scales had been removed from my eyes, forcing me to examine my own tendencies. Similar to Dad, I tended to drift through the major decisions without forcing myself to lead and be accountable. Dad never got comfortable with the major decisions in life. When things got tough, he would retreat into the familiar, to his work or his animals. I saw this tendency in myself and determined to resist the easy path.

Let either the husband or wife forget God's design, and the outcome is less than we were intended to experience. Many families never resolve these thorny issues and operate almost as separate individuals who live in the same house. The need for a family unit is so strong that many cults and gangs are attractive to young people because they offer a family-type group. But when the roles are balanced properly, blessings accrue and successes come that I think are not possible otherwise.

It became clear that we had to implement this model carefully, striving to achieve the right tone and balance. The wife is to voluntarily submit, just as the husband is to lovingly lead and sacrifice. The husband's part is to show up during the times of deep stress, take the leadership role and be accountable for the outcome, blaming no one else. The wife's submission is not a matter of superior versus inferior; rather, it is self-imposed as a matter of obedience to the Lord and of love for her husband.

In wrestling with the concept, the flight into Atsugi during my Air Force years convinced me that the chain of command had to be formalized, both in the cockpit and in marriage. A clear process for making decisions reduces confusion, creates order, allows us to focus on the actual problem—and can even save lives. The experience burned the principle into my heart with greater clarity than anything I had read or been told.

God's Blueprint and Design

The foundation of society is the family. Strong families raise strong individuals, who then make up a strong nation. Ralph Drollinger, who founded Capitol Ministries in 1997, said, "The Bible says the primary role of the wife in marriage is to *build* and *establish* the home while the husband works outside as the breadwinner. It is not as if one is more valuable than the other; both have equal worth; it is just that they have different roles. Ideally, it takes a symbiosis of husband and wife to achieve all of the above. . . . This is how God made marriages and families to function most effectively and productively as the foundation of society."

In Cynthia's words, "It is almost ingrained in my female DNA that the primary goal, the primary urging, is to take care of the home. It is the prime responsibility. . . . There is not even a decision; you just know it comes first."

As I shouldered more decisions and accepted responsibility for our success or failure, it allowed Cynthia to take care of our home. Because of her efforts, our home is orderly and stable, providing a safe sanctuary and offering a retreat from the typical storms of life. With our well managed home as our refuge, I found it possible to wade into the pressures of building our customer base and managing the business because the orderliness and peace inside our home provided renewal each night.

This is not to say that Cynthia was trapped inside the home each day—far from it. She excelled in accounting and was a partner with me in managing our business. But her primary role, attending to the matters of the home as her highest calling, was always very clear in her mind.

Instead of distracting or competing with each other, we have complemented each other's strengths, fitting together as pieces in a puzzle. We have encouraged and developed each other in our specific roles. With the decision process and the home stabilized, I found it possible to find the pathways to prosperity outside of it.

How It Looks

Jesus taught by example that the one in charge is the greatest servant. Cynthia and I intended to pattern our lives after this biblical model, getting the balance right in order to provide a relationship in which we could both thrive and grow to our full potential. The tensions that inevitably occur when either party insists on his or her way disappeared as we developed our trust and coordination. Most of the time, we were in solid agreement how to proceed.

Often, we have moved more slowly than would have been my choice, because I wanted her to be comfortable with the risks and the speed of change. By slowing things down to her pace, we have had more stability than if I had followed just my own heart. Stability is a key ingredient for families, especially as the kids yearn for a sense of routine. On the other hand, because of my influence, we have accomplished things she never would have contemplated.

Cynthia and I flourish because we operate as a team. It is as if neither of us can see a way to the finish line without the other. This mutually shared vision is one of the most fascinating parts of my life, and one of the reasons I am daily amazed by and attracted to my wife.

Only once did I make a major decision without her consent, and it was regarding a matter of discipline for our daughter. We had visited Texas A&M, where we were paying for Lori to attend college, to find out that she was making life choices that were contrary to the values our family taught. As we left College Station for Hobbs, our home in New Mexico, we discussed how to proceed. I suggested that Lori pay her own way, to show her that we would not subsidize a lifestyle that we did not believe was right. Cynthia, with a softness of heart that I cherish, believed that was too harsh.

The discussion was so intense I could not drive and still process the flow of the conversation. We stopped, got a hotel room, and continued the discussion late into the night. Then we woke early and persisted mid-sentence.

It was the most difficult moment of our marriage. Finally, I said, "I love you dearly, but I must make the decision I believe to be right, and that is that Lori can start paying her own way."

Cynthia responded in full anger, "I completely disagree, but you have the right to make that choice. You alone are responsible to God for this decision." In theology and management this is termed "exercising headship"— most of the time the pilot and copilot agree on things, but when they don't, in marriage or in the cockpit, the one in authority must exercise headship.

I took the weight of her words seriously, which left me in an unbearably difficult position—though one I think God intends for us to experience when we, as men, make decisions about the future of our families without the full consent of our wives.

(Our daughter, years later, confirmed that our actions, hard as they were, were right. She said she would have turned out differently had we not gotten involved. Cynthia acknowledges that Lori's admission is valid.)

Though I appreciate my father's good example in many areas—his sensitivity, his gentleness, his work ethic—I had determined to lean into the task of leading in the big decisions. I have worked hard to shoulder responsibilities as the spiritual leader of my family, forcing myself, at times, to take on the difficult choices.

I do not often try to speculate why God has made certain commandments, concentrating instead on following them. But in this one area, I have spent much time wondering why God would have the husband be the one in charge of the family. Studies show that, in marriages, the women make many of the day-to-day decisions; data in fact supports the idea that women make the vast majority of the healthcare, education, and spending choices in their families. Many women juggle multiple responsibilities in the workplace and home, all the while remaining sensitive to the emotions and needs of each family member.

I suspect that, as Mom said, God's intent was, in part, to keep the man involved, to keep him engaged when his normal desires and tendencies would take him in other directions, away from the home.

When I watch the nature programs on television, there seems to be a correlation between the male lion and how a human male, unrestrained, might interact with his family. The lion often sits back, waiting for the females to catch the prey, coming along only to take charge of the meal once the work is done, driving away the females and young and eating his fill before the others. Unchecked, the human male strength could also be used to the disadvantage of the female and the family. Being responsible, being sacrificial, are commandments that take the wild out of the man.

I believe that my wife and I are successful because we choose to pattern our lives and relationship after the biblical blueprint for the home and our respective roles in marriage. I have led Cynthia beyond her safe zones and into the uncharted territory where we often live, and she has tempered my impulsive and spontaneous tendencies.

We committed to the principles of how decisions would be made in our new family. That decision was to play a key role in one of the most critical moments of our business lives that lay just around the corner.

28

PASTOR DEAN AND "GETTING IT"

After Cynthia and I were married, we began looking for a church. We both wanted one that was biblically based and more traditional than the New Age fad that was sweeping the land. She was insistent that we find one that involved the youth so that Lori would grow up in the faith community, too.

As soon as we heard Dr. Dean Mathis preach, we felt that Taylor Memorial Baptist Church in Hobbs was home. Cynthia checked out the youth program, which was active, and we both declared it to be the answer to our prayers. The congregation welcomed us and for the next thirty years it was the primary source of our spiritual maturing and study.

Dean has the magnificent capability of being able to relate the Bible stories to events that occur in our ordinary daily life. That is always the hard part, the connection, the association, the "so what" of any philosophy or theology.

One of the first great points he proved was the difference between scruples and commandments, the latter being absolute and the former being choices made by individuals. It is an important distinction in the lives of Christians. It keeps a legalistic interpretation of the Bible from choking us in a net of restrictions that were never intended.

He answered the question of *how* we are to accomplish "loving our enemies" when we do not feel that love. His exegesis of the subject led me to one of the great "aha" moments of my life, dating back to those discussions with Earl and Shirley Seall over a decade before. The translation of the text does not command us to emotionally love, but instead to do what is possible . . . to show loving acts, to say hello, to wish them a nice day. If loving them was not possible, treating them with compassion was. Another piece of the puzzle was in place for me.

The next great discovery he led us to was the understanding of what makes sin wrong. Why are bad things wrong? What makes them sin?

Dean's teaching was made even clearer to me through a young soldier from New Mexico, whom I happened to encounter in Afghanistan. We were both in a foreign country, and it is always good to find someone from your home state when you are abroad. I didn't know his family, but I knew Las Cruces, where he grew up.

"Did you graduate from Mayfield or Las Cruces High?" I asked, making conversation.

He paused before answering, "Well, I graduated from a school in Arizona."

I responded, "That sounds like a story all in itself and probably not a good one." I could make that observation because the kid in front of me was a soldier, confident and composed, sure of himself. People like that are usually willing to talk about serious things.

He allowed himself a wry grin and said, "You have that pegged right."

Considering that a bit of an invitation, I pushed on, "Drugs?"

"Yes, I got way out of control. My parents sent me there when they did not see any way forward."

"Obviously, you found yourself. What was it that let you see the light? A program, a counselor, religion?"

"Actually, it was not really any of those."

Now my curiosity was piqued. "Getting loose from something that was destroying your life is no small matter. If it was none of those, what was it?"

He was spontaneous and direct. "I came to the understanding that I had separated myself from everyone in my life. It was the recognition of my separation from all who loved me that did it. I quit cold turkey when I realized that."

The problem with wrong things is that they separate us from our loved ones, from everyone around us and—first and foremost—from God. Separation is so serious in society, so serious in our personal lives, that the things that cause it have to be declared as *sin*, as so wrong that we teach children to avoid them and punish adults who commit them. Murder, theft, and false testimonies are all prohibited by law because they are the source of deep rifts in society. Similarly, alcoholism, drug dependency, gambling addiction, and sexual addiction all separate us from those who care about us.

The original Ten Commandments were a listing of things so heinous that they disrupt society, our lives, and our relationships. They separate us from one another. This was one of the most powerful understandings that came from Dean's sermons. It had taken me years to "get it." But the young man I was visiting with had worked it out in his own mind when the pain became great enough.

That may be the strongest point in why I choose to be a Christian. It provides guides for living. Some, such as this young man, work it out in their own minds, but it was a very painful way of learning. The result, if one does not happen to "get it," is a lost life. I think more people are in my situation than his, struggling for understanding and looking for ways to know the pathways we should choose. I think most people need that relationship with a power higher than themselves or their friends to figure life out.

Christians who were looking for a new land established our nation, a land where they could pursue their beliefs without harassment or persecution. John Adams observed, "Our Constitution was made only for a moral and religious people. It is wholly inadequate to the government of any other." Our Founding Fathers had the understanding of the need for ingrained, consistent moral standards in their hearts. Obedience to the laws of the land has to be voluntary.

Dean constantly educated our congregation on the need for Christians to run for office, and during his tenure, the congregation produced two state representatives, one state senator, multiple city and county elected officials, a judge, and a U.S. congressman. His lessons were instrumental to the way Cynthia and I live our lives and the decisions we made, helping us in our decision to run for public office, influencing our business decisions and the maturing of our faith, and affording us a clear understanding of our role in God's kingdom.

Joe and Sarah Yue

America is a beacon of hope to the world—those who have none come here to find it. Destination "hope" is one of the great things to love about this country.

My mom was also hope. She taught ESL (English as a Second Language) in Hobbs. As a result, we got to know most of the people who moved to town from foreign countries. I grew to have a real respect for anyone who would leave everything—their country, their family, their home, their culture—and move to a new place where they had nothing, knew no one, and usually didn't know the language.

The families that moved to Hobbs looked at Mom as more than a teacher, because she appreciated and valued them. Anywhere people were brave enough to emigrate from, she had arms big enough to hug them in welcome into this new land. Seeing the good in each person she taught, she encouraged and lifted them up, included them, pushed them, and became their friend. In short, she treated them as she treated her own kids.

John Adams observed, "Our Constitution was made only for a moral and religious people. It is wholly inadequate to the government of any other."

In response, they shared their appreciation in the only thing they could—native dishes, cooked with care and delivered to our house. Through the years when she was teaching ESL, we had a steady progression of Korean, Chinese, Guatemalan, and Mexican foods. She did not just teach; she involved herself in their outcomes. They visited our house, and we visited theirs. It was like a whirlwind of inclusion until they had developed their own life and their own friends. She saw that their pump was primed and then left them to themselves and went on to the next project needing to learn English.

In 1978, I moved back to Hobbs from Arkansas. Most of my childhood friends had moved away or moved on, and I was looking for someone who could understand the military, the war, and the things I had experienced.

Mom was teaching new residents from Taiwan—Joe Yue, his sister, Chen, and her husband, K. C. Many of the immigrants who moved to town immediately started a small business. Joe was no exception and started the Peking Restaurant. Mom insisted that we had to be among the first to patronize the business.

From the day I met Joe, we connected. We were both trying to move up the economic ladder. I had flown in and around the Asian countries, spending time in Taiwan, so Joe and I had something to talk about immediately. He had also served in the military in Taiwan, and we discovered that military service in any country has many similarities.

Over the next few weeks, I dropped by for afternoon tea, and we became good friends, discussing the military, business, and philosophies of life. I was flying many hours and would be gone for days, but when we got together, it was as though we could start with the same sentence where we left off in the previous discussion. We both love business, and the idea of finding the best and most efficient way to run a business was a bond that pulled us together. He is successful because he works hard.

Sarah, his wife, a native of the Philippines, works equally hard, studying at night and on weekends to graduate from nurse to nurse practitioner. Together, they typify what is wonderful about the infusion of new vitality into any society by immigration.

When I introduced Joe to Cynthia and Lori, he welcomed them into our friendship circle. When Lori was eleven, she worked the cash register in our store, which was next to Joe's restaurant, and he grew to have a great love for her. She refers to him as Uncle Joe.

Cynthia and I were included in the Yue family events. We were there when Joe married Sarah, when their son, Thai, was born, when Joe's sister got married, and we helped him bury his mother. And we have been fellow participants in hundreds of hours of discussions of family matters between our two families, sharing the joys and pains equally. We have been friends for more than thirty years and share the values of family, hard work, trust, and doing the right thing. Our community is a better place because of people such as Joe, Sarah, Chen, K. C., and many others who are like them!

29

REMEMBER ME

"Remember me." Those were the last words I would have from my brother Tom. They were scrawled on the back of a picture from his high-point days, wearing a cowboy hat and a well-trimmed beard before he got sick.

Tom was the outsider when we were growing up. Mike, the oldest brother, always seemed to take up for me, so it was the two of us against Tom. It was not good or bad, just the way it was.

Tom talked about leaving Hobbs as soon as he graduated from high school, and he did. He went first to Lubbock, Texas, the nearest big city. But even that metropolis was not enough to satisfy his hunger for people, excitement, and a fast pace, so he moved very soon to Los Angeles and lived his life there.

When I visited him, he would fly down the freeway in bumper-to-bumper traffic while talking nonstop, a steady stream-of-consciousness talk that always left me exhausted just from listening. He would exclaim, "Look at all these people and stores!"

I would respond dryly, "I see them, Tom. I hate this pace and the crowds. Other than for visiting you, I would never want to come here." I was satisfied on our little five-acre farm, the farm chores, and the oilfield. I thrived on solitude; Tom needed the crowds.

Tom was about fads, always chasing the newest and latest, while I never participated in the latest of anything and was content with traditional beliefs and institutions. He was always energetic, almost flighty, while I was rock solid, tending to plod along. He was a spender; I was a saver. The thing we shared in life was that we both worked hard.

Tom was the older brother who taught me how to shave. He tried to help me in junior high to get through my terrible shyness, and he was the one who got me hired where he worked at Weichmann Nursery.

During our junior high years, the nation administered aptitude tests that tried to help kids find their career paths. The teacher who went over mine with me said that I should never be a doctor or nurse or anything dedicated to serving others. Helping others was my lowest aptitude. So when Tom got sick, I faced a quandary—go to help him or stay inside the comfort zone I had lived in, not responding to the needs of others?

Mike went to California and helped nurse him along when he was at a low point. Mike noticed that his feet were filthy, the toenails long and curving under. Tom, in his weakness, had not been able to reach them to clean them and clip the nails. Mike cleaned his feet.

One day Mom was at work and called Tom's doctor at the hospital. He told her that if Tom was his son, he would be there with him. Mom stood up from her desk and walked to her supervisor's office to let him know she was going to California. She did not find him but just kept walking, not looking back at unfinished work or needed coordination. She walked away from a career and responsibilities to go live with Tom and take care of him. Then one day she called me and said, "You need to come see your brother."

"I know, Mom. It's not something I have ever been good at, being around sick people."

Months later, Tom, still fighting for health, was back in the hospital. Mom was exhausted from helping him by herself. I finally set aside one more of the fears I faced and flew to see him. When Mike found out I was going, he warned me, "They never clean him up. Be sure to help him bathe and check on his feet." Mom used my presence as a chance to take a much-needed rest, flying back to New Mexico.

As I parked the car and walked into the LA County public hospital, I passed homeless people huddled in doorways and saw multiple places where people had defecated in the parking lot and on the sidewalk leading to the hospital. I was ready to leave before I got inside. When I walked in, Tom was emaciated and curled in a ball. I assumed he was medicated and asleep. So I was surprised when he spoke weakly, "Thanks for coming. I wasn't sure you would make it."

It was not an accusation; we knew each other that well. Many times in the previous several years he had used me as a sounding board to communicate with the family. We were close even though we disagreed on most things.

The county hospital was where the indigents came, people with no resources. The staff was overwhelmed with too many sick people and not enough help. When the nurses came in, I stood back, never helping in the process of making him more comfortable. They accomplished the basics of changing his linens, administering medicine, and taking vital signs. It barely qualified as care, but it was better than leaving him on the street. They said when patients reached his condition they did not have much longer to live.

Tom's approaching death was like an abstraction, something I was not processing. Day after day, I visited him, staying around all day and into the night. We talked about significant things; things that we had never gotten around to saying. I told him from early childhood I could not envision the things he did: dressing as the Philip Morris smoke tray boy, performing his pantomime of Tennessee Ernie Ford's "Sixteen Tons" (the rendition of which started for a 4-H talent contest but evolved into many versions over the next twenty years), or coming to our Christmas reunions with the Santa costumes. When he walked in, skinny as a rail with a pillow bulging under the Santa costume, he performed a complex, spontaneous monologue addressed to the kids yet with asides and double entendres that the adults loved. He embodied love for all that Christmas.

In his weakness, Tom would attempt to laugh at some of the funny stories, but the laughter was too difficult, so he ended up smiling the tired smile of the sick and weary.

I, who hated the crowds and excitement, found myself longing for them to show up to visit. I longed to see him full of the life and energy I would never have. Instead, at the end, life had forced him into the solitude for which I usually yearned. The crowd of friends had forgotten him when he needed them.

I never looked at his feet, which made me angry at myself. The time when I should be able to overcome my fears, I was immobile. Frozen. And time was running out . . . for my visit and in his life. My last day there, I resolved to look.

When I arrived, he did not awaken. I looked in alarm at the screen to make sure he had a pulse. It was weak but steady. I worried that he might be dying. He roused briefly and acknowledged my presence but fell back into a deep sleep. I sat for hours immobilized, unable to carry out my promise to myself. Mid afternoon, having seen no medical staff check on him all day, I got up, walked to the side of his bed, and stood looking closely. My brother Mike's imperative to check his feet echoed in my head. For long minutes, I stood. I touched his arm but he did not respond. Gradually, I got used to standing that close to him.

With trepidation, I lifted the sheet off his feet. I was shocked at the condition. Filled with purpose, I looked around for a plastic basin, filled it with warm water, and began to wet his foot. I started with his left foot. Tom, like Dad, was left-handed, and it seemed to be my unconscious acknowledgment that his being left-handed was at last okay. I had never forgiven him in all those years since Little League for being left-handed, for his awkward throw, and for not staying with me on that team.

Finding liquid soap, I began to wash seriously, to clean the filth. I poured the basin out and started again with fresh water. I found some of Dad's gentleness in myself in these moments and began to find peace in the humility of forgiveness and compassion. Inexplicably, tears began to run down my cheeks. Then I noticed Tom had roused . . . and tears were running from the corners of his eyes.

The harsh words of childhood, the judgment of adulthood, the years of unspoken distance, and the sadness of the coming parting began to melt away in the simple, humble, deeply intimate act of washing my brother's feet.

I was on an early flight the next morning. Tom, who was so close to death that day, began to rally and got well enough to go home. We wanted to bring him back near the family, so three of us brothers went the next month, rented a U-Haul, and moved him back to be with family. The prodigal son was back among us with much rejoicing, but he was still very weak and very sick.

He lived for another six months. The thing he and I both learned from Mom was her tenacity, and Tom continued to hold on to life tenaciously. The doctors could not explain it.

In 1987, his last Christmas, we all gathered one last time. The picture of the family shows him emaciated beyond understanding. When I got back to New Mexico, I waited nervously for the call from Mom, with the whispered news that Tom was gone. But still he held on; he could not let go of life.

Finding liquid soap, I began to wash seriously, to clean the filth. I poured the basin out and started again with fresh water. I found some of Dad's gentleness in myself in these moments and began to find peace in the humility of forgiveness and compassion. Inexplicably, tears began to run down my cheeks. Then I noticed Tom had roused . . . and tears were running from the corners of his eyes.

Mom's nerves were frayed, living each day expecting it to be his last. I knew it was time for him to go . . . I think we all sensed that it was Tom's time, and he passed soon thereafter.

This kid from Nadine, who would not be run off the job when the two of us were landscaping a yard, moved to the big-time arena of Los Angeles and created floral extravaganzas for the 1984 Los Angeles Olympics, the Major League Baseball All-Star Game, for Stevie Wonder's release of the album "Journey Through the Secret Life of Plants," and many events for Elizabeth Taylor and other stars. At Tom's memorial service the comment was made that a country boy came in with his boots, big hat, and western attire and just outperformed everyone.

I have never been able to achieve Tom's sheer joy of living or his wildly creative vision, but in his deepest need, I was able to respond with kindness and brotherly love that I had never achieved until he needed me.

30

BUSINESS

After working for X-Pert/B&M as a pilot for a few years, the company announced it was going to sell the King Air 200 airplane, because the oilfield economy had one of its worst collapses ever. They were generous and allowed me to transition into the purchasing manager spot in late October 1985.

The company conducted two main types of oilfield service. X-Pert had workover units that rigged portable derricks over the wells when it was necessary to pull the pipe out of the wells to accomplish downhole work. B&M was a contract company, similar to the one my father worked for as a contractor when we moved to Hobbs back in 1948 and lived on Cecil Street.

If a crew from either side of the business needed anything, a member would come back to the purchasing office and place an order, and I would have it ready the next day. It was a pretty routine job, but it paid the bills. I showed up about 5:30 a.m., was there to take orders before the crews left for their respective job sites, and was there to give them their supplies when they got back to the office in the afternoon between 5 and 6 p.m. In the process, I got to see and know most of the employees.

Eye Surgery

One morning, a smallish, wiry Hispanic worker showed up. He was wearing a bandana around his thigh and a ferocious attitude that oozed hate and confrontation. He was nice enough, but what was unspoken made me very wary. It was impossible not to notice that one of his eyes was obscured by a cloudy film.

"Have you ever had a doctor look at that eye?" I casually inquired. He did not speak but just looked at me with fire burning from his eyes. He finished his business, wheeled around, and left without answering. After I had finished with all the crews and had gone back into my office, with the door open as usual, he suddenly burst through the door, slamming it shut behind him.

"What the f*** are you asking about my eye for? What the f*** business is it of yours?" He was not waiting for answers but was on a total rampage. "Don't you ever stick your nose in my business again. This is my eye. You just don't worry your ass about it." He wheeled around to leave, still firing insults and threats.

I shouted to his back, "You have insurance that will pay to fix it."

He did not seem to hear or care.

Early one morning about a month later, he burst into my office again, starting exactly where he left off. "What the f*** business is it of yours?" He was as angry, threatening, and confrontational as before. This time, though, he stopped to hear the answer.

"Well, most of the guys don't know much about insurance, but I checked with your supervisor just in case you came back to talk about it. You are enrolled and pay each month for the coverage. I figure the problem with your eye is causing you not to see, and I believe it will be pretty simple to fix."

Full of anger, he spit out the words, "I have worked here for more than ten years and not one person has asked me about my eye. What the hell do you care?" All at once, he burst into tears—this fierce, angry guy, with all the signs of being dangerous, was suddenly in full-out tears.

I spoke quietly, "My mom recently had the surgery, so I saw her fix a problem just like it. I just know if you were my brother, I would be trying to help you."

That was apparently the wrong thing to say. He flashed back to the angry guy. "Well, I ain't your f***ing brother. You can forget about my eye." Then he stormed out.

That afternoon as I was walking from the shop to the office just after lunch, I saw a car with a young Hispanic woman and several kids in it. Families often came to check on paychecks or any number of things, so I didn't think much of it. I went outside a couple more times and saw the same car with the woman still in it. Finally, about 6 p.m., I closed the office and headed out to my car. That car was still there, and it was just mine and hers in the lot.

The woman was outside the car in the cool dark. "Are you Mr. Pearce?" she asked shyly, as had been my experience with most of the Hispanics. I realized with chagrin that she had been waiting hours to see me but was too embarrassed to speak when I walked past her.

"Yes."

"You talked to my husband about his eye."

I was suddenly very engaged. "Yes, is there a problem?"

"Mr. Pearce, he is not angry with you but about his eye. He has been afraid for several years as his eyesight gets worse. I just wanted to find out more about the surgery and insurance you mentioned to him."

"Well, neither are complex. My mom just went through the same sort of surgery. She was pretty scared, too, but she said it was simple."

"She did not go blind with the surgery? They did not have to take her eye out?" Her questions revealed the wide range of speculation that the young family had been having and the fear they had been dealing with— how would they feed the family if he became blind?

"No, she is fine and said that it was like someone turned on the light."

"Mr. Pearce, please do not think badly of him. He has just been worried too long. He was not sure what your motivation was. We do not know this country or the people well, and we have been taken advantage of a few times."

I was suddenly taken back to our house on Cecil Street when we first arrived in Hobbs and were very young. A tax man, who was also a family friend, came by to check on rumors that Dad had extra barrels of unrefined—and untaxed—gasoline to run his car, as did nearly every other oilfield worker. When the taxman showed up, he found the barrels, but he also found a poor house on the wrong end of town with the three sick kids who had the measles.

He could see that Mom did not know anything about measles, and he quickly informed her that we needed to be in dark rooms. He helped her put sheets up on the windows to make it darker. Mom invited him to stay for lunch and prepared what she did almost every day—leftover Cream of Wheat from breakfast, flattened into patties and fried. Mom told him that, when it was cut into strips, it tasted just like fried fish.

The state man was considering the options for recourse as he sat their sharing lunch with us. They ranged from having Dad pay the back taxes to sending him to jail. He told Dad that if he would pay the taxes on the gasoline and get the barrels out of the backyard, the case would be closed. (Later, companies developed procedures to capture the drip and get it into the refining stream, so the practice and the tax problem were solved all at once.)

The tax collector had shown up with the fate of my father in his hands and found an unexpected situation, one that required understanding beyond his job description. I saw in this woman standing before me now the fears my mother had for her three sick kids when the tax man knocked on our door. I had the opportunity to pass along this same grace.

Minutes passed as the implications swirled through my mind, until she asked, "Mr. Pearce, are you okay?"

Focusing back on her, I answered, "Yes, I'm okay, just thinking about what you said and how concerned you have been . . ." I trailed off without finishing and continued, "I understand how hard it is for you to trust, but if you want help, I will help you find a doctor who specializes in cataract surgery and set up an appointment. The process and the surgery are not that complex. Your husband is very young to have a cataract, so there may be something that complicates the problem, but I think it will be pretty routine. He will have to wear an eye patch for a week or two, but that's about all."

"Mr. Pearce, we cannot afford any more payments. How will we pay for the doctor and a surgery?"

"That is what your insurance is for. I have already checked, and you are signed up and are current on your payments, so most of the cost will be paid for you. You will have to come up with a couple of hundred dollars to pay a deductible, but the insurance will cover the rest of the costs for the doctor and the surgery. The insurance company will work with you on how to pay for the deductible. I would encourage you to have him see the doctor."

Life has been circular like that for me. I have had many opportunities to repay the kindnesses others showed my family with kindness to strangers.

Rene Reza

Rene Reza was the man who changed tires on our company vehicles. When he realized I cared, he would proudly show me where he had saved five dollars in costs to the company here and fifteen dollars there. I recalled with clarity my own father's pride when he began to save money for his employer, and I praised Rene for his loyalty to the company.

With the recognition, he began to open up and showed me ways we could save more money. One of the most significant examples saved the company hundreds of thousands of dollars. He showed me how to "stick the fuel tanks" before we took delivery of fuel. Because of our attention to detail, our fuel costs dropped significantly as we were charged only for fuel delivered. For the rest of my business career, I made it a habit to watch the small parts of our purchases, and it led to big savings.

One day I commented to Rene about how smart he was and how much he was helping. He responded, "Steve, to most people we are just dumb Mexicans. I didn't get the chance to get much education, but I have learned what I can. Common sense is more important than book sense. Just look at who makes the money for the company. It's not the guys with the book smarts, but the guys who have done things before." Since then, I made it a point to really know the people who made the companies work and pay attention to their contributions. It made my business more successful and life more enjoyable.

With his attention to detail and his interest in cutting costs, we became good friends. Cynthia and I had him and Rosa to our house for dinner, and they reciprocated, introducing us to chicharrones and fiery hot asado. He was my eyes and ears into the Hispanic inner culture at the company. He could always read my questions but never volunteered answers, instead waiting patiently and respectfully until I asked.

One day I asked, "Rene, I never mentioned it, but this young guy came back to the office one day six or eight months ago. I never knew his name, but he had this bandana around his leg. He was pretty hostile. You wouldn't know who I am talking about would you?"

"Sure." He gave me the name immediately. "He had the problem with the eye."

"Yes, that's him. What happened to him? Is he still around? Did he get his eye fixed? I got busy and forgot to check."

Rene had a seriousness about him that noticed things. "He got his eye checked, and the doctor operated." I could tell he wanted to say more, but I knew also that he wanted me to ask him to finish the thought.

"Well, is he okay? Did he get his eyesight back?"

"The surgery turned out fine."

"That's strange. I would have thought he would come back and update me."

"Steve, he is embarrassed for all the things he said. He told me to tell you he appreciates your help."

"He was pretty hostile. Man, he can be a little scary when he goes off. Is he still angry?"

"People get that way when they get treated badly, and he has been treated pretty badly. He is not so angry now. He appreciated your help."

"Rene, how long have you known all this?"

"Since his surgery."

"That was months ago. Why didn't you say something?"

"Steve, if you don't ask questions, you don't get answers. It's the same way with God. If you don't ask, he can't help you. To most people, we are nothing. I was not sure you would remember."

"Of course I remember. How could I forget? He broke into tears in my office, after cussing a lot. Did you know his wife came by, too?"

"Mr. Pearce, we all know his wife came by and that you took the time to talk to her and calm her fears. We know the whole thing . . . how he cussed you out and you helped him. How you explained the insurance to his wife. People watch and know these things. Everybody was waiting to see if the insurance would help. Generally you pay in for ten or twenty years, and when you have a claim they don't want to pay nothing out."

"Rene, you could have told me this sooner."

"I already said you have to ask questions to get answers. I wasn't sure if you would be interested to know."

Over the years I have been hard and demanding but fair. I wondered how many times I have not found the blessings in a story because I became too busy to check back on something important.

Rene and I are still friends. Years later, I got a call from him when his son had died in Hobbs. The answers given by the law enforcement officers did not add up. He was wondering if I could help get him answers. "Steve, my boy died. They are not telling us anything. It seems like they think he is just another Mexican. Rosa just wants to know the truth before we bury him."

"Rene, I will ask, but I need to know if it is drug- or gang-related."

"Steve, I don't think so. My son made lots of mistakes, but that shouldn't keep us from getting an answer. We just want to know the truth about what happened. What they tell us does not make sense. It leaves too many questions."

I was overwhelmed with the sadness of a small family with whom I had shared so much. I watched their children grow up, shared meals with them at their house and at our house. They were unwilling to compromise their dignity in asking for the truth, regardless of the circumstances or any mistakes a child may have made.

Shop Manager

After about six months, I was promoted to manage the shop in addition to doing the purchasing. When the freezing weather of winter arrived, it brought with it chaos. The cold temperatures caused the oil in the big engines to thicken, which made the units hard to start. Starting as early as 5:30 in the morning, the operators would call, one by one, to ask for assistance. The pushers all had jumper cables and spent the winter mornings jumpstarting the big rigs at scattered locations all across the region. It was a miserable way to start each business day.

Rules in business are a form of gravity, giving cohesion, predictability, and purpose. This time, the problem was not too much gravity but too little. When there is insufficient gravity, things come loose; unhinged, they fly around in random fashion. The shop and fleet were missing those gravitational elements that bring stability.

Decisions are easier when there are statistics to show you what to do next, providing a form of guidance. These numbers are only possible when records are kept. We began to measure things, such as engine life versus cost of repairs and lost time and evaluated the lost time each day trying to start the big 12V engines on the equipment.

I called the mechanics together and asked what needed to be done to eliminate the chaos. Based on their input, we changed things, looking at long-term fixes rather than the stopgap measures that were often used. I hired more mechanics, and they bought into the vision of repairing equipment in ways that needed more time but which would noticeably improve the stability of our fleet. Based on the input of our mechanics, we started a yearlong project to repair electrical systems, replace aging alternators, strip the old wiring out, rewire the entire frame, and install stronger batteries.

The next winter the operations supervisors were mad. They didn't have any units to start and worried that the company would decide they were no longer needed. Instead, they began to have more time and energy to take care of the technical problems customers were having on wells.

We got a spare 12V engine, had the block machined, bored, and installed pistons. When an engine started giving us problems, we stuck the new one in and got the old one machined and rebuilt and put it on the shelf. As a result, engine life improved dramatically, because the inside of the engine had tighter tolerances and fit together without the slack that inevitably comes as an engine wears out the crankshaft and piston liners.

I was finally getting the mechanical experience I had sought from my father as an elementary school kid.

One of the signal events occurred one afternoon when an operator called with the news that his engine had started blowing heavy smoke.

Larry, our lead diesel mechanic, went to the field to investigate and called with the news, "The engine is completely shot; it needs to come out."

The operator was beside himself, as they were in the middle of a critical part of the workover, and he needed the engine running by 7 a.m. the next morning. He was forceful in telling us that we could stick a piston or two in and have him ready to run by the next morning, but it would break our new shop principle to avoid halfway repairs. We were in a pinch, because it usually took two days to pull and replace an engine. The mechanics were watching; internal discipline breaks down at precisely these moments. It was a sneaky, low level no-notice exam, but one that was testing my resolve and commitment to a principle that would bear long-term fruit.

On the drive back to the shop, Larry had been thinking and planning and had several of the mechanics with him when he came into the office and said, "If you will give all of us permission to work all night, we will pull the engine, stick the new one in, and still have that unit going by 7 a.m."

I was impressed. Our maintenance team was *asking* to work all night long. I replied, "Well, when you put it that way, how can I say no? But don't make it a habit."

He knew it was my way of kidding, and he grinned. "It will put us all on overtime for the week."

"You get the engine running by 7 a.m., and I'll worry about the over-time."

"Oh, by the way, you get to tell Jim [the operator] that we are going to pull the engine. He was pretty excitable when I was out there."

"I'll talk to Jim. You just make sure you have that engine going by seven!"

The group of mechanics was in as good a mood as I had seen as they gathered tools and nightlights and headed out the door. The human spirit hungers to create standards and to live by them. They had wondered if I would cave in to the pressure and go back to the old way of doing partial repairs, or if I would trust them and stick by the principles we had all agreed upon. I stayed steady, and they responded with vigor and finished the job on time.

When I drove to their location near midnight to take them a meal and check on the progress, they were too busy to talk or eat. But they noticed that I cared enough to come out in the middle of the night to check, and it seemed to give them an extra shot of adrenaline.

I was waiting when Jim pushed into my office early the next morning, ready for conflict. "Jim, the replacement engine is installed. It won't be ready by seven, but we can have you running by eight."

He stood, looking me square in the eye, eventually nodded and walked away.

That ability to stand my ground went all the way back to Coach Shaw insisting that I make the pitchers throw my pitch.

The human spirit is a magnificent and wonderful force in every human life. Sometimes you have to look around for it, but when you awaken it, it will do the rest. You just let the lion out of its cage, and it will do its work. The lion in the mechanics had been let loose, and they responded in a full-throated roar.

Oil Changes

Another decision that proved to be a turning point in the shop was actually a small program. Both companies had policies requiring the crews to change the oil in their equipment. We checked out oil and filters to them each month and kept records to prove that everyone got the oil. If a crew did not get oil, an exception report came out and their bosses would remind them it was time for their oil change. Then they dutifully came and picked up the oil. The system had been in use for decades at the companies without anyone asking if receiving the oil meant they were actually changing the oil.

After it became obvious that maintenance was a high priority in the shop, small details began to emerge. Mechanics showed me oil filters that were plugged with dirt and oil so thick it could not circulate through the engine. One particular truck was operating with less than a quart of oil in the big engine. Each time an instance was brought to my attention, I had the operators come to the shop and show them the evidence, comparing it to the records that they had gotten the oil each month. Some sheepishly admitted that they never changed the oil. But they also expressed a deep vein of resentment at being asked to take time away from their customer to change oil or use their own time to do it.

I suggested to Mr. Eaves that we start changing the oil in the shop, bringing more consistency and certainty that the used oil was not being poured out on location while offering a goodwill gesture to the crews. He agreed. I put out the word that we wanted a disciplined person to apply for the oil-changing position.

Martin Gonzales showed up. He was qualified on all accounts. He had dropped out of high school after marrying Anna, his childhood sweetheart, and they had young children. He had a GED but no major work experience. He was hungry to prove his skills and promised to be the best oil changer in town.

His job: perform a ten-point inspection and change oil in the fleet of company vehicles, trucks, and well-servicing units all day, every day. He was tenacious, going so far as to set up his own system to keep track and coordinate with the operators. Maintenance costs began to fall as we improved on the fundamentals, making sure that all the equipment had oil and operating filters and problems found during the inspections were fixed, thus diminishing downtime due to failures in the field. The mechanics often came to share about a major save of an engine, transmission, or differential as Martin discovered oil leaks, antifreeze in oil, and metal in the oil pan.

B&M bought new Ford trucks to use in the fleet at that time. Ford had developed a plan in which fleets could do their own warranty work. You had to send a mechanic to their regional school for a day of written tests that included mechanical as well as Ford Administrative Warranty Policy. I ordered a set of the manuals, which were daunting—several big binders of policy and technical information, hundreds of pages of technical reading.

I asked Martin to come to my office. "If you didn't have to change oil, could you read all of these in a week and pass a test?"

He looked at the big stack, picked up a couple of the binders and thumbed through them. "Yes, sir."

"Wear dress pants and a clean shirt next Monday. I have a room in the front office for you to use where no one back here can distract you. All day, every day, you are to read these manuals. A week from Monday, I have you scheduled to take the test in Albuquerque."

"How will I get to Albuquerque?"

"That's a crazy question, Martin. The real question is: how are you going to learn all the stuff in those manuals?"

"Well, that question is not too great either. I am just going to read them."

I had to laugh. "Martin, the guy who administers the program in Albuquerque thought I was crazy, sending a twenty-two-year-old guy who is not even a mechanic. He said they have never had anyone in the whole nation that young take the test, much less pass it."

"I still want to know how I am getting to Albuquerque."

"You are going to take my company car and drive up on Sunday. I will give you my credit card for gas, hotel room, and meals."

"That will work."

> The human spirit is a magnificent and wonderful force in every human life. Sometimes you have to look around for it, but when you awaken it, it will do the rest. You just let the lion out of its cage, and it will do its work.

As he was leaving, I said, "The guy in Albuquerque said many guys who have been mechanics for years had failed the test. He assured me that you would fail. You are too young and too inexperienced."

"I didn't see anything in the manuals that looked that difficult. Sir, how did you know I would say yes?"

"It's my job to know things like that."

Monday morning, he showed up dressed for the front office. I led him up to the cubicle and told him to come out only at lunchtime and quitting time. He held up his sack lunch. "I will eat while I read. There are lots of books here."

I checked with him on Thursday. He had books opened up all across the desk, a notepad out, and was busily scribbling on it. He glanced up. "Hello, sir."

"How's it going?"

"Fine."

He kept studying. I left him alone. At noon on Friday, he came back to the shop, carting all the books.

"Finished?"

"Yes, sir."

"You can pass the test?"

"Yes, sir."

"I will get the car to you on Sunday, and you can drive up."

"Sir, could I drive up today?"

"Martin, I can't justify three nights in a hotel for you to take the test."

"Oh, sir, I would pay tonight and tomorrow night. It's just that Anna and I have never had a real vacation, and this is our one chance."

I pitched him the keys, "Take me by the house, and you can leave this afternoon. How long will it take you to pack?"

"We are already packed."

"Pretty sure of yourself, aren't you?"

"Sure of you, sir."

On Monday, he called in the early afternoon. "I'm finished, sir."

"How was your weekend?"

"Fine, sir."

"And the test?" I was afraid to ask but did anyway.

"Oh, fine, sir."

"Did you pass?"

"They don't grade them today. They send them off. The guy offered me a job, so I think I did okay."

"You need to get Miss Anna in that Pontiac and get back to Hobbs. You better not drive our company car to get hired by some big city guy."

He laughed.

Later in the week, the coordinator of the warranty program called with the news. "Your young guy did pretty well, one of the best scores we have ever seen. Youngest guy to ever pass, nationwide. The only non-mechanic to ever pass, nationwide. Congratulations, you are now authorized to do your own warranty work."

After I left X-Pert, the oil change program and the warranty program lost their status. Martin slipped out of orbit, left to work for another company, and eventually came to work for me again. But he was already looking for more challenges and advancement opportunities than he could find in Hobbs. He used his skills learned at X-Pert and Lea Fishing Tools and was further trained by a major international oil service company to become a downhole troubleshooter in South America. He used Hobbs as his base, but he traveled for months at a time across all of South America. When he first started, he was making six figures. He has been promoted through the years and has used his discipline and hard work to become highly specialized in his knowledge. Today, he is regional manager plus performs downhole tech support in Latin America for a European company in the oil service industry. All that from a guy with a GED and no experience.

Martin was hungry for his chance. If you just open the cage, the lion will do its work.

Operations Manager X-Pert Well Service

During this period, I was promoted once again, and this time to Operations Manager for X-Pert. I handpicked a mechanic to manage the shop. We were building a cohesive team.

Harry Eaves, the founder of the company, said company profits were soaring. He credited much of that to changes in purchasing of fuel and improvements in maintenance that meant costs were dropping. The same way that our family had cut the costs in the 4-H projects back in my teenage years, our team was making significant reductions in operating costs at our company. While there were more zeroes in this company than in ours, the concept was the same.

I had gotten raises for the mechanics and was preparing to ask for one myself. I gathered hard data that showed we were saving about four hundred thousand to five hundred thousand dollars a year, not counting the longer life we were getting out of the engines and transmission. I carried the information to the front office, presented it to the president of the company, Raymond Eaves, Harry's son, and asked for a pay raise. I was making about fifty thousand a year and told him I thought the increased performance justified a significant raise. He asked if he could think about it. Two days later, he declared that it was my job to cut the costs, thus implying that there would be no raise.

I thanked him and left the office. If he had given me a suitable raise, I would have leaned into the future with them. But when he didn't, I knew Cynthia and I had to find a different path.

31

LEA FISHING TOOLS, INC.

Based upon my failed effort to get a pay raise at X-Pert and the fact that as the executive director of a local mental health clinic, Cynthia was constantly at odds with the board and wanted to change jobs, we sat down at the kitchen table to look at our long-term future. My family had done the same decades before when we decided to buy the $200 boar to create more cash flow for our 4-H projects.

Having paid off the airplanes and Christmas store debts, we were debt-free besides our home. Neither of us had retirements plans or 401Ks or stock investments, and we had about twenty-five hundred dollars in savings. From the perspective of our early forties, we could see that we would have to survive on Social Security in our retirement years—an unsavory prospect when we looked at couples living on that fixed income—unless we changed course. Neither of us seriously thought that Social Security would be available by the time we retired anyway. We were past the point where we could start new careers in jobs that would provide a comfortable retirement. Time had us in a corner.

I suggested that the only way forward was to create our own retirement by buying a business large and profitable enough to allow us to save for retirement. (The idea of running for Congress had never entered my mind, and we had little idea how it would end up turning that comfortable retirement on its head when I was elected.) With early lessons from my days in 4-H and the experience of owning a crop duster under my belt, I was sure we could be successful owning a business. Cynthia was not as easily convinced, even when I pointed out that we were making decisions every day that made other companies work well. She was managing an office and complex payroll while I was working twelve- to fourteen-hour days making profitable decisions for my employers. I reasoned we could do the same for ourselves.

Over the years, I had watched for business opportunities, and although the airplanes and Christmas store had set me back, the desire to have my own company burned brightly. A basic skills assessment showed that Cynthia had a tremendous accounting and management background with her degree in finance, coupled with her experience in personnel management and her ability to write internal rules, harmonizing business with the many layers of government regulations. My degree in economics, willingness to work long hours, and ability to make decisions complemented her skills, so we began looking all over the country at dozens of possible small businesses to buy, but basic reviews of the financial statements left us with few viable choices.

One morning, Chuck Kittrell, our lead mechanic at X-Pert, mentioned that his father was trying to sell his business located in Lea County, where we lived. Named after the county, it was called Lea Fishing Tools. And as was true of the rest of the county, the business revolved around oil. In simple terms, *fishing* is used to repair pipe in the well and retrieve stuck or dropped equipment from the wellbore. Any of these circumstances within the wellbore obstruct production of oil and require a company to contract with a fishing operation such as ours.

When I asked Chuck to get me a copy of the financial statements, without letting anyone know it was me who was looking, he was a willing agent. As it turned out, the company was practically dead on its feet. In the previous month, total revenues were fourteen hundred dollars. With four employees, it was not paying even one person's salary. The company had two customers—eighty-five percent of the business was with Texaco, fifteen percent was Yates—and was selling at an asking price of half a million dollars.

Cynthia and I researched, talked, analyzed, worried, and prayed over the decision. But no matter how we looked at the company, it did not look promising.

Even though I'd spent several years of my childhood living in an oil camp and had grown up in and around the oilfields of southeastern New Mexico, I had no experience in the oil business other than some summer work. So I went to visit my longtime mentors in Eunice, Roy and Polly McLean. He had moved to Lea County dead broke and had started a small oilfield service company that made him a millionaire. They could provide some insight into the problems we might face in the business.

Roy was lukewarm. He started his company when the oilfield had little competition but had seen the oilfield mature. He observed it would be much tougher if we tried to enter the field now. After much discussion and consideration, he offered the opinion that it would be very difficult, if not impossible, for us to succeed.

The bank seemed to side with him as well. The negotiators there were very clear that they would require our house and cars to be used as collateral on a loan. If the business failed, we lost everything. It was a major risk.

But even with the negative opinions of everyone around us, the belief that we had to change course kept me focused on what it would take to make the business work. There was the memory of the $200 boar and how our entire family believed that if the experiment failed it would sink our family. It did fail, but it did not sink us. I continued to think about the venture, calculating the worst-case scenario to see what it would take to pay off the bank if the business failed.

Long after Cynthia thought the idea was forgotten, I asked, "What do you think about buying the business?"

"It is half a million dollars. That is more than we can make if we work for the rest of our lives. It will make paying off the planes and Christmas store seem like a vacation package."

I showed her a copy of the inventory. "Look at this. I have been going to auctions and watching this stuff sell all the time. Look at what the equipment will bring in if we fail and have to auction it off. I think if things don't go right, we can sell the major pieces of equipment for four hundred thousand dollars. That leaves all the tools, pickups, and trucks to pay off the rest of the note. It seems we might have the chance to buy this company with not a lot of actual downside exposure."

She replied tersely, "I don't know anything about the oilfield. What do you know about the business?"

"Nothing, but I can learn."

"You can learn? We sign over our house as collateral . . . while you learn? What if we lose our home? Where will we live?"

"I told you, I don't think it will come to that. We can sell things at auction and pay off the loan if we can't make the company profitable." I was reaching way back to those days with the pig projects, figuring how to pay off the loans we got each year at the bank.

"What will I do? You know things are not very good at my job. What if I lose that?"

"I think if we buy the business you should quit your job and we'll work together."

"Work together! Do you know how many marriages fail when husband and wife work together? And you are going to sign our house as collateral?"

Our prayers over the next year included specific requests for direction, for answers to these exact questions. The discussions went back and forth. We were both gun-shy after the Christmas store experience.

I began to work on a business plan. When Cynthia figured out what I was doing, she pitched in to help, verifying another of the personal characteristics that caused me to marry her. She might not buy in fully, but she jumps in and uses her analytical skills to help assess possibilities.

We projected how many fishing jobs it would take to break even and make the bank note payments of ten thousand dollars per month. To give us a greater cushion, I made a suggestion, "Why don't we put in the business plan that we will both work for free for the first year."

"No, I absolutely refuse to do that. We cannot sacrifice our family for this company. I will put my foot down on this."

"Since we are living on four thousand dollars per month and using the rest to pay off old debts, would you go along if we each work for two thousand dollars per month?" I asked.

"That will look funny to the bank. Why don't we pay you four thousand a month, and I will work for free? The bankers will think *that's* okay," she said, making a light jab at the male mentality.

My teenage experiences borrowing the money for the pig projects were very important for this phase. I knew what the bank would need to assess the loan, so we assembled our personal financial statements and other documents, which were not great. We scrubbed our names and addresses off everything and carried it to a friend and attorney from 4-H and church, Robert Love. We asked him to apply for a loan at Sunwest Bank but not reveal who was applying.

The loan request was rejected because we did not have enough cash for the twenty percent down payment. Undeterred, I sent word through Chuck of the situation and had him ask his father if he would finance the other twenty percent at the same rate the bank was charging. The answer came back: "Yes."

We were now at the decision point. I approached Cynthia, "We got a yes back from Joe Kittrell. He will carry the twenty percent." I asked her if she was ready to leave the security of a steady paycheck, working for someone else, and go out on our own, beyond certainty. Buy our own business. Only two people in town knew of our inquiries thus far. "It's not too late to turn back," I told her.

We knew that stepping out was a risk, and a big one according to the conventional wisdom around us. But we also knew that we wouldn't be the first ones God had called out of our comfort zones. He called the biblical Abram out of Ur of the Chaldees to wander the land and to spend his life living in tents, so that he might make him into Abraham, the father of many nations. The vision was much greater than the risk. Cynthia and I had to decide whose wisdom we would follow, and whether it was worth the plunge.

Cynthia was cautious. "What do you think?"

"I think I'm ready, but I would like to sleep on it for a day or two. There's no hurry."

"You don't think anyone will buy it out from under us?"

"Everybody in town has apparently looked at it, but no one else has been interested."

Telling my wife that our "hope for the future" had been rejected by all the other businessmen in town was not the best choice of words.

"Then why are we interested?"

I repeated the part about the auctions. "I don't think anyone is looking at the auction value. I don't see many other Hobbs guys when I am at the auctions. Other than that, I can't give an answer."

Even with no experience, other than working on pulling units during my college years, my recent management experiences at X-Pert gave me the confidence that I could make good decisions in almost any field. We decided to buy the company and on March 29, 1989, pledged everything we owned as collateral and showed up at the bank to sign papers.

In deciding to proceed with the purchase, we realized we were going against the advice of my long-term mentor, Roy McLean, as well as the judgment of all the Hobbs businessmen who had considered the company and decided against it. But we felt compelled to move forward and had the peace to do so.

Looking back through the prism of time, placing ourselves in such a risky situation with no background was not the dumbest thing I've ever done, but it probably makes it onto the top ten list. However, when the venture later succeeded, it became one more piece of evidence in our spiritual life that, if we commit and pray, God will show us the way. We had been praying about the matter continuously and felt peaceful proceeding.

LFT—at the Bank

We delivered the business plan to the bank, showing how we would revive the business, and the bankers had studied it well before we arrived for the closing of our purchase of Lea Fishing Tools. On the closing day, all parties gathered in the conference room at the bank. Cynthia and I, the seller (but not his wife), attorneys for both sides, and the bankers were seated around a large conference table, preparing to sign the papers—a process far more imposing and complex than signing the loan papers for the 4-H pig projects had been.

For us, the decision to buy a company had been stressful, because it required getting out of our familiar orbit, letting go of the predictable routine of our lives, and borrowing more money than we thought we could ever earn, much less repay. And now, having scraped together twenty-five hundred dollars as a down payment, we were borrowing more than ninety-nine percent of the value of the company—eighty percent from the bank, with the seller carrying nineteen percent of the loan. Both had equal rights to repossess the company and everything we owned if we could not make it work, since that was our collateral.

It was sinking in: if we failed, we lost everything. If Cynthia's contribution to our relationship was making sense out of my many ideas and working spreadsheets, my contribution was leading us into dangerous and uncharted waters—that could maybe pay off in the end.

During the closing, the banker asked if I was sure Cynthia would be happy with the plan in which I would be paid four thousand dollars per month and she would work for free. They didn't want a surprise after making the loan and find that this husband-wife partnership had discord about pay. It was a valid question. My response was immediate, knowing we were in this thing together. "If my wife ever becomes dissatisfied with the pay arrangement, we will pay her four thousand dollars per month, and I'll work for free." We had not discussed the proposition, but our relationship had evolved to a level of complete trust that I felt qualified to answer. The answer surprised and shocked the bankers, but it also satisfied them. Not only were we committed to repaying the loan but also to each other. And the process of signing papers moved forward.

Suddenly, the seller interrupted the signing of papers as they were making their way around the table. He declared that the price was not enough and began to push for changes to things that had been agreed upon since the beginning. At first, I listened in disbelief and tried to reason with Joe, but he was intractable. Then I got angry, stood abruptly, and declared that everything was off and we would walk away from a deal that had been months in the making.

Cynthia's contribution to our decision-making process was about to kick in. She asked that the meeting take a brief recess, then suggested to me that we leave the room for a brief conference. She asked one of the vice presidents if he would lend us his glass-enclosed office. Once we were alone, she said, "I know what is happening is not right, and I will support any decision you make, but we have invested a lot of time and energy in getting to this point. I would hate to see us lose the deal at this late stage. I believe you have everyone's attention by walking out, but before we walk away, why don't we go back in and offer to finish the purchase on the original terms."

It was classic Cynthia, but it was also the model for all the decisions in our marriage. She fully supported my leadership but felt free to weigh in and offer advice when it was needed. My responsibility was then to make the best judgment possible and ensure we were in agreement before we made a move. We obviously were not in full agreement to walk out on the deal, so I reconsidered the decision based on her point of view.

At her suggestion, we prayed about the matter there in the office. And with her steady support and calm suggestions in hand, we walked back into the room. Everyone waited. Finally, I calmly broke the silence and said, "Cynthia is not in agreement with terminating the deal. Out of respect for her, we will proceed with the closing if the original terms are honored. If there is any disagreement with that, I have Cynthia's full support to walk out."

Heads nodded around the table, and the most momentous financial decision of our life quietly proceeded.

Without my impulsive decision to walk away from the table, the deal would have been wrangled and possibly rewritten with worse conditions. Everyone at the table knew that the purchase was on thin ice, so—with a subdued seller glaringly giving consent—the process moved forward on the original terms. If I had not heeded her input, which we had so recently declared would be our process, we would have walked away from one of the largest financial blessings of our life. It was not the first time our team-work had won a very hard situation, but it remains one of the most vivid and delicately balanced decisions we've made.

It is this strong mix of my sometimes volatile nature with her calm, analytical resolve that has propelled us into a life that always surprises us, a life that has delivered us blessings we could never have imagined for ourselves, given our modest upbringings.

The strength of the biblical relationship began to dawn on both of us that day. If she had been disagreeable or unsupportive, my anger and pride would have intensified an already complicated situation. But her promise of complete and ultimate support allowed me to listen to her calm advice and evaluate the proper response to the seller.

Division of Duties

Being responsible for the decisions is not equivalent to handling every detail. As an aircraft commander, I learned to delegate, assigning important duties to the crew members—a concept that we carried over and used successfully in our business. I hated certain duties of the company that Cynthia happened to love, so she made those decisions. In fourteen years, our company distributed about seventy million dollars in checks, with Cynthia's signature being the only one required.

Likewise, buying vehicles has always been boring to me, while Cynthia has endless energy for it, studying consumer reports and evaluating engine sizes, transmissions, and rear-end ratios. She will drive the vehicle, listening for wind noise that indicates doors were not hung squarely at the factory and noticing vibrations in the drivetrain that indicate problems that will last as long as the vehicle is in service. I was likely to tell the dealer to just bring us a pickup without looking at it. We both agreed she was better at the job and would handle that part of the business. If we had problems with a vehicle or the dealer, it was my duty to intervene and come to a solution. Conflict resolution is no one's favorite task, but I didn't feel I should outsource the duties that were hard or distasteful.

Normally, the strategic vision of new products and services was under my direction, along with buying equipment at auctions. Though I made my share of mistakes, I did not sink our economic ship. My strength is in seeing the unseen, visualizing strategic positions and moves that allowed us to benefit from market forces. That process of visualization, which was so hard for me to master naturally, was possible largely because of Coach Shaw. The high school baseball coach who spent a few minutes a day pushing me to "see the batter and know what he is thinking" had no idea the impact he would have on my life.

There was a mind-set in the oilfield that renting BOPs, or blowout preventers, did not make money. The heavy cast-iron units bolt to the top of the well when its head is removed, keeping it from blowing out when downhole repairs are being completed. When we bought LFT, it had no BOPs, but a quick review of the economics of those rental items showed they could indeed be profitable. So I suggested that we buy fifty of them at a cost of ten thousand dollars each.

> It is this strong mix of my sometimes volatile nature with her calm, analytical resolve that has propelled us into a life that always surprises us, a life that has delivered us blessings we could never have imagined for ourselves, given our modest upbringings.

It was a significant investment for our small business, and Cynthia did not agree to fifty; that was too big a risk for our cash flow. She offered that she was comfortable with ten, so we proceeded with the smaller number, ultimately getting more than fifty. We compromised on the pace of expansion.

I wanted a plane that I could start flying again to give us the freedom to get away, and she readily agreed to that idea, but I deliberated too long. She approached one night while I was poring over the aircraft that were available and announced, "I am going to buy an airplane tomorrow. You can choose one tonight, or I will choose one tomorrow."

I made the decision to buy a Mooney 231. It was fast, fuel-efficient, and reliable, and in the following years, we found it to be our main outlet for freedom from the daily stress of operating a small business. When our first grandchild was born, Cynthia announced that we would need an airplane with five seats, "and because of his precious little ears, it needs to be pressurized." So we bought a 1997 Piper Malibu. I enjoyed the planes, because I love flying; she wanted the planes, because they represented freedom to take off whenever we wanted.

During the years we owned the business, our vacations were rare and infrequent. Our payroll was on two different calendar schedules, so Cynthia was committed each week to processing payroll checks. When the pay periods happened to fall in the same week, Cynthia would call and tell me that she had finished both payrolls, and we were free to go somewhere for the next eight or nine days.

It's the way we made decisions and the way we lived for fourteen years. We could be at our hangar within an hour of her call and could fly to any destination within a thousand miles. We have flown to the Baja Peninsula in Mexico, San Diego, St. Louis, and anywhere in between. The planes gave us freedom to escape the constant and strong gravitational pull any small company exerts on its owners.

Every small business has more decision making than can be handled by one person, so we split the decisions and both of us made our share. But we did so under the guidance of our belief system: if things went wrong, I was ultimately responsible and accountable, no matter which of us had made the mistake.

LFT—the Company

Many times after buying Lea Fishing Tools, we would get calls from people looking for rods and reels, bait or lures. But those of us who grew up in the oilfield knew what *fishing* meant. An oil well is a hole in the ground, about the diameter of a coffee can and anywhere from a thousand to fifteen thousand feet deep in southeast New Mexico. If you drop your car keys down the back of your couch, you reach down inside of the couch and feel around, eventually fishing them out by feel alone. When anything is dropped in a well, it has to be retrieved the same way, by feel alone.

It's like changing a light bulb with one of those extension handles, grabbing the bulb with a mechanical arm to unscrew and replace it. Making repairs in or fishing things from an oil well uses the same concept, except it takes thousands of feet of extensions or mechanical arms. There are dozens of tools, but three main methods: you can grab the "fish" from the outside or the inside, or you can grind it into metal shavings with mills that have tungsten carbide chips imbedded in them.

The wells have blueprints that describe where different components or production zones are in the well. Pipe is run into the well, one joint at a time, until you get to bottom, and the tools are placed in the string so that they function at the exact depth where they need to be. The joints of pipe are about thirty-one-feet long. Each piece has to be measured to one-hundredth of an inch and tallied before it is screwed onto the string and lowered into the hole. You must always know the exact depth of the tools.

Dealing with the dynamic situation downhole as well as the psyche of the crew and customers, the fisherman must have a deep inventory of fishing tools and people skills. A difficult fishing job may cost a half million dollars and last several months, with each day bringing unexpected and new questions and uncertainties. Fishermen generally are high strung, confident, and mysterious prima donnas. They are not unlike pilots. I understood them and got along well with them.

The fisherman is part plumber, mechanic, engineer, counselor, field general, and mystic. He may invoke black magic, superstitions, hard-core logic, faith, or the fast talk of a used car salesman, all while working on the same well. Fishermen in this industry are very specialized, having learned to understand downhole problems from experience in other facets of the oilfield. They are often recruited and hired away from well service or drilling companies, lured by higher pay and the desire to make more decisions and have more responsibility.

The job is high pressure. No company likes to call in a fishing job, since even the simplest job has the potential to turn into an expensive project. Without the ability to see downhole, uncertainty and second-guessing are commonplace among customers, competitors, and even people in the same company. Sometimes the fisherman's decisions will be challenged by his customer, all the way up the chain of command. It was not an everyday occurrence, but more than once the company representative on location in Lea County would get a call from the Texaco Corporate Headquarters in White Plains, New York, to ask, "What the hell is going on out there on that job?" Fishing is not for the faint of heart.

When the fisherman arrives, even though he is a contractor and not an employee of the company that owns the well, he becomes the quarterback on location, the catcher calling the pitches. He runs the job. It requires decisiveness, clarity, discernment—and *cojones.*

The jobs in the field were demanding and took place in all weather, including those New Mexico springs when the winds can regularly blow up to fifty miles an hour. The crews on location are subject to H2S, hydrogen sulfide, which can kill a man with a single whiff if it is present in the right concentrations; concentrations that high are not unusual in Lea County.

Lea Fishing Tools (LFT) was organized back in the 1960s by a handful of men in Lea County. Joe Kittrell, a squat, bowlegged, barrel-chested, part-Cherokee Indian man from Oklahoma, was one of them. He could ingratiate himself to you, offend you, convince you, and freeze you in your tracks, all in the same conversation. It came from years of dealing with the ebb and flow of tensions and emotions on fishing jobs. People in the oilfield either swore by him or swore at him. To solidify his psychological edge, he had a practice of spitting in the well on each trip, which was just strange enough that people did not want to interfere with whatever spell he was placing on the well.

When we bought Lea Fishing Tools, the employees included J. T. Woodard, who had been with the company for more than twenty years, the mild-mannered Carlos Pando, shop manager David Ferrell, and bookkeeper Claudia Workman.

I stumbled into buying the business, but it ended up being a perfect fit for me. My transformation from shy to decisive, introverted to a little in-your-face, had not been perfect, and certainly there was more work to be done. But the company we were buying required that I continue the transition even more dramatically, leaving behind the timid version of myself to own the personality necessary to run our new company. My inability to visualize things in the past would perhaps see the most improvement, since the main job of our company was visualizing what could not be seen miles underground.

32

CHANCE BROTHERS

D uring the first week after the purchase was finalized, I was hard at work at our new acquisition, trying to sort through the thirty years of junk we now owned and beginning to question the wisdom of our decision—when the Chance brothers walked in.

Jim and David Chance had grown up on a side of town that was not unlike where I grew up—poor and rural—and they were the same age as my younger brothers. I'd left town, gone to college, and had now come back home while they had stayed in Hobbs and worked in the oilfields all their lives. They were grown up now. Both were huge, well over six feet tall and over two hundred pounds of sheer muscle, shaped from the hard work of the oilfields.

I was sitting there with doubt, misgivings, and the weight of the world on my shoulders when they strode in. Right after, "Hello," they looked around the shop and shook their heads. "This is about the stupidest thing we ever saw anybody do."

"What's stupid?" I asked, shocked at their directness.

Jim, who appeared to be the spokesman, continued, "We've never seen anyone come in from outside the industry—with no background in a fishing tool company—buy one and try to operate it. Well, we have seen it tried but never succeed."

The fishing tool business is highly segmented, highly specialized, and is built on hard-earned relationships. It's like finding a dentist or a doctor. Once you find one you trust, you don't shop around. Fishing is such volatile and exacting work that the relationship between a company man and his fisherman usually lasts decades. As a result, breaking in and getting new customers in the fishing business was nearly impossible.

I had long since outgrown my unnecessary fears and insecurities, but this was a cold slap of reality. I wasn't exactly positive that buying the company was a good idea when they arrived; now I really questioned it. I knew they were right, and I felt nauseous. Excusing myself, I left them to find their way out. I could smell the fear of my younger life bubbling back to the surface.

I did not have to remind myself that in the biblical decision process, the man is responsible, so I knew that I alone was accountable for the decision to risk everything we had. Cynthia had concurred, but I was responsible. The biblical instructions have practical, day-to-day outcomes that are designed to keep us out of trouble and keep the lines of authority and responsibility clear.

Cynthia knew her part of the business—the accounting and personnel details. I could not burden or alarm her with the details of their visit, but I knew I was going to have to be mentally and emotionally tough enough to deal with the uncertainty, the fear, and my desire to run from the problem. I had a deficiency in my area of responsibility and needed to summon the tenacity to do my job and salvage our investment.

Fear and uncertainty usually look for partners to share the blame, but when the process is right, sharing the blame is not a possibility. Blaming each other is one of the things that collapses partnerships, including marriages. Buying the business was and would be my decision. The years of training for emergencies in an aircraft prepared me with the knowledge that the most important part of this moment was to just fly the plane and stay mentally composed. Stay focused. Make good decisions.

After the visit from the Chance brothers, I admitted the challenges that lay before us. I was overwhelmed. I began to think of failure before the first month was over. Cynthia was the one who got me focused. "We have been broke before. You can only do your best." It relieved the family pressure, but the stress was still intense.

Jim and David Chance worked for one of our large international competitors. They knew the business and the customers. Shortly after our visit, they both quit their jobs with that company and started their own fishing tool company, which looked just like ours. They had the same quantity of equipment and the same downhole services, but they had experience, customers, and were known in the industry. Their business prospered from the beginning.

Meanwhile, I was struggling with our two customers. Relying on an unwritten rule of life—start where you are and work with what you have—Cynthia and I took a little piece of the company at a time and focused on it. We plodded through the problems one by one, bringing much-needed stability where there was none and a bit of gravity to hold things in place.

The Chance brothers' business grew so fast and steadily that they had more work than they could handle and gave us the overflow, a move that helped our cash flow greatly. More importantly, it helped reassure me that their visit was not meant to be hurtful; they were just telling me like it was.

This is a curious thing about people in the West that confuses people from other places. Your neighbor will straight up tell you what you've done wrong and then proceed to help you without much fanfare. That's what was happening between the Chance brothers and me.

There were many days when I thought we wouldn't make it, that we'd go broke, and I had to summon every bit of discipline to not let my fears run away with me. I reined myself in to not transmit them to Cynthia or others in the company. I was in a pressure cooker and uncertain that I was up to the challenge. My childhood was proving to be a blessing in disguise. Growing up poor instills toughness to resist adversity, and that mental resilience was being called on at this moment.

Cynthia did the accounting and ran the office while I ran operations. Early on in our business, I told her that it was reassuring to have her running the office. I had seen other small companies not pay their bills on time, forget to invoice jobs, fail to pay their taxes, or any number of oversights that caused great distractions or even failure. "Your work here in the office allows me to focus on what I'm doing, because I'm confident you have things handled," I said and would find myself repeating.

Together we sorted through complexities and solved the problems. Building on a strong foundation, the business began to stabilize ever so slightly.

Chance Visit

Nearly a decade after we bought Lea Fishing Tools, I heard that Jim Chance, one of the brothers, was in the hospital. We'd been competitors in business but had maintained a good relationship. Having seen him days before when he looked well, I decided to pay him a visit to find out what was wrong.

> The power of healing words and actions was burned into my mind that day. I have tried to keep up to date in my life, clearing up mistakes I have made or things I have said in the past.

When I walked in, I found him in bed, looking just as healthy as he had the week before. With typical oilfield directness I asked, "What's up? What are you here for?"

His answer was equally direct. "Steve, I'm dying."

I was shocked, but my natural introversion and the years of training for inflight emergencies cried out to me, "Show no emotion. Keep steady. Don't let your dismay become his reason for dismay." Without so much as a blink, I asked calmly for him to tell me more, because he looked so healthy.

He responded, "I had been losing weight for no apparent reason. I was eating the same, working the same. Something wasn't right. I went in for a checkup, and they found that I'm full of cancer. I feel fine, but they say I won't last the week."

About that point, Doctor McCormick came in making his rounds. When he saw we were visiting, he told Jim he would come back later. Jim called him back in. "Doc, I have something to say and need a witness to tell it to. You are the only one who is available."

The doctor walked back in with a questioning look as Jim continued, "Doc, when Steve bought his business, my brother and I went to see him. I told him he was stupid for buying his company. Doc, I need to say that Steve was the smart one. He stayed in the office to manage his company. I tried to manage ours from the field. You can't run a business from the field. Steve was smart, and I was the stupid one. I just had to say that and needed a witness to hear it."

I was shocked beyond words but immensely touched. Our initial conversation had never been repeated in the years since it took place, but here was Jim, as one of his last acts, clearing up a burden he'd been carrying. I had never held that initial visit against him, but his confession was one of the noblest gestures I have ever seen.

This time I could not contain my emotions, and with a freedom and release that only comes from confession and forgiveness, I told him, "Jim, you are a good man and a friend. The help you gave us through the years let me know you meant no harm. You were just telling me a truth. I am good with you."

The power of healing words and actions was burned into my mind that day. I have tried to keep up to date in my life, clearing up mistakes I have made or things I have said in the past.

Jim did, in fact, pass away later that same week. Without Jim, Chance Tools was never the same.

Looking back, the brothers were right. Few had ever succeeded in the business with no experience. Cynthia and I had enough tenacity and discipline to make it work, but our faith in God was the mainstay of our success. That faith allowed us to stand still and wait for God to reveal himself, rather than quitting when times got difficult or trying to find our own way out.

The great thing about this country is that you can get ahead if you are willing to sacrifice, work hard enough—and take a risk now and then.

33

FACING THE GIANTS

I mmediately after we signed the papers for the company, the former owner, Joe Kittrell, and I crawled into the company Crown Victoria and started making the rounds to the job sites and company workers who would now be ours. It was gracious of him, and he did not do the deed halfway. With a kindness and friendliness that had been absent in the boardroom, he introduced me to the company's fishermen, J. T. Woodard and Carlos Pando, as part of passing along the reins. Wayne Epperson was our truck driver who delivered all the heavy equipment to locations; David Ferrell was our dispatcher, shop manager, and kept all the heavy downhole tools clean, painted, and organized. I managed the field operations and made sales calls while Cynthia managed the office.

Joe spent the next month riding with me and conducting an intensive, mobile learning lab, spending hours talking about the big picture of the oil well process. He started by detailing what went into drilling the well, the completion (bringing it into production after it is drilled), the stimulation, hydraulic fracturing, fishing, casing repair, and the day-to-day process of getting the oil out of the ground after the well has been completed. He was a technical manual of oil well operations, in human form. I made notes and taped the sessions, studying these at night to understand the business we had purchased.

But when we walked into the customers' offices, I could see he had gone too long without making sales calls. The swagger that was so evident and respected on drilling location was not present in the office setting. He was unsure of himself here. The problem was that he tried to fake it, which compounded the situation. It was uncomfortable for our customers and for both Joe and me—it was an area that would need work.

Sometimes the most obvious things are overlooked in a complex decision. Such was the case in the plan to buy the business. I hated sales, and yet I was the only salesman. My strong introverted nature and normal shyness make the sales calls excruciating. The process of overcoming this obstacle prepared me for the ultimate sales experience, campaigning.

Our contract specified that Joe would work in the business for a month to help us transition, and he did. After that, he quickly became a distant figure in a fast-moving game of survival. Soon, the other side of Joe began to surface again, the side we had briefly glimpsed at the closing. Whispers started coming to me, from customers and the community, "Joe used to be bad about drinking. Once when he was drunk, he drove over to HOMCO [one of our competitors] and shot the place up with the machine gun he carries in his trunk."

Joe's wife, Grace, had not been at the bank closing, which I thought was strange. A month after the sale, she showed up at the office, furtive, maybe even scared. She chatted with Cynthia and then got to the point. "I need a copy of the sales contract."

Cynthia has extraordinary intuition (for Christians this is the Holy Spirit speaking) sensibility in such matters, sticking closely to protocol and ethical standards. Her guard went up. "You will have to get those from your attorney."

Grace pushed, "That attorney is Joe's attorney. They don't share information with me."

Cynthia gently tried to turn her. "Grace, I have no right to give you what you are asking for."

"You do not know what Joe is capable of. You don't know what he has in store for you. I know him." The implication seemed to be that we should help her, and in turn she might help us.

Cynthia would not break her internal code. "I'm not sure what you're talking about, but I can't give you the papers. Maybe you could petition the courts to get a copy."

Grace angrily pushed open the door to leave. "I know what he has planned for you. You'll be sorry."

We learned things later that seemed to indicate that Grace was pursuing her own agenda, and that Cynthia was correct in not being drawn into participation.

Joe began to show up at the yard more frequently. When I happened to come back in to pick up a tool, he and our dispatcher, David, would be there huddled together. They may have been innocent, but against the backdrop of Grace's conversation, these small meetings seemed ominous to us. Occasionally, Joe would stop in the office and talk to Cynthia when I was not there.

The basic trend of the conversation went like this: "You all can't make this company work. Steve does not know the business. You two, husband and wife, working in the business together, is ridiculous. It will never work. I never let my wife come in here." He was very friendly while saying it, but the words alone were threatening. What he said and what he did were incongruent, which has always been one of my signals that things are not harmonized, out of whack. Volatility is often close at hand.

Another thread of the conversation included references to the Mafia. He told Cynthia, "When I started, the company got too big for me. I had to get the Mafia involved to help finance it. They are the ones who gave me my submachine gun. I carry it in the trunk. Do you want to see it?"

We already were worried about survival and making payroll at the end of the month, and suddenly we had to think about machine guns, the Mafia, and hidden surprises that Joe could have waiting for us. When I was in the field, Joe was in the shop, keeping connection with the employees and dropping little pieces of conversation on Cynthia that unsettled her. When

I stayed at the office, he didn't come by, but our shark-like competitors were circling our job sites, eager for the kill, hinting to our employees that we were not going to survive. They were trying to snatch our employees and our customers.

What I did not know at the time was that Joe was making moves that were prescribed in an unwritten playbook, one that had been used many times before in the Hobbs oilfields. Later, in talking to other people who had bought local companies, they faced similar challenges, sometimes succumbing to the pressure and sometimes holding strong. The playbook read like this: a company, whose owner was out of time, money, and ideas, would sell to some unsuspecting person and obligingly carry a portion of the note. When the new owners ran into trouble, the bank would gladly give the original owners control, just to try to get their money back out of the deal.

In our case, Joe had gotten the check for four hundred thousand dollars on the day of the sale, personally loaning us the other one hundred thousand. If we failed to pay him or the bank, either could repossess the company. This playbook may have been useful information, if we had been privy to it, but we were not aware of the history and took the transaction at face value, naively believing everything was normal. Even if we had known, we would still have had to deal with our problem. We understood that Grace's veiled warning and these sudden disruptions were threatening the survival of the company by reintroducing me to an old friend: fear. Once again, life was testing my courage and grit.

One theme from Joe was that we were cheating him. I kept trying to make rational sense of it, but there was none. He had signed the papers the same as we had, stating the price and terms, and we were honoring the terms. He was trying to scare us, but I was looking for the logic. Meanwhile, the situation continued to deteriorate. Cynthia was uncharacteristically nervous. I knew that if I stayed in the office to deal with him, we would lose jobs in the field. That was the more immediate problem, but I could not let him continue to visit with Cynthia. Her peace of mind was at stake.

One afternoon, hustling from one location to the other, I decided the time had come to face the giant. I called her on the way to the office. "I am headed in and will be there about six o'clock. Why don't you wait at the office for me?"

The request was unusual, but she could tell by the tone that it was urgent. When I walked in, everyone else was gone, so we could speak openly. "I have had it with Joe. We need to stand our ground," I said.

She responded, "He was back in today with that whole line, that we don't know what the Mafia would do and all about shooting the place up over at HOMCO. It's getting worse."

It was at this point that the biblical story of Nehemiah came to mind. After the Jews had been in captivity in Babylon for seventy years, Nehemiah went back to Jerusalem to rebuild the wall and the city—but the people who had moved into the city in their absence did not easily give it back. They tried a series of ploys to stop the rebuilding, including derision, threats of attacks, letters of lies to the Persian king, and finally attempted to personally ensnare Nehemiah. Instead of succumbing to the attacks, he stayed the course and completed the work. I determined to stay the course, but we could no longer remain passive.

"He is trying to scare us into quitting. Pull out all the old payable files and the financial statements."

She looked at me, questioning.

"We are going to confront him. I know from the stories that there have been misapplications of funds. We are going to find them. That will be our shield."

She understood immediately and dug out his old files. We began to search for things that were purchased with corporate funds but were used for personal living. It is a way that businesses sometimes use to avoid taxes and reduce living expenses. We both pored over the records, easily finding enough examples to make our point.

The next morning at 5:30, I rang the doorbell at Joe's house. Oilfield guys are always up at that hour. He answered the door, wearing pants and an unbuttoned shirt, no socks or shoes, with a cup of coffee in his hand and one of the long brown cigarettes he smoked clinched in his teeth. The file folder I was carrying caught his attention. When I walked in without an invitation, he motioned me to a chair at the breakfast table.

There was no small talk. "Joe, you have said we are cheating you."

I had moved too quickly into the confrontation. He tried to stall. "I don't know how you did it and how you are doing it, but you are stealing from me."

I produced the first set of papers. "Here is the contract specifying how much the sale is. Here is a copy of the check for four hundred thousand dollars from the bank to you. Your signature is on the back. You cashed it. You are carrying the note for the remaining hundred grand. That note declares that we will make a payment each month to you until that debt is retired. Here are copies of the checks we have sent each month to you with your signature on the back, meaning you have cashed them. I want you to show me where we are stealing from you."

"If it walks like a duck, looks like a duck, and quacks like a duck, it's a duck," he replied.

I knew one of his techniques was to use obscurity to keep the other person off balance, so I avoided the trap. "I don't have a clue what that means. Let me get to my real point. Your visits to the office are interrupting my wife's work. Your signature appears on this contract, indicating you sold the company and have no right to be there. So you need to stay away."

Another technique he used to gain advantage was alternating his personalities from one persona to another, from Jekyll to Hyde, from gracious champion to opponent, back and forth. You could not follow him. I had caught one side of him off balance.

At that moment, his personality stabilized into one vein of hostility, and it was glaring directly at me. He lit another cigarette, and the previous one joined a cluster of stubs in an ashtray emitting a stale tobacco smell. I had tapped into the full intensity of the short little powder keg. His eyes were blazing. "You are cheating me. It is not just me you have to deal with. I have been talking to my friends." The hints of the Mafia again, the unseen enemy and the threat hanging over our head.

"Joe, I don't know who you are or what your connection is with the Mafia or anybody else. But I am telling you that you are not welcome at the office. You will stay away."

"What will you do, call the police? They never did anything when I shot up HOMCO. I have connections." The intimidation was seething from him.

"I brought this little file for you. I am taking a copy by our attorney's office, and I am putting one in our safe deposit box. Today." I pushed it across to him.

He was off balance, surrendering the intensity for curiosity. He eagerly peered through the file and snarled in disdain, "This does not make any sense. There is nothing here. How is this going to keep me from getting my business back?"

"Joe, they didn't get Al Capone for any of the vile things that he did. They got him for tax evasion. What you are looking at are a few transactions where you've used corporate funds personally."

Suddenly, he was very attentive. I let him look while I continued, "We are continuing to go through the financial records. You have signed the checks for each of the transactions on this page. What you did in your business was your business. But if you stop at the office one more time, if you show up on location one more time, I will deliver these to the IRS. You may have local connections; you may not. I don't care. I am going to test whether your connections reach to the IRS."

In the blink of an eye, the appeasing side of Joe was back. "I am sure there has just been a misunderstanding. I am sorry your wife is scared. It's nothing I've caused."

I wanted him to acknowledge our agreement. "Just once more, right?" I pressed.

He was looking at me with a mixture of hatred and timidity. He did not speak.

"Joe, you are going to respond before I leave. One more interruption, one more visit, one more time in the shop, and I turn this over to the IRS. This is not a threat; it's a promise. Your whole financial history goes to the IRS. Do you understand?"

"I UNDERSTAND."

I stood to leave, and he remained seated. "Have a nice day, Mr. Kittrell."

Well before the expiration date of his loan, we paid him in full. He showed up at the bank to receive the payment, warm and gracious. "I hate that you all are paying this off early. I really enjoyed getting the same interest the bank receives. I can't get that anywhere else." He signed our release. It was the last we saw of Joe for some time.

The story of David slaying the giant is well known. We typically see only the ill-equipped boy, becoming victorious. We do not process David's life as a whole, beyond Goliath. After David was anointed to become the next king, King Saul tried repeatedly to kill him, trying to get rid of the threat David represented to his family's ability to maintain the throne. Later, David's own son Absalom drove David out of Jerusalem, trying to kill him and crown himself king. David sometimes retreated, but only for a time. After his faith was tested, God restored to him even greater blessing.

In the Psalms that David wrote, he repeatedly entreats God to defend him from constant threats. He faced giants his entire life. We all do.

The Bible stories of Nehemiah and David were my playbook, teaching me how to respond and that my circumstances were not unusual. Life was not picking on me; it is simply the testing process that prepares each of us for even higher stakes. If you flee from the giants, they win; if you trust God and stand your ground, you find victory and prepare for the next battle.

The Big Test

Just when I thought things could not get worse, they did. In the weeks following the confrontation with Joe, I was making sales calls, still introducing myself to our customers. One of my stops that day was the Texaco Main Office, where the big cheeses worked. I had been making calls on Fred Reynolds and Hollis Cox in the Eunice field office, but I felt a need to meet their bosses.

As soon as I walked in the door of the Texaco offices in the Broadmoor Tower office building, Gary Porter saw me and intercepted me. He shepherded me into his office, looking around to see if anyone had seen me. No one had.

I had gotten to know Gary in my last months with X-Pert. He was a good man, who talked with an air of mystery and with his mouth pinched in from the corners. This time was no different.

When he was seated behind his desk, he nodded and spoke, "You must have some really good friends in town," he said through his pinched lips. Then he fell silent, and his mouth went through motions that were a language all their own. They pursed, puckered, transformed into a slight smile and then a grimace as I waited, trying to read the message. I could not, so I remained silent. It was not the way I hoped the conversation would start.

He continued, "Texaco has an obscure provision in all its contracts that says if a company ownership changes by more than fifty percent, the contract has to be renewed. It is a provision that is seldom enforced, but it looks like someone around here has brought the matter to the attention of higher authorities. Your contract has been set aside for reauthorization."

> The Bible stories of Nehemiah and David were my playbook, teaching me how to respond and that my circumstances were not unusual. Life was not picking on me; it is simply the testing process that prepares each of us for even higher stakes. If you flee from the giants, they win; if you trust God and stand your ground, you find victory and prepare for the next battle.

Warning horns were sounding everywhere in my head. "Can I pick a blank contract up today and fill it out?"

"It's not that simple. Contracts have to be approved here, sent to Midland and approved, then to Houston for approval. If they go through all these steps, White Plains [the home office location in New York] has to sign it. All levels have to sign; if one does not, it sits there waiting until it gets a signature. The big companies have salesmen who call on our main office in New York, and they can get a signature with ease, then everyone downstream gives approval; they don't want to offend anyone in the home office."

"If a contract is sitting on a desk waiting for approval, say, in Houston, can we work until they accept or reject it?"

"I'm afraid not. It works the other way around; you can't work until all signatures are on it."

"What are my chances starting at this level?"

"Not good. We've had no luck getting new contracts originating here through the system for the past year or two."

I was trying to maintain my composure, but that was getting harder. I stood up with the intention of leaving, unable to speak. On this nondescript day, one of the most severe no-notice exams of my life came roaring at me. This test of my character took weeks to complete and would try the very foundations of my life and every ounce of courage and faith I could summon.

He shook my hand. "I like Lea Fishing Tools. They have fished lots of junk out of wells for me through the years. My advice to you is to duck out of here without being noticed, then stay out of sight and out of mind for a few weeks. I think we can work this out, but I can't make any promises." As he said the last sentences, he pinched his lips the tightest I had seen. This seemed especially emphatic. He looked out into the office lobby, waited until the coast was clear, then we walked nonchalantly out the front door. He shook my hand and nodded his head to get out quickly. "Take the stairs, not the elevator."

Someone had really had it out for me. I never found out who did it. It could have been a competitor, the previous owner, or anyone else.

I drove back to the office in confusion. When I walked into Cynthia's office, she closed the door immediately. "Sit down. You look terrible."

"I just came from Texaco. They have cancelled our contract based on a provision that says any time there is a change in ownership the new owners have to get a new contract. Ours has to go up the channel, being signed four times all the way to the head office."

"How long will that take?" She was suddenly as crestfallen as me. Texaco represented eighty-five percent of our revenue.

"There have not been any new contracts in the last two years."

Both of us were silent. We were not lost in thought and in confusion. She spoke first, "I think we should pray."

I looked up in despair. I was not convinced.

"God has gotten us this far. He will see us through."

She came around the desk, sat down beside me, and took my hand. I prayed. "God, we need a solution." It was short and to the point.

A day later, I got a call from one of my friends at X-Pert. "They announced today to continue to treat you well, that you might be back with us in a few weeks."

Two Sundays later, a young attractive brunette walked up to Cynthia and me after church services and said, "I am Pam Hunt. I work in the main office at Texaco for Mr. King. Did you all recently buy Lea Fishing Tools?"

Cynthia spoke, "Yes, that's us."

"I will not say much except that you all have a major problem. If you do not mind, I would like to help, but you can't say anything to anyone."

"We are in desperate need of help. We would appreciate anything you can do."

"I will call you if I need anything. Until then, you just have to stay away and be patient. I know that is hard, but you have to trust me." With that, she turned and melted into the departing crowd.

Cynthia said, "You are an answer to our prayer. Thank you."

We could see she heard by the nod of her head, but she did not turn back. I got the feeling her job could be on the line.

"Be patient," that was her message. It was the same thing Moses was told when the Egyptian army was bearing down on him. Trust God and watch for his power. It is much easier reading about Moses needing to trust God than actually doing it myself. I wanted to make myself a nervous wreck by worrying. Instead, the commandment was to stand still and trust. So we tried to do that with respect to our Texaco contract.

Meanwhile, I was hustling all through the rest of the oilfield, looking for work. Every office I went to had a salesman from one of the competing companies. There were four major competitors, each with multiple salesmen, so I was outnumbered at each office. It felt as though I was competing against the entire world.

These months were as tough a period as any I have ever faced in business or in life. The year in Rocky's math class in high school had only been a training ground for tests such as this one. Despair was at my doorstep every day. As it turned out, surviving the mental roller-coaster ride of this period was simply the testing ground that prepared me for challenges that lay years down the road when I started public service.

Texaco had used our fisherman, J. T., for more than fifteen years continuously, moving him from one job to the next. But when we lost our contract, they could not use him any longer. I worried that he might leave and go to a competitor, so he could go back to work at Texaco. A week passed, then a second, with no word from Pam or Gary.

Harvey Apple worked for Yates, but we had never worked for him. Paul Vega was the manager for 55 Well Service and did most of Harvey's work. Paul watched me come by his locations week after week and finally seemed to take pity on me and steer me to jobs. With Paul's encouragement, Harvey asked if we could do a reentry, which means the company is going to reenter or drill back into a well that has previously been plugged and abandoned. It can involve several weeks of work and lots of tools and produce significant revenue.

I jumped at the chance. When I got back to the office, I called J. T. and explained that we had a reentry for Yates.

"We shouldn't take it," he said matter-of-factly. "Carlos is catching a job now and then and cannot be the operator. And I'm too old to take these twenty-four-hour jobs."

"J. T., we desperately need this work. If we take the travel trailer, you can work days and sleep in the trailer, and I'll work nights."

"You have no experience."

"J. T., I fly jets. I can do it if you show me. Plus, I can wake you if there are problems. Come on, we need your help to get us through this job."

Reluctantly, he agreed. I met him that same day at location, and we spent the rest of that day and the next getting all the equipment there and rigging it up. Then we started the job. I showed up a little after 5 p.m. every day to watch, getting training and instructions. He slept at night while I got my first experience on the reentry process.

J. T. came out to relieve me every day at 7 a.m., and I would drive the hour and a half back to Hobbs, sleep for two or three hours, and then go make sales calls until it was time to go back.

As I was growing up, I learned from watching my dad that work was not just an eight-to-five routine. Like him, I get a strong sense of pleasure from work and seeing things accomplished, despite the sacrifices. My mom always quoted her mother saying, "You can sleep when you're dead." So our entire family seemed to inherit the belief that sleep is overrated.

Because of these early lessons from my family, I have been able to survive on five to six hours of sleep a night. If I get seven hours or more, I am groggy for a full day. I can go months on five hours' sleep, refueling with short five-minute naps a couple times a day. But as the first week gave way to the second, I was beginning to suffer greatly from lack of sleep. The days of worrying about the profit from our 4-H projects were coming back to life, on a larger scale. The fear of not being able to make the payments at the bank was a tremendous motivator, but my body was physically giving out. A couple of the customers on whom I was calling found out what I was doing and shook their heads in disbelief. They thought I was crazy. We had been on the well about three weeks and had more work to do before completing the job.

On a Sunday while we were in the midst of the reentry, Pam came up to me at church. "If you come by the office tomorrow, I will have your contract. Wait until 11 a.m., then call me from the parking lot before you come in. I will meet you at the door and give it to you. I suggest you not come around for several months after that. Just call on the guys in the field."

"I will be there. And thanks."

She did not acknowledge or answer and walked away briskly.

The next day, I called from the parking lot.

"Come on up." She was all business and did not want the process to linger. She met me at the main entry to their offices and handed me the contract with a faint smile.

Years later, I was able to piece together the way it may have happened. Gary Porter had filled out the contract, but it needed Mr. King's signature. Occasionally, Mr. King had a mid morning golf game with a salesman and one or two of the engineers. Gary had delivered the contract to Pam who waited for one of the days when there was both a golf game and lots of paperwork to sign. Mr. King, in a rush to get out the door, just peeled back the corner of each document and signed the stack without looking at each individual paper. Our contract was in the stack.

That answered how we might have gotten the district superintendent's signature, but it does not explain the three other signatures from the higher offices that Gary said we needed. All I know is that we prayed unceasingly for the contract to be approved. It was, and LFT, Inc. was called back to work for our largest customer.

With J. T. going back to work for Texaco, we needed an experienced fisherman in order to finish the reentry that was in progress. Swallowing my pride after the confrontation with Joe Kittrell, I called and asked if he would help. He was affable and welcomed the opportunity to get back out into the field. We completed the job and invoiced the customer. Since Cynthia had been disciplined with our cash, we had paid all the operating expenses on that job without having to borrow more money. When we received the check for the well, Cynthia used it to establish a two-month operating cash balance in the bank. In other words, we could operate for two months without receiving one check and not be concerned about paying our bills.

One of our huge keys to success had just fallen into place, a cash cushion that offered peace of mind. We never spent into that reserve, instead growing it as our business expanded. That cushion made it possible to sleep at night. We still worked just as hard, but without being on the tightrope every day, wondering if we would have enough cash to pay the bills and make payroll checks.

Many small companies find themselves with significant amounts of cash in the early days of their operation, but instead of holding it as a cushion for the inevitable slow periods, they spend it. When the storm comes, they have no safety net.

Our business plan and original loan anticipated the company being paid for in seven years. In reality, we paid it off in three. That is not too extraordinary, but what's amazing is that we expanded the business in the same three years we were paying off the company, doubling the number of employees to eight in the first year, and doubling that again to sixteen in the following year.

Every operator needed a pump, power swivel, drill collars, a pickup, and incidental tools. In other words, for us to provide one more job, we needed to invest almost a quarter of a million dollars in new capital. That money could be borrowed, which would put us more at risk, or we could patiently wait until we could pay cash. Using debt to expand is faster, but it causes companies to go bankrupt if there is a change in demand. Using the same financial principles I learned when we were running the pig enterprise and when I was collecting hot checks for C. R. Anthony's, Cynthia and I disciplined ourselves and expanded only when we could do so without taking on more debt.

We never took money out of the company and constantly saved cash in order to pay our bills on time and pay for new equipment. The result was dramatic growth without much risk from increasing debt during those first two years. It increased our stability greatly, but also provided us with peace and calm in the turbulent world of business.

Several years after Joe helped us with the project, I heard that he was in the hospital, dying of cirrhosis of the liver from too many years of drinking. I went by to see him, to see if there were things that needed to be said. Cynthia and I walked in, unannounced, and said, "Hello, Joe, we heard you were under the weather. Just thought we would drop by and see if there was anything we can do."

The old Joe was back, gracious and accommodating. The demons were gone, and he was quiet and conversational. Joe's mother was full blood Cherokee, and one of her ancestors was a Cherokee chief. Joe returned to the land of his fathers and was buried in the same cemetery as both.

Just as there was strength in the confrontation that needed to happen, there was redemption for both of us in the visit. We made our peace before it was too late. He died within a month.

The Turn

Pay cash. Avoid excess debt. Cynthia and I have MBAs, but all the knowledge came down to one rule: PAY YOUR BILLS ON TIME. Everything else is secondary and stems from that one principle. Living within our means was the crux of our success.

About three years into our operation, the old International truck that came with the company finally died with hundreds of thousands of miles on the odometer. So we bought a worn-out truck from Star Tool, our largest competitor, paying fifteen thousand dollars in cash. The truck was old and had driven almost a million miles, but it was serviceable with a bed, gin poles, and rolling tailboard, all essential to lifting the heavy loads associated with our business.

The day after we bought the truck, it was sitting in the yard with the STAR TOOL logo still on the doors. Johnny Ellis, one of our good friends from Burlington, saw it while he was driving by our yard and wheeled around, pulled in, and walked in to see Cynthia in her office.

"I guess Star Tool is setting up an outpost in your neighborhood. I see they have parked their truck in your yard." Even among friends, you have to hold your own in the rough-and-tumble, give-and-take of the oilfield.

My wife was equal to the task. "They are not parking anything here. We are buying them out, one piece at a time."

Her quick response surprised Johnnie, and he turned on his heels and left. Later in the day, he told me about the visit and her quick wit.

"I have experienced it fully, Johnny. It's the reason I married her."

Johnny and Ed Jackson both worked for Burlington. We had started to work more for Texaco and were getting some Yates work, but the work from Burlington was the turning point that helped us begin to make money.

Johnny called one morning about 9 a.m. from Trinidad, Colorado. "I am talking to the guys up here about providing a unit for us. They are too high-priced. We have several months of work, maybe a year. If I give you the job, will you do it at the same rate you work for us down there? And can you have all the equipment here by 7 a.m.?"

"I will have to charge you for trucking the equipment there. We need some sort of living arrangements for our fisherman, and we need to charge something to you for his meals where we can reimburse him. But other than that, yes to everything. Same rate, and we can be there by 7 a.m."

"He can live in one of the trailers here at the office, and we will pay a food allowance. But the main thing is, can you be here by 7 a.m.?"

"Sure."

"If your equipment is not here, I will run you off. This is all business."

It was a standard oilfield discussion; high stakes, no friendship could get in the way of the job.

"Everything will be there" was my terse reply. I knew there would be no second chances. We had struggled to keep our equipment and operators busy, and this provided full-time work for one person. It was important for us to get the work, but equally important for our little company to make the commitment to solve the problems for our customers.

"What operator will you send?"

"Frank Marquez." He was the only operator whom I knew would go and stay that long. Frank was a new hire but had fallen right into place, doing anything to see that we all succeeded.

"Frank will work. Ed doesn't much care for him, but I'll handle that. Seven o'clock."

I hung up, called Frank, got David and Wayne together with Cynthia, and told them about the job. Cynthia saw the possibilities and Frank was excited, but David and Wayne were skeptical. It would take two truckloads, maybe even a third, driving ten hours one way, thus twenty hours to make one round trip. While we were talking, David called local trucking companies, but no trucks were available to get us there on time.

David spoke, "If you call Johnny back now and tell him we can't make it, he won't be mad. He can give the job to one of the bigger companies that can handle this."

Frank offered to drive a truck all night.

I immediately turned down the offer. "I don't want you to drive a big truck to location. We need to look like we are professionals. Wayne, you and David figure out how to get this stuff on two trucks, then load them both. Wayne, if you leave by noon, you'll be there about ten tonight. I'm going to drive the second truck—the one you have loaded for me. I'll arrive about midnight, and then you can set my equipment before daylight. I'll be back here and on my sales calls by noon."

Wayne answered, "There is one little problem. To cross into Colorado, you have to have your CDL," meaning a commercial driver's license.

I thought about it. "If there is a spot to park, I will get to the border north of Raton about midnight. You can drop your load, come back, get the tank off my truck, and you'll be back to Trinidad about 3 a.m. You can set all the equipment and sleep in Frank's bed after he has gone to work." It was a long shot that would try the very fabric of our company.

Cynthia saw the work that David and Wayne did loading the first truck and was ecstatic. "I can't believe what all you got loaded onto this truck."

David pointed out, "Yeah, and it's still underweight, so we're legal."

Before he left, Wayne asked if I had ever driven a truck.

"No. I fly jets. I'll figure it out."

He was suspicious and had me climb up into the cab, where he took me through the shifting sequence and instructed me to use only the higher gears, because the tank is not too heavy a load. With that he departed.

Several hours later, after making sales calls, I got into the truck and started grinding gears. Through Lovington and on to Tatum, I was not getting any better and was worried about Portales. The main highway runs right through the middle of town with lots of turns, corners, and stoplights. I called Wayne and asked if there was a way around the small town.

From the question, he could tell I was not doing well and gave me the bad news. "There is no way around Portales. Be sure to watch for the turn when you get through town; it is easy to miss. By the way, how do you like flying that jet?"

I didn't answer, not wanting him to know just how badly I was treating his truck.

The thought of Johnny Ellis running us off the job for not being on time kept me moving forward. I could visualize him, laughing at me for turning back at Portales, just before he had us move our equipment off the location. Grinding gears all the way through town, I struggled forward and to our meeting spot north of Raton and found Wayne patiently waiting for me. He was loose and easy as he unloaded my truck in the midnight dark, ready to carry the tank on into location.

"Are you doing okay?" I asked.

"Me? It's you I'm worried about."

"I'll make it just fine. I really appreciate you shouldering the load the way you have and making this thing work."

I drove back to Hobbs, getting there about 9 a.m., never improving on the shifting. I showered and was out on sales calls before noon. Fear and hunger are strong motivators. I was afraid of not being sufficient to the task, of failing to do everything possible to make the company work. We stayed on that work for Burlington for over a year until the project was completed.

It was on that one day, when LFT team members made it work, that the company turned around. At that point, we all began to believe that our company would make it. Our employees began to believe and see a new vision of how we could compete against the well-established companies, by using our nimbleness, enthusiasm, and confidence to win more customers.

David Barton

Sometime around 1992, David Barton visited Taylor Memorial Baptist Church in Hobbs on a Sunday morning to give his historical lesson about the founding fathers and their faith. David was a high school history teacher when he discovered that textbooks differed on their descriptions of our founding fathers and their faiths. So he began to research the founders' original documents and bought them to preserve them. Now he has a collection of over one hundred thousand original source documents of our founding fathers. The Supreme Court sometimes calls him to see the original documents when they have questions.

In his talk before the church, he opened the eyes of all of us about the original intent of the founding fathers. Finally, he asked the big question, "How many of you are disappointed in the direction the country is going?"

My hand, as did most of the rest who were gathered, shot up.

"Do you know why it is going that way?"

Headshakes. No.

"It's simple. It's because people like you all do not run for office."

I was flabbergasted by the truth of his simple explanation. I began to pray that day, not that I would run for office, but that God would reveal to me who, from our church, I should talk into running for office. I did not share the prayer with anyone else. It was my solitary commitment.

Meanwhile, I continued to concentrate on growing our business and developing the people we had working for us. I was very satisfied with my lot in life, even if it was still within five miles of Nadine, the humble place of my youth.

After a couple of months of such praying, I decided one Sunday that I would not leave church that day without following up on the idea planted by David Barton in that now-distant speech. I decided I'd talk someone from the church into running for office.

In almost twenty years of attending church at Taylor, the Sunday school class Cynthia and I attended was set up in the same fashion—thirty people in rows, looking at the back of the person sitting in front of them. When we walked into the room on the Sunday of my decision, for the first time ever, the classroom was laid out in a square that made it possible to look into the eyes of the people whom I would talk into running for office. *Even better*, I thought.

True to my pledge, I sat down in one corner and began to assess the person just to my left, then his wife beside him, finding in my own mind why first this one and then that one should not run for office. Maybe it was young children at home, an inability to speak publicly, being too easily discouraged, or problems at work. Any number of variables existed that were credible reasons for not entering the public arena. I had made it down two sides of the square without having picked anyone when I began to realize it would be harder than I initially thought. I passed over the third leg of the square and still no luck. Now, I was processing each person on the side on which I was sitting. I was becoming a bit nervous. Finally, I was down to just me. *What excuse did I have? What reason did I have?*

Fairly satisfied at the understanding that Christians have a lot of legitimate reasons not to run for office, I committed at that moment to pray about whether I should be the one to run for office. Sharing the question with my wife later that day, she committed to pray about it with me. For another year or two, we prayed about whether that was a direction in life God would have us take.

It has been my experience, since then, that most people need a gestation time to let the idea of running for public office fully materialize in their minds and hearts. Sometimes years are needed to help convince someone to run.

One Sunday night, about nine o'clock, Cynthia and I were visiting as we normally do when the phone rang. Usually it was one of our fishermen who might need a tool or something, but we had no round-the-clock jobs going on. I answered it.

Cynthia, absently listening, asked who it was when I hung up.

"It was Ken Batson." His wife, Ann, had been the chairman of the Republican Party in Lea County for years.

"What'd he want?"

"Oh, he asked me to run for state representative. Seems like Bobby Wallach is not going to run for reelection."

She sat forward in her chair. "What did you tell him?"

"No. Why?" The obvious still does not always connect with me.

"Why?" Now my lovely and spirited wife was fully engaged. "Why? What do you think we have been praying about all these years?"

Suddenly, I was defensive. "Cynthia, it was just state representative. If it was an answer to our prayers, I think it would have been something . . . well, bigger." In my mind I was visualizing something like emperor, for all I knew. (I should mention that state legislators are volunteer, unpaid positions in New Mexico.)

"If that is your response, I am going to stop praying about it."

Not only was my decision in question, but also my logic. Nothing galvanizes action in a man like a wife's sudden introduction of an objection. Not one to hesitate, I hurriedly and sheepishly called Ken back, less than ten minutes after his call to me. It was a no-notice exam with big stakes.

"Ken, you haven't found anyone to run in that state rep slot have you?"

"No, Steve, not yet." He tried to be serious when he surely wanted to burst out laughing. The fact that it takes years to make such a decision, and it was after 9 p.m. on a Sunday night, did not matter. I could not survive if he had found someone. Domestic tranquility was at stake.

"Well, Ken, I would like to run for that position."

We discussed the details, and the next day Ken had an announcement in the paper that I would run. That afternoon, I walked the street on which

I live to get the required signatures. State law mandates the number of signatures required to run for each specific office in the state and for each district—thirty-six signatures were necessary in mine. It took me about an hour to gather them. The date for filing came and went with no one filing against me.

So with one hour of work and thirty-six signatures, I became a state representative. When God is ready for something to occur in your life, all you need to do is say yes. In saying yes, I began what would become a life of service.

When I called to tell Mom, her response was all business. She seemed to suggest that I should have made the decision long before. "Steve, you have shown you can run a successful business. It is time to give something back."

During the campaign, I knocked on doors and introduced myself, even though I was uncontested. I had seen an unopposed candidate on a congressional ballot lose to a write-in candidate years before and would not fall victim to the same fate.

I served four years in the state legislature, getting an assignment on the Appropriating Committee as a freshman, where I could use my business background and natural skill with numbers. Interim committee assignments included the group that considered water issues. With two Democrats, G. X. McSherry and Joe Stell, taking valuable time instructing me on water issues, I learned more in four years than I could ever have expected.

Three simple bills were all killed in committee and gave an indication of which way I was headed versus the way the Raymond Sanchez-controlled state legislature was going.

In New Mexico, schools are paid by the student and don't get paid when students are kicked out. So when a teacher takes a student to the principal's office for suspension, the kid beats the teacher back to the classroom. One bill would have given the teacher the final decision on discipline in the classroom. The teachers unions killed that bill.

I submitted a bill that would create a five-acre demonstration project in the forest above the Santa Fe drinking water lake. We had testimony that a one hundred-acre fire would destroy that critical water source, so I thought we should start mechanically thinning the forest before it burned and damaged the water system. The environmental groups killed that bill. Now the forests throughout the West are burning, the trees will not grow back for over a hundred years, and the drinking water systems in the mountains are being destroyed by silt and ash.

I also approached the petroleum exploration companies that produced oil in Dagger Draw between Carlsbad and Artesia. I asked them if they would give the water that is brought to the surface to the state of New Mexico rather than dispose of it through their usual methods. Since it is less salty than the Pecos River, I reasoned that the hydrocarbons could be removed fairly cheaply. The state then would have new water to help make the water deliveries required by law to the state of Texas. That bill was killed by the State Engineer due to environmental groups lobbying against it.

Now, fifteen years later, teachers tell me they spend sixty percent of their day trying to establish discipline. Watersheds across the West are starving for water because the massive forest fires create topsoil runoff into the streams and rivers, choking them with mud and killing the fish population. And the New Mexico State Engineer is pumping aquifer water into a lake trying desperately to make the required deliveries of water to Texas during the extended drought of 2013. The aquifers across the West are drying up, but this one is being pumped dry to try make up for the rain that is not falling.

After four years in the state legislature, I could see that the big decisions were being made in Washington, D.C., so I ran unsuccessfully for the U.S. Senate in 2000. With that loss, I believed I had fulfilled my obligation for service that Mom had insisted was mandatory, and I threw myself into our business.

34

SNOWPLOWING
THE SLOPES

Ruidoso, a popular destination among skiers from our part of New Mexico, is home to the twelve thousand-foot Sierra Blanca Peak, the highest point in the state. The mountain is less than two hundred miles from Hobbs and gets plenty of snow despite the semiarid region that surrounds it. Many kids in Hobbs were avid skiers because of this proximity to the slopes, but the issue of skiing never came up in our family, as we were always short of resources for superfluous trips.

My first experience came in college when buddies convinced me to go. We sat in our dorm rooms, plotting out the trips. Knowing I didn't have the money for ski lessons, I listened intently as they discussed stem Christies (an advanced technique for sharply turning the skis that was popular in the 1960s) and other things I needed to know. It sounded easy and fun, and I visualized myself traversing the steep slopes, pivoting sharply at the edge of the trail.

But all those instructions evaporated on the mountain, as gravity took over and spilled me onto the snow time after time. Finally, out of options, I learned how to snowplow, turning the skis in at the tip and leaving a wide wake of freshly flattened powder behind me. With powerful legs from working on our farm and being the catcher on the baseball team, I could snowplow down all except the steepest slopes.

Stem Christies never interrupted my central nervous system again. Fighting the gravity to keep my speed in control was tremendously hard work. While all my friends zigzagged down the mountain with ease, my thighs burned with pain from the first run until the last. I hated the cold from the days of milking our cow, and the cold of skiing was no different, except the intense exercise caused full body sweat that left me soaked. Without proper clothing, I was miserable the entire day. The colder I got, the more I hated the slopes. It was not as much fun as it had sounded in the dorm rooms.

During this college period, overcoming the childhood fears and developing confidence and strength became a priority. I started grabbing hold of life. I accepted and embraced that I would fly airplanes, go to war, that I would face my fears and accept leadership positions. I began to solve problems on my own and accept responsibility for the outcomes in my life. But I stopped skiing after college.

From our first days of marriage, however, Cynthia insisted that I take her skiing. When we wound up with the business bills paid and a few free days ahead of us, we would jump in the plane and head to the slopes at Ruidoso. She loved to go fast. Her natural coordination and physical abilities gave her confidence and grace on the mountains that I envied. Instead, I still snowplowed down the mountain, legs burning, sweating, cold, and miserable.

Eventually, as age crept up, my legs lost some of their strength. One weekend, in my mid 40s, Cynthia suggested we take advantage of the fresh snow on the mountains at Ruidoso. On the hills that day, I faced a dramatic reality. My legs were no longer strong enough to hold the snowplow. Headed down the slopes, my skis slid parallel, and I began to glide—effortlessly—back and forth, across the decline, using the slope to increase or decrease my speed. *I was skiing.* The strenuous effort, the sweat and pain were gone. The gravity that had been my enemy now was my source of strength. It was unforced and graceful compared to the tremendous exertion I was used to. Without the running sweat, my body stayed warm. I found comfort in the snow I had never known before.

Irony of ironies, the thing that improved my skiing the most was losing the strength of my legs. My strength had been an impediment as it allowed me to pursue bad habits. I knew I would never be good, but I was lighthearted at the discovery of how it was supposed to work.

The lesson learned from my skiing became the way to visualize other parts of my life. I saw clearly how fear, overexertion, and relying on my own strength made the challenges of life more difficult.

At that same time, Cynthia and I were in the midst of experiencing the heavy burden of owning our company, Lea Fishing Tools. All our skills, confidence, and abilities were challenged to the fullest. No longer were we in the protected zone of a small business run from the relative safety of our home, with the ability to supplement the cash flow as needed with steady paychecks from our jobs. Now our paychecks came solely from our success; our house and everything we owned were at stake.

Each day brought questions about replacing worn-out equipment, personnel problems, or deadlines to deliver equipment to locations. Every day was consumed by questions; every month required continued focus to ensure we reached breakeven or made money.

There is a saying in the churches: "If you want to walk on water, you have to get out of the boat." I did not think of myself as walking on water, but I was way outside the boat. I was overwhelmed with decisions and responsibilities, in water that was too deep and turbulent to tread.

Snowplowing Through Life

I grew up in the Church of Christ. Mom and Dad had us in church Sunday morning, Sunday night, and Wednesday night. I learned discipline in that regimen, and I learned to respect God and his Word. I gravitate naturally to the stability and orderliness of a society based on verities, truths that cannot be changed.

What I was missing, though, was an understanding of a God who answered prayer, who would deliver me from obstacles and enemies in my everyday life. I didn't really understand the need to trust God through these prayers. I understood religion, but I did not know God.

Wrestling with the problems at our company was sapping me of my energy and joy. I found myself looking for the God whom David found when he declared:

The Lord is my shepherd; I shall not want. He maketh me to lie down in green pastures . . . He restoreth my soul.

I looked desperately for rest and restoration amid the challenges of making decisions and calculations every day.

Until we owned the company, Cynthia and I thought ourselves able to solve all our problems on our own. We were independent, strong and committed, embracing the challenges at Lea Fishing Tools with the same strength, intensity, and zeal that had gotten us this far. Faced with the heavy burdens of business, I worked harder and longer, hoping deep down that our strength and self-sufficiency would keep it afloat. But after the visit from the Chance brothers, the turbulence from the previous owner, and the loss of the Texaco contract, I admitted strength and tenacity could not solve the problems.

> The problem with depending on personal strength and independence is that eventually they are insufficient and keep us from experiencing the supernatural power that God wants to reveal in and around us. When I realized that my strength could be a drawback, I achieved a spiritual maturity that took me places I could never have gone on my own.

Cynthia and I started praying together regularly for help and acknowledged our own insufficiency. I began to pray for wisdom and discernment in my daily prayers.

Similar to my experience on the ski slopes, I was working far harder than I needed to. I came to realize I was snowplowing in my spiritual life, missing the promises God offers to us—to be our strength, our shield, and to give us rest.

I saw lessons I had missed in my Bible reading. In the book of Exodus, Moses is leading the Israelites out of slavery and gets trapped between the Egyptian army behind him and the Red Sea in front of him. In desperation, he prayed, "Lord, what should I do now?" God gave him a curious answer. "Stand still, so I can show you my glory." I had never learned that, occasionally, when faced with a tremendous challenge, I should stand still to see God's glory and simply receive his power.

The first major "stand still" moment came when we lost the Texaco contract, and Pam told us we would have to be patient. When I saw the power of God come through in that instance, I learned to let go of the reins in other ways. We stopped straining against life. Trusting God to sustain us provided us with a calm that had been missing. As I had learned to use the energy of the mountain when skiing, I slowly learned what it was to let God's strength be my strength and work on my behalf. As I relaxed and released the daily worries, I began to glide much more effortlessly through life than ever before, finding the rest and peace that comes from the Good Shepherd.

It is important to note that before this time of great stress, we went to church regularly and never really struggled with doubt. But until then, we never understood the abundant blessing of receiving His peace during trials. I didn't know that letting go and letting God's gravity do its part in my spiritual life could be as exhilarating as letting gravity work on the ski slopes.

Our personal effort to do the things only God can do consumes our energy and tires us. It leaves us winded and cold as we go through life. The problem with depending on personal strength and independence is that eventually they are insufficient and keep us from experiencing the supernatural power that God wants to reveal in and around us. When I realized that my strength could be a drawback, I achieved a spiritual maturity that took me places I could never have gone on my own.

In such moments of trust, I feel peace and strength, not doubt and weakness. I feel I can take on the challenges for which the strength of my own legs is insufficient. I go where I do not know the way or have the answer. I can walk by faith, not by sight.

As my faith life evolved more toward knowing God and away from practicing religion, concepts in the Bible began to come to life. One of the most vivid is the story of Joseph, who many years after he was sold into slavery by his brothers, declared to them, "You intended it for evil against me, but God meant it for good." The lessons of many such stories became crystal clear as I saw similar principles at work in my own life.

In elected office, I find prayer sustains me when all seems out of control. When chaos and insurmountable obstacles face me, I find myself able to look for God's glory to be manifested, just as I learned to do amid the challenges of operating the business.

35

JULY 4—
INDEPENDENCE DAY

When our daughter, Lori, graduated from Texas A&M in 1993, she took a job as a buyer for Walmart in northwest Arkansas. We were at College Station for her graduation with the U-Haul truck loaded, waiting for the parchment before we hit the road.

But Lori was a wreck as we waited for her last grade to be posted; anything less than a "B" would require a retake and make walking the stage symbolic. After a rocky start in college, she had finished big but needed that one grade to graduate. For the third time, we parked and waited so she could run into the building and check the grade. Her nerves were so frayed that she would not survive another dry run.

It was obvious the moment she came back out into the sunlight that an enormous burden had been lifted, a weight that had been building for years. She soared and shouted her way back to the car; her spirit was un-tethered. Her comment as she got into the car reflected the struggle it had been: "If I can graduate from Texas A&M, I can do anything." The lion had been uncaged.

Lori was a lot like me. She had made excellent grades up until a specific point in school, and then it seemed she could not break free and her grades began to drop. She had the brains but lost the confidence she had in her younger years. I had experienced the same thing, but found myself powerless to help her. For me, watching her struggle to get free, to believe in herself, was a painful replay of my own trials. Gratefully, her confidence began to rebuild that day.

Schools across America work to teach kids self-esteem, but these efforts are misplaced. Confidence is what they need, which is not the same as self-esteem. I frequently interview young people who apply for jobs and have high self-esteem, believing they can do anything. The problem is that they cannot do everything. Their self-image is not built on real accomplishments but on the self-esteem lessons they've been taught in school. When they find out the truth, their delicately nurtured confidence goes into a tailspin.

Confidence can only be instilled by doing. For me, confidence began to build as I competed in various venues and finished well—4-H, the baseball lessons under Coach Shaw, and the National Youth Conference. Lori began her serious competition at the university but had a long way to go. Life is where the gun goes off, and we prove ourselves or drown in the deeper water.

Down into the Depths

When we arrived in Arkansas with our U-Haul truck, Lori felt like one of those "One-Day Millionaires" in the Philippines—except she was buying on credit while they paid cash for lack of credit. Today, credit card companies and banks, eager to lend America's youth as much as they will borrow, begin to seduce them the minute they have financial independence. Such was the case with Lori as well.

Lori bought a new car, a new insurance policy to go with it, and rented one of the newest and best apartments. I didn't ask how much she was making or spending, figuring that with a degree from A&M she could figure it out. That was a mistaken assumption that cost us both dearly.

Two years later, I began to notice the strain in her voice when we would talk over the phone. When we talked in person, she seemed jumpy, on edge. Finally, I asked if she was on drugs. "No" was her plaintive reply.

"Pregnant?"

"No." Even more sadness colored her words.

"Then it has to be money," I said, and she immediately burst into tears. I asked what the problem was.

"I have a cash flow problem," she explained.

I asked for explicit details but got lost in the explanation, gleaning only that it was bad enough that she could not quantify it in her own mind. "Get your bills and your checkbook, and let's see what you have," I said as kindly as possible.

As we pored over the documents, Cynthia, who had joined the conversation, observed, "You don't have a cash flow problem; you don't have any cash."

Her situation was dire enough that the financial consolidators refused to take her as a client. Her student loan payment, car payment, apartment rent, credit card bills, Dillard's account, Sears . . . she owed them all. For me, who pays off every credit card each month, it was unimaginable. I had forgotten to teach her my rule about setting aside money in checking to pay for each purchase she made with a credit card.

As any parent would, I made her a deal. I told Lori I would take her car and its payment and sell her our Jeep Wagoneer for five hundred dollars in cash. It was several years old but clean and very reliable. Most importantly, it would free her from the six hundred dollar a month car payments and another five hundred dollars a month payment for her insurance. I told her I'd help move her across town to the apartments where the rent is two hundred dollars a month less.

Even with these changes and with thirteen hundred dollars of her income freed up each month, she could just barely pay the minimum on her credit cards. I pulled out her latest credit card bill and said, "Show me how much you owe." She had never paid attention to that number and looked around to find it. "When you find it, divide the payment each month into that balance owed."

Lori did that, her hand trembling as she did the math on the bill itself.

I asked her, "What does that number mean."

Her voice trembled. "I don't know."

"Divide that number by twelve, and it should give you a hint."

She still did not know what it was all about.

"I'll give you a clue. The twelve is the months in a year. So it is twenty years."

I could tell from all the trembling that Lori could not know where all this was going. She was off balance and could not process.

"Add your age to that number."

"Forty-five." It still had not hit her.

"Forty-five. That's how old you'll be when you pay off this credit card bill, if you only pay the minimum amount each month and do not buy another thing for twenty years. More purchases will make you older when you pay it off."

The color drained from her face, and the shakes in her hands moved to the rest of her body. The years of financial stress were coming to the surface as she realized that she was in a self-imposed debtor's prison—and would be for years. There was no way out. Her youth would be gone by the time she paid off the shoes, knickknacks, and other consumable items that, by then, would be in landfills or thrift shops. That's what too much credit does for you; it steals your independence.

Lori began to sob, sorrowful and repentant. I consoled her, but I did not help her beyond taking her car and its payment and selling her my vehicle. *Discipline cannot be bought.* It cannot be given from me to her. She was learning a very hard lesson in life that can only be learned by getting one's self under control.

She needed to practice financial discipline now or she never would. Each month, she made her payments on time. She did without when it came to things she wanted; she sacrificed. Each time she paid off one small bill, she added that cash to what she was paying on other cards, accelerating the payoffs. She called exuberant each time she paid off another loan and said, "I just paid off the Sears credit card. I have twenty dollars to apply to the credit card bill!"

Each time she paid off a bill, she built a little more confidence that she could work her own way out of the jam, lessons that were just as powerful as the confidence gained from graduating from Texas A&M. She was developing the confidence that she could live with financial discipline, that she could manage her financial life.

Watching from a distance, I saw her live with perfect discipline for four years. Each time she paid off a bill, she applied the free dollars to a new bill. She still owed fifteen thousand dollars and had years to go to be debt free, but I figured she had learned to live within her means.

Independence Day

On July 4, I called and observed, "Today is the day you get out of the water."

"What does that mean?"

"Cynthia and I are giving you swimming lessons, not drowning lessons, and today is the day you get out of the water."

"I'm sorry, but I still don't know what you're talking about."

"What day is it?"

"July fourth."

"What day is that?"

"Independence Day."

One of the hardest things for a parent to learn is that his or her children will make mistakes. If we are not careful with our help, we enable a lifetime of dependence.

"That's right, Independence Day. Debt owns you, but I am going to buy your financial freedom back . . . by paying your debt in full. You'll be free tomorrow, but never let yourself get pulled into spending more than you make again, because I won't bail you out of your problems next time."

The drowning man pulled from the water does not leap for joy; he lays exhausted, trying to get more oxygen. Such was Lori's response. Only through the next weeks and years did I see much tangible evidence of the joy and lightness of step we had given her, which was tempered by knowing how close she had come to catastrophe.

The biblical stories of kinsmen redeemers are about people who buy the debt or provide other saving acts for a family member, such as Roy

McLean had done for our family. In the book of Ruth, a kind and wealthy Boaz agrees to redeem the widowed Ruth by marrying her in a culture that afforded few other options to widows. Boaz agreed to take care of Ruth and her mother-in-law, Naomi, and to free them from a life of servitude.

The story is from centuries gone by and maybe doesn't seem to apply today, but seeing the effect this brand of redemption had on Lori was dramatic. The stories had never conveyed to me the sheer joy of the one who is set free, similar to one being let out of a jail cell with lost hope restored.

The story of Ruth is a preview of the way Jesus would pay our debt of sin on the cross and redeem us to a right relationship with him and should be met with the same enthusiasm that Lori found from her release.

For me, watching my daughter develop the understanding that she could live a life of financial freedom is what parenting is all about. In the sudden restoration to full financial health, I could see her slip the surly bonds that had trapped her spirit, and she found freedom years before it was anticipated. Her lesson was well learned; she has not fallen into the debt trap again.

One of the hardest things for a parent to learn is that his or her children will make mistakes. If we are not careful with our help, we enable a lifetime of dependence. Lori only learned her lesson because I gave her time to wrestle with her own problems and develop the habits of spending control and the belief that she was capable of working her way out of a serious problem. Parents who protect their children from such lessons do them no favors.

36

CYNTHIA AND
THE LFT STOCK

After we paid off our company and it began to make money, Cynthia came to me with a quiet and respectful question, yet it threatened to bring volatility into our newly settled life. She proceeded carefully; the shyness that lies deep inside her surfaced and controlled her observations. I encouraged her to say what was on her mind. Backing into it, she pointed out that the organization of our duties put me in constant contact with our fishermen (the income producers) and with the customers (the income generators), and that I alone had an intimate knowledge of the exact inventory of our company.

In other words, even though she was satisfied with the pay arrangements and our division of responsibility, the organization inherently placed me in a more favored position than her, should something go awry with our working or marriage relationship. In my mind, I was thinking, *So what? We are married. It's a community property state.* Fortunately, I didn't say what I was thinking.

Since my youth, the connecting of dots, the reading of meaning into conversations, has been one of my weakest areas. This discussion had the makings of one of the most dot-filled of our life together, and I was not at all sure what point she was making.

I am usually dismissive of people's doubts and concerns, and in similar circumstances I have all too often proceeded carelessly. In the past, I might have scoffed at or ignored her heartfelt concerns or rushed to reassure her in a way that could come off as dismissive, but I fought my lifelong tendencies. Something about her carefulness and shyness caused me to be just as cautious in my response. The discussions between us at the beginning of our marriage, about submission and the husband's responsibility to not make his wife angry or bitter, replayed in my mind right then, granting me the restraint I needed.

Besides, I had watched casual conversations between my mom and dad result in months and years of distress. I had watched friends ruin marriages with thoughtless and hurried responses. *So I did something unprecedented for me. I responded with, "Let me think about that."*

She agreed, and I left for work. I tried to consider what would have caused this discussion, seemingly out of the blue. It was not something that had come up before. *Why now?* The entire tone of it, her worried demeanor, was foreign to me.

I don't work well with nuances; I just want the answer. But I silently vowed to figure this out. Something about it seemed to suggest that we were establishing the framework for either future happiness or future bitterness. Weeks passed, and I slowly came to see it from her perspective. I realized this conversation was a continuation of one we had had before, right after we were married, about life insurance.

We were still operating under the agreement we had given the bank at the beginning, with me making four thousand dollars a month and her still working "for free." Cynthia had done that for several years now, investing all her time with not much to show for it outside of us.

The thought of a failed marriage or desertion was as foreign to me as our conversation. When I commit, I commit; there is no looking back. But she had only my words to reassure her, and memories of a previous broken marriage. She had years of watching similar promises to other women wind up differently. In her initial conversation, she was being very careful not to offend me. But she was also not willing to blindly go along for years building a business where I had full advantage because of the division of responsibilities—as much as she trusted and loved me.

As I wrestled with my potential response, I thought sequentially, about telling her that she got and deposited our paycheck, that even though the paycheck was in my name, she controlled the money, both at the company and at our home. I thought about simply reminding her that we both owned equal amounts of stock and were, therefore, equal partners in the venture.

Slowly, the built-in disadvantage she had pointed out became clearer to me: if something should happen to our marriage, I had the one hundred percent advantage. If we split up, the most equitable split would be fifty-fifty. But within days, my half would have far more value than hers. The customers knew me, not her, and their loyalty would be to me. The same was true with our operations guys. So I would have an operating fifty percent, and she would have a shell.

I was getting it. But understanding the problem is not the same as knowing how to fix it. Everything I contemplated seemed too combative or felt as though it didn't really address her fear or her exposure. It was one of the most subtle of my no-notice exams, but it was testing my preparation for life's questions that would challenge the very foundations and principles of my life.

I had gotten married later in life, which gave me the luxury of processing the problems in other people's marriages, including my parents, from a distance for years. I knew the stakes were much higher than the question at hand. We were working on the structure not only of company ownership, but also of our marriage. Looking around, I could see that she had cause for concern. We knew women who had put their husbands through medical school, only to be jilted; successful businessmen left their wives for younger women, taking the company with them.

I wanted to get it right; I wanted our marriage to be right. I knew from the biblical teaching that I needed to respect my wife. She was to be an equal partner in reality and not just on paper.

The innocuous conversation had brought me, once again face-to-face with the major life questions: "Who am I, and who will I be? How, now, shall I live?"

I struggled to find an answer that would give her reassurance and peace of mind. When I think about strategic matters, I do not discuss them out loud. It's as though I'm boiling the issue in my mind, rendering it down to the final element. Others are not let in on the process.

The discussion was several months behind us, and Cynthia had never brought it up again. She has an incredible capacity for patience that makes life with her pleasant—especially for me, as I take my time sorting through matters that others might solve quickly. Gradually, I saw my way clear and found a possible solution.

I waited for a time when we could talk without interruption and without turbulence from other discussions obscuring the details of this one. Six months after the initial discussion, I had my chance. No recent storms of controversy threatened to cloud the topic at hand. We were sitting snuggled on the sofa with my arm around her, the way we always do when things are calm between us.

I asked, "Do you remember your question about me having a great advantage in the company?"

I felt her body stiffen. She remembered.

"I think I have a solution."

She waited without a response. I could tell from the sudden tension in the air that she had suffered quietly over the past six months. She wondered if I had gotten mad and would offer a sullen response or had decided to ignore the question completely. Or maybe her worst fears would play out—maybe I would just split that day. It had been a difficult waiting period for her, but I could not apologize for the delay. I work slowly through these matters.

I continued with the thesis of my long-simmering solution: "If you will prepare the paperwork, I will give you one of my shares of stock today."

Her response was one of hurt and surprise, as though I had slapped her across the face. She withdrew from my arm and moved away on the couch. The fiery part of her nature, the part she rarely displays, was just below the surface . . . waiting for the spark to set it off.

I was thrown off by her response. What I was suggesting was right; I was sure. I was ready to react in anger, but instead tried to understand her reaction. I realized she didn't see the full implication of my suggestion. What she was seeing was that we each had one thousand shares of stock, and that one share changing hands had little value. Math equations were running loose in my head, and I was fighting my urge to smugly prove her wrong. But instead of accelerating the argument, I offered an explanation.

"Cynthia, in small, closely held companies, the majority owner has one hundred percent control. If I give you one more share, you'll have 1,001 shares and I'll have 999. You can outvote me at every board meeting. You will be in full control. I would not be able to do anything without your approval—not sell the company, not sell equipment. If we split up, you'd make all the decisions. You'd own the company."

In other words, I was giving up control of everything to give her the reassurance she needed. But she seemed unconvinced that it could be that simple. She remained distant and quiet. But it was the right thing to do, so I pushed forward.

This was a principle that went all the way back to my childhood Bible lessons. The sheep and cattle ranchers of biblical Israel were commanded to give the very best of the herd as a sacrifice to God. I had thought a lot about that as we improved our pig herd in 4-H. When we try to maintain control, when we try to keep the best, we are choosing an idol, the god of our herds and our possessions.

If I chose to maintain the advantage, in this case with my wife, I would be choosing control and possessions over her peace of mind and security. If that were my choice, what would be my answer in life's other questions? If I were to maintain total control, how could later reassurances be more than the ringing of a bell? The words for the rest of our life together would be muted by my actions in this one instance. This is what vows and commitments are about, valuing the good of the other before yourself.

It's not that I would be satisfying her worries by putting myself totally at risk. I still had de facto control of the company because of my relationships with the employees and the customers. I still knew the inventory and what it would do. My offer simply yielded to her a counterweight that would only matter if we decided to sell the company or if our relationship did not work.

Once she saw it, she prepared the papers for the transfer. James Francis, our accountant, carefully cautioned me that there was no going back. I could not get the share back without her signature. I knew what it meant: my position in the company would depend on maintaining a good marriage. I could not slip into the undisciplined lifestyle of disrespecting her or neglecting my work for hobbies or pastimes. My only strength was my performance. It was a challenge with which I was completely comfortable.

I signed the paperwork, knowing it represented a very large investment in the happiness and trust of our married life. Nothing changed after the papers were signed; we operated exactly as we had before. She never outvoted me in a business meeting. It was more of a safety net for her. For me, there was the inner knowledge that I had passed a critical test, that the trust and peace of mind of my wife were more important than money or control. It made me feel more in tune with her and also with God. I sensed that I had come to understand one of the deepest mysteries taught by Christ—that in giving up all, you gain more.

Happiness, peace, trust, and contentment do not come easily in a relationship. Financial infidelity is one of the biggest stressors on a marriage.

In the years following that discussion, the subject only came up once more, and that was in a very positive light. A couple of years after our decision, Texaco announced it was going to channel a certain percent of its contract business to minority and women-owned companies. Cynthia was the one who researched the issue and found that since she owned more than fifty percent of our company's stock, we qualified for the preference.

Our decision ended up paying unintended dividends, but the real benefit was my understanding of how well God's principles work if they are implemented the way they are intended.

Surprise #1

It's not that I'm not good at buying gifts and giving surprises; I just don't do it on schedule. I am more of a spontaneous gift giver. And my spontaneity does not surface on command at Christmas, birthdays, or anniversaries. Cynthia knows that about me and has rarely made an issue of it.

A few years after we bought the business, we were still living in the townhouse I bought before we married. Cynthia had been looking at houses for seven years with the same real estate saleswoman, Anita Cheney. They'd looked at dozens, and if it passed Cynthia's tests, they would call me to come see it. For seven years I had dutifully gone, taken the tour, listened to Cynthia's observations about how the house would look after we moved in. I very rarely explained why I did not like a house; I would just shake my head no and we would leave. Not once did she ask for my reason, not once did I offer to explain, and not once did Anita complain about our failure to buy.

I wanted to honor Cynthia's desire for a larger and better home. It was just not high on my priority list, and I didn't want to accept just anything. My years in the Air Force and as a corporate pilot had kept me on the road, and the last thing I wanted was to move with the idea that we would move again when we found a better house. I wanted to feel right about a house and only move once.

One morning, I got the familiar call and, with a sigh, said I would meet them. Almost the moment I walked into the house, I felt comfortable. The house was well designed and well constructed, and I had an immeasurably good feeling about it. I didn't say much but asked Cynthia if she liked it. She did. As we left, I made the comment that we might just have to build a house to decrease her expectations, but I knew we both liked this one.

Later that day, I stopped by Anita's office and explained that I wanted to make an offer on the house but did not want Cynthia to know. I wanted to buy it as a complete surprise. Anita was shocked. At first, she said it was not possible. I pointed out that it might not be usual, but it was possible. She reluctantly agreed. So I made an offer, received a counteroffer, and refused that. The weeks wore on and not a word had slipped out to Cynthia. Finally, I got the breathless call from Anita. We had reached an agreement with the sellers.

I said I wanted to sign the papers, get the loan, and have the house in hand before telling Cynthia. I wanted it to be a complete surprise and wanted her to be free from the hassles involved in the transfer. Anita convinced me that now I was way out of bounds. It could still be a complete surprise, but the surprise would have to be played out right then, because we needed Cynthia's signature to move forward on the loan and closing. We decided that I would bring Cynthia by her office that night after I got off work, and we would spring the news on her.

I got to the house about 6 p.m. and told Cynthia that Anita had some ideas on how we could move forward in this search for a house. Cynthia was resistant. She was tired of looking and a little discouraged that I could never be pleased. After more effort than I anticipated, she agreed and we drove to the meeting.

Anita and I had already orchestrated the entire process. We walked in, sat down, and after some small talk, Anita announced that our offer on the house had been accepted. She needed a check for the earnest money. We were set to close the next week and would be the proud owners of the house on McKinley Street.

To my complete surprise, Cynthia was very upset. "What kind of cruel joke are you two playing?" It was turning out to be too big of a surprise, and she could not believe Anita. Cynthia was staring daggers, first at me, then at Anita.

Then I took her hand and said, "I knew the minute I saw the house on McKinley that I liked it, and if you wanted it, I would buy it for you as a surprise. I have been working with Anita for weeks making offers and counteroffers. You said you liked it."

At that point the full realization and belief hit her, and she broke into tears. Real tears. It was one of the few times I have seen her cry. Then, in typical Cynthia fashion, she stopped crying and declared that if it was going to be our house, we would sleep there that night. At this point, neither Anita nor I wanted to test any part of Cynthia's support, so Anita somehow made it work.

We bought a blowup mattress that night, and Cynthia slept in the home for which she had been patiently shopping for seven years. We still live in that same house, and it has been the perfect fit for us.

Surprise #2

I find my wife just as fascinating and interesting today as the day I married her more than thirty years ago. The year 2011 was an unusual one for us, because we were spending more time apart than at any time in our married life. This was what I had wanted to avoid during my military years and part of the reason I had delayed settling down. It's a sacrifice we both have learned to make, but neither of us like. Text messages, email, and phone calls do not get the job done.

During a work period in our district that year, I was traveling without her to a series of events. Tim Keithley and I were rolling into Clovis for an evening event and were, as usual, right on time. The air conditioner in the vehicle had not been working properly, which made for a sweaty New Mexico car ride, even in September, and I was frustrated. Cynthia always has an eye on my schedule, and knowing I had a couple of minutes before the event, she called to see how things were going. I finished the conversation quickly so I'd have time to check under the hood before it got dark. I wanted to see if there was a busted hose, a broken belt, or other noticeable problem.

> To have the wife of my youth evoke such a strong response of laugh-out-loud joy at the sudden unexpected sight of her is a rare gift indeed. This is the blessing my wife brings to me—the light and laughter poured into me just from her presence.

As we pulled into the parking lot, I saw Bob and Glenda Carter waiting to attend the event with us. He is an excellent mechanic, and I waved for him to meet us in the back corner of the parking lot to look under the hood. By the time he walked over, I had the hood up and was peering into the engine compartment.

We finished the inspection, and I started weaving my way through the cars to the event. In my natural state, I can focus on things so closely that I am totally unaware of my surroundings. This was happening now as I tucked my head down into the BlackBerry messages that needed answers. Watching my feet and the fenders over the top of the BlackBerry, I knew we had arrived at Bob's car because I saw his feet stop. I was going to look up from my phone to give Glenda the customary hug and then hurry into the waiting crowd. At the last second, I looked up.

Beside Glenda, to my great surprise, was Cynthia! Without my knowledge, she had ridden with the Carters. She had quietly waited for us to finish looking at the car and for me to walk across the lot to her. She was leaning casually against the car, amused that I had not seen her. It was a replay of younger days when the girl waits to see if the guy will notice her, knowing that if he does, she will sweep him off his feet. She did.

I am rarely surprised in life, but this was one of the times. Her presence alone was a shock. I had no clue she was going to ride two hours just to listen to me give a speech. But the big surprise was my response. I broke into loud and spontaneous laughter of sheer joy as we embraced. Then I could not stop squeezing her or stop the outpouring of laughter as we walked into the building with her under my arm. I do not cry, but I was emotional and very near tears.

After the speech, she and the Carters drove the two hours back to Hobbs. When they had departed and the crowd had dissipated, I reflected in the stillness of the cool desert evening.  To have the wife of my youth evoke such a strong response of laugh-out-loud joy at the sudden unexpected sight of her is a rare gift indeed. This is the blessing my wife brings to me—the light and laughter poured into me just from her presence. These easygoing qualities do not come naturally to me. Intensity, focus, and heavy lifting are my lot in life, and Cynthia brings me the balance of joy.

37

THIS IS WHAT IT'S ALL ABOUT

Shortly after buying Lea Fishing Tools, I had an opening for someone to work our steam bay. The job entailed using hot steam to clean oil and paraffin off the tools used on the oil wells. It's lowly, dirty, hard work.

Albert DeLeon applied. He had loads of shop experience and had been a truck driver, yet he was available to start work that day. I have learned not to ask too many questions in such circumstances. I hired him on the spot. He was dependable and efficient. Months went by, and I was still impressed with his work, so I promoted him to work in the shop and found a new steam bay worker.

Typically, I arrived at the office about 5:30 a.m. I would visit with the operators, see that all the jobs were covered and that the truck drivers got out of the yard. Around 8:30, the hard buzz of activity from the morning would slow, and I would then "manage by walking around" the shop, visiting with the employees, and touring the yard and steam bay with the tools waiting to be cleaned. I'd make lists of things the guys told me we needed to buy, equipment that needed repair, or decisions that needed to be made.

The process suited me perfectly. It allowed me to be accessible while keeping my finger on the pulse of the company. Many people are uncomfortable talking to the boss. The office and the desk they sit behind make it harder. But during my walk around, they felt free to make their comments while accomplishing the business of the day. Very seldom did these conversations seem official, and almost always they were contained to a sentence or two. I wanted communication to be open and easy, so I chatted and asked about families and the weather. Inevitably, I learned much more if I just listened to what was really being said.

Albert and I had been working weeks on improving our shop, using his knowledge of procedures from the international competitor for whom he'd worked previously. One day we were sorting tools, placing overshots on the racks, and checking grapples to see if they were worn or would do their job of picking up pipe in the next fishing operation. Sorting the heavy tools is tedious.

We were both looking for a breather, so we stood up and paused there in the middle of the shop floor. He suddenly glanced my way and burst out, "Boss, this is what it's all about, isn't it?"

Still panting from the hard physical exercise, I cautiously looked at him. "Albert, I have no clue what you're talking about." I thought he was joking until I saw the concern and the question in his face. We both looked back at the tools waiting to be painted and racked, but neither of us moved as he continued.

"This . . . all of this. This is what it's all about, isn't it?"

"Sorry, Albert, you are way over my head." I still didn't know what he meant, though I assumed he wasn't talking about the tools before us. I knew it was serious, that I needed to be careful not to scare him off the issue.

"Boss, I watch you. You come to work at 5:30 every morning. You do your work; you come back here with us; you do your work up front, and you are here all day long. You go home in the evening to be with your family. The next day you come back in to work and do it all again."

I was nodding my head in silent agreement. "It sounds boring when you say it that way, but, yes, I guess I do."

"No, boss, I'm serious. This is what life is all about. A person comes to work every day; they do their job, and go home to the family every night. That's what life is all about."

"Yeah, now that you say it that way, that is what it's all about," I said, processing and wanting to work in "the why" for how I live my life. "I go to church to try to learn how to live better, but otherwise you have it summarized about right. I guess I learned it growing up. My family struggled to make ends meet. We lived out at Nadine. Dad worked all day for Exxon, then came home and farmed until dark, every day of my life. That is what I saw, and it's all I know."

"Boss, I just needed to know . . . I don't know what life's all about. I've lived my life drinking up my money. I am thirty-four and don't own my own house. I can't even buy shoes for my kids." He was getting emotional but continued, "Boss, I have a confession. I had to come to work for you because I got fired. I got a DWI and lost my CDL license and can't drive a truck anymore. I didn't know what life was all about. My father died when I was young and was never around to teach me these things, so I just did what all the other guys did when we were growing up. But they didn't have dads either. I just need to know. Watching you, I think I have finally figured it out; this is what life is all about."

He moved back to the rack and picked up another tool. I did not want to spoil the mood, so we slung tools together for a while longer. I didn't want him to feel as though he had talked about something that was off-limits. As I was turning to leave, I said, "I'm glad you're here, Albert. You are a good man, doing a good job."

After a time, I promoted Albert to shop manager and, finally, to dispatcher, which is the heartbeat of a service company. Once he started dispatching, I sat down at the counter with him one day when things were kind of slow. "How are things going with you, Albert? At home?"

"Real good, Boss. I go home most nights. I save a lot of money that I used to spend, out with the guys. My wife is trying to get me to go to church with the family. I can't quite pull that off, but I have gone on some church trips with my girls as a chaperone. Those kids, they can't fool me. I know all the tricks. Boss, it feels real good."

"I know, Albert. Real good." I got up to leave and said, "Oh yeah, Albert, Cynthia says you are going to have to learn this computer program if you are going to dispatch. She is transitioning to a new computerized process and insists that you learn it."

"I know, Boss, you have been telling me, but I never did too good in school. I'm not sure I can learn."

"You're pretty smart; you can learn."

"I don't know, Boss. I've been talking it over with my wife. My oldest daughter said she will help me learn the program, but we don't have a computer."

"I'll get with Cynthia, and we will check one out to you."

I was suddenly flooded with memories of sitting at night with my own father, figuring the tallies on his tank gauges made during the day. He would hustle from one tank battery to the next and come home to finish the paperwork at night after dinner. I was always good with math and could run through the numbers and fill in the totals for him while he filled in the rest of the report. At eleven and twelve years old, I felt I was contributing to the family.

With the help from his daughter, Albert learned the dispatching program and helped us move into a new technological phase of the company.

Haarmeyer Electric

After about a decade at the business, things were going well. We had developed accounting, invoicing, and sales and were beginning to understand the business. So much so that Joe Yue wondered if we wanted to buy another business: Haarmeyer Electric.

"Sure. Send them by."

Andy Haarmeyer came by first, and the meeting did not go well. Two hardheaded guys would not work well in the same venture, so I politely declined to get involved. Then Andy's wife, Mary, called and asked me to reconsider. I was frank with my observation that I didn't think I could work with Andy. She reassured me that, even though Andy had a dominant side, he was an honest and hardworking man. After listening to this woman whom I had never met plead her case, I laughed and said, "If you are involved, I could probably work with my worst enemy. Why don't the two of you come back—together!"

So Andy and Mary set up an appointment and showed up at our offices to meet about selling us their business. They brought with them their company financial statements. Andy's father was a lineman for Lea County Electric and had taught Andy about electricity from his early childhood. He knew the trade well and had the license. Mary, like Cynthia, ran the office and did all the accounting work.

They anxiously spread their reports out in front of us. I knew none of their background and wanted to start out with a little introduction to break the ice, as it was obvious they were nervous and scared. "How did you start your business?"

Andy was the first to speak. "We just need to sell. We don't have enough money to continue."

"I can see that. I just wanted to know how you got started."

"Listen, we have some hard decisions coming up. We just need to know if you're interested." He had gotten in over his head and was grasping for a lifeline.

I turned to Mary. "Did you all start the business?"

Mary hastily shared their story: "Andy and I talked about starting the company while we were dating. We both agreed it would be great to pursue Andy's dream of owning his own company, so we began making plans. We picked up our first service truck on our wedding day. For our honeymoon, we went to Santa Fe to take his contractor's test. We were only gone two days for our honeymoon, because we had to get back home and rig out the new service truck to start work that Monday. So we have both been committed to this company from our first day together . . . and it has run our lives ever since."

"But it's just the two of you now?"

"Yes."

Andy has a strong introverted side, and he retreated back inside his shell after his first few bold statements.

We could see from the quick looks through the financial statements that the company was in bad shape for cash but had solid revenues. Several large customers had gone belly up in the oilfield recession or just closed up shop and vanished, leaving the Haarmeyers to pay employees and suppliers without being paid for the work they had done.

"You know you could file for reorganization and not pay those bills."

Andy responded, "We have to pay those who trusted us with their services, even if it means liquidating the company."

I could tell from the emotion that this would be hard on him, especially since he was losing the company due to the actions of others. After some questions from Cynthia about the documents, I wrapped the meeting up. "We need a couple of days to review the documents, but we are interested. I know you are nervous and scared. Can you wait that long?"

Andy just said okay and got up. He thought we were putting them off and was ready to leave. He and Mary exchanged deep looks, silent questions moving back and forth in their eyes. They were defeated.

"Look," I continued, since they had not responded, "we are interested, but this is a big decision for us and for you. We need to study your financials to see what's wrong. It may not be possible to fix it, even for us. Neither Cynthia nor I know anything about the business. I don't want to jeopardize our business either. Two days. You be back here in two days. No longer."

"Two days? You're sure? You're not just putting us off?" Andy was suspicious.

Cynthia, more compassionate than me, jumped in. "We have been right where you two are. We have risked losing everything before and were uncertain about the outcome. We are interested, but we just have to work up a business plan. We are here to help."

Her softer tone and more personal approach seemed to reassure them, and Mary, who intuitively understood we needed the time to look at the financials, finished the discussion. "We'll be back in two days."

It's my job to sort through strategic decisions, so I carried the financials into the office and began to pore over them, jotting notes down, making observations. Numbers have a language all their own, and I had always been able to interpret it. When I had my notes made, Cynthia took the information and worked it into a business plan. The night before they showed up, we had our usual prayer about the decision, and we felt good about the chance to turn the business around.

The next morning Cynthia came into the office and said, "I don't feel good about this deal."

I agreed. "Yeah, something is out of place. I just can't figure out what it is."

"If we buy their business, who are they, and what do they do?"

"Say that a different way. I'm not sure what you're getting at."

"I don't have it all the way worked out in my mind either, but they are scared. If we buy the business, Andy will have to go to work for another contractor, working for wages. He will see things that could be done better but will have to keep quiet because he is giving up. Mary has talent that is not yet harnessed, but she will have given up."

"You've got it—that's what was bothering me. Their spirit is about broken. When we buy their business, we will break their spirit in the process."

"I'll leave the decision up to you as to what we do and how we respond," she said and went back to her desk and duties.

I usually handle this type of thing after she has kicked them off, so I prayed for understanding, then set about organizing the response in my mind.

They showed up, right on schedule, more anxious and scared than before. The process was very difficult for them.

"Please, sit down. Can I get you water or coffee?" I am usually more to the point, but their turmoil was very close and personal to me. I remembered the fears and doubts and feelings of insufficiency that riddled my own childhood and surfaced when we got our business. That's what they were feeling as they were giving up their dreams—falling short.

They were too nervous. They didn't want anything—no coffee, no small talk.

Andy blurted out, "What did you decide?"

I ignored the aggressiveness. I understood. "Well, we have a business plan here. I think you have a good company. With the right moves, it will make a profit."

"Does that mean you are going to buy it?"

Mary jumped in. "Excuse Andy. He is just anxious."

"Don't worry. I know exactly how he feels." Then I got to the solution. "We will be happy to buy the business, but we have a proposition. Are you interested in hearing the proposition, or is this all just too painful?"

Mary responded before Andy could bull his way through. "We are interested in the proposition. Tell us more." Andy looked at her sharply.

"Cynthia observed this morning that she did not feel right about buying this without considering other alternatives."

"I knew it!" Andy exclaimed.

"Andy, I am about as volatile as you are, so you need to calm down a bit," I said. My patience was almost gone. "In normal circumstances, I would have already told you to shove it. I think you stand to gain or lose more than the business about now."

He sank back, and Mary leaned into the discussion. "Please continue."

I filled in the details of what we had come up with. "Cynthia and I were ready to buy the business last night, but we prayed about it just before bedtime. Each of us woke up with a question. That question was about your spirit. We can buy your company and take it over, pulling you in the boat, or . . . we can throw you a life raft and you can save yourselves. We will go through with the purchase if that's what you decide, but we want you to try to work this thing out on your own. We have a business plan that I believe will make your business work. I will go through that with you right now, then give you the business plan to provide you a blueprint of exactly how we would turn this thing around.

"If you decide you are too far gone, we will buy it and hire both of you to do exactly what you are doing now for exactly the same amount of money you pay yourselves now. But once we buy it, it is ours. In other words, we will help you, but we will not take the risk, fix it, and then give it back. If we buy it, the company will remain ours."

Years later, Mary confirmed her response, "In my head I was like, 'Throw me the raft, and I'm on it!' I wanted to save the company more for my husband and his dream than for any other reason."

But Andy was still suspicious and spoke for them, "If we take the proposition and succeed, what do you want out of it?"

"Andy, that is your first good question." I was feeling hopeful. The right question being asked is a leading indicator that the listener is processing. "We do not want anything. We have been blessed beyond anything we ever imagined. The county or the country will not be any better off if we fix your business. What the country needs are more people like the two of you who will take chances and figure things out. The country needs small business owners more than Cynthia and I need the financial gain. I don't have anything against the big conglomerates, but the strength of the country comes from strong individuals. If the two of you let your company go, I think you will lose part of yourselves and will live a lifetime of defeat rather than a lifetime of giving back."

Mary spoke quietly, "You're right about it breaking our spirit. We have worked so hard and have not taken a vacation or paid ourselves more than minimum wage, trying to take care of our employees and the company. And you have heard what kind of honeymoon we had. From the start, we have sacrificed to make this work and have done everything right . . . been honest, not taken advantage of anyone. And because of the selfish or bad decisions of others, we are going to lose our company. But we want to honor the debt we owe, even if we have to sell our company to do it."

It was my turn to be surprised. "That is exactly what we need—people in the country who will honor their obligations and commitments. So all I want in return is for you to show up at the county fairs and buy a 4-H pig or steer for the next couple of years."

Andy retorted angrily, "Are you kidding me? You want us to buy a pig at the county fair?"

Mary was obviously thrilled and jumped in, "I was one of those 4-Hers standing in the ring. I know how much it means to help the kids grow with their hard work. Andy, he wants us to succeed and give back." It was clear she had gotten the picture, while Andy was still trapped in his suspicions. She continued, "Can you show us the plan?"

I slid their copy over to them.

"First, I would try to sell the rewind shop. It is pulling profit from your commercial electric operation. But if it does not sell in a week or two, shut it down. It's an anchor pulling you and the company down. You are better off if you just cut the chain and let it sink rather than trying to hold out and get something for it."

Mary looked at Andy and said, "I told you we should close this."

Andy's response was immediate. "I don't think I could close it."

Cynthia chimed in, "Business can't be personal or emotional. You have to be decisive enough to jettison things that need to be thrown overboard. The reason you don't have cash is you're pouring it into this piece of the operation. Close it, and you'll have cash within sixty days. Leave it open, and you lose the business. Also, you are operating from two different locations. You need to merge those."

Again, Mary responded, "I told you we needed to do that."

We continued until the business plan had been laid completely out.

"What do you think?" I asked.

Mary was still taking the lead. "It looks good. I just don't know if we can do it."

"I am certain you can do it, which is why I am going to offer to keep you both in your positions if we buy it. The only thing you have to decide is if you want to do it for us or for yourselves."

Mary was looking at Andy, who was still prepared to bluster about it.

Cynthia surprised me then. "Andy, we wish nothing but the best for the two of you, but you need to know one thing."

"What's that?"

"Steve and I work well together. It is one of our successes. He recognizes what I have to offer. If you continue on your own, you need to let Mary be more of an equal partner. She has a lot to offer."

I saw the wisdom of her counsel and added, "Andy, you are like a sports star. You are good at your work, but you are not managing very well. Very few players can play and be managers. Mostly, their skills have to be managed. I do not work in the field; I manage. You work in the field. That is your strong suit. Mary is your best asset. Mary, have you been to college, or is all this your natural talent?"

She admitted she only had a high school education and no accounting background at all.

"Get into college and get the accounting degree, and it will increase your profits dramatically. Andy, you need to let Mary take over the management of the company—all of it—until your company is on solid ground. Then you can gradually pull yourself out of the starting lineup. Right now, you must stay and do the work in the field. Your company can't survive the loss of any customers. In fact, I think your aggressiveness is coming from being stretched too thin."

He took these latest assaults in fairly good graces. In fact, he seemed relieved that he did not have to hide any longer, that the stress of doing everything was about to overwhelm him.

"Which is it going to be?" I was wrapping up the sale.

They looked at each other, unable to answer, but the fear was dissipating from their eyes.

"Let me suggest one more thing. You all go back to your business and use the plan or not. If you just don't have it in you to continue the fight, call us and we'll buy it." That seemed to be the assurance they needed. They agreed that they would give it a try.

The next year, right on schedule, they showed up and split the cost of a pig with me at the county fair. We continue to work together on various projects as they have found their success and the joy of giving back.

Mary did enroll in college and made all "A"s in the accounting and business classes. But before she could complete her degree, tragedy struck. Andy's father was killed, her brother was hit by a semitruck, and Mary's best friend died in an accident, all within a four-month period. She dropped out of school and never made it back. But her natural skill—coupled with that year and a half of business and accounting school—provided enough of a foundation for the success of their business.

Today, Andy and I are good friends. The pressure-induced anger and aggressiveness are gone, and we consult together on business and life questions often.

The Haarmeyers are now helping a young couple who have started two companies—the wife owns a restaurant and the husband, whom Andy trained as a young man right out of high school, owns his own company. Andy and Mary want to share the kindness, compassion, and knowledge they have received in business. This is precisely the outcome Cynthia and I hoped for when we helped. This is what it is all about, helping and healing one family at a time.

Several years later, without any training in the field, Mary decided to go into film production. She bought professional equipment and set up a studio in Lovington. The lion inside her had been uncaged. Her creative genius is too strong to sit forever doing accounting. She still watches over the contracting business, but Andy has transitioned to full-time management.

Their dreams and aspirations quietly add to the spirit, strength, and vitality of their small town and of our nation.

Browbeating

In the oilfield service business, there are never enough managers. The work is too hard and dirty to attract the MBA types out of the big cities. Consequently, I had to promote line workers to supervisory positions. Most were very intelligent, but few had any college education, and none had formal training in management.

I promoted mechanics to be shop foremen, truck drivers to supervise the drivers, and operators to be operations managers. People who work with their hands have a hard time fighting the urge to just do the job themselves. Shop foremen invariably ended up under a truck with a wrench in their hands. On such occasions, I uttered one of my most repeated instructions to managers: "When you pick up a wrench, you quit being a manager and become a mechanic." It was my way of trying to say, you must train others to do while you manage. I had ongoing discussions about management with everyone I placed in supervisory positions. It was a perpetual training program.

One year, on the Wednesday before Thanksgiving, I was having just such a meeting with Lynn and Albert. I looked down at my watch and saw that it was 2 p.m. I asked the two men, "I thought we always shut the office down at noon the day before Thanksgiving. Aren't you two headed out?"

Albert was quick to respond, "Not if you keep browbeating us."

I laughed at his quick wit and ran them out of the office so they could be with family.

Usually, the Friday after Thanksgiving was a light day, so we let as many people as possible take that day off. I was in early as usual, but I was surprised to find Albert and Lynn both there. "What's up? What are you guys doing here this morning?"

Albert took the lead. "Boss, we discussed it and had to talk to you this morning."

"Can't it wait until Monday?"

"No, Boss. We need to talk to you today."

"Okay, talk."

"Not here, Boss. It needs to be in your office. With the door closed."

That spelled trouble. My door was rarely closed. It was my sign to everyone that the seriousness had just been kicked up a notch or two. They were upgrading the seriousness from their side. I was very surprised, but we walked down the hall from the dispatch desk, I led them into the small office and closed the door behind them.

"What's on your mind?"

Albert led off their side of the conversation. "Boss, I was trying to be funny the other day when I said that thing about you browbeating us."

"I know, Albert. It was a pretty good joke, and I laughed at it, so what's the problem?"

"Boss, we are proud that you are taking the time with us and are afraid if we don't clear this up that you might not take the time with us anymore. None of us guys in the back had any kind of home life. None of us had fathers who spent any time trying to teach us anything. You are the only one who has ever cared enough to try to help us know things and understand."

Lynn broke into the conversation. "Boss, all of us had bad homes, and you treat us like we wish our fathers had. We don't want you to stop browbeating us. We want to learn."

Lynn was an athletic-looking man who had worked hard his whole life. He had a cocky attitude and a mouth to go with it, but I had always appreciated his dependability and hard work.

Albert added, "All Lynn's dad did for him was beat him . . . hard."

Lynn lost his cockiness and was transformed back to his youthful self, almost cowering at the thought of his father. It was obvious the two young men sitting in front of me had contemplated this conversation together.

"So, Boss, I was just trying to be funny when I said that about browbeating, but we want you to browbeat us."

Lynn chimed in, "Boss, I know how to drive a truck, and I'm good at it, but my father is sixty years old and still driving a truck. I don't want to be like him. I want to learn what you teach us."

At that point, I was about as emotionally overwhelmed as I get. In one of the roughest professions in the country, the oilfield, on a nondescript Friday morning, great meaning was attributed to the life values my parents taught me by their actions. To have a couple of guys straight out of the oil patch put it into words was one of the most profound experiences of my life.

I kicked them out of the office with a slap on the back and an admonishment to get on home to their families. They both had a smile on their faces and a bounce in their step as they left. Yelling after them, I told them not to worry, I was not nearly finished browbeating them.

Alone, I reflected on the blessing of my own father, who had had such patience and who helped so many kids in the 4-H program. I had a sense of fulfillment that I could not describe. When I got home, I told Cynthia, "I am not sure where life will take us, but after Lynn and Albert made their comments today, life makes a little more sense." I concluded that if this is the life that God intended to be our calling, I was completely satisfied.

When we sold the company, Albert stayed on as dispatcher for the new owners, but they never saw Lynn's potential and busted him back to driver. He could not get used to being back on the line where he once managed, so he quit and started driving a hot-oiler (a unit that heats oil and circulates it down a well to treat it). Less than two years after leaving the company, Lynn was on location operating his unit, which somehow caught fire, and he was burned to death. When Albert called to tell me, I wept.

Rosa

After we had worked several years in our business, it became obvious that we needed to get more sophisticated with our invoicing process. I visualized that each morning we could have someone call the operators and fill out a spreadsheet on the tools used the day before. Typically, the operator would keep a daily journal of tools run, and when the job ended—sometimes days, weeks, or months later—we would try to sort through the pages of reports to invoice the tools used. We could be filling out the spreadsheet as we went along if I had someone dedicated to the job.

Rosa Munoz was the only one available, so I told her my plan. "Rosa, I am going to assign you a new duty to go with your bookkeeping and payroll responsibilities. You can allot half a day, every day, to the new task." I tried to explain the duties briefly, but the discussion went on for the next week.

"Rosa, are you ready to start?"

"Mr. Pearce, I can't do that."

"Why?"

"I'm so shy."

"Rosa, you will not be asking the operators anything personal. You are just talking about the jobs."

"Mr. Pearce, my accent is too strong."

"Everybody out here has an accent. Can't you hear mine? Don't let that bother you."

"These men, they have been here a long time, and I'm a nobody."

"Rosa, everyone here is the same. There are no prima donnas here. Besides, I have been watching your work, and you are very precise. I need someone who pays attention to detail and is very precise."

"I just can't do it, Mr. Pearce."

"Rosa, I'll give you a day or two to think it over, but you are the only one I have. So we really don't have a choice."

I had spent so many years afraid of talking to people that I knew first-hand what she was struggling with. But we needed the job done, and Rosa was the person to do it. I told Albert to talk to her.

He told me that he already had. "I've been watching how you always talk to people about things like that, and I tried to encourage her, too, but she just won't do it. Boss, I think she is just scared and embarrassed."

"Albert, we're all scared. I am the most scared of all. I spent all my life feeling like I was in a jail cell, afraid just like Rosa."

"You, Boss?"

"Yes, me. Man, I have spent what feels like a century confined. I found out later that the jail cell door was unlocked the whole time. Now that I am free, I just want to help others get free."

"Boss, I don't want you to get mad or anything, but Norman asked me once if you are a preacher."

I looked over at him and laughed out loud. Norman was much younger than Albert, and Albert had brought him on to help in the steam bay. One day, I saw the young man go into some sort of trance and asked Albert about it. He told me Norman had fallen on his head when he was a kid and that ever since this "thing" happens to him: "It's like something catches in his head, and he goes to shakin' and his eyes roll back. He snaps out of it and doesn't hurt nobody," he told me, before pleading with me to keep him on in spite of this. Norman worked for us for a while and then moved on. I was still shaking my head and laughed at Albert's question. "No, I am not a preacher."

"Boss, Norman's point was that you talk different from most of the bosses."

"Well, Albert, I consider that a compliment." As I turned to leave, I said, "Don't forget to talk to Rosa again."

I never knew if Albert talked to her, but that same week Rosa came into my office and asked to speak to me. She closed the door right behind her and stood there with her back almost up against it. "Mr. Pearce, I have been talking to my husband. We have prayed about what you want me to do. I just don't think I can do it."

"Rosa, I know you can do it, but I won't make you try. Why don't we do this—you try it for two weeks. If it doesn't work, I'll find someone else. Also, I'll call each operator and let them know what you're doing and that you're doing it to make their lives easier and my life easier."

"You'll do that?" she asked with great surprise.

"Sure."

"Well, then I'll try. But you have to tell them it's not my idea."

"Rosa, you don't have to worry about that. Everybody is used to us trying crazy new things, and they always know to blame me."

So with that agreement, we moved forward. We set her up at a table where nothing else was to take place but those calls. Discipline was the key. Every day, the calls had to be made and the tool sheets filled out.

"Mr. Pearce, call J. T. first. He scares me."

"J. T. scares everybody at first," I told her, but he was one of the nicest guys there. I told her how, during our first month of owning the company, J. T. helped deliver his own equipment, driving the truck and setting it off the float with the winch truck. Somehow, the pump had gotten caught on the edge of the truck once and broke the piece that drives the winch. He called me to report it and said that if I would bring a new one out, he would install it. Sure enough, when I got there, he had the old one off and rolled under the truck to put the new one on.

"If you just let him know you are uncomfortable, J. T. will help you."

I got him on the phone. "J. T., we are going to a new process. I am going to have Rosa call you and every other operator each day and mark down the tools you used the day before. Should take only a couple of minutes, but it will save you a lot of hassle when we start to invoice."

"It sounds good to me. Put her on the phone, and we can start now."

Rosa was hesitant but tried it. J. T. helped her through the process. I sat there and helped her fill out her spreadsheet each morning for the rest of the week. She seemed to get the hang of it.

Months later, she showed up to work earlier than normal. I was in my office, and people were just starting to make their way in. She once again closed the door, standing all the way back against it as though she was afraid it might fly open, her hands holding the door handle behind her. "Mr. Pearce, I have to talk to you." She was breathless.

I waited, nodding my head.

"Mr. Pearce, can I say something?" She had been waiting for permission, and I had only nodded.

"Sure, Rosa. Go ahead."

It was clear she was very nervous. I began to have a sinking feeling that the experiment might fail, and I would have to start looking for someone else. "Rosa, you are doing a fine job. I have been talking to the operators. The system is working well for them, so what's the problem?"

"It's not that, Mr. Pearce. Everything is going fine." She began to breathe hard. Whatever she wanted to say was very emotional to her. Finally, she burst out, "Mr. Pearce," quickly calming her emotions and becoming focused on the words, "I have been waking up early every morning the last week and . . . and . . . I just have to say this. . . . Mr. Pearce, I have been telling my husband that I would work for you for free!" She emphasized the word *free* by pumping her fist, as though she was hammering it onto a table.

I tried to lighten things up. "Rosa, you don't have to work for free."

But she did not hear me; she was on a mission. She continued on as if I had not spoken. All you have to do is let the lion out of the cage, and it will have its way. Now she was possessed. There was nothing else in the world for her but the need to express her deepest emotions.

"Mr. Pearce, I would work for you for free." She repeated the assertion, with all the intensity of a courtroom lawyer making her closing arguments. "I told my husband, I would work for you for free because you believed in me when I did not even believe in myself. You believed I could do things when I didn't even believe I could do them."

She stopped for emphasis, but I could tell she was not finished. This time, I had the good sense to wait quietly. I could see the wave building inside her, like a breaker that forms offshore and moves in, gathering speed and height and mass.

"Mr. Pearce, the other girls in the office say, 'Rosa came here a Chihuahua, and now she is a pit bull.' I am changed, because you believed in me.

> "Mr. Pearce, the other girls in the office say, 'Rosa came here a Chihuahua, and now she is a pit bull.' I am changed, because you believed in me. You believed I could do those calls, even when I did not believe it. I did not like being a Chihuahua; I like the ladies calling me a pit bull. I love my job!"

You believed I could do those calls, even when I did not believe it. I did not like being a Chihuahua; I like the ladies calling me a pit bull. I love my job!" She finished with her closing argument. "So, Mr. Pearce, I told my husband this morning I was going to talk to you, and I have. I told him I was going to tell you I would work for you for free."

My own memories of trying to break out, to be more than a Chihuahua, were crowding back into my mind. I was close to becoming emotional and euphoric at the same time. "Rosa, you are doing a great job."

She could tell the message had hit the target, and she opened the door to leave. We both needed to be alone with our thoughts. Her spirit was soaring with the freedom of expressing her gratitude.

"Rosa, could you pull that door closed?" She nodded in understanding. "And Rosa, one more thing. . . ." She pushed the door back open. "Rosa, you are filling a key role, and you don't have to work for free. The comments you made just now make my job worthwhile and give meaning to my life."

She laughed out loud with the sheer joy of redemption, the fulfillment of being transformed. I was, at that moment, being transformed, too, finding even more freedom and release in the barren desert land of eastern New Mexico.

38

BURNOUT

I have lots of stamina. I can keep going long past the time when others would stop. It's just the way I am and the way I work. I work fourteen or fifteen hours every day. It seems normal to me. It's what I saw my parents do.

One year, Cynthia and I had taken four days off for Thanksgiving. Normally, I would have been impatient to get back to work the following Monday. But this Monday was different. I couldn't identify what was going on. I did not want to be at work. I suddenly did not even care whether or not jobs got out the door.

That morning, I left the workers to do their jobs, got in my car, and began driving. About 6 a.m., I called Ed Jackson, a friend who worked for Burlington. He had one of our units and fishermen working on his wells in Trinidad, Colorado. "Ed, what are you up to?"

"Just sitting at the house."

"I thought you were supposed to be in Colorado."

"That's what my boss said."

Something was amiss. Ed and Johnny Ellis were a lot like me; they, too, worked constantly. They ran their jobs on location. Now, Ed was not even in the right state, and he appeared to have blown it off.

"Are you up?"

"Yep. You're talking to me."

That pinched me just a bit. "I mean, if I stop by, are you going to throw me out the door?"

"Nope."

"See you in about twenty minutes."

"I'm not going anywhere." Click. He had hung up. That was not unusual, but his tone was. Ed lived at Loco Hills and had grown up in the Maljamar area that lies between Hobbs and Artesia. It's remote, even for New Mexico, and very small. We had been friends for a long time.

One Friday, we were together on a well. When he asked me to watch our fisherman on his job the next day, I looked at him funny.

"My son is getting married. I need to be there."

"Your son? The one I met a couple of months ago?"

"Yep."

"Ed, he's a sophomore in high school. He's not old enough to breed."

"That's not what the girl's parents are saying." Ed always distilled things to their essence.

I was curious about him being in New Mexico when he was supposed to be watching several rigs operating in southern Colorado. I pulled up and walked in the back screen door without knocking. "What's up?" I asked.

He was sitting at the breakfast table in his pants with no shoes or a shirt. "I just burned out, man. Just woke up yesterday and realized I did not want to be there. The feeling was so strong, I didn't care if they fired me or not. So I just got in the vehicle and started driving back here."

"What did your boss say when you called him?"

"I didn't call him. I figured he would find out soon enough."

"So you are just cruisin' down the road, not a care in the world?"

"Yeah, more or less."

"Man, I know just what you're feeling," I said, surprised that I could relate. "I just got back from four days off. Normally, I am ready to go. I woke up this morning and did not want to make one more decision. I don't think I can face making my sales calls or taking questions from employees. I was thinking of driving to Colorado to see you when I called early. Just the drive up would take a day. The drive back would be another day. If you are burned out, I must be burned out. Everything you are saying sounds as though you've been reading my mail."

"Steve, if I'm burned out, that's one thing. They can replace me, and I can get another job. If you are burned out, your whole company is at stake. If I get fired, I will just lay out for two or three months, but you lose your business." He was suddenly engaged in my problem and asked, "What would you do if you didn't have to work for the next month?"

Without blinking, as if my mind had already thought it through, I responded, "I would buy a pass to travel the whole month on a train. Then I would upgrade it to a sleeping compartment. I would take Cynthia, and we would just ride the train for the whole month."

"Your company will be okay for a month, but it won't be okay if you lose your desire permanently. If you want my advice, go get that train ticket today. Now, get out of here before I run you out. Every minute you delay makes it more likely that you won't do it. Go get your bearings back."

I saw the wisdom in what he was saying.

On the hour-long drive back to Hobbs, I called and priced the passes. I got to the house about 9 a.m. I had called Cynthia to meet me there, and she met me at the door, still wondering at what was going on. "What are you doing home?" It was very unusual for me.

"I just don't think I can even go through the motions of work. I have never felt this way, but I don't have any interest in anything this morning. I don't think it's going to be better tomorrow. I am burned out. Ed Jackson advised me to take some time off, or he says I may get to the point where I will never want to come back. So I'm going to take his advice and take a month off, starting right now. If you can take off, I want you to come, but if you can't, I can't wait. I'm going to pack and leave within the hour."

"Where would we go? What would we do?" She was trying to process this sudden change in me.

"I've reserved a train pass, like the Eurorail Pass you and Lori used when y'all went to Europe. I've reserved a sleeper car, and I'm going to stay on the train until I feel like getting off. I will circle the U.S. until the month has passed."

Cynthia replied, "I just started the computer program conversion at work. I can be finished in two or three weeks."

"I'm sorry, but I can't wait. I think this is serious. I've worked twelve to fifteen hours a day almost my whole life. Something has snapped inside, and I need time away."

"I really wish you would wait. I could use the time off, too."

"I would if I could, but I can't. I'm sorry. You can take a month when I get back."

I packed and was gone within an hour. I flew to Houston, rented a car, and drove up to see my folks in College Station. I drove back to Houston that afternoon, boarded the train, threw my bags in the sleeper car, crawled into bed, and fell asleep. I brought several books along. I would wake up, read for a few minutes, and fall asleep again.

When we got to Tucson, I got off the train and tried to go see the Air Force boneyard at Davis Monthan AFB. I had wanted to see it since my days in the Air Force, but it was closed until the next day. I couldn't wait. I caught the next train out of town that was headed west. When I got to Los Angeles, I called my longtime friend Rebecca Allen.

I spent about a day in L.A. before climbing back on a train. I slept and read until we hit Las Vegas, and then stayed on the train headed east. I would sometimes eat at the dining car, but I was just as likely to sleep through mealtime. I had never slept this much.

Generally, I can function well on five or six hours of sleep a night and keep that schedule up indefinitely. But I felt like a battery that has not recharged sufficiently and suddenly has no more power. When that happens, it needs to be deep cycled, charged slowly for a very long time. If the power drain hadn't damaged the cells too badly, it should recharge.

I continued east through the Rockies. It was snowing across much of the country, and I was beginning to stay awake longer. I would open a book, then sit and watch the countryside go by without reading a word; even that mental exercise was too much. Mile after mile. I did not want to think.

I did not call home or write letters. I did not want the pressure of having to check in. I just hoped everyone understood. It was all I could do.

The Bible speaks of times like this and declares that God can hear the gasps and grunts of our lives when we are too empty to pray. I prayed that he would hear my groans and remember his covenant with me. That is as coherent a prayer as I could offer.

When I got to Chicago, I got on a train headed south. At Walnut Ridge, Arkansas, I got off. My old friends James and Joyce Price drove several hours to pick me up. While I was there in Blytheville and Leachville, I saw Doc Rodman from the old poker club. He had retired and started painting—real live art. I was shocked. Of all the things I expected this "belligerous" man to do, art was not one of them. He took me to his garage where canvas after canvas was stacked up. "I paint seagulls. I don't have the patience to use those little bitty artist brushes. I use a four-inch-wide house brush to paint the canvas blue. Then I use a two-inch paint brush to paint the sea gulls." He then demonstrated the technique, slapping blue house paint on a fresh canvas, dipped the smaller brush in the white and splashed two strokes, making a V, the way we did in grade school. "I charge five bucks a gull. If you want five gulls, it's twenty-five bucks."

"How's the gang?" I asked, changing the subject before I was forced to compliment his work. "Do you all still play poker out at the cabin?"

"No, the boys don't gather much anymore."

Seeing the garage full of unsold seagull canvases and hearing the news that the gang didn't get together any longer was more than I could handle. I had to ship out, get back on the move. Two burnouts together did not seem to be a good combination. I have often heard of people who just snapped, who could not face life anymore. I was hoping I had not gone that far, but I could not be sure. On the train, I fell asleep and slept for hours.

With about nine days left in my month, I got back home. Cynthia watched closely to see how I was. There was still no light in my eyes. I could have told her that.

"Are you going to work tomorrow?"

"The month is not up."

"Customers . . . employees . . . everyone is asking about you."

"I'm sorry. I just can't carry the load any longer. I will go back on the thirty-second day." I was not so sure. Cynthia was not so sure.

The next morning I got up early and began to dig out boxes that held the accumulation of decades of personal notes, projects that had not been finished, and letters I had not answered. I began to examine the flotsam and jetsam of my life, discarding stuff, answering letters (no matter how long ago they were written), and filing financial records that needed attention. I spent the next nine days throwing overboard the junk of years passed. I began to feel lighter, as though the cargo thrown overboard would make it possible to clear the mountains ahead.

On the thirty-second day, I returned to work. I was tender, as if recovering from an operation, still not ready for the challenges, the decisions, and problems of being a small business owner. Gradually, I got to the point where I could take on the day-to-day tasks of running things again, making the decisions on routine matters. It took about a week to hit full stride, but I hit it. I came through, thankful for the healing, thankful that God had heard my groans.

It was not long after the burnout that I needed every ounce of energy I could muster.

Six-Dollar Oil

In 1999, the international price of oil fell from twenty dollars to ten. The oil in southeast New Mexico is not as high quality of oil as in the rest of the world. Some of our customers were only getting six dollars a barrel, for oil that cost thirteen dollars or more to produce.

Saudi Arabia and the OPEC were flooding the market, trying to kill the stripper wells in the U.S. If they could do that, they could sell us another million barrels of oil a day. Lea County, where I live, has lots of these marginal wells and found itself on the front lines of a battle between nations—and forces we knew nothing about.

Work on oil wells stopped immediately. The day the price fell, the work stopped. Our business lost eighty percent of its revenue—just like that. Companies like ours began to lay off people and give pay cuts. The layoffs claimed up to seventy percent of people's payrolls, along with thirty percent pay cuts to those who were kept on.

Cynthia and I had a board meeting, the two of us sitting at our kitchen table.

"What's happening? Why is everyone in the yard all of a sudden?" she asked.

"I don't know. The company men are telling me the price of oil has been falling, but they don't know much more than we do. How much are revenues off?" I asked.

"Eighty percent, more or less," she said, looking at the spreadsheets we had on the table.

"How much cash do we have?" was my next inquiry. "How long can we continue at these revenues?"

"I will have to check more closely, but a ballpark figure is about five or six months. How are other companies managing?" she wondered.

"Layoffs . . . and pay cuts."

"What are you thinking we should do?"

"Not sure. We need to think about the health of the company," I said. "But we convinced each person here to come to us rather than stay with the major companies. J. T. could have gone anywhere when we bought the company, but he hung around and treated us well. David, Richard, Kelly, Kelli, Billie, Albert, Frank, Mike—all of them. They all came with us because of who we are. They believe in us, believed we would treat them right, treat them fairly. We can't just ignore that."

Cynthia replied, "We can't ignore the people, but the question becomes, are we ready to jeopardize the future of the company? Remember, if this thing fails, we have nothing. We have signed everything—our house, our cars, and our savings—as collateral against the bank loan. The bank gets everything if we guess wrong." She was referring to loans we had taken out for equipment after paying off our initial loan for the company. They had never released the personal guarantees that we would give everything over if we failed to pay. "You are fifty-three years old, and I am fifty-one. Can we go out and get a job? What will we do for retirement if we let the company go broke?"

"I know, I know, I know," I said and sighed, the frustration beginning to build.

Life tests us in exactly this way. What are our priorities? How now do we live? What are our values? The process is guaranteed to entail stress and pain as long as we value any two things equally. We valued the company and invested our lives in it, and we valued the employees who invested their lives in it. We could not make a decision right then but agreed to have another dining room table board meeting the following week.

Over the next week, the tensions mounted at the company and inside the two of us. We were acting as if nothing was going on, but we, and everyone who worked for us, knew better. They saw the evidence around them, as one company after another began to do layoffs or go out of business. Our employees were wondering when the inevitable would happen.

From time to time, I would consider one option and then another as I passed through the hallways of the office and shop. The problem with a small business is that you can never get away from it. Day and night, the questions are on your mind. With both of us working for the same company, our company, all other conversation had ceased. We did not want to talk about it, but we could not disengage from it enough to talk about anything else.

"You know Mike Williams had that heart surgery and won't be able to get on anyone else's insurance," Cynthia said.

"What are you getting at?" I asked.

"Well, if we do this thing, if we try to make it work, we can't do it halfway. We can't just keep them employed. We need to keep the insurance and pay them about the same pay as they have been making. Otherwise, they lose their houses. What kind of life is that? We are not the only ones who stand to lose everything we have worked for."

That tied my stomach into a deeper and harder knot. The conversation would end right there. Later that day or the next day, first one of us and then the other would make an observation: "Richard is raising his grandkids. J. T.'s kids have been having trouble, and he is helping them. Albert is getting himself on the right track, starting to learn what life is all about.

Lynn is starting to see the big picture." One after another, we began to realize how much we had come to value each person there, and what the uncertainty was doing to them.

We wondered, each of us alone, just what God was doing and why. My prayers were basically a plea. "God, I just need to know what to do. Every person at this company works hard; they are good people. What is this all about?"

Every person who had come to work for us came from a competitor, choosing our lowly company over the big, well-funded ones. They had chosen to invest their lives with us. We considered our biblical responsibilities and our hearts and realized we did not have the choice or the desire to lay people off. We had a moral obligation to those who chose us to now choose them.

Gradually, we came to a joint conclusion that we had not yet put into words. We met again at the dining room table. Cynthia, in her magnificent clarity, had already identified areas we could cut back and extend our ability to weather the storm. I knew what I had in mind, and the proactive way in which she was looking for savings indicated her vote. Now that the decision was made, the pressure was temporarily off. At least we had certainty about our course of action. Now we had to make it work.

We called a 5:30 a.m. meeting with employees. Both Cynthia and I were there, which was unusual. I would normally handle these early morning meetings alone. That sent a message that this was not an ordinary meeting.

Because we had not been sure what we were going to do before this morning, not even our trusted advisors in the company knew what was up. The employees showed up on time—and the tension, too. People had seen their friends lose longtime jobs, had seen others get pay cuts—first five percent, then ten percent a week later, and another fifteen percent after that. They expected the same this morning for themselves. The normal good-natured crabbing about the early morning meeting was gone. No one smiled or chatted with Cynthia or me. This is what the loneliness of leadership can feel like at times.

I began the meeting: "We are on the front lines of some sort of attempt by OPEC to drive the stripper wells out of the world market. They are flooding the world with oil in order to artificially drive the price down. The low price has shut off all work in the oilfield, and our revenues are down by eighty percent. All the service companies are experiencing the same thing. That's why you are seeing layoffs all around Hobbs and Lea County. Through no fault of our own, lives are being destroyed. No one knows just how long this will last."

Cynthia continued, "Steve and I appreciate each person who works here; each one of you has chosen to leave a good job to work with us. We cannot, in good conscience, lay off one person. Further, though you are seeing your friends with other companies take pay cuts, we are not going to give pay cuts."

No one breathed; the stillness in the room revealed the level of pain they saw in others who had been cut—and the news they had been bracing themselves for.

"We know each of you personally," Cynthia explained. "We know your personal lives, who has bought a house and is paying off medical bills. We cannot bear to see anyone lose a house or children go hungry. We have made a decision and commitment to hold out as long as we can, making no changes in pay, benefits, or the number of workers."

It was my turn again. "I have been in your shoes. When the service companies sold their airplanes, I had to wonder when I was going to be cut. Here, it is my job to worry, not yours. Do not worry about this job. You should work hard when we do have work; make the customer know we appreciate their business. But then you should not worry. We will tell you when to worry. Go home to your spouses, raise your children. I want you to show up every day, paint tools, cut weeds, do something productive. At night, I want you at home with your family. Reassure your family that everything will be okay. Be the calm in the storm that is sweeping across Hobbs and the oilfields nationwide."

Cynthia filled in the specifics. "Everyone paid by the hour will get the same overtime as when we were busy. If you averaged seventy hours a week for the last year, that's what you will be paid for." There was a murmur as people contemplated that. "Operators will get the same base operator pay for the days when you are out on a job. If the customers insist on cutting the daily rates they pay for our services, we may have to visit this more. But for now, we will absorb any short-term rate cuts."

I gave them one last promise. "I will give you thirty-days' notice before changing one thing we have talked about today. I will let you know when you should worry. Until I give you that notice, I do not want you to be concerned with the talk in the coffee shops. We don't have absentee owners or shareholders looking for dividends. You all can see we are very careful; our business is solid. We can weather a pretty big storm. Thirty days! You have my word. Now go make your sales calls, repair your equipment. Prepare for the rain. Be ready, because some day the work will start again."

When Cynthia and I discussed this solution, we anticipated the problem would last two or three months. We thought that is about how long we could last and how long the Saudis could suffer the reduction in revenues without giving up their attempt to shut down production and gain market share. But three months came and went. Cynthia calculated we were paying out fifty thousand dollars per month more than we had work for. We set up a pilot operation in Farmington and rented an apartment there, rotating people to that distant location, cross training them to get a few days' work each month.

As the weeks dragged on, we pointed out that we were paying enough for one salary a month to have others change oil in their vehicles. If they would change their own oil, we could string this out longer. They began to change their oil. Big Dan, who graduated a year behind me in school, was too large to fit under his truck. No one said a thing, but one of the other operators pulled his vehicle into the shop one day and changed the oil for him. It was that day that I knew we would fly the company into the dirt before we called it quits. It was also that day that I believe the employees decided they would make any sacrifice to see us all through the turbulent times.

The weeks continued to drag on. I pointed out that the cell phone bill for all the employees combined was eight thousand dollars per month. If we could cut back a few calls each, we could use the savings to last longer. They cut the bill in half. The four thousand dollars per month was another testament to how much everyone was willing to give to make it work.

Even with less work to do, the company began to perform better with what it had. When the salesmen from other companies were sitting in coffee shops complaining about low pay and worrying with salesmen from other companies about being laid off, our salesmen and fishermen were out hustling jobs, turning over every rock. Our market share and revenues began to gradually creep up. But just like the plane ride without power the year before, we still did not have flying speed. We were still headed for a rough landing; we were just extending the splash further into the future.

Operators started to resent having to make the long drive to Farmington, five hundred miles and nine hours northwest. I was beginning to feel the pressure of dwindling cash and facing the loss of everything for which we had worked. Everyone was feeling the stress. We were at nine months and counting since work had fallen so precipitously. There was no sign that the price would move anytime soon.

Customers began to notice what we were doing with and for our employees. A small margin of new work began to come our way out of sheer respect for our commitment to a principle. But inside, I could tell we could not make it much longer. Finally, about the middle of May, I told Cynthia that if things did not improve by the end of the month, I would have to tell our guys that they should start worrying. I calculated that we had forty-five days of cash left.

The strain of not worrying our employees and keeping the problems between Cynthia and me was taking a toll on both of us. The thought of losing our business and home was becoming a crushing reality. But we had made the decision ten months earlier and committed to it. There was no turning back. All our airspeed was gone; our altitude was above us. It was all I could do to stay positive and remember my statement that the employees were not to worry, and that I would tell them when to worry.

It was equally as dark and frightening as that night flight just a year and a half before. I could tell people did not think we were going to make it. I did not think we would make it.

Less than two weeks after making the statement to Cynthia that we would tell our employees the end was near, before we had the conversation with them, the price of oil began to climb.

The work came back quickly. The pent-up demand that comes from eleven months of not repairing wells hit like a flood. The price now allowed companies to repair the stripper wells that had suffered problems, putting them back into production.

We had the only team that was intact. We had fishermen, reverse unit operators, steam bay technicians, shop workers, drivers, hotshot drivers, invoicing, and payroll clerks. Other companies were desperate to find experienced employees to fill the sudden demand. Our employees were courted heavily. Their response when approached by the other companies: "Everyone knows how you treated your employees."

The loyalty we showed was returned in kind by our employees. I told them if they would keep me advised of the offers that they were getting, we would match the pay. Work was pouring in. The offers were pouring in to them. I gave a ten percent pay increase to match the competition, and a month later another ten percent. It took months for other companies to hire and train new employees.

> The thought of losing our business and home was becoming a crushing reality. But we had made the decision ten months earlier and committed to it. There was no turning back. All our airspeed was gone; our altitude was above us.

In less than six months, we made back the cash we had lost in eleven months. But Cynthia and I got more than the stability. Our step got a little firmer and more confident. It's not that we were smarter than others, but we had lived out our values, learning to walk by faith, even in the most uncertain and turbulent times of our life. When faced with the question of where our hearts were, we could say we chose God and our employees over money in the bank.

We passed one of the most severe no-notice exams we had faced, and it prepared us for the greater challenges that were to come.

39

KEEPING THE COMPANY
GOING IN OUR ABSENCE

I have never been very big on layers of bureaucracy, and our company structure was very flat. I ran operations, and Cynthia ran the office. Each of us had trusted advisors, but our processes were simple, direct, and uncomplicated.

Through the years, I had made operations decisions with strong input from the fishermen: J. T. Woodard, Mike Etheridge, Richard Frederick, Mike Allen, Robert Maxwell, Bill Seymour, and others. In the shop and trucking, I likewise sought out good counsel from "Mr. Bill," Bill Campbell, a workhorse in his late seventies who continued to work because he loved it. In sales, Mike Williams, Ralph Stewart, and Mike Clampitt had strong inputs. Our operations were successful because everyone was engaged in making it work.

But the ability to serve in public office was made possible by the addition of four women who seemingly were delivered to us. I had long before stopped believing that such appearances were coincidental. Rosa's contribution has been previously described, but three more showed up about the same time; all were essential to the coming challenges.

Kelli

As I transitioned into the duties at the state legislature, my days become much more complex. Cynthia suggested I needed someone to help me do my job. Kelli Ruthardt applied for the position of executive assistant. She had worked for several lawyers at the district attorney's office, keeping up with all of them. We hired her, and she proved to be a hard worker, which was nice. But what I appreciated most was her ability to translate my instructions into action. Often my vision outpaces my ability to describe things in detail, let alone act on them, so it takes someone who can fill in major gaps.

I asked Kelli to build a schedule that organized my life into combined work, public service, and volunteer efforts, such as serving on the Lea County Fair Board. She planned my days for maximum efficiency, making it possible to get our work done in much less time.

At another juncture, I asked Kelli to set up the inventory of all our downhole fishing tools for the business. The complexity was overwhelming, but the two of us worked out a numbering system and assigned each tool a specific spot on the racks in the warehouse. She donned coveralls and worked with the guys to stamp numbers on every tool, so they could be placed and found in a specific spot in the shop. If the spot was empty, we knew the tool was out; we no longer had to look around to find it. She created the whole system in-house and with near perfect discipline. It functioned perfectly, saving an enormous amount of time.

Kelli often commented that she did more work for me than all the attorneys could assign her. I was not sure if that was a compliment or a complaint. She kept up and always looked for more. She was so valuable to my productivity that I asked her to accompany me to Washington when we won the election for Congress. She politely declined. I think she could see the workload that lay ahead.

Billie

Billie Charo was an energetic, chatty young mother who came on board with minor bookkeeping experience but without a college degree. She had a mind that breezed through things easily and quickly recognized the pattern of my questions each month as we pored over the financial reports. She anticipated my questions and began to do the same analysis of the reports as I would expect from someone with an MBA. Billie, Kelli, and Rosa each, with little formal education, began to fill roles that allowed me to devote increasing time to the state legislative duties while continuing to oversee our company.

People have wonderful spirits that, when let loose, can move mountains. Too often these great human assets in our country are overlooked by the large corporate structures that naturally weed out any except those with college degrees. Small local businesses such as ours can see the talent develop in local people and promote them accordingly.

Joyce

Cynthia and I had been operating Lea Fishing Tools for more than ten years when a friend showed up out of the blue. We knew Joyce Connolly from her work as the vice president of a local bank, but more than that, we knew her from her volunteer work with multiple nonprofit activities in our town. She was a leader in Hobbs and Lovington.

She had called for an appointment, and we assumed she wanted to try to ease her way into getting our banking business. The three of us were having a friendly chat when Joyce suddenly started sobbing. It turned out that she was not there in her role as a banker. Through tears she said that she had just burned out at the bank. She knew our values and the reputation we had developed for fair play and square dealing and said she wanted to come to work for us.

I told her we could never afford the salary she was making at the bank. She explained that she was not after the money; she wanted to work for us. Cynthia pointed out that we did not have the kind of work she was qualified to do. Joyce then offered to do clerical work for clerical pay.

Both Cynthia and I could see that there was a lot happening in her life. We suspected she wanted to get back to the values that she learned at home on the hardscrabble farm in Lovington. I remembered my own strong need to get back to my values when I was in Arkansas, and we hired her on the spot for about a third of what she was making at the bank.

Joyce started by doing basic clerical work and threw herself into the job. She was hungry to return to the basics. Very soon, Cynthia started shifting more to a management role, giving Joyce many of the day-to-day tasks, doubling her responsibilities and her pay.

Joyce later confirmed our observations, stating that we helped her change the course of her life. She, like Cynthia, had never finished college. But she was also feeling adrift spiritually. Joyce stated that she knew we were both spiritually mature and that we advocated education for our employees. In the next three years, she completed her bachelor's degree as well as strengthened her spiritual life, describing that she now has the "peace and contentment" she hungered for the day she came to our office, and that made possible her transitions to the coming challenges.

All four women were with us when we decided to run for Congress and were essential in helping Cynthia manage during the year I was absent on the campaign trail. Contemplating what we would do if we were successful, Cynthia and I hired a manager for the operations and assumed Joyce would be the office manager.

> People have wonderful spirits that, when let loose, can move mountains. Too often these great human assets in our country are overlooked by the large corporate structures that naturally weed out any except those with college degrees.

As the election wound down and it looked as though we were going to need to implement the succession plan, something had not fallen into place in my mind. After weeks of praying about it, I still could not figure out what was nagging at me.

After the election, I left on a four-day trip to Washington, D.C., for orientation. Without knowing exactly why, I stopped in Joyce's office on the way out the door. "How do you get along with Richard?" I asked, referring to Richard Fredrick, our lead fisherman.

"Okay, I guess. Why?"

"As I passed your office, I just felt like I should ask. Not sure why." At the door I paused again, turned back and told her to spend the next few days developing communications with Richard. Joyce had a questioning look, but no more than I did.

I wondered what it was about but quickly forgot the question and set off on my trip to Washington. When I returned a week later, as I walked by Joyce's office, I felt the tug again and walked in. "How did it go with Richard?"

"Fine. Can I ask what's going on?"

"I don't know what. Something just moved me when I walked by your office."

Later Cynthia came into the office to inquire what I was working on with Joyce, but I had no answer. It was still not clear to me. We resumed our planning to set up our managers and getting ready for the move to Washington. I kept avoiding the meeting to solidify the management plan. Finally, just days before our departure, Cynthia insisted we get things finalized with our organizational chart. I told her I was going to the shop, and we would do it when I finished visiting with the guys. Something was still not worked out in my mind, so I stopped when I saw Richard and asked how he was getting along with Joyce. They had gotten along fine. I was dragging my feet, and I knew it, but I did not know why.

Coup D'oeil

Suddenly, I stood up and walked briskly to the front, got Cynthia, walked into Joyce's office, and closed the door. They both looked at me with deep questioning looks.

"I finally figured out what is bothering me. I have been uncomfortable with our succession plan." Looking at Cynthia, I told her that if she did not have great objections, I was going to pull Joyce out of the role as office manager and assign her my spot as the operations manager.

Management is more about decisions and less about the actual work. With no experience in the downhole work, it was essential for Joyce to work in concert with an operations guy, otherwise we were right back at the point the Chance brothers warned about. Richard was to be that link. Mike Williams was a natural fit to coordinate with her about sales. Joyce had developed good instincts and judgment in her job as a bank vice president. Her decisions were solid, consistent, and fair. She used those qualities to operate our company in our absence.

All our employees helped us transition from owning a business to serving in elected office. Later, when we sold the company, Richard became the district fishing supervisor, Mike became the district sales director, and Joyce earned her way to become operations manager over all New Mexico for the company that purchased our business.

Joyce had showed up looking to leave the bank in seeming disarray and looking for gravity. We thought we were doing her a favor; instead, I wonder if she was sent by God to help us find stability amid the transition. In fact, each person in the company seemed to have made their way to the company and was in place prior to our need. Some call it coincidence; I choose to believe it was God's favor blessing us with the people who would make it possible to take on the next challenge.

40

THIS REALLY IS WHAT
LIFE IS ALL ABOUT

T he pull of gravity can be terrifying or exhilarating, depending on
the circumstance. I have experienced both.

In trying to capture the essence of my life, I realize my stories
are mirrors that help me see my reflection and arrive at essential truths
and the meaning of certain events.

Be Strong and Courageous

In the Bible, when Joshua took over the leadership of the Israelites
from Moses, God commanded him to be strong and courageous. It is a
lesson I have restudied my entire life.

The difficult part of my change from being shy, introverted, and fearful was making a decision to act; to start where I was with what I had. I
realized one of the elements that kept me immobile was the fear of not
measuring up, of making a mistake or looking foolish.

My oldest brother, Mike, was exceedingly smart, and my next older
brother, Tom, was tremendously outgoing and had a wonderful voice. My
fears manifested themselves in the early understanding that I could never

be as smart as Mike or sing or be totally immersed in others as Tom. My fears kept me quiet, withdrawn, and afraid to try. But after several failed attempts, I realized the glaring truth that if I failed to act, the fear would never go away.

When I was about thirteen years old, I had a sense that time was running out—that the song in my heart would be extinguished before I worked up the courage to try. I realized that I might never see the vivid colors of life—that at some point the layered refusals to try would become set in shades of gray. I was afraid others would grow tired of trying to help and would let me live life under the bed with my feet being the only visible part of my life.

My vision quest had the beginning place that only looks within, but also had strong tendencies of the mouse that is fearful and tentative. If I only stayed there in that spot, I would have been content scurrying from home to work, gathering food and bringing it back to the nest, limited to seeing the world directly in front of me, never experiencing the sheer joy of understanding or connecting the things I saw. I longed to be a whole person.

We only grow by seeking understanding. We can't wait for the right time or for someone to lead us. If necessary, we must move alone. Immediacy is an essential part of change. Fears multiply when left unchecked. When Joyce sought us out, she understood the need for immediate action and left a high paying job to make a change.

Watching my brother Philip learn to function in a wheelchair, I realized his limitations were visible . . . mine were more invisible, but they were just as confining. We all have to learn to overcome whatever challenges life throws at us.

If we are to know big things, we must first learn small things. I began to sing and paint a few paintings—safe things, such as the T-38, which connected me to the truth that I could escape the gravitational freezing in place of the past.

The scales fell off; my eyes began to see, and my ears began to hear. It was exhilarating.

It's not that I was good at singing or painting, but I discovered the song and voice inside me and the vision that had escaped me. I never achieved

Dad's natural artistic talent, Mike's intellect, or Tom's voice, but the release inside me that came from trying was as great as if I had.

My small escapes, encouraged by parents, friends, and mentors who never gave up on me, helped me develop the ability to see from the vantage point of the eagle, to act with the strength of the bear and the understanding of the buffalo. In the process, I discovered the wholeness of leaving my natural beginning point; learning to see and understand from all vantage points. That is my strength—the wholeness found by seeing life from multiple points of view.

Although I rarely read advertisements, one captured my attention during college. It depicted a tombstone with the inscription: "Here lies the mind of John Doe. Died age 21. Buried age 75." It spoke to the slothfulness and fear that kept me immobilized. It became one of my motivations for a life of questioning, hard work, and continuing to learn.

Our pastor, Dean Mathis, taught a lesson that involved the same principle. Every tombstone has three elements—the date you were born, the date you die, and a dash in between. For the rest of time, our life is summarized on stone by a dash. But each of us is the architect of what that dash means—choosing to live free or in slavery to substances or fear, choosing to live by faith or by sight, choosing to live each day or die each day.

The "Parable of the Talents" taught by Jesus began to make sense to me. Some have several talents, some have less (I definitely fell into the "have less" category), but we are called to use the talents we have. As did Rosa, I learned that all it takes is old-fashioned guts to take the chance.

If we choose to play it safe, make excuses, or give in to fear, we die every day. That is the most painful death, the spiritual death, where we bury our talents and never work up the courage to try.

I have watched other lives and learned that one of the saddest stories is to live a long life and tell the story of the person who could have been, the things that could have been done, and the things that could have been different. I determined to not let that be my story.

I experienced the terror and the exhilaration of conquering my fear by flying supersonic jets and traveling into Phnom Penh and on the trip of a lifetime to South America. I have cast off, beyond certainty, so many times in my life that I find myself longing for the time when there are no trials and tests and yearning for times of rest, when I am not continually under pressure to learn new things or pilot in uncharted territory. Yet it is the willingness to move beyond certainty, out of my safe zones, that has given my life fulfillment and the rich blessings that accrue from letting our lives serve as the hands and feet of God.

I learned in years of trying that life will beat you up mercilessly. In looking back, I am amazed at the number of times I have fallen and gotten back up. I am mediocre at most things, but tenacity and resilience are valuable lessons I learned from my parents and their dignity in the face of failures and disappointments.

I have many faults, but I try to stay engaged every day. Even when I am getting the stuffing beat out of me, I am trying and giving it my all. The only answer I know, when life is almost out of control, is to do what I can with what I have.

I distilled my rules of life to understand that when the trials and uncertainty come, I can survive by holding steady and trusting God—by staying focused and not panicking, being strong and not giving in to despair, not hesitating or being paralyzed with fear, and not backing down or vacillating. I can survive and thrive in every new circumstance with one rule: Just fly the plane.

Not by Bread Alone

I am truly blessed to have a wife with whom I can look outward. Her kind and giving heart has led me to find the same in myself. We are partners in our faith, our business, and in life. Cynthia has been beside me wherever life has taken us. We face the unknown with only our faith in God and the courage to try. It has made the journey beyond certainty less lonely.

When the price of oil fell from twenty dollars to ten dollars, we learned even more truth—that in troubled times, we depend not on our bank account but on the understanding and faith in our lives. Our associates at the company looked to Cynthia and me as a source of peace, calm, and understanding during that period. Chaos requires finding the gravity in our lives as we experience the greatest trials. Our security came from internal strength, ingenuity, and courage. I find those in my faith.

The upheaval and uncertainty we faced brought amazing clarity and made us understand that when life was distilled to the essence, we face the unknown with only our faith in God. Jesus' teaching that we cannot live by bread alone made more sense, and I achieved a deeper understanding of another of life's critical truths.

I began life as one who had no aptitude for serving others. But during my years in management, I found that aptitude as I worked with people who were struggling to understand what life was all about. That was indeed rich stuff, helping others recognize and overcome their fears, to help give them sight.

When Lynn and Albert professed that their own fathers had been absent in their lives and how they yearned for the time I was investing in them, I realized that there is the need in each of us for the perfect Father, our "Father in heaven."

From my own loneliness, I knew that the thing people crave most is understanding, and the only way to understanding is through touching. I was being touched by the humble lives there in our small company. I found fulfillment in discovering the special power that exists in each person— power that gives each of us the capability of achieving nearly anything if we will but be the pilot in our life, not just a passenger.

The company provided Cynthia and me with our daily bread, but loving others enough to help them in their pain and fear was a profound transformation of my basic spirit. Only God can bring that sort of transformation.

Love Your Neighbor

I grew to love the simplicity of Nadine and the ordinary, real people who lived there. When Tom moved to L.A., he was heralded as a real person, but over time, surrounded by the fantasy, the freeways, and fast pace, he seemed to lose his connection with real things; so when I visited, he and others referred to me as a real person.

America is hungry for real people, for real leadership, for ordinary people who live real lives, instead of the make-believe, made-for-TV lives the media presents to us every day.

During this season of helping others find their strength and develop an understanding of their potential, I prayed prayers of thanksgiving, admitting to God that I was satisfied with my lot in life. I was convinced that at fifty-four years old, the quiet, peaceful life in that dusty, dry corner of southeast New Mexico was my final destination. I understood that this was indeed the day the Lord had made, and I was content.

In these quiet lessons, in the barren drought-stricken edge of the Permian Basin, in shepherding the small flock of families at Lea Fishing Tools, a blue-collar workforce with no fancy degrees, just ordinary people living ordinary lives with the basic challenges we all face, I learned the most significant lesson of all—one that my introverted, shy, and fearful beginning self had resisted up to this point:

"Love your neighbor as yourself."

Loving your neighbor brings peace and harmony to our otherwise chaotic lives. It is a truth older than life itself.

Coincidence?

At some point, I stopped believing that coincidence was the determinant of my life. The scattered events that began to channel toward outcomes I never considered have been too numerous.

The assignment of Coach Shaw to help in the baseball program for one year . . . the year I was ready to implement his instructions.

The change in direction of the country's policies that put into motion the search across the nation for kids who had picked up trash along the highways. The declining of the chairmanship by the young man who won the election, thus putting me as the second place finisher in the White House multiple times in a year and causing me to see so much more I could do in life.

The local draft lottery that forced me to fly and go to war and face some of my deepest fears. The reprogramming of missions that took me away from almost certain destruction at An Loc and Kontum.

The call from a congressman's son to fly for the family, later exposing me to the campaign of his mother for the office and her encouragement for me to seek out public service.

The only five minutes that Rosie and the girls ever spent talking to me that opened my eyes to the woman whom I was about to meet and who is the perfect life mate for me. The almost haphazard process when Cynthia and I decided to base our marriage on the biblical order, which within days provided the decision framework that facilitated the largest financial decision in our lives.

The cancelled Texaco contract that was renewed when none were making their way up the chain of command. The facing of fears in the attempts by the previous owner to scare us into giving up our business. Overcoming the fear of approaching customers as a salesman that placed me perfectly into being able to campaign for public office.

> America is hungry for real people, for real leadership, for ordinary people who live real lives, instead of the make-believe, made-for-TV lives the media presents to us every day.

The late night call asking me to run for state representative when no one knew about the prayers my wife and I had been praying.

All these lead me to believe that what has occurred has been more than coincidence; indeed, they have been God's plan for my life.

Up, up the long, delirious, burning blue
I've topped the wind-swept heights with easy grace.
Where never the lark, or even eagle flew—
And, while with silent, lifting mind I've trod
The high untrespassed sanctity of space,
—Put out my hand, and touched the face of God.

"High Flight" by John Gillespie Magee Jr.

41

9-11-2001—
PARIS, FRANCE

C ynthia and I arrived in Paris for a ten-day vacation with our friends Jack and Michelle LaBree on September 10, 2001. Jack had been an American soldier in France during WWII and married one of the lovely French girls, bringing her back to America. She had grown up in Paris and wanted to make a trip back to her home, but they were both in their eighties at the time. Our presence helped them to make a safe trip in their aging years, and their presence would help us negotiate France without speaking the language.

With the time difference, we were just returning to the hotel on the September 11 when American Airlines Flight 11 slammed into the North Tower of the World Trade Center in New York. We did not know anything had happened as we reached our hotel and approached the front desk. The attendant at the Paris hotel verified that we were Americans, then strongly suggested we go immediately to our room and watch the news. He wouldn't tell us what had happened but said, "God is sovereign. He will prevail."

Splitting off from our friends, we sat on the bed in the hotel room and watched in horror as the second plane hit the South Tower, and both buildings collapsed. As with every other American, we were in disbelief.

The French people were wonderful in their caring responses. They easily recognize Americans and have a reputation for using that recognition to offend them. But in those days of world turmoil, they were warm, gracious, and caring, giving reassurance and encouragement.

Of course, all flights in and out of the U.S. were cancelled immediately. TWA, our airline, which had been acquired by American Airlines, used the occasion to announce that all their international flights would be suspended and rolled into the American Airlines system. So our flight home no longer existed.

Since the call centers did not answer, we took the train daily to and from the airport trying to reschedule a flight. The lines of people extended through the terminal and out the doors, but people were curiously accomodating. No loud protests of passenger anger; people were aware that something fundamental had changed.

Back in the U.S., Vivian Flemmons, our travel agent, stayed on the phone all day every day, getting one seat at a time, and succeeded in rebooking us before we got to the front of the line in France. Our flight was only one day beyond our original departure date. Others ran out of money for hotels and did what they had to, taking their entire families to sleep in the terminal for days.

It was in that setting, on the night of the attacks, that Cynthia displayed incredible foresight. She noted that the United States was in trouble and might end up in war and drilled this down to how it might impact our own lives: Joe Skeen (the sitting U.S. congressman from southern New Mexico) had health problems. The state would need new leadership.

Our relationship had grown to the point where Cynthia, even though she hungers for security and hates the continual challenges, suggested that we launch beyond certainty into a new and perilous journey.

"If he decides not to run, you should run for U.S. Congress," she said as we processed what would be a life-changing event for all Americans. "You have the military background, an economics degree, and the business background. Your voice will be important in this new phase for the United States." It was one more no-notice exam, testing our preparation, our character, and our very foundations.

> It was there that we made the mutual and spontaneous decision to once again let loose of the familiar and go into uncharted skies and in faith say one more time, "Yes, we will go."

It was there, that night in Paris, France, during one of the worst attacks on U.S. soil ever to occur, that we prayed and made the commitment to run for the office (if Joe Skeen did, in fact, retire). It was there that we committed to change our lives from one of business management to one of service if called upon.

It was there that we made the mutual and spontaneous decision to once again let loose of the familiar and go into uncharted skies and in faith say one more time, "Yes, we will go."